THE WIDENING GAP

DEVELOPMENT IN THE 1970's

The Widening Gap

DEVELOPMENT IN THE 1970'S

Edited by BARBARA WARD,

J. D. RUNNALLS, *and* LENORE D'ANJOU

A Report on the Columbia Conference
on International Economic Development
Williamsburg, Virginia, and New York
February 15–21, 1970

COLUMBIA UNIVERSITY PRESS
NEW YORK AND LONDON
1971

FOREWORD

IN FEBRUARY, 1970, Columbia University called a conference on international economic development in response to the recommendations put forward in *Partners in Development,* a report prepared for the international community at the invitation of the World Bank. This report had been drawn up the previous year by a distinguished commission of experts, chaired by The Right Honourable Lester B. Pearson, and has come to be known as the Pearson Report.

The Albert Schweitzer Chair in International Economic Development, which is funded by the State of New York, organized and convened the Conference for Columbia University, with generous financial assistance from the Ford Foundation, the Kellogg Foundation, the International Bank for Reconstruction and Development (the World Bank), and the Inter-American Development Bank. This assistance made it possible to insure the representation of a very wide cross section of views on development.

The debates, which lasted from February 15 to February 21, 1970, followed the general outline of the Pearson Report and took four main topics for discussion. These were the implications of aiming at a 6% rate of growth in the developing world, the structural changes such a rate might impose or require, the world framework of trade and liquidity in which growth would have to be undertaken and the kind of aid relationship between developed and developing nations that might or might not be achieved in the process. Preparatory papers were written to cover each of these themes, both from a general and a regional point of view.

The Conference itself was divided into two parts. A majority of the participants—chiefly from the academic community—gathered at Williamsburg, Virginia, for three days of discussions. They then moved to New York, where they were joined at Columbia University by a further group who, in the main, represented governments, international institutions, and public and private agencies actively engaged in international development. The Williamsburg participants took up again the themes already discussed, and the newcomers brought their practical experience to bear on them.

This book is a report of this conference.

ACKNOWLEDGMENTS

SINCE *The Widening Gap* is derived from the papers and discussions of Columbia University's Conference on International Economic Development, the editors wish to express their gratitude both to those who were concerned with the Conference and also to those who have helped in the preparation of this book.

Special recognition must be given to:

W. A. Marianne Boelen, Assistant to the Convenor of the Conference, and to Jane Aptekar and Paula Bregman, for organization of the Conference.

Brian Johnson, who organized the Conference rapportage.

Mrs. J. Tessier and H. R. Cantave, Canadian International Development Agency, who served as interpreters for the Conference.

Several of the papers included in this volume were published in Columbia University journals, whose editors and staffs made many helpful suggestions in preparing the texts. Thank are due to:

The *Journal of International Affairs,* edited by Paul Shapiro, in which the articles by The Right Honourable Lester B. Pearson, Richard Jolly, Laurence Whitehead, Samir Amin, and Max Nicholson appeared under the general title "International Economic Development in the 1970's."

The staff of the *Columbia Journal of World Business*—Courtney C. Brown, George Browne, Richard Greenbaum, Carol Rogovin —in which the article by Harry G. Johnson appeared.

Gratitude is also due to various publishers who released material under copyright for publication in this volume:

Praeger Publishers, Inc., for permission to quote liberally from *Partners in Development: Report of the Commission on International Development,* Lester B. Pearson, Chairman (© Praeger Publishers, Inc., New York, and Pall Mall Press, Ltd., London, 1969).

International Finance Section, Princeton University, which previously published the article "How to Divest in Latin America and Why."

The University of Chicago Press for permission to quote from M. Bronfenbrenner, "The Appeal of Confiscation in Economic Development," *Economic Development and Cultural Change:* no. 1 (April, 1955) in "The Aid Relationship in Latin America."

Finally, major credit for both Conference and book must be given to the staff of Columbia University's Albert Schweitzer Chair who gave helpful suggestions and unstinting assistance at every stage:

Suzanne Springstead Haigh, Irene Hunter, Dorothy Schlotthauer, and Nadine Seltzer.

CONTENTS

THE WIDENING GAP

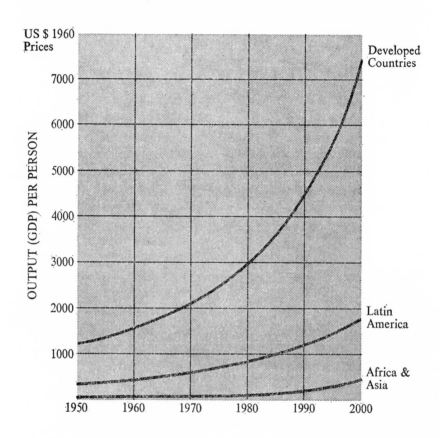

THE BACKGROUND OF THE CONFERENCE

The "Grand Assize"

The Columbia Conference on International Economic Development was convened to discuss the implications of *Partners in Development* * —the report of the Pearson Commission. To understand the emphasis of the conference, it is necessary to know how the Pearson Report came to be published. In essence, the Report is a high-level examination or "grand assize" of the whole issue of foreign aid, and it came into being as a result of the initiative of one president of the World Bank and the active and sustained support of his successor.

At Stockholm in October, 1967, George Woods, then president of the World Bank, first called for a "grand assize" to inquire into the realities of foreign aid. He asked that an international commission, composed of men of commanding ability and reputation, be invited to examine the whole issue of assistance to development—the record, the results, the lessons. They should, he suggested, report to the international community on achievements and failures with equal candor and give their unbiased counsel on what should be put right and what should be

---

* Lester B. Pearson, et al., *Partners in Development: Report of the Commission on International Development* (New York: Praeger Publishers, 1969); hereafter referred to as the Pearson Report.

carried further. Their reputations would insure their objectivity, and this in turn would give genuine authority to their advice.

Mr. Woods had become convinced of the need for some new departure in the field of aid because it was no longer possible to overlook a growing trend toward disillusion with the whole policy. The 1960's began bravely with a doubling of official assistance and a general sense of new commitments in what could reasonably be described as an emerging planetary community. But by 1967 the brave visions were fading, the transfer of resources had ceased to grow, and, in the case of the largest and therefore pace-setting donor, the United States, there were signs of decline.

This was the situation to which Mr. Woods addressed his Stockholm speech. He emphasized two different and apparently opposite elements in the crisis. On the one hand, the donor countries did not seem to realize just how much progress had in fact been made. It was already clear, in 1967, that average growth rates in the developing world had been running for over a decade at a higher sustained level—4.8% a year—than the Atlantic world achieved during its earlier stages of development in the nineteenth century. Could an aid effort that had contributed substantially to such a result be called a failure?

This failure to recognize achievement was, in Mr. Wood's analysis, all the more irrational and misleading in that popular opinion almost certainly *underestimated* the difficulties faced by nations attempting to modernize their economic and social structure in the last third of the twentieth century. In a somber passage, he pointed out that the analogies of rapid transformation, most of them drawn from the experience of the previous century, were not in fact valid.

In the nineteenth century, the major developed powers experienced their greatest expansion only *after* the processes of modernization had set in. One thinks of Britain with six million people in the middle of the eighteenth century and, even more astonishingly, America with only five million and a virtually empty continent in 1789. The first spurt of rapid population growth provided a new mass of laborers in industry and new markets for food and helped to populate the new industrial cities. Later on, public health began to lengthen life and lessen infant mortality. Later still, a more sophisticated work force became necessary to man increasingly labor-saving machines. But by that time, family size had shrunk and, in farm or town, population growth had slowed down. The pioneer nations were trebly fortunate. On the whole, their trends of population growth, urbanization, and mechanization helped and reinforced each other.

For present day developers the opposite is the case. All the various elements—population, patterns of technology, urban expansion—contradict and impede the others. A measure of public health activity has preceded modernization in developing lands. The spurt of population is taking place *ahead* of the means of feeding and absorbing it—at a time when farming is still insufficiently modernized to provide increasing food for the whole population and at a time when the trend in industry is to need fewer but more highly skilled workers. A refinery at Port Harcourt in Nigeria may cost $36 million. But it will only employ 350 men. These unlucky disproportions are due not to vice or incompetence or perversity. They are due to a certain historical timing, to a certain place, if you like, in the queue of world development, in which newcomers cannot follow the favorable patterns of the pioneers simply because the world has moved on, conditions have changed, and the same advantages are no longer there to be seized.

The "grand assize" had, therefore, a double purpose—to assess the success or failure of the whole effort of international assistance to development and to set the effort in its proper perspective of seeking to modernize social and economic systems in a world already radically transformed by the successful and prior modernization of the pioneers.

When Robert McNamara succeeded Mr. Woods in 1968, he took up the establishment of an expert and distinguished commission of inquiry as a first priority. The Right Honourable Lester B. Pearson, who had just retired as Prime Minister of Canada, agreed to chair the Commission, and seven other distinguished experts * accepted the invitation to join him as Commissioners. They, and their secretariat headed by Edward K. Hamilton, set to work in November, 1968, and a year later the Pearson Report was made public.

The main thrust and intention of the Report can best be described by W. Arthur Lewis, himself one of the Pearson Commissioners and a participant in the Columbia Conference.

* Sir Edward Boyle, Roberto de Oliveira Campos, C. Douglas Dillon, Wilfried Guth, W. Arthur Lewis, Robert E. Marjolin, Saburo Okita.

The Purposes of the Pearson Report

BY W. ARTHUR LEWIS

The Pearson Commission was appointed because of the crisis in foreign aid. As measured by the Development Assistance Committee (DAC) of the Organisation for Economic Cooperation and Development (OECD), the net flow of official development assistance, which between 1961 and 1967 had been rising not much faster than prices, actually fell between 1967 and 1968. The downward movement was led by the United States, where it seemed likely to accelerate. If United States aid falls significantly, other countries are likely to follow; so a review of the situation is clearly urgent.

The Commission's first task was to satisfy itself that foreign aid serves a useful purpose and serves it well. One reason for the stagnation of aid is that some of those whose opinions influence the volume of aid are not convinced that this is so. They accept the desirability of the purpose—to improve the productive capacity of the less developed countries—but they doubt that this purpose is served by foreign aid. Disillusionment with the effectiveness of foreign aid is widespread. Some of it is due to disappointment with the political effects of aid, but much of it springs from the belief that the less developed countries show very little economic result from the aid which they have received in the past; foreign aid thus appears as a bottomless pit. Some proponents of larger aid have contributed to this disillusionment by spreading the gospel that "the poor countries are getting poorer while the rich are getting richer," as part of their case for larger aid. If it were indeed true that the poor countries were getting poorer, despite the great opportunities offered by expanding world trade, and despite official development assistance averaging $6 billion a year during the 1960's, then the opponents of aid would indeed have a plausible case. Some of the papers in this volume seem to exaggerate to the point of falling into this trap.

The Commission tried to clarify the facts. It found that the rate of growth of the incomes of less developed countries was both unexpectedly and unprecedentedly high, whether in total or per capita. The total growth rate was about the same in developed and less developed countries, but the per capita growth rate was lower in the less developed because of the unprecedentedly high rates of population growth. Thus, the per capita income of the less developed countries is growing rapidly by any historical standards; nevertheless the gap between developed and less developed is widening because the former are growing even faster.

The Commission's next task was to establish that foreign aid does contribute to economic growth. This could not be done historically for all foreign aid, since so much of foreign aid has in the past been given for purely political reasons, without much concern that it be spent on increasing productive capacity. It is easy to list countries which have clearly benefited economically from foreign aid, but it is also possible to list examples where foreign aid has increased the consumption or political or military power of some classes, without increasing productive capacity. The Commission was convinced that foreign aid could make an enormous difference to productive capacity; this proposition is hardly disputed. But it also concluded that it could not justifiably recommend a large increase in foreign aid without safeguards that would insure that such aid would be effective in raising productive capacity. This is why its report associates the allocation of aid with performance and emphasizes a multilateral framework for the continual assessment of economic performance.

The Commission's approach does not give universal satisfaction. The linking of foreign aid with performance displeases several groups: those who think that aid should be distributed according to need, rather than according to effective use; those who fear that assessment of performance may degenerate into a new form of imperialism; and those who put greater emphasis on raising consumption levels than on increasing productive capacity. These groups, who are well represented in the following papers, can be categorized under the slogan "Give them the money and shut up," though they normally express themselves in much more elegant language. They may have superior morality on their side, but it is to be doubted whether they have superior persuasive power in the crisis now upon us. The Commission's task was to persuade opinion makers, who are somewhat disillusioned with aid, that within a strengthened framework aid could be effective in raising the productive capacity of the less developed countries. In this context "Give them the money and shut up" is a non-starter.

Given an effective framework linking foreign aid to productive capacity, how large should foreign aid be in the 1970's? Here the Commission's task was relatively simple. What is feasible is bounded by two constraints, namely the absorptive capacity of the developing countries and the consensus of potential donors. The Commission did not need to do original work in either area, since others had fully explored the ground.

The question of absorptive capacity had been studied at length by a United Nations committee making recommendations for the Second Development Decade, under Professor Jan Tinbergen. This committee had concluded that it was feasible to set a minimum target growth for national income during the decade of 6% per annum. Foreign aid is not, of course, the only constraint; in most countries, in practice, the most obstinate constraint is the rate of change of agricultural output that can be achieved by the small farmers who constitute 60% or more of the population. The omens for agricultural change are now highly favorable, so the 6% target does not now seem as unattainable as it would generally have been thought to be as recently as five years ago.

The Tinbergen Committee also asked itself how much foreign aid was required for 6% growth and, after volumes of arithmetic, decided to endorse the recommendation of a net transfer of resources equal to 1% of the GNPs of developed countries, which developed and less developed countries had agreed to at the United Nations Conference on Trade and Development meetings in New Delhi in 1968. So here we have a happy coincidence of two constraints—that of absorptive capacity and that of political acceptability.

Unlike some writers in this volume, the Pearson Commissioners felt themselves bound by these constraints. One can pick any targets one likes from the air—say 10% growth and 3% transfer—once these constraints are abandoned.

From the political point of view, the 1% transfer target has the advantage that it has already been very widely endorsed by the governments which must put it into effect. It also represents a drastic reversal of recent trends. Actual achievement in 1968 was only 0.77%. Assuming that national income grows by 5% per annum, a net flow equal to 1% in 1975 would represent an absolute increase in transfers of 87%, or from $13.0 billion to $24.2 billion. This is by no means a low target, when seen in the light of current trends.

In 1969 five of the sixteen OECD countries were already exceeding the 1% target, and several others had already announced their intention of getting there. To endorse the 1% target would bring very wide support among OECD governments; to adopt a significantly higher target would alienate this support and be totally ineffective. The Pearson Commission therefore recommended that the president of the World Bank call on each developed country to state, at the World Bank meeting in September, 1971, the precise measures which its government will take to insure that 1% is reached by 1975. Possibly all but two countries will be able to report concrete measures in 1971, thus putting the pressure of the entire world community on those two.

It is still too early to say whether the Pearson Commission is doing an effective job, since its job is essentially one of persuading opinion makers. The audience for the report is quite small. It is not aimed at the general public, since much of its argument has to be technical and statistical, and the general public does not read 400-page technical reports. Neither is the report aimed at the U.S. congressman, who so largely responds to the opinions coming from the constituency which he represents. It is aimed rather at those who make public opinion—at editors, clergymen, and other such public persons, who are willing to give careful study to facts and figures, and then to offer leadership. The Commission felt that it was this group of people who most needed, at this time, an objective review of all the issues of foreign aid, leading (as such a review fortunately does) to the conclusion that there is no need for disillusionment. The less developed countries, on the contrary, have demonstrated that they can grow rapidly; we now have a framework for multilateral supervision of aid which reinforces the chances of effective use. We have learned much in the 1960's, both about the processes of economic growth and about the possibilities for international cooperation in this sphere. As a result we are now in a position to make a major effective thrust toward helping the less developed countries to achieve ultimate economic independence at high levels of growth. Having got thus far, to turn back would be absurd.

Or so the Commission thought. But to show that aid is viable, useful, and effective is not to prove that it should be given priority over other uses for scarce resources. Insofar as the Commission addressed itself to those who needed the facts, it did a competent job. But what about those other opinion makers who have known all along that foreign aid is effective, but who simply do not consider it as important as other uses for funds? Here the Commission had no special contribution to make. The case for foreign aid is basically moral: the obligation of the rich to help the poor. When all is said that can be said of a technical nature, the supreme task still remains that of persuading the peoples and governments of developed countries to continue in the worldwide crusade against poverty. This is where the opinion makers take over from bodies like the Commission, trying to reach the public in millions, through meetings, sermons, newspaper articles, books, and other forms of communication. If these activists find help in the Pearson Report, the Commission will have justified itself.

The Recommendations of the Pearson Commissioners

The report of the Pearson Commissioners runs some 400 pages and contains 68 specific recommendations. These recommendations cover the four broad categories examined in this volume: proposals for an accelerated rate of growth for the developing world as a whole; proposals for the liberalization of trade among the developing countries themselves and between the developed and developing areas of the world; proposals for new attitudes toward private investment; and proposals for a complete rethinking of the aid relationship.

The Report suggests a 6% rate of growth per annum for the developing countries throughout the 1970's.

Developed countries are urged to eliminate duties and taxes on products of special interest to the developing countries which are not produced in the developed world. The developed world is also enjoined to draw up long-term plans for the reduction of tariffs to insure a much larger market for goods from the developing world. Buffer stocks and supplementary financing to enable primary producers to withstand the shock of price fluctuations are also encouraged. Institutions promoting trade between the developing countries are singled out as worthy recipients of increased aid.

The Commissioners felt that private capital could be of considerable assistance to development, and they urge developing countries to restructure their laws to remove obstacles to domestic private investment, to provide stability in their regulations affecting foreign investment, and to strengthen their investment incentive schemes. International agencies, such as the World Bank's International Finance Corporation and the United Nations Industrial Development Organization, are urged to expand advisory service and project identification.

The recommendations for a new definition of the aid relationship are perhaps the most exhaustive of all the Report's proposals. The Commissioners recommend that each developed country increase its resource transfers to developing countries to at least 1% of its GNP by 1975 at the latest. An amount equal to at least 0.7% of its GNP should be devoted to official development assistance by 1980 at the latest, with 20% of this contribution to be given through multilateral agencies. The terms of official development assistance loans should be limited to 2% (with twenty-five–forty-year maturity). The Commissioners were very suspicious of the value of tied aid. They recommend: a conference of major donors to consider the progressive untying of aid; the suspension of provisions limiting the rights of recipients to call competitive bids; and the exclusion from aid calculations of costs resulting from the tying of aid to use of the donors' ships to transport it.

Present technical assistance programs were also seen to be insufficient. The budget period for technical assistance should be extended to at least three years, financial assistance should be extended to cover the local costs of projects, and national and international corps of technical assistance personnel created.

The role of the World Bank should be expanded. Developed countries should commit at least one-half of all interest payments due them on official bilateral loans to subsidize the interest rates on Bank lending. The International Development Association (IDA), the Bank's "soft-loan window," should be reorganized, and contributions to it by developed countries should reach $1 billion annually by 1972 and $1.5 billion by 1975. The Bank should convene a conference of all multilateral aid-giving agencies and major bilateral donors in 1970 to "discuss the creation of improved machinery for coordination capable of relating aid and development policies to other relevant areas of foreign economic policy, moving toward standardized assessments of development performance, making clear, regular, and reasonably authoritative estimates of aid requirements, and providing balanced and impartial reviews of donor aid policies and programs" (Pearson Report, p. 230).

The Columbia Declaration

These major recommendations of the Pearson Report formed the basis for the discussions of the Columbia Conference on International Economic Development, February 15–21, 1970.

It had not been the intention of the conveners to try to secure an agreed communiqué or any kind of consensus from the discussions. The representation seemed much too diverse. It included heads of agencies, government officials, academic experts, traditionalists, young radicals from both developed and developing nations, businessmen, publicists, participants of all political persuasions. How could such a heterogeneous assembly come to any agreed conclusions? Could they even agree on the facts or the issues? The most that seemed possible was a confrontation, hopefully enlightening, between deeply divergent points of view.

However, as the debate moved back and forth, there began to emerge a framework of fact, an analysis of difficulty, a sense of direction, even perhaps a first sketch of strategy. Spontaneously, a small group * set to work to draft a Declaration which attempted to embody the conclusions that were taking shape. A very large majority of those present at the final sessions signed the Declaration. Many of those who abstained did so because they hold official posts. The Declaration can therefore be taken as a genuine "sense of meeting" of the Columbia Conference.

The text of the Declaration read:

"We the undersigned,** of a wide spectrum of political opinions and from developed and developing countries in all parts of the world, have just concluded a week's discussion of the report of the Pearson Commission on International Development, published a few months ago.

"The widening gap between the rich and poor countries of the world has—in the words of the Pearson Report—become a central issue of

---

* Michael Bruno, Reginald Green, Mahbub ul Haq, Gerald K. Helleiner, Branko Horvat, Enrique Iglesias, Richard Jolly, and H. M. A. Onitiri.

** Signatories to the statement are indicated by an asterisk in the list of Conference participants at the end of this volume.

our time. In incomes, living standards, economic and political power, one-third of the world has in recent decades been pulling steadily ahead, leaving the remainder of mankind in relative poverty, in many cases to live without clean water, education, basic medical facilities or adequate housing. Yet with modern technology and existing productive capacity, none of this need continue if mankind would develop the will and organization to use the resources at hand.

"There is already a deep sense of frustration in the developing countries and this is bound to rise rapidly in the 1970's as the gap continues to widen and as urbanization, literacy, and the spread of technology break down the barriers of communication. A growth rate of 6% in GNP will not be adequate to deal with the situation. In the Indo-Pakistan subcontinent, for instance, 6% growth until the turn of the century would still leave one and a half billion people with an average per capita income of only $200 per year.

"The Pearson Report, by setting forth proposals to meet this situation which will appear 'acceptable' and 'reasonable,' leans far toward reluctant public opinion in the developed countries. A frank report by the developing countries would have revealed a more pessimistic picture, especially when attention is directed: to the losses from changes in terms of trade which often exceed annual gains from aid; to the prospect of growing numbers of unemployed; to the inequities in the distribution of aid under bilateral political influences; to the weaknesses in the existing institutional framework of aid; and to the growing strength of the multinational corporations which often distort the pattern of national development.

"The Pearson Report emphasizes a partnership between the developed and developing countries which too often is simply an illusion. The Report is, however, a starting point and its implementation could improve the chances for a meaningful partnership. For this reason, we support many of the Pearson proposals while emphasizing that they still fall short of what is required and that they ought to be supplemented. In particular, priority should be given to the following points:

"(1) *Multilateral international framework*: There is an urgent need to strengthen the multilateral international framework in the fields of trade, aid, and relations between rich and poor nations. This must cover the United Nations as well as other international and regional institutions. Such strengthening necessarily involves the channeling of increased and independent finance and moves toward compulsory contributions by member countries. International power must increasingly be shared democratically; and this objective can only be attained by strengthening the role of institutions in which the developing economies have a representative vote.

"(2) *The future of aid*: Massive increases in aid remain a necessary condition for rapid economic development. Greater levels of *net* capital inflow must particularly be effected in the coming decade for countries with per capita incomes below $300. In a world in which military expenditures exceed by twenty-five times the total of aid expenditures, the claim that these increases are impossible is blatant hypocrisy.

"At the same time, new objective criteria for effective development assistance are required. An overall minimum growth rate for all countries is, no doubt, a desirable objective. But it is essential also to develop targets designed to achieve a minimum average per capita income of $400 to be reached by all countries not later than the end of the century. Criteria are also needed which focus on the living standards of the bottom quarter of each country's population. We also suggest setting up of a special fund devoted specifically to the fulfillment of social objectives in the areas of education, health, family planning, rural and urban works, housing, and other related social programs.

"Increasing proportions and amounts of aid must be provided multilaterally through the expansion of IDA, the strengthening of regional development banks, and the use of SDR * backing for such aid.

"(3) *Market access*: The developing countries cannot achieve growth rates of 6% and above without a major expansion in their exports. This must be facilitated by a wide variety of means: unilateral reductions in tariffs and other trade barriers and policies to restructure production within the developed world; repayment of a part of debt obligation in the form of goods or local currency balances; provision of financial cover for intraregional trade between developing countries; and an end to present discrimination against the exports of the developing nations. These measures have the particular merit of being in the general immediate economic interests of the developed economies.

---

* Special Drawing Rights in the International Monetary Fund. See Chapter 3 for further discussion.

"(4) *Economic and social change within developing countries*: None of us underestimates the need for major changes in political, social, and economic policies and institutions within the developing countries. Without them, international efforts will be to no avail. Performance criteria should increasingly focus on income distribution, land and tax reforms, ineffective trade and exchange rate policies, size of military expenditures, and the promotion of social justice.

"We leave this Conference with the conviction that nothing is more unrealistic than the apparent realism of those who argue that the Pearson Report is fully adequate or even overambitious in terms of the future prospects. Such realism can only lead to growing confrontation between the developing and developed countries of the world, and to growing misery and frustration for a majority of mankind. Dependence in the modern world must be ended and give way to a framework which will allow genuine interdependence and partnership. The Pearson proposals are important if taken seriously as a point of departure toward this vital goal."

The Shape of the Debate

A comparison between the Columbia Declaration and W. Arthur Lewis's summary brings out clearly the dilemmas faced by any person or group —teacher, practitioner, publicist, commission, conference, or government—involved these days in the enterprise of foreign aid. If the full scale of the crisis underlying world development is underlined, if the historical realities of the context are stressed—as Mr. Woods stressed them at Stockholm—there is a risk of the donors losing heart. But if the rising impatience and resentment at injustice and discrimination felt by the developing peoples is glossed over so as not to rock the planetary boat, they may decide that the only course is to scuttle it. The Pearson Commission felt its task to lie primarily in an appeal to the generosity and self-interest of the donors. The Columbia Conference looked further. The risk in the undertaking was a useless confrontation. The gain was to achieve some insights, some analysis, and some proposals upon which rich and poor, developed and developing, satisfied and radical, could in some measure agree.

The following pages attempt to illustrate how the various points of analysis and agreement emerged. A number of key papers are given in full. Others are used for extensive quotation. The chapter on "Growth and Structural Change" sets the problem. What happens to developing societies as they begin to modernize? How are their chances helped or impeded by the fact of developing in a world already partially modernized by other more powerful states? What are the critical thresholds of growth or frustration? Are there strategies available for turning these dangerous corners? The second chapter, "The Development Sectors," deals with those interrelated structural issues which threaten to obstruct development and deepen the crisis in the societies of the Third World. The chapter on "Trade and Liquidity" looks at the international environment within which development has to take place. Does the particular pattern of world trade, dominated as it is by the already developed states, help or hinder modernization elsewhere? Are the normal methods of the traditional world market—comparative advantage in the exchange of goods, the flow of private capital—adequate to bring today's developing nations to the state of "self-sustained growth" said to characterize mature economies? A short chapter, "Private Investment," then assesses the opportunities and limitations presented by dependence upon the flow of private capital. And finally, "The Aid Relationship" examines the possibility that new types of economic relations may have to be maintained and evolved for any genuine planetary community. The question is asked whether market mechanisms alone can achieve stability and growth at the world level any more than they can do so within each domestic economy. The debate is joined to determine, given the present balance of power in the world, whether aid can come to express the normal obligations of interdependence between citizens. Or does it perpetuate at best a paternalism, at worst a dependent "neo-colonialism," no longer acceptable to the post-colonial peoples?

CHAPTER ONE

GROWTH AND STRUCTURAL CHANGE

The Debate

THE SPECTRUM

Both "developing nations" and a "6% growth target" are concepts of a very high order of abstraction. The countries run from the mini-states of Africa to the Indian Union with its 600 million people. Per capita income varies from below $50 to at least $600. Some states depend upon international trade for 30% of their GNP; in others, trade accounts for less than 10%. It follows that strategies for growth, strategies for aid, and the difficulties to be encountered in both can be usefully discussed only within a context of greater diversity and elaboration.

This was provided by Hollis B. Chenery's paper, "Targets for Development," which opened the Conference and set the direction for much of the debate. His table (Table 2) gives in summary form the types of transformation which a society experiences as it grows. Increases in per capita income imply increases in literacy and school enrollment; steady growth of industry, services, utilities, and urbanization; a balancing decline in agriculture and rural population; an increasing proportion of GNP devoted to savings, investment, and taxation; and the rise of both imports and exports to approximately one-quarter of GNP. These transformations are, of course, well known. But Professor Chenery's chart makes clear how closely and uniformly they follow the pattern of rising per capita income.

Statistical evidence of this kind plots the course of change. It does not measure the exact path by which nations accomplish their transitions. Nor does it define the obstacles which lie in wait along the road. It was on these problems of transformation that discussions tended to concentrate since most participants agreed with Professor Chenery's judgment that the developing nations are finding transformation more difficult than accumulation, the proper deployment of resources more testing than their mobilization.

This was, of course, a sharp departure from earlier thinking on development. The key problem in developing lands had been held to be the change from a rate of investment equivalent to 5% of GNP to one of 15%. This problem of primary accumulation was seen to spring from the extreme poverty of traditional society, its shortage of skills and managerial competence, its lack of financial mechanisms for saving and investment, and its almost complete dependence upon an agriculture in which a host of small farmers could be coaxed only with difficulty into rapid increases in productivity. In the older view, the chief role of external aid was to help break these early bottlenecks and to create both the margin of productivity required for saving and the habit of investment needed to take advantage of it.

The discussions did not ignore or contradict these difficulties. In fact, particular stress was laid on the problem of rapid growth where agriculture now provides more than 50% of GNP. In spite of the hopes raised by new techniques in agriculture (the "Green Revolution"), a growth rate of more than 4% a year in agriculture is quite exceptional. Thus, if more than 50% of GNP is produced on the farms, it becomes almost impossible to achieve a 6% rate of growth overall. However, such early and well-documented obstacles to growth received less attention in the discussions than did the problems of the next stage, which arise when momentum begins to gather behind the transfer of manpower and resources out of agriculture into new urban and industrial sectors.

The starting point for an industrial sector is local processing of domestic raw materials or the manufacture of industrial goods hitherto imported from abroad or some mixture of both. If an overall growth rate of 6% is the aim, the industrial sector has to attempt to grow by not much less than 8% a year. This rate is not unusual in the developing world, but to sustain it calls for some fairly remarkable obstacle-jumping. For instance, The Honourable Philip Ndegwa argued strongly that the size of most African states imposes drastic limits on the local market for manufactures. Yet common markets, whether in Africa or Latin America, confront particular difficulties in allocating industry on an extra-national basis.

Even where the scale of market offers no difficulty, the substitution of local for foreign manufacture tends to be purchased at an exorbitant cost. Additions of 300% to 400% to the price of locally manufactured goods are not unknown in areas of massive import substitution. Stanislaw Wellisz's paper (in this chapter) vividly described the costs imposed on the Indian economy by a policy of protection á l'outrance.

In Latin America, the same strains have appeared. Daniel Schydlowsky gave the conference this analysis:

"Import substitution was implemented throughout Latin America by the use of high and increasing import duties, combined at times with quantitative restrictions, pre-import deposits, multiple exchange rates, and other devices. Import duties of 100% or more, or their equivalent in terms of quantitative restrictions or multiple exchange rates, became the rule rather than the exception and were justified very often in terms of the traditional infant industry argument but just as commonly as a measure of generalized protection of the balance of payments.

"By external measures of success, the policy of import substitution for some time brought satisfactory results. The ratio of imports to income fell considerably in the early stages of import substitution in those countries that assiduously practiced the policy and, although after a time the ratio ceased falling, it stabilized on a level substantially below its initial one. . . . In terms of the growth of industry, the policy can also chalk up rather substantial successes. . . . In almost all the Latin American nations, the rate of growth of industry substantially exceeded the rate of growth of total GNP. Thus the countries which applied an import-substitution strategy should on the whole be expected to be very satisfied with the outcome of their policy. Such, however, is not the case.

"The first major difficulty arising out of the import-substitution strategy appeared in connection with the external dependence of Latin American nations. It had been expected that import substitution would isolate the Latin American economies from the fluctuations of their external accounts. In the event, however, they have become, if anything, more dependent. Rather than being importers of a wide variety of consumer and producer commodities, some of which could be temporarily restricted with little pain in the event of a balance of payments crisis, Latin American countries after import substitution found themselves importing only essential raw materials and capital goods. This implied that if a reduction of imports became necessary, it would perforce take place in the form of lower imports of raw materials and capital goods, . . . thus directly affecting the growth rate and/or the level of industrial employment in the economy. Thus, prior to import substitution a decline in imports implied a tighter belt for consumers; after import substitution a reduction of imports meant unemployment and a lower rate of growth. . . .

"The second unexpected and undesirable consequence of this policy of import substitution followed directly from the first. As a result of the greater dependence on imported raw materials resulting from the first round of import substitution, a renewed effort was made to cut down the dependence on imported inputs by means of further substitution. This, however, required diverting scarce foreign exchange from "maintenance imports" (raw materials and intermediate goods for existing industries) to the import of capital goods for the installation of additional capacity. A restriction of the availability of maintenance imports, however, led to increasing excess capacity in established industrial plants. Thus, Latin America found itself suddenly with industrial plants being operated at a fraction of rated capacity. The increase in industrial costs that ensued was validated with further protection. With the industrial sector often contributing upwards of 20% of GNP, the magnitude of the social waste implied by excess capacity is rather substantial. An estimate of its size can be derived from Argentinian data where capacity utilization has fluctuated between 55% and 67% from 1961 to 1965.[1] Taking an average of 60% utilization and considering a target of 90%, Argentina could have had a 50% higher industrial output. Since industry contributes 30% to 35% of GNP, this implies that total (and per capita) national income could have been some 15% higher each year. Thus, even excluding investment effects out of the higher income, excess capacity meant that Argentina lost one year's worth of GNP every six years."

This building up of overprotected industrial sectors adversely affects the next stage of transformation. No nation, however vast, can continue to expand its industrial sector without a return to the world market. As W. Arthur Lewis repeatedly stressed, there has been a phenomenal growth of exports in the world market. But high-cost industry competes only with great difficulty in international trade, especially when exchange rates are overvalued. Moreover, as Professor Wellisz's paper made clear, an industrial sector that absorbs more resources than it subsequently makes available is not only a poor competitor internationally. It is also in no position to provide a margin for further investments, particularly in agriculture where modernization is required if food supplies are to keep pace with growing demand and if rising food imports, eating up scarce foreign exchange, are to be avoided.

This constraint—of inadequate exports and a lag in local agricultural supplies—has appeared throughout Latin America and in the Indian subcontinent. Both farm and export sectors have suffered from planners' and administrators' neglect until crises, marked by internal inflation and external pressure on the balance of payments, have virtually blown up in their faces. But a crisis point is not the easiest time for the elaboration of alternative policies; in some cases it has led to a melancholy spiral—devaluation, further inflation, increased costs, renewed balance of payment problems, and yet another devaluation. The economy spins round and round the same unconquered obstacles like a gramophone record with the needle jammed.

However, at the Conference the experts from Latin America itself were far more impressed by the *external* difficulties involved in successful industrialization, in particular by the problem of getting their manufactures into a world market restricted and controlled by the developed powers. They underlined repeatedly the fact that the already industrialized nations, by tariff and quota policies designed to keep out competitive manufactures from developing lands, make nonsense of the whole theory of comparative advantage upon which the classical case for free trade is based. As one participant put it: "At least abide by your own rules."

All this is not to say that economic difficulties of transformation cannot be overcome. Professor Chenery's list of thirty-one countries which, over the last two decades, have surpassed or nearly reached the Pearson target figure of a 6% annual growth includes a wide spectrum of size, culture, geographical distribution, and original per capita income. Moreover, they have, as he pointed out in his paper, followed very different strategies in coping with the problems of transformation—some with high aid and some with high exports; some with less capital inflow and more internal mobilization; some with almost no external dependence at all. Yet they have not only grown. Half of them grew more rapidly in the 1960's than in the 1950's. Two-thirds saved a higher proportion of their GNP in the second decade. These are the figures which underpin both George Woods' earlier assertion of success in development and the Pearson Report's conclusion that an unprecedented surge of growth *is* taking place.

SOCIAL TRANSFORMATION

Yet, in spite of such well-documented evidence, most of the participants concluded that growth as such can be considered a necessary but not sufficient target of development strategy. The insufficiency of growth alone is not rooted in the difficulties inherent in the various economic stages of transformation. Indeed, these difficulties can hardly be surmounted without a strong thrust of expansion. The trouble lies in the whole variety of social, political, and historical changes which both determine and are determined by the process of economic growth. Peter Williams' reminder in his paper, "Education for Development," that "developing *societies* and not developing *economies* . . . ought to form the subject of discussion" accurately reflected the main thrust of the debate.

The early stages of modernization are always times of upheaval and tension. In the pre-technological society, incomes, rights, and opportunities are determined more by tradition than by skill. Once efficiency and productivity become the criteria—as they must if growth is to begin—the weak, the unskilled, the marginal men of all kinds lose the safeguards of custom. Farm laborers can no longer graze a couple of animals on neglected hedgerows or fallow land. A host of retainers hired for display, not work, are dismissed as the landowner gets down to profit and loss. These uprooted country people drift off to the harsh, unfamiliar conditions of raw, new, industrial towns, where, at first, by sheer numbers, they push wages down to bare subsistence. Meanwhile, the increasing rewards of an economy which is beginning to expand go to the skillful, the adventurous, the lucky, and the rich, who have the immediate gifts and resources needed in the dynamic new sectors. For a time—and it may be a long time—the gaps between classes, groups, and regions tend to widen. At this early stage, the old "welfare" systems of clan and village are disrupted, economic "trickle-down" has had little effect, often no political effort toward redistribution has been undertaken. Such impoverishment of the many and success of the few can lead to violent confrontation and unrest.

This cycle of early modernization, first played out in Europe, had, by the 1840's, set in motion an almost continuous tremor of social protest and led, in 1848, to the "year of revolutions." It can be argued —and it was forcibly so argued at the Conference—that the social consequences of economic growth for developing nations are potentially even more disruptive today.

There are two reasons for this risk. The first is historical. The first developers escaped from the "contradictions" of early transformation not only by skill but by enormous good fortune. Developing nations today have no guarantee that they will be able to repeat it. It may be a "one shot" historical event. As The Honourable Lester B. Pearson suggested in his Conference address (see Chapter 5), the phase of disruption in early Atlantic development was mitigated and overcome by several specific strokes of political good luck, above all by the ability of the Americans and the Europeans to take over all the planet's remaining unconquered or unsettled fertile, temperate land. As he put it, this "bonanza" was secured "with little more cost than that of running the Indians and the Aborigines and the Bantu off their ancestral lands." This eased the most critical of all pressures on early development which was, in the view of contemporary critics, fundamentally a crisis of population pressing on food supplies. Demand pushed food prices upward, prices pushed up wages, rising wages threatened to squeeze out the profit margins needed for reinvestment.

Other specifically nineteenth-century phenomena also played a part in easing population pressure. Birthrates and death rates remained high for at least half of the century, and population growth rarely exceeded 1.8% a year. Moreover—again, the historical good fortune— some 40 million migrants left the cramped cities and consolidated farms of Europe for the free land and almost unlimited labor market of the

United States. The annual growth in the labor force seems to have remained well below 1% a year. And, as Mr. Woods pointed out in his Stockholm speech, the early nineteenth-century growth of the labor force coincided with crude mechanization using thousands upon thousands of unskilled "hands," so unskilled indeed that they could be the hands of pauper children. Some six or seven decades later, when technology had begun its steady advance toward greater sophistication and called for a smaller, more skilled labor force, family size had become stable and education was becoming available for more and more children. In short, the "transformations," difficult as they were, had an inner tendency toward a measure of balance.

The exact opposite is the case today. The measures of public health and epidemic control invented and introduced by the pioneers have sent population rocketing ahead of every other form of growth. Population grows on the average by 2.8% a year, by 3% and more in many areas. The annual entry into the labor force is roughly 2% a year. Yet, in any but the short run, highly productive agriculture tends to release labor. In industry, the new techniques, again invented by the pioneers and designed for societies rich in capital and stable in numbers, are, virtually without exception, capital-intensive. Yet it is claimed that these are the techniques that must be adopted if developing industry is to be efficient enough to compete in world markets dominated by super-efficient producers from America, Europe, and Japan.

Migration is no longer any solution since the "empty" fertile lands are used up—again the historical, "one-shot" chance—and rigid limits are, in any case, set on the movement of peoples of alien culture or color. This does not mean that migration is not occurring. It is doing so in a human avalanche resembling the old "Völkerwanderungen" from the Asian steppes. But the migrants move, in the main, not across frontiers but within nations. They stream away from underemployment on the farms to the risk of unemployment in the cities. Cities are growing two and three times as rapidly as population itself, and the trend of unemployment is steadily upward. In the all but unanimous view of the Conference, the continuous piling up of unemployed millions in these miserable, hungry megalopolises brings together, in a concentrated risk of explosion, all the contradictions of current transformation— too many people and too few jobs, too many births and not enough food, too much labor and too little capital, cities ahead of jobs, technologies which do not fit, markets blocked at home by poverty and abroad by the protectionism of the already developed nations.

In the view of the majority of the Conference participants, the simple pursuit of economic growth would fail to overcome most of these critical social and political obstacles to long-term development and stability. In the poorest communities, such as the African mini-states, even a 6% rate of growth over the next decade would raise the per capita income only from $80 to $167, as G. K. Helleiner pointed out (see "Structural Change in Africa" in this chapter). In most developing countries, large or small, at least a quarter of the population would, with almost mathematical certainty, be left behind in the movement toward higher income and would subsist, in despairing unemployment, on the margins of life in farm and city.

Moreover, in the world at large, the already developed states, with widespread control of the world's resources, an overwhelming concentration of the world's capital, and a virtual monopoly in the world's research, will be bound to leave the developing nations (even if they grow at 6% a year) further and further behind with all that this disparity entails in terms of unequal world privilege, control, and bargaining power. The most succinct definition of this gap was given by Robert McNamara, President of the World Bank, in his address to the Conference:

In the developing world, at the end of the [first] decade [of development] malnutrition is common. The FAO [Food and Agriculture Organization] estimates that at least a third to a half of the world's people suffer from hunger or nutritional deprivation. The average person in a high standard area consumes four pounds of food a day as compared with an average pound and a quarter in a low standard area. . . .

Illiteracy is widespread. There are 100 million more illiterates today than there were 20 years ago, bringing the total number to some 800 million.

Unemployment is endemic and growing. The equivalent of approximately 20% of the entire male labor force is unemployed, and in many areas the urban population is growing twice as fast as the number of urban jobs.

The distribution of income and wealth is severely skewed. In India, 12% of the rural families control more than half of the cultivated land. And in Brazil, less than 10% of the families control 75% of the land.

The gap between the per capita incomes of the rich nations and the poor nations is widening rather than narrowing, both relatively and absolutely. At the extremes that gap is already more than $3,000. Present projections indicate it may well widen to $9,000 by the end of the century. In the year 2000, per capita income in the United States is expected to be approximately $10,000; in Brazil, $500; and in India $200.

To sum up, one can say that there was general acceptance of the judgment which opens the Pearson Report: "The widening gap between the developed and developing countries has become a central issue of our time." The controversy turned on the question of whether the Pearson Report, by suggesting continuities of experience between developed and developing states, by leaving out the critical influence of the historical record, and by "soft-pedaling" the extraordinary privileges of the rich donor countries, had not presented the "central issue" in terms which underplay the full scale of the world's crisis and tragedy. In fact, the whole thrust of the Conference, "to go beyond the Report," sprang from a feeling of need to supplement targets of growth and economic criteria with the social and historical realities that lie behind modernization in the late twentieth century.

AIMS AND POLICIES

These preoccupations helped to fix the pattern of the debates. Whatever the topic—growth and structural change, trade and liquidity, private investment, the aid relationship—a common theme and common divisions tended to appear. A minority continued to believe that, both locally and internationally, rapid economic growth within the market would provide the chief stimulus and resources for a better life. At the other end of the spectrum, a larger minority argued for the breaking of all links with established market economies in practice as in theory. Aid should be rejected as a possible contamination by false ideals and an almost certain loss of political and economic control; trade should be drastically redirected away from developed markets and toward strong regional groupings in the new continents; domestic economic policy should be strictly subordinated to social and political needs. Between these opposite views, the majority came to develop the "sense of the meeting" set down in the Columbia Declaration.

The later chapters of this book examine the implications of the debate from the international perspective of trade, investment, and aid. In this section it only remains to give some idea of the various proposals for domestic policy in developing lands which emerged from the debate.

Naturally, specific targets can only be related to specific countries. Conclusions on policy have, therefore, to be stated fairly broadly:

1. There was general support for the call made by both Mr. Mc-Namara and Professor Jan Tinbergen for the inclusion of social objectives in development planning. In Mr. McNamara's words:

In setting the objectives, planning the programs, and measuring the progress of development in the 1970's, we must look to more than gross measures of economic growth. What we require are relevant "development indicators" that go beyond the measure of total growth in total output and provide practical yardsticks of change in the other economic, social, and moral dimensions of the modernizing process. To limit our attention to expanding GNP, even though it be from 5% per year to 6% or 7%, can only lead to greater political, social, and economic disequilibrium. However important an increase in GNP may be as a necessary condition of development, it is not a sufficient condition.

2. There were various proposals for mitigating the social disruptions of early growth. In his paper Professor Chenery suggested that it might be wise to look not for a maximum growth rate but for an optimum one. For instance, in countries with a per capita income of less than $500, a 6% to 7% rate of growth might produce excessive social strain; a lower rate could be desirable. This found an echo particularly among the African participants who argued that noneconomic values such as a sense of community, the preservation of stability in rural life, and measures of purposive control over the exodus to the cities should be given equal weight with targets for growth.

3. Specific social objectives included population control virtually as a matter of course. Many participants, however, argued against approaching population policy simply in terms of stemming the fatal tide of uncontrollable expansion. They felt much more emphasis should be put upon small family size as a key to genuine family welfare and argued that measures for improving health, education, and housing should be closely linked to population control, particularly in the international approach to the question.

4. A lively debate developed on the possibilities of using purposive policies of controlled urban development in order to secure better regional balance, to check the risk of avoidable pollution, to slow down the hemorrhage of people, particularly young people, to the largest

cities, and to use more widely the labor-intensive possibilities of urban construction. There was some emphasis on the likelihood that such a policy could be firmly rooted in self-help projects, both for work and for financing.

5. In a sense, these approaches to a positive policy of urban construction can be seen as part of a wider and exceptionally vivid concern for the problem of unemployment in the 1970's. To quote Mr. Mc-Namara once more: "Just as the censuses of the 1950's helped to alert us to the scale of the population explosion, the urban and employment crises of the 1960's are alerting us to the scale of social displacement and general uprootedness of populations which are exploding not only in numbers but in movement as well."

Formal strategies for creating employment cannot, of course, be divorced from rising economic growth rates. But much more emphasis should be placed on finding effective labor-intensive technologies; on planning rural and urban public works; on selecting the kinds of education that encourage self-help and decentralized initiative; on lessening, without loss of efficiency, the concentration of resources in too few hands.

6. This last suggestion points to the larger issue of the proper distribution of gains from economic growth. There appeared to be virtual unanimity that it was no longer morally acceptable or politically possible to encourage rapid growth by concentrating its rewards on a dominant few and postponing its redistribution to some future condition of much increased national wealth. Unproductive feudal farm ownership and management, agricultural policies which consolidate farm ownership and pauperize the smaller peasants, industrial policies which draw vast, unskilled migrations into towns ahead of any hope of employment, taxation which bypasses the rich in the name of encouraging enterprise, incentives to foreign business in the shape of the free movement of capital which permit a local elite to send their wealth to "safe havens" overseas—all these are incompatible with hopes of stable development in the years ahead. As a warning, many cited Pakistan's violent social explosion after nearly a decade of high economic growth.

Any policy strongly designed to keep social reform and economic growth in balance would demand decisive and dedicated political leadership. This was not questioned. But few participants felt that they knew enough to determine exactly what the trade-offs between the two might be. Professor Chenery drew attention to the lack of concrete data in this field. As Professor Wellisz made clear in his paper, the pursuit of social justice, either in the form of wider distribution or of public control over the "commanding heights" of the economy, cannot be combined in any easy way with policies for rapid growth and increasing efficiency. India's struggles with this problem show how easy it is to miss an effective combination of the two and possibly produce less of either as a result.

7. These uncertainties underline a final conclusion of the Conference—the need for more knowledge, more interdisciplinary exchanges, better analysis, and new working strategies for all these critical points at which economic growth and social change impinge upon each other with still unpredictable results. Once again, Mr. McNamara's conclusion can be quoted to sum up the matter: "We should be frank about this. As we enter the 1970's, in field after field, we have more questions than answers. Our urgent need is for new instruments of research and analysis with which to dispel our ignorance of the social dimensions of economic change and help us formulate a more comprehensive strategy for the decade ahead."

Targets for Development

BY HOLLIS B. CHENERY

To show what might be achieved with more effective development policies and more adequate external assistance, the Pearson Commission sets out some general targets: a 6% rate of growth in as many countries as possible, an approach toward independence of concessional aid, and the modernization of the economic and social structure. While these

I am indebted to Hazel Elkington for research assistance and to Branko Horvat, Michael Bruno, Richard Jolly, and other participants in the Columbia Conference for helpful comments.

The background research on this paper was supported by the Project for Quantitative Research in Economic Development through funds provided by the Agency for International Development under Contract CSD-1543. The views expressed in this paper do not, however, necessarily reflect the views of AID.

seem to be the right general objectives, they need to be further differentiated according to the conditions of each country. It is difficult to judge the validity of the 6% growth target for the future without a clearer understanding of how accelerated growth has been achieved in the past.

In this paper I shall try to distinguish among countries according to their levels of income, economic structures, and development strategies. I shall try in this way to identify the differences in the development targets that may be appropriate for different types of country without having to treat each country as a unique case. The analytical framework is provided by recent econometric work on the sources of economic growth and the nature of the structural changes that accompany it.

The analysis is in three parts: the nature of structural changes that affect the rate of growth and the utilization of external resources; the results of econometric studies of the sources of growth; and a classification of the development strategies of thirty-one countries that have experienced successful development over the past two decades into four principal types. The results are brought together in the concluding section, which proposes a differentiated set of development targets and some specific criteria for judging performance.

GROWTH AND STRUCTURAL CHANGE

The Annexes to the Pearson Report contain many illustrations of the effects of differences in economic structure on a country's rate of development and need for assistance. For example, small countries rely much more heavily on international trade than large ones, their growth is correspondingly more affected by trade, and they receive larger capital inflows per capita. Countries having favorable raw material exports need aid only to supplement domestic savings and investment, while those with less favorable resources may find the import-supplementing aspect of aid to be of greater importance. Countries having a large agricultural sector and little industry find it more difficult to raise the growth rate to 6% than do those in which the share of agriculture has been reduced to a smaller proportion. These are examples of structural features that need to be taken into account in an analysis of development targets and strategies.

In order to determine the interrelations between growth and the structure of an economy, we need to have an idea of the variation in the structure of production and trade that normally takes place as income rises. Empirical studies such as those of Kuznets have shown that almost all aspects of the economic structure—rates of saving and investment, the composition of demand and production, the pattern of trade, the allocation of capital and labor—change systematically as the level of income rises.[1] These normal patterns of development can be traced to similarities among societies in their tastes, access to technology and international trade, and common elements of development policy. We can measure both the normal variation with income and the effects of other factors (such as size, resources, capital inflow) by means of multiple regression analysis based on statistics for all countries.[2]

When we think of "development" as distinct from "growth," we normally have in mind the set of structural changes that are needed to sustain future growth of output and to respond to the changing needs of the society. While in the long run growth and development go together, they need not do so over periods as short as a decade. Thus an expansion of GNP based on the growth of primary exports without other changes in resource allocation constitutes growth with little development, while large increases in infrastructure and education that have not led to increased output in other sectors represent development without much growth. In determining the success of countries in achieving their long-term economic objectives, one must take account of both current growth and the structural changes that will facilitate—or impede—future growth.

Table 1 lists a number of measures of structural characteristics that may affect the present and future rate of growth. The factors that receive most attention in theories of growth are the accumulation of capital, skills, and other productive factors, all of which are included in the first group.

In addition to increasing the supply of inputs, a country must allocate them according to its changing pattern of demand and its opportunities for international trade. As development progresses, a country's difficulties in transforming the structure of its economy in order to maintain a balance between supply and demand in each sector are often greater than its difficulties in accumulation. Aggregate measures of the composition of production, labor use, and trade are given in the re-

TABLE 1. NORMAL VARIATIONS IN ECONOMIC STRUCTURE WITH LEVEL OF DEVELOPMENT

	Level of GNP per capita (in 1964 U.S. dollars)								
	$50	$100	$200	$300	$400	$600	$800	$1,000	$2,000
I—Accumulation									
1. Gross National Savings, as % of GNP	9.4	12.0	14.8	16.4	17.6	19.3	20.5	21.5	24.6
2. Gross Domestic Investment, as % of GDP	11.7	15.1	18.2	19.7	20.8	22.2	23.0	23.7	25.4
3. Tax revenue, as % of national income	9.8	12.7	16.7	19.5	21.8	25.3	28.0	30.3	28.0
4. School enrollment rate	17.5	36.2	52.6	61.2	66.9	74.2	78.9	82.3	91.4
5. Adult literacy rate	15.3	36.5	55.2	65.0	71.5	80.0	85.4	89.4	93.0
II—Output Composition									
6. Primary share of GDP	58.1	46.4	36.0	30.4	26.7	21.8	18.6	16.3	9.8
7. Industry share of GDP	7.3	13.5	19.6	23.1	25.5	29.0	31.4	33.2	38.9
8. Services share of GDP	29.9	34.6	37.9	39.2	39.9	40.4	40.5	40.4	39.3
9. Utilities share of GDP	4.6	5.7	7.0	7.7	8.3	9.1	9.7	10.2	11.7
III—Labor Force									
10. Primary labor, as % of total labor force	75.3	68.1	58.7	49.9	43.6	34.8	28.6	23.7	8.3
11. Industrial labor, as % of total labor force	4.1	9.6	16.6	20.5	23.4	27.6	30.7	33.2	40.1
12. Services labor, as % of total labor force	20.6	22.3	26.7	29.3	31.7	35.8	39.2	42.2	51.6
13. Urban population, as % of total population	4.1	20.0	33.8	40.9	45.5	51.5	55.3	58.0	65.1

IV—Trade

14. Exports of goods & services as % of GDP	9.9	13.2	16.3	18.0	19.1	20.7	21.8	22.5	24.8
15. Imports of goods & services as % of GDP	16.6	18.7	20.6	21.6	22.3	23.2	23.8	24.3	25.5
16. Primary exports as % of total exports	89	78	68	61	56	50	46	42	33
17. Primary imports as % of total imports	10	18	25	27	28	29	30	30	30

Source: All values are computed from multiple regressions for a sample of about 100 countries over the period 1950–65. The values shown apply to a country of 10 million population in the year 1960. Underlying data are taken from the International Bank for Reconstruction and Development, *World Tables*, December, 1968. Further details are given in Hollis Chenery, Hazel Elkington, and Christopher Sims, "A Uniform Analysis of Development Patterns," Economic Development Report no. 148, Harvard University, January, 1970, multilith.

Note: Levels for $50, $100, and $1,000 have been adjusted proportionately to total 100%.

maining sections. Table 1 gives the normal variation on each index with the level of income, abstracting from differences in size and resources.

The following discussion illustrates the changing importance of several aspects of accumulation and transformation as the level of income rises. "Early development" can be thought of as the increase of per capita GNP from $50 to $300. "Later development" covers the range from $300 to $800, a point at which the effects of increases in capital accumulation, industrialization, education, and urbanization have largely run their course. Concessionary loans ("aid") are largely limited to the early stages and are later replaced as sources of capital and foreign exchange by exports and by other types of foreign investment.

In an intercountry comparison, gross savings (line 1) rises fairly steadily from 10% of GNP at the lowest income levels to over 20% for developed countries. The transfer of capital normally adds 2½% to 3% to domestic resources at lower incomes, so that investment rates (line 2) rise from 12% to 19% in the early stages. Government tax revenue (line 3) shows an even greater increase—from 10% to 20% of GNP—between $50 and $300 per capita and continues to rise thereafter. This greater government control over resources affects development primarily through expenditures on education, health, and other public services rather than through increased investment.

The accumulation of skills can be measured by indices of enrollment or literacy. They show that education is now stressed at early stages of development (a few countries with income levels below $200 have educational attainments comparable to the advanced countries). The normal relationships given in Table 1 are also among the few that show a marked upward trend in the postwar period. While there is considerable evidence that an increase in education and skills is needed to sustain rapid growth, statistical estimates of this requirement are less satisfactory than those for capital.

The data in Table 1 indicate that by the time a country reaches the middle income level of $300 it is typically investing 50% more of its national income and educating three times as large a proportion of its children as the poorest countries. Since the capital and skills required per unit of output do not increase significantly at this level of income, higher rates of accumulation should lead to higher rates of growth if the resources are properly used. It is therefore reasonable to expect

higher growth and to set higher targets for middle income countries
than for very low income countries.

Transformation

Continued growth requires a reallocation of labor and capital in
accordance with changes in demand and comparative advantage. The
average transformation of the economy is shown in Table 1 by the
changes in the composition of output, trade, and the labor force. The
possibilities for deviation from these normal patterns arise primarily
through international trade, which enables small countries to follow
a pattern of output growth that may differ substantially from the pattern of domestic demand. Large countries are much more constrained
by the need for balanced growth, since trade constitutes a much smaller
proportion of GNP.

The existing composition of demand and output provides an additional set of constraints that affects the overall rate of growth. Since
agriculture typically comprises more than half of the output of the poorest countries, its growth potential is a predominant factor in the total.
More than other sectors, the growth of agriculture is constrained by the
rate at which new techniques can be adopted, cropping patterns changed,
and organizational changes carried out. Sustained growth rates of agriculture in excess of 5% are rare, whereas growth of industry at 10%
or more is common. Although the difference is partly explained by a
lower income elasticity of demand for foodstuffs, there appears to be a
limit to agricultural growth from the supply side that is determined by
the knowledge and entrepreneurial ability of the many small productive
units involved. In support of this hypothesis is the fact that the Ivory
Coast appears to be the only country that has sustained a 6% rate of
growth for as much as a decade starting with an agricultural sector of
more than 50% of GNP.

As industry (plus mining) approaches agriculture in size, countries
become capable of more rapid growth, particularly during the period
in which domestic manufacturing is substituting for imported goods.
This transformation can only take place as per capita income rises and
the share of food in total demand declines substantially, since it is rarely
economical to exchange manufactured goods for imported food at low
income levels.

Some of the effects of the changing structure of output on the potential rate of growth of total production can be illustrated by the following example. If we make the favorable assumptions of a 4.5% growth potential in agriculture, a 9.5% growth of industry and utilities and a constant share of services over the lower income range from $50 to $300 per capita,[3] the growth potential rises from 5.4% to 7% as the shares of industry, utilities, and primary production vary as shown in Table 1. Although an increase in accumulation and other conditions are required to achieve this result, enough countries have been able to accelerate growth in this way so that it may be regarded as a norm for a well-functioning economy in the lower income range—provided foreign assistance is available in the early stages.

The principal obstacles to accelerated growth in the middle income range also arise from the changing structure of demand and supply.[4] These are summarized in the theory of balanced growth. Although theories of this type typically underestimate the opportunities for maintaining balance through changing the composition of trade, many countries have been unable to carry out the policy changes required, which include a shift from protection to promotion of industrial exports, through devaluation or otherwise. Countries having a pronounced comparative advantage in primary exports (such as Argentina or Venezuela) can maintain growth on this basis for some time, but they usually encounter the same difficulties of transformation (perhaps in more acute form) at a higher level of income. Such variations from the average patterns of transformation are considered later.

Urbanization and Employment

There are a number of other aspects of structural change that are relevant to the setting of development targets but can only be mentioned here. Most important for human welfare are the possibilities of providing full employment for the labor force. As shown in Table 1, the pattern of employment differs from the production patterns already discussed. At lower income levels, the share of labor employed in primary sectors is much higher than the share of output, but the disparities in labor productivity are reduced as income rises. Urbanization often proceeds more rapidly than the rise of industrial employment unless GNP is growing in excess of 6% per year.[5] This phenomenon—which is analyzed in the dual economy, surplus labor theories of Lewis and of Fei and Ranis [6]—provides an opportunity for rapid growth during the interval in which urban real wages remain fairly constant because of the rapid migration to cities. Furthermore, it is hard to see how the problems created by urbanization can be solved without rapid growth of income.

Ultimately, successful development requires a fall in birthrates as well as death rates and a slowing down of population growth. Although the social and economic factors affecting the birthrate are not well understood, there is considerable evidence connecting lower fertility rates to both education and urbanization. A more complete understanding of alternative population policies may well show that these structural changes are important in lowering the denominator as well as raising the numerator of the income per head index.

STATISTICAL EXPLANATIONS OF GROWTH

There have been a number of attempts to measure the effects of several of the factors considered above on the rates of growth of both underdeveloped and advanced countries. Although these studies have had only partial success in explaining the causes of growth, they provide some perspective on the relative importance of the factors considered and also provide indices of the relative efficiency of different countries.

Time Series Estimates

The predominant methodology for analyzing the sources of growth in advanced countries is that developed by Solow and others for the United States and extended to Europe by Denison.[7] The technique consists essentially in estimating statistically the contribution of increases in capital and labor to growth under the assumption that each factor receives its marginal product and then attributing the unexplained residual to technological change. The most notable results for the advanced countries are that: (1) growth of the capital stock accounts for less than a quarter of the total growth of GNP; (2) the residual—technological change—typically accounts for half of a total growth of 4% to 5%.

This methodology must be modified to apply it to less developed countries because the assumption that the relative contributions of labor and capital to growth are measured by their shares of GNP is more dubious. Most studies of developing countries have concluded that the labor share of income exceeds its marginal product and therefore the share of capital understates its contribution to growth. When allowance is made for this fact, capital accumulation has been shown to be much more important to the growth of middle income countries and to account for 40% to 50% or more of the total increase.[8]

The residual growth that is unexplained by increased inputs is less important in most of the low income countries than in the advanced ones. These results should discourage the uncritical application to less developed countries of the conclusion from Europe and the United States that growth can be secured primarily by technological change. The only recorded cases in which more than two percentage points of growth can be attributed to technological change are Israel, Yugoslavia, and Japan, in which overall growth has averaged 9% to 10%, half of which is attributable to capital formation.

The existing methodology of aggregate time-series analysis explains growth by increases in inputs and makes little allowance for the types of disequilibrium that result from difficulties in transformation and resource allocation. Although these effects can be captured in development plans and programming models, they have not yet been incorporated into the techniques of growth accounting because of the short time-series available for each country. The best evidence as to their relative importance therefore comes from intercountry comparisons.

Cross-Country Estimates

A number of attempts have been made to associate differences in rates of growth with structural factors through statistical analysis of growth data for a number of countries. Here the assumptions of equilibrium growth can be dropped and allowance made for the initial composition of output, the possibility of balance of payments disequilibrium, and other aspects of structural change. The main weaknesses of the intercountry estimates are: (1) their assumption that the explanatory factors affect each country in the same way; (2) the lack of an adequate model of disequilibrium growth on which to base the analysis. Despite these limitations, regression analyses can identify factors that are important to growth even though they do not determine the nature of the causal relationships.

Such studies test the effects of the increase in capital and labor, the level of income, and several aspects of structural disequilibrium. They also bring out some significant differences between underdeveloped and advanced countries. The latter conform more closely to neoclassical assumptions and show less effect of surplus labor, trade bottlenecks, or other disequilibrium forces.

The following findings are particularly significant for the assessment of development targets of underdeveloped countries:

1. The rate of investment and the level of income are the largest single influences on the rate of growth.

2. The inflow of capital (net foreign balance) contributes to the explanation of the variation in growth rates over and above its contribution to the financing of investment. This result is consistent with the two-gap analysis of the effects of foreign assistance.[9] Robinson has shown that the effect of capital inflow on the growth of large countries is particularly marked, reflecting the fact that they receive less aid per capita.[10]

3. The results support the hypothesis of a normal rise in growth rates up to income levels of $300 as the share of agriculture declines, even when allowance is made for variation in investment rates and other factors.

4. Taken together, these factors explain 70% of the variation in growth rates of less developed countries in the decade 1951–59 but a smaller proportion in more recent periods.

In addition to showing the average effects of the several explanatory variables considered, the intercountry regressions also provide a rough basis for judging the development performance of each country. There are few countries whose performance diverges by much more than 1% from the predicted growth rates. The notably efficient countries in this sense are Israel, Taiwan, and Mexico, while the relatively inefficient ones are Algeria, Peru, Uruguay, and Ceylon.[11] There are few surprises in either group. It is notable, however, that the high growth rates of Japan, Greece, Spain, and Thailand are not much more than would be predicted by their level of income, rates of investment, and capital inflow.

Since the regression equations reflect the performance of all countries, they tend to overstate the amount of increase in aid or investment that would be needed to sustain a higher growth rate in a country with relatively efficient policies. To get at this question, I will analyze the development strategies followed by the more successful performers over the past two decades.

THE VARIETIES OF SUCCESS

While formal statistical analysis can identify factors that have a significant effect on growth, it cannot capture the interaction among various elements in a successful development strategy. For this purpose we must resort to less formal methods and depend more heavily on judgment of the factors that are important to each country.

As a starting point, I have taken sixty countries which had a per capita income of less than $600 (in 1964 prices) in 1950 and for which the World Bank has been able to compile relatively complete information on the major components of the GNP covering most of the period 1950–67.[12] From this sample, I have chosen thirty-one countries that have shown the ability to sustain a relatively high rate of growth for the whole period, making some allowance for countries having a very large agricultural sector to start with. More specifically, the sample includes twenty-nine countries having an average growth rate of at least 5.5% for the seventeen years plus Nigeria and Pakistan (initial agriculture of over 55%) which have attained this rate in the last decade of the period.[13]

In analyzing the sources of this successful performance, I will be primarily interested in three aspects: (1) the financing of investment as among domestic savings, private foreign investment, and public external sources; (2) the role of natural resources, as evidenced by primary exports; (3) the transformation of the economy, as evidenced by the lead or lag of industrialization compared to normal patterns. Measures of the deviations of trade and production patterns from the normal for a given income level (and country size) were used to measure the last two characteristics. Indicators of all the three characteristics are given in Table 2.

To get an idea of the role of external resources in these cases, we need to know the extent to which investment was financed by external capital in different parts of the seventeen-year period, the extent to which external dependence was reduced, and the way in which the productive structure was adapted to maintain sectoral balance. Several measures of structural change relevant to these processes are given in Table 2.

A preliminary analysis of these data shows that there are basic differences in patterns of resource allocation between the countries enjoying large supplies of foreign exchange through aid or primary exports (primarily small countries) and countries lacking these external sources (mainly large countries). Such considerations led to a grouping of the cases of successful development into the four types of strategy:

A. *High Capital Inflow:* More than 35% of investment financed by aid or other foreign sources for at least the first decade.

B. *High Primary Exports:* Levels of primary exports at least 50% above normal values (and typically twice as high).[14] The existence of high primary exports seems to be more important in characterizing the pattern of resource allocation than the capital inflow, although they sometimes go together.[15]

C. *Moderate Capital Inflow:* Countries having external financing to the extent of 10% to 30% of investment during most of the period.

D. *Low External Dependence:* Countries having none of the above.

As the following discussion shows, these features are associated with characteristic leads and lags in the growth of industry and primary production and hence can be described as different strategies of development.

Strategy A: High Aid

The seven countries that have been able to achieve high growth rates on the basis of large amounts of external capital are all small (except Korea) and have received support for a variety of political reasons. Typically they started the period in difficult political circumstances and with unfavorable resource bases. The capital inflow has amounted to 5% to 10% of GNP for substantial periods and was largely public. In almost all cases there has been a substantial rise in investment in the second decade, reduced dependence on capital inflow, and a shift toward private sources of financing.

The essence of the high aid strategy is to permit the country to expand the sectors that can grow most readily without having to worry about balance of payments problems in the near future. In most of these

TABLE 2. A CLASSIFICATION OF DEVELOPMENT STRATEGIES OF HIGH GROWTH COUNTRIES

Country	1950 GNP per Capita	Pop. (1960) (mill.)	GNP Growth 1951–59	GNP Growth 1960–67	Pop. Growth	Per Cap. GNP Increase (1950–67)	Investment Ratio 1950–55	Investment Ratio 1960–65
(1)	(2)	(3)	(4)	(5)	(6)	(7)	(8)	(9)
A–Strategy: High Aid								
1. Israel	$506	2.1	11.5%	7.5%	4.8%	2.23%	.310	.237
2. Taiwan	105	10.6	8.2	9.4	3.3	2.21	.138	.220
3. Jordan	106	1.7	8.8	8.2	3.1	2.00	—	.165
4. Greece	261	8.3	6.2	7.3	0.9	2.41	.177	.249
5. Puerto Rico	441	2.4	5.5	8.1	1.5	2.52	.196	.252
6. Korea	99	24.7	5.4	6.9	2.8	1.48	.120	.164
7. Panama	313	1.1	4.4	8.5	3.1	1.56	.107	.191
B–Strategy: High Primary Exports								
1. Thailand	64	26.4	6.9	7.5	3.0	1.98	.181	.213
2. Trinidad	282	0.8	9.0	6.4	2.9	2.15	.229	.264
3. Jamaica	293	1.6	8.3	4.5	1.8	1.50	.135	.217
4. Malaysia	155	8.1	—	6.7	3.0	1.77	—	—
5. Iran	156	21.5	—	7.8	2.7	1.60	—	.172
6. Nicaragua	190	1.4	5.7	6.8	3.1	1.64	.171	.175
7. Venezuela	537	7.3	8.3	4.2	3.8	1.51	.251	.189
8. Ivory Coast	181	3.3	—	19.1	2.6	—	—	.172
9. Iraq	172	6.9	5.8	7.2	2.8	1.49	.215	.173
10. Zambia	121	3.2	*6.0	6.0	2.9	1.46	.240	.259
11. Rhodesia	151	3.6	6.7	5.3	3.2	1.38	.352	.175
C–Strategy: Moderate Capital Inflow								
1. Mexico	285	36.0	6.0	6.5	3.3	1.60	.130	.161
2. Turkey	159	27.5	6.8	5.3	2.7	1.75	.166	.164
3. UAR	80	25.8	6.2	5.5	2.8	1.83	—	.142
4. Peru	183	10.0	4.7	6.5	2.7	1.74	.198	.203
5. Philippines	106	27.4	6.1	4.7	3.2	1.41	.119	.182
6. Pakistan*	70	92.7	2.9	6.1	2.2	1.24	(.08)	.13
7. Sudan*	63	11.8	4.3	7.3	2.8	1.49	.053	.113
8. Nigeria*	54	—	3.5	6.0	2.1	1.44	—	—
D–Strategy: Low External Dependence								
1. Japan	329	93.2	8.1	11.0	1.0	2.89	.252	.268
2. Yugoslavia	233	18.4	8.9	6.6	1.2	2.55	.314	.375
3. Spain	274	30.3	5.1	8.7	0.8	2.24	.179	.213
4. Bulgaria	269	7.9	8.8	7.3	0.8	2.22	—	.392
5. Brazil	160	69.7	5.9	4.5	3.1	1.43	.135	.150

* Countries having more than 50 percent of GNP from agriculture in 1950.
# Columns 17 and 19: 1950 except 1955.
§ Columns 17 and 19: 1950 except 1960.

Sources: The basic data were compiled and circulated in December, 1968, by the Economics Department, Comparative Data Unit, International Bank for Reconstruction and Development, under the title, *World Tables*. References are to that volume unless otherwise noted. The data came from UN, IBRD Country Reports and national sources. The sample includes all countries having a growth rate of 5.5% or more in GDP plus several borderline cases (see text).

Col. 2: 1950 GNP per capita in 1964 U.S. dollars from Table IV, Col. 17.
Col. 3: 1960 (midyear) population (Table II, Col. 1).

External Fin. 1951–59 (10)	External Fin. 1960–67 (11)	Capital/ Output Ratio (12)	Primary Exports GNP (1960) (13)	Trade Orientation (14)	Export Growth 1951–59 (15)	Export Growth 1960–67 (16)	Industrial Production Ratio to Norm. ('50) (17)	Industrial Production Growth ('50–'67) (18)	Primary Production Ratio to Norm. ('50) (19)	Primary Production Growth ('50–'67) (20)
.68	.52	3.2	.061	M	21.0%	15.0%	1.28	8.3%	.42	7.5%
.37	.21	2.0	.103	M	7.0	20.0	1.22	15.2	.77	6.5
1.00	1.00	1.6	.145	B	15.0	10.0	.91§	n/a	.40§	8.3
.46	.36	3.1	.084	B	12.0	12.0	.90	7.8	.93	5.0
.80	.79	3.3	n.a.	M	7.0	10.0	.90	9.7	.80	−1.0
.67	.63	2.7	.044	M	7.0	27.0	.80#	14.8	1.03#	5.9
.53	.29	2.4	.340	P	4.0	9.0	1.02	7.9	.80	4.9
.13	.07	2.6	.171	P	2.7	12.7	1.08#	8.5	.91#	5.6
.24	.31	—	.630	—	10.8	12.7	.96	8.5	1.32	6.4
.51	.21	3.3	.330	P	13.1	6.5	1.19#	7.9	1.32#	6.7
.82	.13	3.0	.316	P	0.4	2.2	.58§	5.8	1.23§	2.6
—	0	2.2	.202	P	1.2	9.9	—	10.8	—	n/a
.23	.18	2.4	.261	P	10.2	9.2	—	7.1	—	4.9
.07	−.21	3.2	.310	P	8.3	0.7	—	10.9	—	6.0
−.31	−.12	—	.312	P	3.6	11.5	.60§	n/a	1.41§	−0.4
−.11	.13	—	.126	P	15.6	4.3	.71#	13.4	1.49#	5.8
0	−.36	4.0	.454	P	—	—	.76#	15.9	1.53#	2.5
.47	.02	3.6	.269	P	—	—	1.38#	5.9	.75#	3.8
.09	.12	2.4	.078	B	5.5	5.4	.93	7.2	.90	4.3
.14	.17	2.7	.022	B	5.2	7.0	.72	10.4	1.26	4.3
—	.27	—	.169	P	0	3.0	.74	9.8	.81	4.2
.16	.08	4.2	.141	B	6.6	12.8	.95	7.8	1.02	3.2
.19	.18	2.0	.143	P	2.8	9.0	.71	8.8	.90	4.1
—	.25	(2.5)	.041	B	0.1	6.7	.58	16.2	1.13	2.8
−.15	.19	2.4	.184	P	7.3	2.6	.94#	7.0	1.15#	4.6
−.02	.42	—	n.a.	B	6.8	5.3	.38	11.1	1.19	3.5
0	0	3.5	.010	B	16.6	12.6	.91#	11.2	.92#	4.0
—	—	—	.014	M	13.6	16.2	—	10.5	—	7.2
.06	.01	—	.066	B	—	15.3	1.06#	4.1	—	2.7
—	—	—	.045	M	14.6	15.2	—	13.7	—	10.0
—	.09	—	.084	B	0.3	2.8	1.02	7.0	.81	5.5

Cols. 4 and 5: Annual average growth rate of total Gross Domestic Product: at constant market prices whenever possible, otherwise at constant factor cost (Table I, Col. 2).
Col. 6: Annual average growth rate of population, 1950–67 (Table I, Col. 1).
Col. 7: Increase in per capita GNP, 1950–67 (Table IV, Col. 17).
Cols. 8 and 9: Investment ratios 1950–55 and 1960–67, from Table IV, Col. 1 (Gross Domestic Product) and Col. 2 (Gross Domestic Investment).
Cols. 10 and 11: Balance of payments current deficit, 1950–59 and 1960–65, from Table V, Col. 8.
Col. 12: Gross marginal capital/output ratio, (Table III, Col. 16). Ratios were obtained by dividing the gross addition to capital stock in each period by the increase in GDP in the same period and averaging the two values.

countries, aid has substituted initially for agricultural production, but both industry and primary production have grown very rapidly. The effect on trade is to bypass the normal stage of specialization in primary exports and to develop manufactured exports or services (tourism) instead.

Success in a high aid strategy normally requires a substantial reduction in the dependence on capital inflows after a decade or so, even in these special situations. All except Puerto Rico and Jordan have brought about such a reduction by high rates of growth of both savings and exports, and in most cases the growth rates have increased further in the second decade.

The high aid strategy has not always been so successful. Other countries that would fall in this category (and their decade growth rates) are: Cyprus (4.5%, 4.7%), Tunisia (n.a., 4.4%), and Bolivia (n.a., 5.1%). On the whole, however, the high aid strategy has turned out remarkably well, considering the unsettled political and economic conditions in which it has typically been attempted. However, the total

---

SOURCES FOR TABLE 2 *(continued)*

Col. 13: Primary exports/GNP. Percent primary of total value of exports, derived from United Nations, Dept. of Economic and Social Affairs, *Yearbook of International Trade Statistics 1967* (ST/STAT/SER.G/18) New York, 1969. Primary exports were defined as Food (O), Unmanufactured tobacco leaf (121), Inedible (2–266 Synthetic Fabrics), Crude or partly refined oil (331), Natural gas (341.1), Oils and fats (4), Wild animals (941). Percent exports of GDP is as taken from IBRD, Table III, Col. 4. Figures for Iran, Iraq, Trinidad, and Venezuela revised to include refined petroleum products: Rhodesia and Zambia revised to include copper products.

Col. 14: Trade orientation indicates the deviation from the normal proportion of manufactured goods and primary products in exports, as measured in Hollis B. Chenery and Lance Taylor, "Development Patterns: Among Countries and Over Time," *Review of Economics and Statistics* 50, no. 4 (November, 1968): 391–416. M = manufacturing orientation, B = balanced, P = primary orientation.

Cols. 15 and 16: Annual average growth rate of exports of goods and services from Table I, Col. 8. These are defined to exclude factor and transfer payments to and from abroad.

Col. 17: Industrial production: ratio of observed performance to that predicted by factors included in regression BT.

Col. 18: Annual average growth rate of manufacturing production, 1950–67, from Table I, Col. 7. Generally computed from country indices of manufacturing production published by UN Statistical Office.

Col. 19: Primary production: ratio of observed performance to that predicted by factors included in regression BT.

Col. 20: Annual average growth rate of primary production, 1950–66. Primary is defined as agriculture plus mining. Percent shares of GDP were obtained from Table IV, Cols. 6 and 7, and applied against the IBRD total GNP (Table IV, Col. 16). To extend the series, data were augmented with UN figures for Jordan, Korea, Thailand, Jamaica, Malaysia, Venezuela, Iraq, Japan, and Spain.

population of the countries in group A is only 50 million and there is little likelihood that a large country would have access to such substantial resources from abroad.

Strategy B: High Primary Exports

Development that is led and financed by primary exports is the traditional colonial strategy. Eleven successful countries having a total population of 85 million fall into this group. Although their natural resources normally attract private investment, after several decades the net inflow is typically reduced to low or negative amounts by amortization and remittance of profits.

Although the primary exporters resemble aid recipients in having relatively high import levels, their structure of production is strikingly different. Industry is typically lower than normal, and primary production significantly higher. The rate of growth is closely linked to the growth of the exports even in the successful cases shown here. (In recent years tourism has played the same role as primary exports in a few favored countries.)

Successful development by this route eventually requires a country to become less dependent on primary exports and to shift toward a more balanced structure of production and trade. In successful cases like Thailand, Trinidad, and Iran, this reduced dependence has been achieved—as in the case of the high aid recipients—by rapid industrialization without lowering the rate of growth. A smooth transition is fairly exceptional, however, since most countries wait until demand for their primary exports drops off before undertaking the needed change in the structure of production. This was true of Argentina, Brazil, and Chile in the prewar period and of Colombia, Uruguay, and Ghana in the postwar period.

Strategy C: Moderate Capital Inflow

Eight countries have achieved success with only moderate dependence on external capital and with only moderate levels of primary exports. This strategy is typical of medium and large countries in which primary exports are less than 15% of GNP (see column 13) and in which trade has less effect on the structure of production than in the smaller export-oriented countries. Aid may finance a substantial proportion of imports in these cases and prevent a balance of payments bottleneck from developing in the early years of accelerated growth.

Most countries in this group were previously heavily dependent on primary exports but have undergone sufficient industrialization to achieve an average productive structure for their level of income. In the countries starting below $100 per capita—Pakistan, the United Arab Republic, Nigeria, and the Sudan—relative levels of industrialization have increased substantially over this period.

The performance of the successful members of the moderate aid group resembles that of the high aid group but has been less spectacular. In most cases, both savings rates and exports have risen in the second decade to levels that are adequate to sustain fairly rapid growth. The poorest countries still need to finance more than 20% of investment (and a considerably higher proportion of imports) from external sources in order to sustain growth rates of 6%.

Since only a few countries have the option of a high aid or high primary export strategy, most of the rest have attempted the development strategy outlined here. Transforming the economic structure to a more balanced pattern has proved particularly difficult in medium and small economies such as Ceylon, Ghana, Kenya, Colombia, Chile, and Uruguay, which had previously developed in the B pattern of dependence on primary exports. Since the possibilities for economical import substitution in manufacturing are limited, continued growth requires a shift to manufactured exports (or new primary exports) that has not yet been accomplished.

Strategy D: Low External Dependence

The list of successful countries that have had little dependence on either primary exports or external capital is relatively short. This strategy requires the early development of manufactured exports to cover minimum import needs and can hardly be adopted by very poor countries. The more autarkic pattern typically requires a somewhat higher than average capital/output ratio and hence high rates of investment for rapid growth.

The most successful practitioners of this strategy are Japan and Yugoslavia, which have achieved high growth rates through very high levels of domestic savings and investment. Japan has long since left the category of underdeveloped economies, but Yugoslavia comes closer to providing a model of the possibilities—and problems—of relatively autarkic development.

It is notable that rates of export growth in this group have been very high except for Brazil, in which growth slowed down in the 1960's because of a failure to develop new exports. More notable failures in the execution of this type of strategy have been Argentina, Burma, and India, which also attempted to sustain a pattern of autarkic development without sufficient stress (until recently) on exports or agricultural development. In the case of India, however, the responsibility must be shared by the aid donors, who have provided considerably less capital than that allocated to other countries with comparable performance.

India was following a moderate aid strategy in its Second and Third Five-Year Plans but has been forced to shift to a more autarkic D pattern in its Fourth Plan (1969/70–1974/75) because of the increasingly poor prospects for external capital. As the Pearson Report indicates (p. 298), it is one of the least favored countries because of its large size. I would go further and suggest that it is the outstanding example of aid shortages contributing to reduced growth—which is not to say that the Indian government would not have done better by favoring agriculture and exports much earlier than it has.

These four successful strategies are distinguished primarily by the varying priorities in resource allocation through which the economy is transformed to meet the needs of development. In terms of accumulation of capital and skills, the development patterns have greater similarities. In virtually every case, rapid growth has been accompanied by a rising savings rate, which permits the inflow of capital to be reduced unless the growth rate accelerates further. This experience contrasts with that of slower growing countries and suggests that the greater profitability of investment at higher rates of growth has a significant effect on the supply of savings. In the experience to date, therefore, increased self-reliance accompanies rapid growth; it is only the slow-growing countries whose dependence on aid tends to be perpetuated.

A second feature of importance to aid allocation is the fact that it is the rapidly growing countries that become attractive to private investment. Furthermore, private capital has become available for manufacturing investments in a number of successful countries (for example,

Taiwan, Korea, Thailand) which a decade earlier held little interest for foreign investors. Private capital and hard loans can increasingly replace concessional lending in these cases.

CONCLUSIONS

This discussion has attempted to bring out the effects of differing resource endowments, income levels, and development strategies on development targets. In some respects it merely leads to a refinement of the Pearson Commission recommendations, while in others I would put the emphasis a bit differently.

Objectives

The objectives of development can be best stated in terms of the long-term transformation of the economy and the society. Achievable rates of progress toward this goal depend to a large extent on the starting point. I would suggest that it is as difficult for the poorest countries to achieve 5% growth in GNP as it is for the $300 country to achieve 7%, and that the overall 6% target would be better conceived in these terms. In fact, when we come to understand social change better, it may turn out that growth rates in excess of 5% to 6% in the more primitive societies produce stresses that are not conducive to sustained growth. If this is true, we should be looking not for a maximum but for an optimum rate of development.

Possibilities of Accelerated Growth

On the whole, it has turned out to be easier to achieve higher rates of growth than was imagined ten or fifteen years ago. Over the observed range, capital requirements per unit of output tend to fall (not rise) at higher rates of growth. Developing countries frequently achieve 7% growth with a gross investment ratio to GNP of 20% or less. Since savings have usually risen in response to higher growth rates, the financing of self-sustaining growth becomes more feasible once the initial momentum has been achieved.

While accumulation thus appears to have been easier than anticipated, transformation has, on the whole, been harder. In comparing the thirty countries that did not qualify as "successes" for Table 2 to those that did, I would judge that the management of the balance of payments had been a greater source of failure than the financing of investment, although this proposition is difficult to demonstrate statistically. In the successful cases, aid (and primary exports) have permitted many countries to develop industrial capacity and skills in a rapidly growing domestic market which could then provide the basis for manufactured exports. Frequently, the less successful countries have not been able to bring themselves to take the steps needed to shift output from domestic to foreign markets.

The Allocation of Aid

In retrospect, I think it is clear that the importance of aid is usually understated by measuring its ratio to investment in cases where it has led to rapid growth and a subsequent rise in savings. Conversely, its importance is often overstated in countries where growth has not been accelerated and aid in effect merely substitutes for domestic savings. The real test of aid effectiveness therefore is accelerated growth.

In a period of stagnant aid levels, this observation emphasizes the need to be more penetrating in assessing performance and likelihood of accelerating growth. In general, there should be a presumption that aid is provided for the purpose of accelerating growth, which would result in the highest per capita amounts going to countries in the income range of $100–$300. At higher income levels, exports and private investment should be able to finance imports, and adequate domestic savings are mainly a question of government policy.

The Implications of a Six Percent Growth Target
for India and Pakistan
BY STANISLAW WELLISZ

It is the purpose of this paper to explore the implications of the 6% growth target for India and Pakistan. In accordance with the spirit of the United Nations Development Decade report and of the Pearson Report, I shall take the numerical target to signify not an absolute objective but a rapid pace of development—faster than hitherto achieved by either country on a sustained basis, and faster than the countries which are now highly developed achieved as a group in their early stages of growth. The 6% target means short-cutting the process of development and catching up. As a precise goal it means very little, and I shall not spend much time on numerological exercises proving or disproving its feasibility.

For India and Pakistan, two of the world's most populous countries and two of the world's poorest ones, rapid economic growth means the lifting of the masses from a condition of abject poverty which has prevailed over centuries, not merely the production of more commodities which satisfy consumer needs but do not necessarily improve the quality of life. Yet even for India and Pakistan rapid growth is just one of many policy goals: neither country can neglect such targets as national sovereignty, self-reliance, social justice, or political stability and concentrate exclusively on rapid development. This paper will inquire whether, given the broad socio-political context, the two countries are likely to grow in the 1970's at a markedly accelerated pace and will suggest measures which could promote faster growth without running counter to the other national goals.

INDIA

Criticism of India's economic performance and advice on how to improve the state of the country are perennial pastimes for professional and amateur economists, inside India and out.* Critics on the right catalog the shortcomings of India's administrative approach toward economic problems; they call for liberalization and contrast India's poor performance with that of countries such as Japan with well-functioning market economies. Critics on the left concentrate their fire on India's antiquated social system and on the barriers which democracy and pluralism impose on the government's efforts to modernize and develop the country. In their view a social revolution and a Soviet-type mobiliza-

* From the flood of critical writings I would single out three works of outstanding merit, upon which much of my discussion is based. These are: A. H. Hanson, *The Process of Planning* (New York: Oxford University Press, 1966); Paul Streeten and Michael Lipton, eds., *The Crisis of Indian Planning* (London: Oxford University Press, 1968); and J. N. Bhagwati and P. Desai, *Planning for Industrialization* (OECD, forthcoming). I am especially grateful to Professors Bhagwati and Desai for permission to read their book in manuscript form and to quote from it in this paper.

tion of resources are necessary to pull India out of its economic back-wardness and abolish economic inequities.

Much can be said for the arguments of both the "right" and the "left"—and India listens to them with an infinite patience—yet the basic criticism, that India is stagnant, is clearly incorrect. During the first three Five Year Plans India's real GDP grew at an average rate of 3.4% per annum. A major part of the improvement was "eaten up" by population growth, yet even per capita income increased, the compound rate averaging 1.2%. If we neglect the final year of the Third Plan, the GDP grew at 3.9% and the per capita income at close to 1.8%. These figures (which incidentally are likely to be underestimates rather than overestimates [1]) place India in the middle group of developing nations in terms of performance, far behind such leaders as Mexico, Taiwan, or South Korea but well ahead of the laggards. India's recent performance also contrasts favorably with the country's development in the first half of this century: it has been estimated that between 1900 and 1947 un-divided India's total product grew at approximately 1¼% per annum and its per capita income at 0.4% per annum.[2] The income figures do not give a complete picture of the increase in well-being, for they neglect the remarkable improvements in public health, the notable progress in education, and other social gains.

During the first three Five Year Plans there was an increasing channeling of resources to investment: domestic savings as a proportion of national income rose from 5.5% in 1950/51 to approximately 9% in 1960/61 and to 10.5% in 1965/66. With foreign aid, the investment/income ratio rose even faster: from 5.5% in 1950/51 (a year in which virtually the whole investment was financed out of domestic savings) to 14% at the end of the Third Plan. There was also a corresponding in-crease in the ratio of tax receipts to national income—from 6.6% in 1950/51 to 9.6% in 1960/61 and over 14% in 1965/66.[3] The in-creasing mobilization of resources was reflected by an increasing tempo of growth. While under the First Plan net national product rose at 3.5% per annum, under the Second Plan and during the first four years of the Third Plan it rose respectively at 4.0% and 4.2% per annum.[4]

The growth process was brought to a temporary halt during the last year of the Third Plan and what was scheduled to be the first year of the Fourth Plan. Two disastrous droughts and a war were the main causes of the recession, but the crisis was aggravated by a policy which overemphasized investment in heavy industry and large-scale projects and did not provide agriculture with the proper incentives—or the proper means—for rapid growth in output.

The crisis has been largely overcome; growth has resumed and is accelerating—largely because of very marked improvements in the agricultural picture which promise to have long-lasting positive effects. Agriculture still accounts for over 40% of India's GNP, and the sector's performance determines, to a large extent, the overall performance of the economy.[5] During the first three Five Year Plans (neglecting the disastrous harvest in the last year of the Third Plan) agricultural production grew at an average rate of 3% per annum. Thus, despite the slow pace of introduction of new agricultural technology, shortages of fertilizer, and a policy which limited rewards to farmers, output rose markedly faster than in the previous half century.

The latter half of the 1960's was a period of droughts, but also the beginning of the "Green Revolution." In 1963/64 the first small trials were carried out with Mexican dwarf wheat varieties. By 1967/68 the new wheats covered about six million acres, and by 1968/69 an estimated twelve million acres—or over 85% of all irrigated area under wheat. The increases in yields are equally spectacular. An all-India survey of crops on farms where both local and high-yielding varieties of wheat (mostly the Mexican Lerma Rojo variety) were grown shows that the new varieties on the average give a 77% higher yield per acre than the old ones.[6] Optimistically, one may hope that new high-yielding varieties of rice, jowar, and lesser field crops will spread rapidly and that, with increasing supplies of fertilizer, pesticides, and tools, with further gains in minor irrigation and greater mastery of the new techniques, the "Green Revolution" will gather impetus. The other high-yielding grains have met with greater consumer and producer resistance and present greater technical difficulties. There is also danger that the yields of the new varieties will be diminished as new strains of plant disease develop; it is not certain that the supply and distribution of the requisite inputs and the provision of credit to procure such inputs will grow at a pace needed to achieve the high target growth.

The "Green Revolution" is, of course, not a fortuitous occurrence —it was preceded by years of research in many countries including

India, and its realization required that other factors needed by the new technology (such as fertilizers and pesticides), be provided and that farmers be given credit for the required purchases and incentives to increase crops. Since December, 1965, India has greatly liberalized its hitherto restrictive policies toward fertilizer manufacturing, imports, and distribution. Minor irrigation, somewhat neglected during the first three plans, was also given encouragement, and the farm extension program was streamlined and concentrated largely on areas most likely to benefit from the new technology.[7]

Forecasting agricultural progress is always difficult—especially in a period of rapid technological change—but a growth rate of 4.5% over the next few years appears to be likely, and a 5% growth rate high, but not beyond the realm of possibility. If agricultural expectations are realized, the 1970/71 plan target of a 5.5% increase in national income may be achieved. (The Annual Plan calls for a 5% increase in agricultural output and an 8% increase in industrial production.) Such a growth rate—and even somewhat faster growth—is not inconceivable for the decade to come; if agriculture grows at 4.5% per annum, a 7% growth in the other sectors will suffice to reach the 6% target. During the first four years of the Third Plan growth of the non-agricultural sectors averaged 8% per annum.

Will India generate enough domestic savings and receive enough foreign aid to sustain such a fast rate of growth? On the foreign aid side, the situation is somewhat disturbing; over the years, India's dependence on aid has been increasing, while currently (and probably for some years to come) the donors have been more and more reluctant to meet the mounting needs. Yet even here there is some reason for cautious optimism. Over the period of the three plans the volume of imports steadily mounted (despite great efforts at import substitution), while exports remained virtually stagnant, but in 1968/69 exports rose by 13% over the previous year, while imports declined by 7%, resulting in a narrowing of the trade gap from Rs. 7,535 million in 1967/68 to Rs. 4,362 million in 1968/69. A further increase in exports of Rs. 1,000 million (7.4%) is forecast for 1969/70.[8] The improvement can be largely attributed to the effects of the 1966 devaluation and of export-incentive schemes. This does much to destroy the myth of inelastic demand facing India's products. Whether the improvement will be maintained depends largely on India's willingness to set and maintain its currency at levels insuring the profitability of exports, and to pursue policies encouraging the growth of industries capable of competing on world markets. Conflicts arise between the goal of encouraging such industries and other socio-economic goals, or, to be more precise, about the approach adopted by India in its pursuit of such goals.

The problem of sufficiency of domestic savings appears to be more serious. With the expansion of large-scale industry one would hope and expect that corporate savings would *increase* as a percentage of GNP, or at least keep pace. Yet during the first two years of the Third Plan corporate savings amounted to only 0.7%, and a peak was reached in 1962/63 with 0.8%. The next year a decline set in—more than two years ahead of the generally acknowledged recession. Government savings maintained their upward trend for one year longer, peaked in 1963/64 at 2.9% of the GNP, and then declined; only individual savings remained relatively stable. The fact that the decline in institutional savings preceded the recession of the late 1960's points to the need to re-evaluate the causes of the recession, but it also raises disturbing questions of longer-term significance. The decline in the importance of corporate sector savings strongly points up the decline in private corporate profitability. This may be a transitional phenomenon—or it may be the result of long-range government policies to control the private sector. The latter is likely to be the case.

In the government sector the savings come (potentially) from two sources: taxation and profits on government enterprises. Government enterprises have been running at a loss which in 1967/68 amounted to Rs. 340 million on a total capital investment of Rs. 33,000 million (about 1.03%). Though the government is in the process of streamlining the public sector, and though there is an intention to raise uneconomically low prices and to achieve an 11%–12% return on public investment, the chances of any radical improvement are not very great. While tax yields have risen over the first three plans, the mounting cost of debt service, administrative expenses, and armaments has meant that a decreasing proportion of the total tax take has been translated into government savings. Although year-to-year fluctuations somewhat obscure the trend, the proportion has been declining since 1961/62, when government savings amounted to 20% of the tax take.[9]

This decline is also reflected in the ratio of central government outlay for development to the tax revenue retained by the center. In 1961/62, 33.8% of the retained taxes were spent on development purposes; by 1964/65 the proportion declined to 15.1%, and the increase in the subsequent years has been insignificant. For the near future there is little hope that the government will be able to increase its savings-to-tax-take ratio greatly. To increase the tax take as a percentage of national income, the government would probably have to resort to taxation of the agricultural sector, which is taxed far more lightly than other sectors of the economy.[10] Yet increased taxation of agriculture presents political problems, and it runs counter to the current program of encouraging the small cultivators to greater investment and production efforts. The problem of how to enforce land reform and simultaneously promote increased investment in agriculture while increasing taxation which would mop up part of the investable agricultural surplus is a difficult one, indeed. Thus, although higher taxes and higher government savings cannot be ruled out, there are signs that the current low rate of savings may be more than a transitional phenomenon. If this is true, the ambitious growth program might be difficult to achieve.

The difficulties encountered in mobilizing internal resources for growth are common to all countries which are poor. In India these difficulties are aggravated by the growth of what I call parasitic industries. To inquire into the causes and manifestations of such growth, a brief digression is necessary.

India is a large and heterogeneous country with complex and sometimes competing national goals. It seeks to develop modern large-scale industries but also to protect small and cottage industries. It wants rapid development but also an equitable geographic growth pattern. Its goal is the achievement of the "socialist way of life," which includes public control over major economic activities, but it appreciates the benefits from, and wishes to take advantage of, private initiative. However, the growth of private business is to be channeled in a way compatible with other national purposes, and excessive concentration of economic power in private hands and the growth of private monopolies is to be controlled, and, if possible, avoided. These national goals must be weighed against each other. The result of this weighing process is embodied in an economic strategy expressed in the successive plans. Because of this complexity, policies which are deemed best for the country are not always those which lead to the fastest possible growth.

The rapid development of a publicly owned heavy industrial sector is the cause of the "too large and too early" type of parasitism. Public control of basic industries is for India an important policy objective, and India has both the market and the human and material resources to develop such a sector. What went wrong is that, instead of building what was needed and when, project selection followed a "Grand Strategy" based on a confusion between the sequential interindustry flows and the optimal timing.[11] It is true that to produce consumer goods one needs machines, and to produce machines one needs machines producing capital goods, and these, in turn, require steel. But if imports are possible, it does not necessarily follow that industrialization should start with steel production followed by capital-goods-producing machines and consumer-goods-producing machines. The "Grand Strategy" was designed with little attention to the optimal distribution of imports and even less attention to the optimal export strategy, with the result that the consumer goods sector relied largely on imported machinery, while the heavy industry sector remained a virtually self-contained cell feeding upon itself, and exports stagnated. With the progress of industrialization the gap is closing, but much of the basic investments turned out to be inappropriate or rapidly became obsolete. Heavy Electricals Ltd. of Bhopal, which in six years of operation accumulated a loss of Rs. 330 million on an investment of Rs. 620 million, is an example of a parasitic growth resulting from the "Grand Strategy." The enterprise (by no means a unique example of its kind) is expected to chalk up another Rs. 210 million in losses by 1970/71.[12]

It is often claimed that, were it not for the assignment of responsibility for heavy industry development to the government, heavy industrial development would have lagged behind, causing bottlenecks in other sectors. Whether this is so is a moot point; it is by no means certain, moreover, that building somewhat behind demand is necessarily more costly to the economy in terms of resources and growth than building ahead of demand.

The cumbersomeness of bureaucratic management is another reason why many public sector enterprises, which are economically sound in conception, fail to make a satisfactory contribution to the economy.

In the case of many enterprises in the government sector, financial results underestimate the real economic contribution because output prices
are set at extremely low levels: this is the case with steel, coal, rail rates,
and the prices of such enterprises as Hindustan Machine Tools which,
unlike private companies making similar products, follows a policy of
pricing based on the landed cost of comparable imports. However,
uneconomically low prices lead to misallocation and real losses elsewhere
in the economy.

The slowness of government sector project planning stretches
gestation periods and adds to the cumulative capital cost. Even more
important is the problem of the cumbersome nature of bureaucratic
management of the going enterprise. There is a basic contradiction between principles of sound public administration, which rest on the
routinization of procedures, and principles of sound business management, which require constant adaptation to changing circumstances and
involve much improvisation. For a public servant improvisation does
not pay.

The tendency toward routinization, together with the susceptibility
of public enterprise to social pressures (which manifests itself in over-
staffing, in the inability to discharge excess or incompetent personnel,
in vulnerability to labor union pressures, etc.), almost inevitably leads
to low efficiency, and it is high tribute to Indian management and technicians that some of the government enterprises do show excellent
financial results.

The government and the public are keenly aware of the shortcomings of the public sector enterprises, and it is enormously to the
credit of India that the doubts and criticisms are publicly aired instead
of being swept under the carpet (or branded as seditious and unpatri-
otic) as happens in many nations. Yet, while many detailed improvements in the procedures and routines are made, the basic question is
whether old-fashioned nationalization is the proper vehicle for the advancement of social goals. Such questions are being raised even in
Soviet-type economies where the "socialist way of life" is rigidly interpreted in terms of Party supremacy and political orthodoxy. In India,
where the "socialist way of life" means social justice, increasing equality,
and lack of dominance by a business oligarchy, the question is more
pertinent and can be examined more dispassionately. This is not being

done; the existing proposals aim at the replacement of procedures and routines by better procedures and routines, or sometimes even stop at the enumeration of *desiderata* without going to the heart of the matter.

The inefficiency of many of the public sector industries is so evident that it is easy to lose sight of parasitic industries in the private sector—industries which make private profits at public expense. The growth of such parasitic industries is fostered and protected by the licensing system and by the price policies adopted by the government.

In the absence of controls the private investors would strive to foster their own interests *as they perceive them*. Given the complexity of national goals and the perennial overvaluation of the rupee, the results would not necessarily coincide with the national interest. For example, it is likely that private investment would gravitate to areas which are already highly developed, with the resulting neglect of the backward regions, and that cottage industries would be wiped out through the competition of large mechanized units. Moreover, it is often claimed that in developing countries, where economic and technical information is scarce, and managerial talent in short supply, private investment tends to bunch up in traditional industries to the neglect of new possibilities—resulting in private as well as social loss.

To implement the social goals, policy makers may take measures to improve market efficiency and to modify market allocation via indirect controls,[13] or they may replace market allocation by administrative allocation. Both approaches are utilized in India, but main reliance is placed on administrative controls. Thus, the government created a number of special agencies, such as the Industrial Finance Corporation, the National Industrial Development Corporation, the Refinance Corporation, and the Industrial Credit and Investment Corporation, which fulfill a useful role in mobilizing capital for large-scale private investment. Even the role of the Directorate General of Technical Development, whose reports help the licensing authorities decide on the soundness of the industrial license applicants' schemes, can be interpreted as helping the private entrepreneur in rational individual enterprise planning by providing centralized techno-economic services.

The basic document entitling the government to extend administrative control over private investment is the Industries (Development and Regulation) Act, 1951, whose aim is "to provide for government control over the location, expansion and setting up of private industrial under-takings with a view *inter alia* to channel investments into desired directions, promote balanced regional development, protect small and cottage industries and prevent concentration of ownership and control to the common detriment." [14] Hazari comments that "the major assumption implicit in the Act was that growth and allocation of resources should be looked after wholly or mainly by administrative guidance, promotion and control." [15] Hence market mechanism considerations are relegated to a distinctly subordinate role. The principal policy tool used for the enforcement of the 1951 Act is the licensing system, which provides limits to investment as determined by the sectoral plans, as well as incentives to invest. The licensees are virtually assured that their operation will be profitable regardless of economic efficiency, since competing imports are excluded quasi-automatically under the "indigenous availability" principle (no import licenses are issued if comparable products are available from domestic sources) while capacity licensing limits internal competition.

Thus a licensing policy not only channels investment but induces it, by creating investment opportunities which otherwise might not have been available. The result is accelerated growth in the licensed sector, but growth which may be, and often is, parasitic. Some industries fostered by the licensing system are so inefficient that their cost is 300% to 400% higher (or even more) than the landed prices of competing foreign goods.[16] It is inconceivable that Indian manufacturing is at such a comparative disadvantage; under a more efficient resource allocation scheme the products made by the parasitic industries could be obtained either from home sources or through foreign trade at a fraction of the resource cost. Another drawback of the policy is that it encourages the production of shoddy goods. Manufacturers sheltered from external as well as internal competition have no incentive to maintain quality; indeed, as long as excess demand prevails, there is incentive to cut costs at the expense of quality and to produce shoddy goods which are "good enough for India."

The licensing system, for all its high economic cost, could be justified in terms of social policy achievements, but such achievements have not been very impressive. Perhaps the best results were obtained in sheltering cottage and very small industries, many of which would have failed were larger units permitted to compete. Yet, even from that point of view, licensing is defective, since it gives total protection in selected fields and none at all in others. Moreover, the system condemns small enterprises to dwarfism: were they to grow, they would run across the same barriers which promoted their existence in the first place. A rational policy designed to nurture small-scale enterprises would require the creation of sliding-scale subsidies and taxes, giving greatest encouragement to the smallest units: the subsidies and taxes should be so designed as to encourage growth, i.e., they should less than fully equalize the decreasing costs to scale.

Other social goals were not so well served. In the absence of genuine regional planning, which exploits the comparative advantages of the various regions and creates conditions for the growth of the most appropriate industries, "licensing as it has operated during the last ten years has not been effective except in a very limited way for the attainment of the objective of regional dispersal." [17] Contrary to the opinion that the licensing system favors the large industrial houses, a careful study shows that "the Large Industrial Sector, as a whole, did not obtain a disproportionate share of the overall licenses in any significant sense of the term," [18] yet there is no evidence whatsoever that the system reduced the power of large capitalists or that it fostered in any significant way the growth of a countervailing group of smaller capitalists.

Instead of controlling monopolies, the licensing system in effect creates legal monopolies, even if licenses are issued to seemingly competitive units in the same field. In the passenger automobile sector, for example, licenses were issued to three manufacturers, with a total capacity of 30,000 units per year; actual production reached 24,500 units in 1965/66. The small scale of manufacturing and the high native component content make for extremely high-cost production. Imports are banned, and, even at the high ex-factory prices, demand is far from being satisfied, and substantial premia over official retail prices are offered on the free market.[19] If there were a single manufacturer, the consumer would pay no more, and, given the economies of scale, the social cost of production (i.e., the resources used) would be smaller. The licensing system thus creates a semblance of competition, but in reality it gives rise to a monopoly more pernicious (because less efficient) than a classic one-producer case. The example is not an isolated one; the same pattern prevails in other fields as well.

Allocative distortions are aggravated by formal and informal price controls. The principle guiding price controls is not allocative efficiency but "fairness" to the producer and to the consumer. In practice the "fair" price, designed to give the producer a modest profit, often is maintained at an unchanged level long after it has stopped satisfying even that modest role. For instance, steel prices were calculated in the early 1960's on the basis of the oldest mills' capital costs per ton of output. Hindustan Steel's current capital costs per ton are twice that level, and even at full operation they will surpass it by 70%. For similar historical reasons, coal (especially coking coal) prices are too low relative to the increased output needed. When price adjustments take place, it is through bilateral bargaining, with the government acting as an arbiter of fairness and, sometimes, as an advocate for one or both sides.[20] The adjustment may take years of haggling.

The "just price" system is currently being extended to such fields as banking, and proposals are afoot to extend it to hitherto uncontrolled major industries and to set prices on a "rational and scientific basis," which presumably means prices yielding a fair return over costs regardless of supply and demand conditions.

The "just price" system protects parasitic industries since every unit, regardless of efficiency, is entitled to a fair return. Insofar as prices of basic industrial commodities tend to become frozen, subsidies are granted to enterprises using the price-controlled inputs, often amounting to an unplanned transfer from the public to the private sector. As distortions mount, the results of market allocations become progressively less satisfactory, calling for increased administrative action. Price distortions are one of the main reasons why liberalization moves in the USSR, Poland, and other Soviet-type economies have largely failed: as administrative controls are removed, and mistaken signals are given by the (controlled) price system, pursuit of profit leads to the wrong product mix. Yet, as prices depart from opportunity cost, rational calculus for determining administrative action becomes progressively more difficult.

With all this havoc, it is even a moot point whether justice is served. For example, on September 8, 1969, the passenger car manufacturers announced substantial price increases, which, however, were smaller than the differential between official retail prices and free market prices. The increase in effect transferred a part of the surplus now accruing to the direct purchasers (many of whom are individuals on

official priority lists) to the manufacturers, with no effect on the pur-
chaser-at-large. The government thereupon imposed price ceilings. It is
clear that if the government wanted to be "fair to the public" and did not
want the producers' profits to increase, it should have imposed not a
price ceiling but a sales tax, mopping up the surplus and increasing
government revenues.

The process of parasitism, nurtured by physical controls and aided
by price distortions, gives a mistaken semblance of vigor, but it tends to
be self-destructive in the end. Insofar as that growth takes the form of
import substitution, it becomes less and less effective as imports are
successively replaced, and as domestic industry is forced to utilize high-
priced domestic machinery and materials instead of imports. Declining
investment opportunities and declining profits follow. Data are too
fragmentary and the situation too complex to advance this as a satisfactory explanation for the decline in India's corporate savings sector
which started in the early 1960's. Yet the decreasing profitability
hypothesis (if not this diagnosis of its causes) finds supporting evidence.
Thus Raj Krishna and S. S. Mehta have found that in large-scale industry the ratio of capital (at constant prices) per worker doubled between
1948–53 and 1958–63, while the value added per worker increased
only by 42%, and the value added to capital ratio decreased by 18%.[21]
Another disturbing piece of evidence is that despite an enormous and
increasing investment effort, the economic contribution of industry,
even when measured at internal prices, is relatively small. Total outlay
on organized industry rose from 2.8% in the First Plan period to 20.1%
in the Second Plan, 20.5% in the Third Plan, and a scheduled 25% in
the Fourth Plan.[23] If we include village and cottage industries, the rise
is less precipitous but nevertheless impressive, from an initial 6% in
the First Plan period to a planned 27.4% in the Fourth Plan. Yet value
added by mining, manufacturing, and small-scale and cottage industries
as a percentage of net national product increased very little. Official
estimates show that the sector's contribution in 1964/65 is identical to
that of 1950/51: 16.7%. Performance in recent years has been marred
by crop failures and the recession, but statistics fail to reveal any strong
upward industrial trend. Large-scale industry contributed 8.4% of the
GDP in the first year of the Third Plan (1960/61) and 9.1% in
1964/65, but only 8.1% in 1967/68. These figures, to repeat, are not

advanced as proof positive of the inefficiency or of the decreasing efficiency of Indian industrial investment. They merely confirm what economic theory and common sense strongly suggest: arbitrary controls decrease efficiency, inefficiency impedes growth, and the cumulation of inefficiency thwarts it.

Measures put into effect since the 1966 devaluation gave Indian industry a greater degree of freedom of action and simultaneously exposed it to greater pressures from internal and external competition. The results of the reforms, not unexpectedly, have been mixed: some enterprises managed to take advantage of the new opportunities to streamline production and improve products sufficiently to penetrate new and highly competitive foreign markets. Others found survival very difficult, and their decline contributed to the country's economic crisis. The victims of reforms naturally clamor for their repeal and join their voices to those whose personal careers are connected with the administrative control mechanism or who advocate direct controls for ideological reasons. Simultaneously there is mounting concern on the part of the government to foster social justice and to promote the "socialist way of life," and this concern is expressed largely in the form of imposition of, or proposals for, further controls.

It is most unfortunate that many of the measures proposed as a means of fostering social progress and of achieving important national goals should be such that their impact on growth is almost certain to be negative. In India, as virtually everywhere, the reliance on the market mechanism and allocative efficiency is all too easily identified with "Manchester liberalism," inimical to all planning and indifferent to social justice, while administrative fiats, controls, and restrictions are symbols of progress and equity.

India enters the decade of the 1970's with a new strength and a new growth potential based on unprecedented development in agriculture. Its growth, therefore, is likely to be substantially more rapid than it has been over the past years. India also enters the new decade with a great awareness of its urgent social problems—the greatest of which is the widespread poverty of its rapidly increasing population—and with a will to better the lot not of a selected few, but of the many. Since independence, in spite of the objective difficulties and often mistaken policies, it has made notable progress. That there will be further progress cannot be doubted. Whether policy instruments will be found to utilize the new strength to foster social aims while building a strong and efficient industry capable of holding its own in competition with the advanced industrial nations remains to be seen.

PAKISTAN

Pakistan's Third Five Year Plan (1965–70) called for a 6.5% average annual rate of growth. As in the case of India, the 1965 hostilities and bad harvests disrupted the growth process. A revised version of the plan acknowledged the need for development outlay reduction and project rephasing, and tried to preserve the original overall objectives by concentrating investments where large and rapid returns were likely to be obtained and by emphasizing the need for greater efficiency. The growth targets were not met, but Pakistan succeeded in maintaining the remarkable growth record established during its Second Plan period (1959/60 to 1964/65) when GNP increased on the average by an estimated 5.2% per year. During the first four years of the Third Plan the GNP at constant factor cost increased 4.6% in 1965/66, 5.0% in 1966/67, 7.5% in 1967/68, and 5.2% in 1968/69. Thus, despite an alarmingly rapid population growth (estimated at over 2.7% per year), the nation's well-being improved steadily.

There are good prospects for continued rapid growth, and the 6% annual growth target may well be reached within a few years. Developments in the field of agriculture are particularly encouraging. Over the 1959/60 to 1967/68 period the crop output of the former Punjab rose at an average rate of 4.5% per year; formerly a food deficit area, West Pakistan is turning into a food surplus area. Though future gains in productivity might be more difficult to attain,[23] there are excellent prospects for continued vigorous agricultural growth in the West Wing of the country. The agricultural performance of East Pakistan has been less spectacular, but there, too, gains have been made.[24] The introduction of new rice strains, increased application of fertilizer, more pesticides, and better water control should increase the rate of growth of the East Wing's rice output during the 1970's.

There are, of course, difficulties to be overcome. Foreign aid, which financed a substantial proportion of Pakistan's gross investment (nearly 40% in the mid-1960's),[25] has been tapering off. Therefore, Pakistan has increased the internal mobilization of resources through higher taxation and has stepped up its export drive to earn more foreign currency. These efforts appear to be paying off, and neither the "savings gap" nor the "foreign exchange gap" is likely to be a serious block to development in the period to come.

Despite its remarkable growth record, Pakistan is beset by economic difficulties—one more reminder that "numerology" is a dangerous game. For all its progress, the country is still extremely poor, with an average per capita income of approximately 400 rupees per year.[26] Growth did not bring equal benefits to all regions and all classes; the disparities between the East and West Wings of the country and the inequality of income distribution continue to create serious social tensions.

In the pre-plan period the per capita income of East Pakistan, which contains more than half the country's population but only one-seventh of the territory, was estimated at 82% of the per capita income in the West Wing. Over the 1949/50 to 1959/60 decade West Pakistan's per capita income increased at 0.8% per annum, while that of East Pakistan decreased by 0.3% per year, and by 1959/60 the East Wing's per capita income dropped to 73% of that of the West Wing. During the Second Plan period the per capita income in the East Wing increased at a rate of 2.7% per annum, and that in the West Wing at 2.4%. In the first four years of the Third Plan, progress was once again largely concentrated in the West Wing, where the Gross Provincial Product increased on the average of 6.2% per year. By contrast, growth of the East Wing has been disappointing, and in 1968/69, largely because of poor harvests, the growth of per capita income once again fell behind the rate of population increase.

The trends in income distribution are impossible to judge in the absence of reliable statistics. However, it is clear that, prior to the onset of the "Green Revolution," the gains were mainly concentrated in urban areas, and even those largely bypassed the wage earners. In 1959/60 the per capita income in Karachi was 35% above that of rural West Pakistan and almost 60% above that of rural East Pakistan. The wealthiest 5% of Karachi's population enjoyed an income seven times as high as the national average, but 50% of Karachi dwellers had lower incomes than the poorer half of the rural population of either wing.

The inequities in the distribution of the gains from growth can be largely explained in terms of differences in the natural and man-made environment of the two wings, and by the nature of the growth process itself. Topography (a good harbor in Karachi, abundance of high-lying land), the patterns of human agglomeration (in such major cities as Karachi and Lahore), and social overhead capital (rail and road links, many of them established in the pre-independence period) favor industrialization of the West over the East Wing. The human factor also plays a major role. In the course of population movements which took place during and after the partition of the subcontinent, a sizable group of people with a long tradition of successful entrepreneurship and with skills which, previously applied to commerce and banking, could easily be transferred to industrial management, settled in West Pakistan. By contrast, East Pakistan was virtually denuded of people with entrepreneurial skills. The industrial growth that gave the greatest impetus to Pakistan's development occurred mostly in the West Wing and was primarily concentrated in and around Karachi and a few other urban areas. With the large and growing population, conditions approximating an "unlimited supply of labor" prevailed. Since any number of unskilled workers could be hired at the going wage, there was no pressure for wages to rise, and most of the gains accrued to the skilled personnel and the capital owners.

The West Wing is also favored in agriculture. Though East Pakistan has an abundance of natural water, water control presents very serious technological problems. Rice-growing technology is improving, but until now at a disappointingly slow pace. Jute, the East Wing's most important commercial crop, faces a relatively stagnant world demand. Remarkable gains have been made, but the situation is still one of a race between population growth and agricultural output. By contrast, the wheat output in the irrigated areas of former West Punjab has been growing at a rapid pace, even prior to the "Green Revolution," and in the most recent years the growth has been truly remarkable.

Government policy has been notably successful in promoting industrial growth, but less so in combating social inequities. Indeed, some policies have tended to accentuate the inequalities. One can argue that such policies were necessary in order to promote growth in a country which seemed doomed to stagnation upon gaining independence. However, some features of the policy seem to have aggravated the social and regional problems without a corresponding payoff in terms of growth.

Until the mid-1950's Pakistan's development strategy put primary emphasis on industrial growth. The strategy relied primarily on (1) the public provision of social overhead facilities, and (2) the creation of attractive investment opportunities in industry by turning the internal terms of trade against agriculture and in favor of industry. (Public investment in industry also occurred, but it does not seem to have had a major development impact.) Prices of agricultural goods, including food (the major wage good), and of agricultural inputs into industry (jute and cotton) were kept low,[27] as were the prices of imported inputs for industry, while import prohibitions and limitation of internal competition along with export bonuses yielded high domestic prices and high profits to industry. The industry-favoring policy reflected a development strategy which was widely accepted in the 1950's and 1960's and which rests on the twin hypotheses that (1) rapid industrialization is the most efficient way to foster development and (2) underdeveloped countries which exploit their comparative advantage (which, in most cases, means production and export of primary products and import of manufactured goods) are condemned to stagnation. The path to development rests in the nurturing of new activities with a view to the future development of a new "comparative advantage."

The industrial growth which resulted from Pakistan's policy confounded the skeptics and surpassed even the most optimistic expectations. Value at constant prices added by manufacturing increased almost fourfold between 1949/50 and 1954/55 and almost doubled in each of the two successive five-year periods. High industrial profits attracted capital from commerce (and to a lesser extent from large-scale agriculture) into industry and prodded commercial entrepreneurs to switch their activities to industrial management. Reinvestment out of profits earned through industrial activities soon became an important source of finance for industry, generating "self-sustained growth." (A survey conducted by Papanek shows that 44% of the estimated total industrial assets which existed in 1959 were financed out of reinvested industrial profits.[28]) The income transfers from agriculture to industry were instrumental in overcoming the initial reluctance to embrace industry as a career or as a profitable placement of investable funds. Once

over this threshold, industrial expansion continued in the face of reforms which lessened the discrimination against agriculture and resulted
in a decline of industrial profit rates. The Pakistani experience also
seems to lend support to the classic infant industry arguments; some
branches of Pakistani industry have chalked up marked gains in efficiency and have become internationally competitive.

The policy of promotion of industry had a serious adverse impact
on East Pakistan where jute, Pakistan's major industrial export crop, is
grown, and where natural conditions do not favor industrial growth.
Before partition, jute was grown mainly in East Bengal (now East
Pakistan) while jute mills were located in West Bengal (now part of
India). To exploit its quasi-monopolistic position as a jute grower in
the face of relatively inelastic, short-run world demand, and to promote
the growth of native jute mills, the government pursued a policy of en-
forcing high effective exchange rates on jute exports. In the short run
the policy was undoubtedly successful; raw jute exports brought considerable foreign exchange earnings, while the value of jute manufactures rose rapidly, as did jute manufacture exports.[29] Moreover, the jute
manufacture industry, which had been extremely inefficient, became
more and more competitive with the expansion of scale and the acquisition of skills. There were, however, adverse effects. Buoyed by high
prices, jute growing in India expanded rapidly, while Pakistan's jute
crops remained virtually stationary, with the consequent erosion of
Pakistan's near-monopoly position. Moreover, high jute prices encouraged substitution for jute and the development of alternate products.
The changes, insofar as they are the result of technological innovation,
are largely irreversible.[30] The jute strategy thus took advantage of short-
run opportunities at the expense of the long run. Such a strategy is
defensible in view of the uncertainty of long-run prospects. (The alternative was to foster jute growing, attempt to make radical improvements
in growing methods, and develop new uses for jute. A strategy of this
sort was adopted by the natural rubber growers who until now have
been able to match the competition of artificial rubber.) For East Pakistan the strategy was a costly one, since the area presented few attractive, alternate investment opportunities. Consequently, the earnings
reaped tended to flow to the West Wing.[31]

The nurturing of industry, and the resulting high profits, inevitably
led to the amassment of industrial fortunes. It also led to a concentration

of development around urban foci, particularly around Karachi. The causal chain leading to locational concentration is very familiar. Potential entrepreneurs gravitate to areas with the most intense economic activity. Such areas also attract workers in search of jobs. Human concentration requires the provision of social overhead capital (water supply and other essential services). The presence of entrepreneurs and workers and the availability of social overhead capital create conditions favorable to industrial activity. As the volume of such activity builds up, economies of agglomeration are realized, thus increasing the attractiveness of the area to potential entrepreneurs and job-seekers and further accentuating the advantages of the initial foci over other locations. Where the government exerts a strong control over industry, the proximity of the administrative seat is also an important locational factor. No wonder then that, until the transfer of the capital to Islamabad, industry tended to concentrate heavily in the Karachi area. It is estimated that, in 1963, 26% of the nation's industrial establishments were located in Karachi. In the April, 1959 to June, 1963 period alone the Investment Promotion Wing of the Government of Pakistan issued 48% of all industrial licenses for establishments in the Karachi area, 30% for establishments elsewhere in West Pakistan, and only 22% for East Pakistan.

From the Second Plan onward, the government made increasing efforts to attain a better regional balance, with special attention to the East Wing situation. In 1949/50, only 26% of public sector development expenditure was allocated to East Pakistan. The proportion rose to 36% in 1959/60 and to 50% in 1963/64. After the war, in the revised version of the Third Plan, the proportion was raised to 53.5%. Efforts are also being made to direct a larger proportion of private industrial investment to the East Wing. Thus, an Industrial Investment Schedule published in 1960, which enumerated licenses available to private industry, provided for licenses of twice the value for West Pakistan of those for East Pakistan; in a 1963 revised schedule the proportions were reversed. The actual investment pattern does not conform to the schedules [32] but the seriousness of intent is unmistakable, and there is no doubt that, other things being equal, it is easier to obtain permission to establish a new plant in East Pakistan than in West Pakistan. A system of differential "tax holidays" was also instituted to discourage further expansion of the well-developed areas and to industrialize the relatively backward areas of both wings.[33] Yet, despite all the efforts, a serious problem remains. The initial conditions, favoring the industrialization of the West Wing over that of the East Wing, still largely pertain, and the head start enjoyed by the West Wing industries has put the East Wing at a serious disadvantage. Industrialization of East Pakistan without the imposition of excessive burdens on the entire economy—and possibly a slowdown of its overall growth rate—remains a serious problem.

Income transfers from agriculture to industry are justifiable in terms of future improvements in the economic levels of the polity insofar as the productivity of investment in industry is higher than the productivity of investment in agriculture (account being taken of the "learning by doing" effects and of the long-run comparative advantage flowing from the restructuring of the economy). High industrial profits and the amass-ing of large fortunes are tolerable if there is a positive contribution to real economic growth. Although the global results of the industrialization policy largely seem to justify the social sacrifices, indiscriminate pro-tection offered to all types of ventures has resulted in the growth of many enterprises which are extremely costly to the economy. One study of 32 industrial sectors reveals, for instance, that 12 sectors would be competitive at world prices if the rupee exchange rate were set at Rs. 10 per dollar or lower; another 12 at a rate of Rs. 10 to Rs. 20 per dollar. (The current exchange rate for the Pakistani rupee is Rs. 4.76 per dollar. But most transactions take place at approximately Rs. 8.5 per dollar.) Of the remaining eighteen, some would only become com-petitive at very high exchange rates—Rs. 63 per dollar for electric appli-ances, and over Rs. 1,000 per dollar for silk. Some industries, including sugar, edible oils, and motor vehicles, would not be competitive at any exchange rate since the value of tradable inputs exceeds the value of output at world prices.[34] Moreover, enormous differences in the relation between private value added (wages plus profits) and social value added (computed at world prices) exist among individual industries and among commodities within each industry group. Such differentials would be justifiable if it were true that industries which are relatively costly to the economy are those which, in the long run, contribute most to growth, but this does not seem to be the case.

Then, too, if Pakistan's aim were to develop a closed economy, its industrial strategy would have to aim at "balance," meaning the domestic satisfaction of domestic wants. Yet this is not the case: Pakistan's size, its geographic position, and its natural endowments strongly point to the need for an "open economy" approach, in which trade plays a substantial role. Indeed, industrial exports are an increasingly important source of foreign exchange earnings. Initially Pakistan's exports consisted almost entirely of agricultural products; in 1968/69 the value of manufactured exports exceeded for the first time the value of agricultural exports. A study by Nurul Islam shows that "there is no significant correlation between the net foreign exchange earnings of a manufactured export and its rate of growth over time." [35] Therefore, the foreign exchange is earned at an excessively high (and very likely at an increasing) social cost, and a part of the social burden finds no justification in terms of overall growth of the economy. Growth aims, social equity goals, and efficiency considerations all point to the need for rationalization of the system guiding and channeling investment.

With the passage of time rationalization of the industrial structure assumes a growing importance. In the past industrialization consisted mostly of import substitution for consumption goods and of promotion of export-oriented industries (mainly jute and cotton textiles) based on processing domestic agricultural products with the aid of imported machinery. If the next stage of industrialization consists mainly of substitution for imported capital goods (as is likely to take place, given the gradual exhaustion of the relatively easy opportunities for consumer goods import substitution), then, unless finer discernment is exercised, inefficiencies will cumulate. With the growth of industry, the vested interests in the existing pattern become entrenched, making any reorientation more difficult to carry out.

Earlier than most of the other developing countries, Pakistan came to appreciate that agriculture, no less than industry, is important for growth, and that, widespread opinion to the contrary, traditional farming is highly responsive to economic incentives. The government took steps to provide such incentives first through the gradual removal of controls, then increasingly through a system of input subsidies and price guarantees. A highly efficient extension program was also instituted. The success story is well known and needs no re-telling. What is somewhat less well known is that the success itself brought out new and intricate problems of social equity. The policy of subsidizing fertilizers, pesticides, electricity, and water has brought the greatest benefits to large-scale farmers in irrigated areas and relatively small benefits to small-scale farmers, but dry farming benefited hardly at all. A price support policy designed to maintain incomes of wheat farmers in *barani* areas and of rice farmers in the Sind would create a large exportable surplus in the Punjab. This, in itself, would be no cause for concern except for two facts. Pakistan's wheat prices are above world levels, and the ratio of foreign exchange to domestic factor use earned on marginal areas, where wheat would not be grown if world prices prevailed domestically, would be relatively low. High wheat prices would cause switching from cotton to wheat. Domestic prices of cotton are kept low (exports are made at the official exchange rate) in order to subsidize the domestic cotton industry. In terms of comparative advantage (in terms of domestic factor use to foreign exchange earned), cotton is an extremely important crop for Pakistan. The shrinkage of the cotton output in favor of wheat growing would thus be likely to have an adverse effect on Pakistan's overall welfare. An increase in domestic cotton prices (which would follow if export bonuses were extended to raw cotton) would counter the trend of switching production from cotton to food grains and strengthen Pakistan's foreign exchange position, yet it would handicap Pakistan's domestic cotton textile industries. Thus problems of efficiency, problems of social equity, and problems created by a policy of fostering industry at the expense of agriculture are intricately linked in a way which requires great caution in devising an efficient, yet socially equitable and politically acceptable, solution.

Pakistan's past growth was based on a semi-open economy approach: imports required for development were allowed in, but the development pattern itself was only loosely related to the country's comparative advantage, actual or potential. While the government made efforts to promote a fair distribution of gains (especially concerning the East-Wing–West-Wing problem), the major emphasis was on growth. As the country becomes increasingly self-reliant, the efficiency of the various branches of the economy, in world-price terms, becomes increasingly important. Problems of social equity also assume an increasingly crucial role. Given the growth impetus and resilience which the Pakistani economy has demonstrated, these are the problems which, surely, are even more crucial than a further acceleration of the already remarkable rate of growth.

SOME CONCLUDING REMARKS

Economists as well as policy makers are apt to draw half-true dichotomies between growth and efficiency, and between growth and equity. For poor countries the prescription usually runs: achieve rapid growth first, then take care of social justice, and only later, having grown relatively rich and having achieved social fairness, can one afford the luxury of being efficient. It is beyond doubt that little can be achieved until a country is wealthy enough to do more than take care of its most immediate needs and that efficiency in a subsistence economy does not lead to growth. Yet it is equally true that inefficiency frustrates growth and that growth which distributes gains in an inequitable fashion may be socially and politically unacceptable.

It would be a gross oversimplification to say that India sacrifices growth and efficiency for the sake of social equity and that Pakistan sacrifices social equity and efficiency for the sake of growth. The two countries share many of the same problems, have similar concerns and traditions, and have many similarities in their approach to economic development. In both countries policies to promote growth have achieved notable results but, by simultaneously promoting inefficiencies, they have also placed new obstacles in the way of further growth. It is not open to serious doubt that further growth will occur, and that, with the new developments in agriculture, it is likely to accelerate. Yet, given the prevailing poverty and the urgency of economic and social problems, can either country afford the luxury of policy-fostered inefficiency?

A review of the recent progress and of the prospects for further growth raises a broad strategy issue. Free enterprise in an economically underdeveloped country with an imperfect market mechanism is unlikely to result in a rate of return and pattern of development which are socially acceptable. Should government policy be primarily directed to measures controlling and modifying the market (as was done in both countries) and to substitution of administrative regulations for market allocation (as was done in both countries, though primarily in India), or should it concentrate on resource redistribution (as contrasted with resource transformation), on the satisfaction of collective needs, and on measures to improve market efficiency? Dogmatic and old-fashioned *laissez-faire,* regardless of its theoretical efficiency, is clearly unacceptable as a development strategy. But *dirigisme,* pursued with or without the blessing of theoretical economic constructs, does not seem to provide a viable alternative. India and Pakistan have made notable progress because the respective governments created an appropriate framework for growth and because they helped in mobilizing resources for growth. But where administrative judgment was substituted for economic calculus or where administrative action modified the working of economic forces, the results have often been of dubious value. Frequently there has been much waste and sometimes near disaster. And the sacrifice of real (as against statistical) growth and efficiency has failed to make a major dent in the overwhelming social problems of the two countries. These problems—population increase, which eats up most of the gains in output; education, the lack of which contributes to inequality and cuts off vast millions from the opportunities for self-betterment of economic conditions; regional imbalance, which weakens the political fabric of society, and many others—require a *planned* frontal attack. The forging and application of efficient tools for their solution are perhaps more important for the next decade than the goal of a 6% rate of growth.

A Dialogue on Africa's Development Pattern
BETWEEN THE HONOURABLE PHILIP NDEGWA
AND DAVID NEWBERY

THE SHAPE OF THE PROBLEM

In the words of Mr. Ndegwa:

"It is usual these days to lump together Africa, Asia, and Latin America as the underdeveloped regions of the world. It is true that compared with the rest of the world these areas are "poor." They also

The extracts used in this section are from a Conference paper by Mr. Ndegwa titled "Requirements of More Rapid Growth in 'Black Africa' During the Next Decade." The paper was of considerable scope, detailing suggested changes in infrastructure; education and manpower; intra-country, inter-country, and international trade; and aid relationships and uses. Since many of these issues are considered elsewhere in this volume, the extracts presented here are primarily concerned with the points debated in "A Comment on Philip Ndegwa's Paper," which was distributed at the Conference by David Newbery.

have some identical problems, such as very high rates of population growth, fluctuations in the prices offered for their commodity exports, and so forth. However, despite the similarity of most of their problems, we must at all times keep in mind the significant differences among them. This is especially important when one is discussing the role of foreign assistance in the development of these countries—differences in the kind of foreign assistance required for each region.

"What are the differences? First, in view of most indicators Africa is more underdeveloped than either Latin America or Asia, particularly the former. Per capita income in Latin America is, on average, about three times that prevailing in Africa. For some of the really poor African countries the gap is even greater—per capita incomes in Latin America are well over six times greater and certainly even larger if one takes only the richer countries of Latin America into account. . . .

"Second, structural transformation has gone much further in other developing regions, especially Latin America, than in Africa. For example, while secondary industry accounts for more than 20% of GDP in Latin America (and in some cases well in excess of 30%), in Africa it is insignificant. Even for the more developed African countries, such as Kenya, it is only about 10%. And although such countries as India have the same income level as some African countries, their modern sectors are much larger. This gives them a much better foundation for further development as foreign markets for their industrial products become available. In fact, a major way of assisting such countries during the next decade would be to offer them markets for their industrial products. In the case of Africa, this stage has not yet been reached.

"Third, the human resources in Africa are less developed than in Latin America and Asia. In Africa technical assistance has to cover the needs of virtually every category of high-level and middle-level manpower—from hospital nurses to doctors, from secondary school teachers to university professors, and from draughtsmen to architects and engineers. . . . Lack of the necessary manpower in Black Africa is not only noticeable in government programs but also in other areas. Of particular significance is the small size of the entrepreneurial class, development of which must be given high priority.

"Fourth, most African countries are much smaller, both in area and in population, than those of Latin America or Asia. Many African countries have populations of less than one million. Moderate size nations, such as Uganda, have populations about the size of some Indian cities. This small size means that without economic cooperation on a really wide front, there is little hope of more rapid and sustained growth rates in many African countries. A somewhat related problem is the large number of countries in Africa. . . .

"Finally, both Asian and Latin American countries have had a good deal of experience in administration and in building the necessary institutions for development (even if it is only the central bank!). In contrast, most of the African countries became politically independent only recently—some of them are not independent yet. Given the serious shortage of educated manpower, African countries have to build their institutions with inadequately prepared personnel and with expatriates."

THE TYPE OF DEVELOPMENT STRATEGY

Despite these enormous difficulties, Mr. Ndegwa believes higher growth rates can be achieved in Africa if there is "a firm commitment on the part of the African governments to rapid economic and social development." This commitment should cover at least some of the following:

"1. Recognition of the importance of, and substantial support for planned development . . . [It] must involve acceptance of discipline which planned development calls for. Further, in their planning, the importance of not forgetting the long-term requirements because of the political attractiveness of doing things to meet current demands must be kept in mind. . . .

"2. Preparedness to use foreign resources (capital and manpower) in their development programs . . .

"3. Acceptance of the fact that economic cooperation among African countries on a wide range of areas is necessary not only for each one of them but also for the area as a whole . . .

"4. Willingness to undertake those institutional reforms necessary for rapid development. In some cases this will include such measures as land reforms, reorganization of the civil service, and more control over local authorities. In most countries it will also be necessary to introduce deliberate measures to overcome certain traditional barriers to national integration. One such barrier is tribalism. . . . Elimination of tribalism is, in my view, a major precondition of more rapid development in many African countries."

Mr. Ndegwa judges the gravest obstacles to African growth to lie in its minute industrial sector, its unfavorable scale of internal market, and the relative unattractiveness of its primary exports. His analysis and his recommendations are designed to identify and offset these constraints. First, on the side of primary production, he suggests:

"African countries will continue to depend more than many other developing countries on primary commodities for some years to come. Special efforts are therefore necessary to increase the participation of these countries in the field of international trade. Among the possible measures which can be taken are the following:

"1. African countries should undertake—and the donor countries should assist in—processing of primary (especially agricultural) commodities before export. Assistance from the industrial nations should not only cover the establishment of processing industries but also removal of various tariffs they have imposed on processed products. Processing of primary products before export would enable African countries to play a greater part in international trade, increase their foreign exchange earnings, and reduce fluctuations in the prices offered for these exports.

"2. Efforts should be made to diversify the economies of these countries. The importance of industrialization is known and accepted; what has not yet been fully recognized is the importance of diversification in the primary sector itself. In particular, Black Africa could become a major supplier of food, especially grain and livestock products, to the world. However, in order to do this, a special 'food program' covering production aspects, research, storage, and marketing of the food surpluses would need to be mounted on an international basis. At present many of these countries cannot, in a sense, afford to produce food surpluses—because of marketing and storage problems. . . .

"3. African countries should be assisted in carrying out detailed investigations and surveys of their natural resources. If such investigations are carried out, some African countries may find that they have certain resources (particularly minerals) which could increase their participation in world trade."

Thus the main thrust in the primary sector is toward processing and diversification. In the tiny industrial sector, the inhibitions to growth are seen to lie, above all, in the small scale of local markets which gives import substitution—a normal first stage of transformation—a very limited field of opportunity. Mr. Ndegwa's chief emphasis is, therefore, upon the creation of wider regions of cooperation inside Africa:

"Given the small size of most African countries in terms of the markets for products, it is clear that the potentialities for manufacturing and commercialization of agriculture cannot be exploited fully unless markets are extended through the creation of common markets, or preferential trading blocs to start with. Indeed, greater intra-African trade must be regarded as an important source of growth which has not yet been exploited. This is not to deny the importance of other ways in which African governments can cooperate. But what I regard to be a major constraint on the rapid development of most African countries south of the Sahara—the size of the market—cannot be overcome in the absence of common markets. The effectiveness of other measures of economic cooperation will, in fact, depend on whether or not they are undertaken in the context of a common market or other effective forms of trade preferences.

"Regional groupings are necessary to foster interregional trade and industrialization. In a sense greater trade and a more rapid rate of industrialization are different sides of the same coin in the African context. This is not necessarily true of other developing regions where industrialization has proceeded much further and the ability to exploit opportunities for export of manufactured goods to other developing regions as well as to the developed countries is much greater. . . . At present, intra-African trade accounts for less than 10% of total African trade, and it is composed mainly of primary products. While there is substantial scope for increased interregional trade in primary products and in particular foodstuffs, it is doubtful if trade among countries producing broadly similar primary products can be increased at a very rapid rate unless the exchange of manufactured goods plays a growing role. There is thus a two-way relationship between interregional trade and industrialization. . . .

"In the majority of African countries, the scope for import substitution is much smaller than in Latin America because of their abject poverty and small populations. The optimal scale of operations will certainly be too large in relation to domestic demand for many products and will be reflected in excess capacity. Excess-capacity industries and others established by each country under increasing degrees of protection would subsequently be formidable barriers to economic integration; not every country might be prepared to see some of its industries contracting and perhaps even collapsing due to competition of goods from the partner states. Moreover, in the absence of larger trading areas, many industries may not come to Africa at all, or their establishment may be seriously delayed. . . .

"The East African Community provides a good illustration of the problems that can arise and solutions that may be adopted in efforts to promote integration. The scheme of economic cooperation established during the colonial era was relatively unregulated—that is, free of mechanisms for bringing about an equitable distribution of benefits. This gave rise to dissatisfaction when the three countries gained political independence, and it was found necessary to examine how the arrangements then prevailing could be modified to take account of the changed status of its members. A commission that came to be known as the 'Raisman Commission' was established. The Commission's major conclusion was that the common market benefited Kenya to a greater extent than Tanzania and Uganda, and that, in particular, the latter countries had sustained a loss of import duty revenue. The Commission recommended a fiscal redistribution from Kenya to Tanzania and Uganda. This recommendation was accepted and implemented.

"However, with the passage of time, it was thought to be inadequate and was replaced, as provided for in the second Treaty for East African Cooperation, by 'transfer taxes,' the East African Development Bank, and reorganization and reallocation of the headquarters of the Common Services. Transfer taxes are internal taxes, whose rationale is to enable Tanzania and Uganda to increase their rate of industrial development. The Development Bank has a broadly similar purpose, since it is required to give priority to industrial development in the relatively less industrially developed partner states. In the case of the Common Services, most of them had their headquarters in Kenya, and it was agreed that they be allocated equitably among the three partners.

"I have spent some time discussing the mechanism for an equitable sharing of benefits because this problem is likely to be uppermost in the minds of nations considering economic integration. But the East African Community is much more than a mere common market. A number of services (E.A. Railways, E.A. Harbors, E.A. Posts and Telecommunications, E.A. Airways, the collection of income tax and customs and excise duties, and research in agriculture, forestry, and industry are the major examples) are undertaken jointly and an institutional framework has been established for consultation on matters ranging from fiscal and monetary policies to economic planning. The East African Community provides a good example of the kind of cooperation required in Africa. The cooperation required must extend beyond tariff preferences if it is to lead to higher and sustained growth rates and overcome the serious disadvantages of the small size of most African countries. One can actually go further and state that the wider the front of economic cooperation, the easier it would be to ensure that each member country benefits."

Mr. Newbery does not dissent from the need for larger cooperative units. But he challenges the priority given to regional associations and puts much more emphasis upon the crucial role of the primary sector. First, he suggests that export prospects are not too unpromising:

"High growth rates are usually associated with the industrial sector, and, as Mr. Ndegwa has pointed out, the industrial sector is so small in Africa that it cannot significantly affect the overall growth rate. More particularly, the great mass of the population outside the industrial wage labor force will not benefit from high rates of expansion in the industrial sector, and in all probability will lose, to the extent that, directly or indirectly, industrial expansion is financed by the rural population. In short, the main determinant of Africa's development performance is the performance of the primary sector. With some exceptions, the constraint occurs on the supply side and not on the demand side—which has important implications for the balance of payments.

In Table 1, I have tried to obtain a measure of world market shares held by Africa with its main agricultural exports. Quick back-of-the-envelope calculations show that Africa could enjoy an average annual rate of growth of these exports of 7.5% for a decade while not exceeding

TABLE 1. DEMAND PROSPECTS FOR AGRICULTURAL PRODUCE

Projected Rate of Growth in World Exports, 1960/61 to 1975 * (% per annum)	Commodity	Africa's Share of World Exports 1965–67 (to nearest 5%)
Group I		
Under 1.5	Sugar	10
	Tea	5
Group II		
1.5–2.5	Cereals	
	excluding maize	5
	Maize	10
	Vegetable oils	15
	Oil seeds	10
	Sisal	40
	Fish	10
	Bananas	10
Group III		
2.5–5.0	Coffee	30
	Fruit	20
	Tobacco	15
	Raw cotton	10
	Cocoa	85
	Meat—cattle †	10
	Sheep, goats	30
	Natural rubber	10
Group IV		
5.0–7.5	Fishmeal	10
	Hardwood	15

* Maizels, p. 153, mean of assumptions A (1950's trend), and B (published national targets and plans).

† Figures relate to *numbers* of cattle, etc., not to volume or value of meat. Wine, dairy produce, broadleaved logs, pulses, tinned fruit, spices, hides, and skins have been omitted because of lack of data or projections.

Sources: Alfred Maizels, *Exports and Economic Growth of Developing Countries,* National Institute of Economic and Social Research (London: Cambridge University Press, 1968); and Food and Agriculture Organization, *The State of Food and Agriculture 1969* (Rome, 1970).

TABLE 2.   PROJECTED GROWTH RATES, SUPPLY UNCONSTRAINED

	Value of Exports, Average 1965–67 (1) (millions of dollars)	Assumed Growth Rate (% per annum)	Projected Value, 1975–77 (millions of dollars)
Quota Crops			
Sugar	200	1.0	220
Coffee	600	5.5 (2)	1,000
Dominant Crops (3)			
Cocoa	500	3.5 (4)	700
Sisal	50	1.0	55
Other agricultural products	1,300	9.5 (5)	3,250
Fishery products	170	9.5 (5)	420
Forest products	170	13.0 (6)	600
Total	2,990	7.6	6,245

Notes: (1) Calculated from FAO, *Food and Agriculture 1969*, Table 1C, p. 141, and 6D, p. 171; figures rounded.
(2) Maizels, *Exports and Economic Growth*, p. 293.
(3) Crops with a market share of more than 20%.
(4) Maizels, *Exports and Economic Growth*, p. 288.
(5) Based on the assumption that the average market share doubles from 15% to 30% of the world market, while the total grows at 2% per annum.
(6) Market share doubles but total grows at 6%.

projected world rates of growth of demand for quota crops, or crops in which Africa has a high market share, and also not more than doubling her market share of the remaining commodities. The details of this calculation are given in Table 2. If, in addition, we assume that mineral exports are not likely to be much restrained by a lack of demand, the *demand* prospects for Africa's primary exports look very good, so we can presume that the constraints lie on the supply side—a hypothesis borne out by the figures in Table 3 which report the past decade's performance.

"Another aspect of the dominant importance of agriculture relative to industry is that it is not too clear that the small size of the countries is such a drawback as might be supposed. The economic case for increased cooperation and market integration rests primarily on the indus-

TABLE 3. PAST PERFORMANCE IN EXPORTS, 1957–59 TO 1966–68

	Annual Growth Rate
	%
Agricultural products	
Africa (ex. S.A.)	1.3
World *	3.6
Fishery products	
Africa (ex. S.A.)	3.5
World *	6.6
Forestry products	
Africa (incl. S.A.)	8.6
World *	6.4

Note: Unit values almost unchanged, except for fishery products, where inflation = 0.7% per annum.

  * Excluding mainland China.

Source: Same as Table 1.

trial benefits engendered. If these are small, then so is the attractiveness of forming common markets—unless, that is, a common export marketing policy were worked out for those commodities whose price could be affected. Past experience and the figures in Table 1 suggest that this aspect is not of great importance either."

Second, Mr. Newbery asks whether priority for industrialization at this stage may not be given at the expense of essential development in the primary sector:

"It is argued that industrialization enables high rates of growth, is the only cure for unemployment, is capable of generating high rates of saving and reinvestment, and causes (in conjunction with urbanization) various significant social changes in the population. How far are these benefits available to Africa? . . . I would judge that unemployment in Africa is significantly different from that in Asia, is a consequence of high real wages in the industrial sector, and is, therefore, in part a *consequence* of industrialization. The cure is to change the relative attractiveness of rural and urban employment by reducing the direct and indirect benefits of living in the modern sector. The cure is emphatically not to expand employment by creating jobs in industry—this will only increase the attractiveness of migration. The other advantage of industrialization—the generation of savings—remains as yet unreaped and is linked to the former point that wage rates are too high. A cynical view of the last decade would be that income has been taxed away from the poorer rural population to support extravagant consumption in the urban and elite sectors. The converse ought to be so. The case for industrialization can only be made if there is evidence that these problems are likely to be solved."

SOME IMPLICATIONS FOR AID POLICY

Nonetheless, there is considerable agreement in the proposals for aid policy. Both writers stress the need for capital assistance to the transport links which are a precondition of either integration or greater inter-African trade. In Mr. Ndegwa's words:

"In the field of transportation, the continent faces a number of major problems. First, in practically all cases, the transportation network is inadequate for internal use. Colonial transport policy was concerned mainly with the development of facilities for international trade. With the growth of internal trade, the policy became increasingly unrealistic for it failed to take sufficient account of the facilities required for the promotion of internal trade. The rural areas have had to bear the main brunt of these adverse effects. Expansion and diversification of exports, balanced growth of manufacturing, and accelerated rural development will all call for substantial investment in internal transport . . .

"Second, interconnection routes for general trade between adjacent countries are inadequate and often non-existent. This problem is made worse by factors such as differences in highway codes and incompatible railway gauges. In many cases the improvement or establishment of a transportation link between two adjacent countries will result in increased trade even in the absence of trade preferences. Additionally, better connections should make the countries involved more attractive to foreign investment.

"A third problem is that of landlocked countries. Zambia's recent and painful experience indicates the difficulties that political change in other countries can create for a landlocked country with a single access route to the sea. . . .

"The cost of transporting goods is as important as the availability of physical facilities so far as the trade-promoting effects of transport development are concerned. It is important, therefore, that costs of alternative modes of transport should be properly analyzed before a choice is made. Although the main reliance will probably have to be placed on road development, rail, water and air links may be more appropriate in some cases. The importance of better air links for the promotion of tourism needs no elaboration. . . .

"External finance has played a very important role in financing economic infrastructure projects in Africa in the past. Africa must continue to rely on external assistance for such projects, given the magnitude of their cost and import content. Provision of adequate assistance in this field (and such assistance should include the engineers, surveyors, and the like needed) would be one of the most effective ways in which the donors can help Africa to accelerate her development."

Mr. Newbery accepts the critical role of external aid in accelerating regional integration by way of a workable infrastructure. He does not believe that African governments have done enough to mobilize internal resources:

"It is not immediately clear that finance is a major constraint, given the reasonable foreign trade prospects and the present burden of taxation. This is more contentious, but I would argue that the growing disparity between the income levels of the modern and the traditional sectors is an indication of the failure of governments to use resources available for development; instead they allow inequities to arise and consumption rather than investment to increase."

Nevertheless, large-scale expenditures on regional transport, on electricity grids, and on improved communications do demand much greater reliance on external resources:

"It does, however, remain true that it is probably easier for aid donors to help in the industrial sector than elsewhere, or, more precisely, that they have a comparative advantage in this sector. How can they best help in the African context? Mr. Ndegwa stresses the barriers to marketing industrial goods—poor transport networks and national fragmentation. I think political realities within Africa will constrain local efforts to remove these, and consequently aid directed at these problems will have great effectiveness and will not replace local efforts. I would suggest that priority be given to projects which, in the ordinary course of events, would only be undertaken if agreement could be reached among two or more countries. An example would be the building of two factories, each capable of supplying the total demand for its product by both countries, locating one in each country. The same should be true of transport projects—they should be conceived on a regional basis. This suggests that donors should operate at the regional rather than at the country level. The compliance of recipient countries to regional agreements would be rewarded by the allocation of more aid, and conversely.

"One major sector which could be of overriding importance to some African countries is the tourist industry, as Mr. Ndegwa points out. With world tourism growing at about 15% per annum, and substantially faster in some regions, this could be far more important than most alternative exports for those countries lucky enough to have the appropriate tourist attractions. This implies a need for the International Air Traffic Agreement to negotiate more favorable fares, and for finance and (possibly even more important) management services to be provided for hotels."

EDUCATED MANPOWER

Finally, both Mr. Ndegwa and Mr. Newbery stress the need for technical assistance in the shape of trained manpower. In Mr. Ndegwa's words:

"The acute shortage of high-level manpower is probably a more serious constraint on the development of Black Africa than even the insufficiency of capital. There is a great and growing demand for virtually all skills requiring secondary and post-secondary education. The current situation is a direct consequence of the colonial governments' neglect of education and failure to gear the educational system to manpower requirements. This is well known and need not be labored. It is the acute shortage of high-level and middle-level manpower that distinguishes Africa sharply from the other developing regions. It also makes the task of rapid development in Africa more difficult, since the creation of capital in the form of high-level manpower is often a more time-consuming process than the creation of physical capital. A major problem here is that in certain fields of high-level manpower (medicine, engineering, hydrology, architecture, and the like), there is almost a worldwide shortage. This is making it increasingly difficult for African countries to get the necessary manpower either on a technical assistance basis or through direct recruitment. Provision of reasonably adequate high-level manpower in such fields would be one of the most effective ways in which donors can assist Black Africa to achieve higher growth rates. We in Kenya have been unable (and I am sure this is true in many other African countries) to get, for example, enough doctors, engineers, architects, and hydrologists. The ultimate solution is, of course, for Africa to produce her requirements herself. The donors can make the achievement of this objective relatively easy if aid is given in sufficient quantities for the purpose."

But Mr. Newbery has one or two reservations about the use of external experts and their relevance to African conditions, particularly in the field of planning and administration:

"Most African countries do not have a complex industrial structure and, therefore, do not need the sophisticated inter-industrial balance sheet planning of textbooks. The prime role of the major economic ministry is to collect the relevant information and make sure that it reaches the right people and is correctly used, to ensure that only profitable projects are selected and that they are efficiently operated, and to make sensible fiscal decisions. A plan document is only needed to the extent that some of the information needed to select the right projects concerns the future, and so projections are required for such quantities as future commodity prices, debt servicing commitments, the balance of payments, and the size of the investment program. As far as I can see, the only project which is of such long gestation and which has such far-reaching effects on other parts of the economy that it needs to be treated in the normal comprehensive plan framework is education and manpower planning.

"This has important implications for technical assistance and aid generally. The international organizations are voracious devourers of statistical information, which they usually ask member countries to supply, placing a considerable burden on local data processing agencies. Some of the major aid donors (AID, for example) do much the same thing. It would be far more help if these bodies first decided what information was really vital in the sense of making significant differences to decisions and distinguished this from data which are merely of interest for international comparisons, or which are only of interest in a developed economy, and, second, provided field help to collect this important information. (This would also include surveys of natural resources, mapping, land use surveys, and so on, which require special skills and equipment unlikely to be found locally.)

"In the same vein, if aid donors could assume more of the responsibility for seeking out profitable projects and drawing up project appraisals, the administrative burden would be lightened at the point where there is the most pressing shortage of high-level specialist staff. This would have two other advantages—the foreign staff would not be part of the decision-making process, so that the political problems normally associated with technical assistance would be reduced, and there would be more hope that projects would be chosen on viable economic grounds, rather than on grounds of sectional interest. One final remark on planning: a plea for more competent fiscal advice. To judge the effect of taxes, tariffs, and exchange rates, or to assess their incidence, requires considerable knowledge of the way the particular economy works. It is not clear that either academic economists or the professional economists of the IMF have fully appreciated this, and I would make a plea for more research on this subject, and more sophistication in advising countries on their financial policies. This point is, of course, not specific to Africa."

Structural Change in Africa

BY GERALD K. HELLEINER

In the 1960's most tropical African governments were primarily absorbed in the effort to consolidate their newly regained independence. Their efforts aimed at the development of national political loyalties, the Africanization of their key governmental and other decision-making posts, and the creation of stable political bases for those in power. These attempts have neither been totally successful nor in any way abandoned. The "inevitability of instability" unfortunately remains. (The phrase is James O'Connell's. His *caveat* is apposite here. "Political instability upsets particularly those observers whose own countries have had no experience of it for many generations. They often exaggerate its effects on social and economic life and expect the activities of society practically to cease, where governments topple." [1])

One must hope, however, that time will be found in Africa in the 1970's for more concentrated attention to the objectives of economic and social progress, which frequently were paid only extravagant lip service during the 1960's, and to the formulation of coherent sets of policies to those ends.

The discussion here is intended to generate debate on some of the social, political, and institutional aspects of the expected drive toward African economic progress in the coming decade. The first section is concerned with national socio-political objectives, both internal and external to the nation. The second part deals with those structural changes which relate to some of the institutions of development.

PART I—SOCIO-POLITICAL OBJECTIVES [2]

Growth, Welfare, and Distribution

Per capita income is usually said to average about $80 in tropical Africa.[3] The Pearson Commission outlines a target rate of GNP growth of 6%—despite the fact that aggregate growth rates have been largely discredited in Africa (if not elsewhere) today. This means that "success" is achieved (assuming population grows at 3% a year) if per capita income rises to about $107 by 1980! It is doubtful whether GNP aggregates are a useful way of summarizing levels of living or progress in Africa, but these rough data offer some indication of the magnitude and intractability of the poverty problem.

More meaningful, perhaps, is the fact that physical measures of poverty—infant mortality, literacy rate, hospital beds per 1,000, electric power capacity per person, and the like—all place Africa at the bottom end of the development spectrum. One might convert the targets for per capita GNP growth to physical measures and assume that everything is to grow at the same rate as per capita GNP, i.e., 34% by 1980. If this improvement were evenly spread, and "outputs" were directly proportional to inputs, by 1980 the rural infant mortality rate might fall from about 250 to about 165, the number of rural inhabitants per doctor from about 30,000 to about 20,000, and so forth. But these assumptions are simplistic. In particular, they overstate vastly the progress which would be achieved with 6% GNP growth in such "social" spheres and in rural areas. The dimensions of the poverty that will remain in most parts of rural Africa, even after the Second Development Decade, are staggering.

In the face of economic constraints this severe, does it make sense to carry on *only* the traditional variety of discussion as to optimum allocation? Some would say that this degree of poverty requires even *closer* attention to allocation; misallocation is a luxury which societies that poor can ill afford.[4] This is indeed true. But perhaps more compelling still is the argument that the difference between an income of $95 in 1980 and one of $107 in 1980—which in this context represents doubling the per capita growth rate—looks fairly insignificant relative to the level of poverty which these figures portray. As long as material levels of living are and will remain *so* low, may there not be something to be said, even by economists, for thinking more about "the quality of life"? (An analogous though qualitatively different case is made by Galbraith for the materially very wealthy states.)

What contributes to "quality" in this sense? Here the economist *qua* economist rapidly loses whatever comparative advantage he might otherwise possess. The crux of the matter is whether there are unmeasurable aspects of individual (particularly rural) welfare which can be improved without the insertion of the heavy material inputs which African states are not likely to have. Can satisfaction be derived from an increased sense of involvement in the nation or ethnic group, increased ideological involvement, a greater sense of shared effort? If so, and here the economist returns, can these be achieved without significant material inputs? Many of us may be inclined to doubt whether this line of argument leads very far, but the questions must be asked.

Some hypothesize that increased "consciousness," apart from the satisfaction it provides, may significantly affect the total quantity of material inputs or at least the uses to which they are put (even at the micro-level). African politicians evidently believe this, as they continually exhort their people to alter their behavior in the interest of national development, but it is probably a rather more questionable proposition. Attention to such unmeasurable and non-economic aspects of welfare and incentive structures is likely, however, to be of greater moment in Africa today than in many other parts of the world because of the relative youth of its population and the relative malleability of its social structures. The rapid rate of African population growth implies an age structure in which fully 40% of the population is likely to be between five and nineteen years of age.[5] (Moreover, overt urban unemployment and dissatisfaction are heavily concentrated in the school-leaver age category.) This suggests that national service, youth leagues, boy scouts, young farmers' clubs, or whatever—all of which can draw upon reserves of idealism, self-sacrifice, and the commitment rarer among older people—may have greater chances of influencing aggregate attitudes and behavior in Africa than in "older" nations. Reliance upon these devices must, of course, be carefully planned and balanced against alternative possibilities. It will not do simply to equip youth movements with expensive uniforms or simply to train them in the chanting of political slogans. The risk of these measures must make one pause before embarking too vigorously in this direction.

The main argument here is not based, however, on the possible productive power of ideology as another input but on the possible insertion of some nonmaterial component as part of individual and social welfare functions. The need for such a component may have been among the motivations for the early weak efforts to sell "African socialism." It certainly explains the demand for rapid localization of posts and may even account for some so-called "prestige projects." It is unquestionably now a significant element in a second, more serious, round of ideological efforts, represented by the Arusha Declaration in Tanzania, the Mulungushi Declaration in Zambia, and the new Ugandan "Common Man's Charter." Fundamental to the credibility of such a component is honest government leadership and government behavior which reflects the tenets it espouses. Corruption and dishonesty may not carry any short-term economic disadvantages (they may even be economically beneficial), but they undercut any attempt to construct a society with which its members identify and in which they can take pride.

The most significant aspects of the recent Tanzanian socialist experience were not the nationalizations which received the bulk of press attention but the reductions in leadership income and privilege, the incomes policy to hold down the rate of urban wage increase, and the clear determination to do more for the rural people. These moves have been widely understood and appreciated in rural Tanzania. These policies, relating essentially to income distribution, have to do with the "quality of life"; they may make it easier for many Tanzanians to tolerate their low material levels of living. In this case, moreover, it is unlikely that any aggregate material benefit was traded off against the "quality" gain. Equity in the distribution of income and rights, the tax burden, and government-provided services are fundamental to the quality of a society's development. The main tools which economists have applied to consideration of development problems have not usually incorporated these considerations: growth rates and benefit/cost ratios are singularly lacking in distributional content. But distribution is one of the oldest concerns of the economics profession, and there is a growing recognition that it has been underplayed in recent years. Even the Pearson Report, although its overall tone is quite "orthodox," does address itself quite vigorously to this subject at one point: "In many developing countries, increases in income have been highly concentrated in relatively few hands. . . . Policies which serve to distribute income more equitably must therefore become as important as those designed to accelerate growth." (p. 54).

Planners in Africa have tended to ignore distributional questions partly because of the apparent strength of indigenous security systems (the extended family system) and the relative absence of the grinding poverty found in Asia, partly because of calculations that redistributing the income of the wealthy would have a minor effect on the rest of society, or simply because of a preoccupation with raising the growth rate. Yet the strength of the indigenous welfare system is waning while the prospect of extreme poverty, urban and rural, is rising. The fact that leveling the peak of income distribution has had little effect elsewhere is irrelevant since the policy's principal purpose in Africa would be to create a unity of purpose and a greater sense of public participation in a growing economy. Finally, there is no firm evidence which relates the distribution of income to the rate of growth.[6] In Africa there are even some reasons (profligacy among the newly rich and dramatic self-improvement among smallholders) for predicting an increased aggregate savings rate from redistribution down and toward the rural areas. Moreover, the incentives created by existing wage structures are frequently counterproductive, not least in their relation to paper qualifications of dubious value.[7] In many African nations it may be too much to expect the political and bureaucratic leadership to push for reductions in its own privileges. Therefore the planners must speak vigorously for both efficiency and considerations of equity.

It is well known that civil service and other professional salaries in Africa are inflated as a legacy of colonial salary structures. Upward pressures on rates of professional remuneration continue because of the great international mobility of highly skilled labor. In order to induce engineers, doctors, managers, and others not to emigrate and not to accept employment with an international agency or a multinational firm, poor African governments feel compelled to pay them salaries approaching internationally competitive rates. Yet the "brain drain" common in Asia has not assumed large dimensions in Africa, nor is it likely to for some time. The local demand for skills will remain strong in most African nations during the 1970's, and Africans have, in any case, not shown the same interest in leaving their homes as have others. (This lack of interest could simply be a function of employment opportunities.) It therefore seems likely that African civil servants and professionals are earning substantial economic rents. If it is politically too difficult to cut money salaries and perquisites (Tanzania, however, managed it successfully), they must at least be frozen at present levels. Increases in the cost of living should no longer constitute justification for salary increases but should consciously be permitted to erode the highest levels of money income. In anticipation of future "brain drain" problems, African states should now be devising programs and policies to avert them. Above all, this is a matter of education policy. But it is also a matter of erecting selective barriers—bonding provisions, emigration taxes, or whatever—to potential loss of professionals. If rich nations pursue selective immigration policies, it should not appear unseemly for poor ones to control or tax their emigrants selectively.

It is not simply the elite who have fared disproportionately well in independent Africa. Urban, mining, and estate wages, even for unskilled workers, have usually risen at very rapid rates—much more rapid than the rates of growth of per capita income.[8] In some instances these increases were the product of trade union pressure, governmental conscience, and a tradition of minimum wage legislation; in others they were the product of calculated self-interest on the part of private employers. The effect has been a steady widening of the rural-urban income gap. This gap has been still further extended by the continuing "urban bias" of government expenditures. Health facilities, water supplies, education, paved roads, entertainment, new buildings, all tend to be concentrated in the few urban centers.[9] This urban concentration is probably the most "efficient" means of providing the services because it minimizes per capita costs. But its effect, together with that of the rapid wage rate increases in organized urban labor markets, is to stimulate the flow of rural dwellers into the cities. At the same time, the rising urban labor costs have damped the rate at which urban employment can be expanded. The ultimate result is rapidly rising, overt urban unemployment.

These unemployed and, more important, the rural dwellers have largely been left behind by recent growth in Africa. The urban unemployed have at least derived some benefits from the expanding urban services and have probably shared in the rising incomes of the fortunate job holders. Many, if not most, rural dwellers have not shared in national progress at all, unless they increased their own efforts. Yet in many tropical African countries smallholder farmers are among the most dynamic forces working for economic progress. Equity demands that they share in the progress which, in many cases, they have been instrumental in achieving; efficiency may demand it as well.

Distributional equity is a key element in the quality of a nation's life; the more is this so when poverty levels are extreme. Policies relating to it are essential in the 1970's if Africa is not to re-create the Latin America development pattern.

The rigidity of social structure characteristic of Latin America and Asia does not yet curse the tropical African scene. This is not to say that traditional authority structures and ethnic loyalties are unimportant or that there exist no social or economic classes. One does sense, however, a much greater social malleability, at least in the monetized sectors of the economy. The social divisions in most of tropical Africa have not hardened. Nor have the national or ideological lines. (Ethnic boundaries probably remain the most powerful.) It may, therefore, still be possible to mobilize the interest of many people, even a large portion of the older population, for broad social objectives, provided the goals are both plausible and not hypocritically proclaimed. More equitable distribution of national income gains is a major social objective which could play this role. Its pursuit, moreover, is quite consistent with the other aims of a wide variety of political systems.

Unfortunately the elites and the employed urban dwellers who stand to lose from incomes policies can be expected to oppose them vigorously. Clashes between trade unions and governments attempting to modify existing patterns of income distribution are inevitable. Moreover, incomes policies are particularly difficult to implement where there exists a large private sector. Perhaps only exceptional leadership can succeed in such policies. But as development proceeds and inequalities increase, they become increasingly difficult to introduce. The African political scene is already volatile enough; it would be most unfortunate if extreme inequality were added to other potential sources of political instability in the coming decades.

Employment

Increased equity in income distribution is the key element in this concern with the quality of progress. Urban unemployment is but one aspect of the distribution question. Yet it deserves attention in its own right, whatever one's views on the distribution question. Alleviation of this new scourge of urban Africa is not a priority matter only for reasons of equity (or, more cold-bloodedly, of political survival), but also because it is a source of obvious economic waste. Unemployment in Africa, where the key constraint on agricultural production usually is peak season labor, is much more obviously wasteful than in other parts of the world where the marginal product of rural labor may be quite small. How can the urban unemployed be put to productive use, or, at least, how can their number be prevented from increasing? There appear to be few prospects for their absorption into urban employment in the next decade. Industrialization turns out to have insignificant employment effects, and the service sector (including government) cannot now absorb the present labor force, let alone the large net additions expected from the school systems' output. Employment can only be expanded in sufficient quantity in the rural areas.

The present heavy net rural-urban flow in Africa [10] *may* fall off when the potential migrant faces a risk of unemployment high enough to offset the lure of high urban wages.[11] (The gross flow would probably even then remain heavy, as young people would still come to the cities to look for employment and enjoy urban living before drifting back to the land to "settle down.") But the level of unemployment may be exceedingly high—higher than the society can tolerate. There is little evidence from other parts of the world to support the hope that the flow will eventually ease off, although Africa, because of the greater availability of land, is probably more likely to produce such an outcome than other areas. Governments must, therefore, devise policies to reduce this flow and to stimulate employment in every possible way. The plans usually offered include the maintenance of low urban wage rates; subsidies to or tax allowances for employment; improvement of rural earning opportunities through a reduction in the "urban bias" of governmental expenditures (perhaps through programs of rural works); extra encouragement to agricultural development, particularly to increases in productivity; the payment of higher prices for agricultural output and subsidies to agricultural inputs; the reorientation of school syllabi, and the like. Most of these are desirable policies in their own right; however, such measures may not be sufficient. It may be necessary to consider physical controls over rural-urban migration (for instance, a requirement that urban dwellers possess employment cards, though this obviously would lend itself to abuse [12]), the creation of "workers' brigades" for rural works projects, and other such drastic measures. The time to think through these possibilities and to experiment with employment policies is now, for the unemployment situation is fast deteriorating in most parts of Africa.

This discussion of the "quality" of life has focused on income distribution with respect to "horizontal" lines of cleavage. In Africa today one must also, of course, consider those problems relating to regional and/or ethnic income and rights distribution within nation-states. These too bear on the "quality" of development. The Nigerian tragedy is largely attributable to failure to resolve them adequately.

Some Aspects of Foreign Economic Policy

There can be no escape from the dominant political fact bearing on the relations between rich nations and poor African ones, as a group: the extent of Western trade with and investment in racist Southern Africa. By 1965 foreign private investment totaled over $4 billion in the Republic of South Africa.[13] Total investment in all independent Africa at the end of 1966 was $4,916 million.[14] When monies invested in Rhodesia and the Portuguese colonies are included with those in South Africa, it is safe to say that at least half of the West's investment in the continent is in white Southern Africa. (Southern Africa does not enjoy the same relative importance in world trade, where it makes up only about one-quarter the total value that independent Africa does.)

So it is not obvious to independent tropical Africa which side the rich nations of the West will back when the racial war, which so many predict for the area, finally erupts. This puts severe strains on the development of a meaningful "partnership in development" between the poor African states and the developed West. The presence of powerful and unfriendly states on the southern borders of independent Africa also carries implications for defense and development budgets in Africa. One cannot simply ignore these facts, as the Pearson Commission largely does.[15] African states have to reckon with them. The costly development of transport facilities (pipeline, railway, and paved road) between Lusaka and Dar es Salaam reflects concern with these broader politico-economic issues even in ostensibly developmental matters.

More recently, they have also had to reckon with South Africa's attempt to "open to the north." Not only are Lesotho, Botswana, and Swaziland, which have little choice in the matter, now in the South African orbit, but so is Malawi. Malagasy and the Ivory Coast may be next. There are also strong pressures in Zambia for a more southward orientation. No discussion of an African strategy for the 1970's could be complete without at least raising the question of future independent African economic relations with Southern Africa.

The second major external political fact is the close economic bond (trade, investment, and aid) between Europe and Africa. The product of Africa's colonial past is now perpetuated by treaties of association with the European Economic Community and by Commonwealth preferences. The Yaoundé Convention and the other EEC association agreements providing reciprocal tariff preferences were renegotiated in 1969 despite their apparent conflict with the Algiers Charter. One must have serious doubts about both the political and the economic wisdom of perpetuating such special North-South arrangements, particularly if they lead ultimately to the creation of others—in the Western Hemisphere and Asia. The Pearson Commission notes their existence but is silent about their implications. There is now a serious risk that the Third World will be divided into "zones of influence," [16] with the United States taking responsibility for Latin America, Japan for Southeast Asia, and Europe for Africa. This outcome is most unlikely to be in the poor nations' interest. Africa is thus setting an unfortunate precedent.

The African position on this issue is complicated by the fact that most of its nations are among the least developed in the Third World. They therefore understand their position as requiring *special* arrangements and fear that global preferences in favor of *all* developing countries are likely to benefit others the most. For example, 80% to 90% of the gains which Africa might now reap from the introduction of global preferences have already been excluded through the New Delhi decision to withhold concessions from processed and semiprocessed agricultural products.[17]

Some compensation for Africa's poverty seems already to exist in the form of higher-than-average per capita official aid receipts. (When the North African countries are excluded, the African average falls from $6.1 to about $5.5, but this remains much higher than Asia's $3.2.) However, the disparities are considerable; Nigeria, for example, receives less aid per capita than India! [18]

At the very least, the concessions some African states have extended to the EEC in order to acquire preferential entry to European markets should immediately be granted to one another. In future negotiations a united African front should be presented to the EEC rather than the present queue of needy supplicants. In the meantime, strenuous efforts should be made to further diversify export markets (and aid sources), particularly to the East, where there should still be scope for considerable increases in demand for tropical products.

PART II—INSTITUTIONAL AND OTHER ASPECTS OF STRUCTURAL CHANGE

"Learning"

Studies of aggregative economic growth in the West conclude that the major source of material progress has not been multiplication of capital, as strictly defined, and other factor inputs but an amalgam of "residual" influences including, above all, technological progress, education, and knowledge. Much of Africa's progress in the 1970's, and even more in the long run, will stem from the latter set of influences. If rapid African growth is to be achieved, far more attention will have to be devoted to technology, education, and research than has been customary in the past. But "attention" to these subjects must no longer be associated *merely* with increased inputs to them. Vastly increased expenditures are not sufficient for improvement; often they are not even necessary. A careful benefit-cost analysis of the aggregate of present African educational programs or agricultural research and extension efforts might well produce very low benefit/cost ratios. In that case mere replication of the existing system with more inputs would do little for growth.

Research and Extension. Research *can* provide very high payoffs in Africa if it is sufficiently problem-centered and multidisciplinary in its orientation. Applied and adaptive research is probably one sphere in which mere expansion of inputs *could* go quite a long way; for effective research and experimentation is risky and expensive, and Africa lags far behind the rest of the world. It has already become trite to point to the recent breakthroughs achieved with Asian and Mexican wheat and rice with fairly modest inputs. It should not be beyond human capability to achieve a variety of similar successes in tropical African agriculture.[19]

Foreign assistance could contribute substantially to the building of an enlarged and effective research effort relevant to Africa. Certainly applied research directed to the problems of poor countries is relatively insignificant, and their already tiny share of the world research effort will fall as their share of world income falls. A study of commodity problems last year estimated that $1 billion is spent annually on research which is intended to develop *substitutes* for tropical agricultural products.[20] It is doubtful that the total annual budget for *all* research in tropical Africa approaches one-twentieth of that sum. More resources for this purpose *would* be extremely useful, and the World Bank and the International Development Association should be prepared to move into this area. (The only research for which the Pearson Commission recommended World Bank support was in the area of population control. See the Pearson Report, p. 199.)

Sophisticated integration of the work of physical and social scientists will be required if these expanded research efforts are to be fruitful. The temptation simply to transplant the technology of temperate agriculture to the tropical environment is probably no longer serious, but the danger of failing to gear agricultural innovations *sufficiently* to local factor endowments remains. During the 1970's African agriculture will continue to be characterized by fairly small-scale operations, severely limited capital, and sharp seasonal fluctuations in labor demand, together with an extraordinary variety of climatic and soil conditions. Innovations that are not adapted to the smallholder's physical and social environment and factor availabilities (and that are not communicated effectively to him) will have little bearing on rural progress. Coordinated research in agriculture should be capable of producing dramatic results in crop production, transport and storage, animal husbandry, and soil and water management,[21] all at the local smallholder level. (The Appendix to the Pearson Report [p. 267] conveys the totally misleading impression that African smallholder agriculture has been "sluggish" in its growth, whereas plantations, "usually under expatriate management," have done better.)

One of the most important and previously neglected features of any program to raise agricultural productivity is a monitoring and evaluation component. Carefully controlled and properly focused experiments on research stations are only one aspect of the research effort. At least as important are the daily results of activities of extension offices, credit agencies, cooperatives, settlement schemes, and the like, all of which should be constantly evaluated, and all of which could constitute important learning experiences. It has taken many years for agriculturalists to appreciate that the low rate of smallholder adoption of some innovations was frequently not the result of rural backwardness or conservatism but the result of their unprofitability or riskiness or both. With rising literacy rates, smallholder response will presumably become increasingly sophisticated. Somehow, skill-saving means of evaluation and thereby learning must be devised and incorporated into Agricultural Ministry activities. These learning experiences must be more closely knit with the "purer" activities of the research stations so that the latter are increasingly engaged in the broad learning, communication, and extension processes. A recent study has stated the need in excellent terms: "The fundamental problem confronting agriculture is not so much the adoption and spread of any particular set of physical inputs or of economic arrangements or of organizational patterns or of research institutions; rather it is to build into the whole agricultural process—from the farmer to the university research institute, from the field extension agent to the minister of agriculture—an attitude of experiment, trial and error, continued innovation, and adaptation of new ideas." [22]

Research in areas other than agriculture is also likely to have a high payoff. For instance, much remains to be learned about the potential for natural resource development in Africa. There is still a considerable propensity to transfer, with minimal adaptation, non-agricultural technology from rich countries to poor rather than to develop new techniques. There is an urgent need for development of intermediate technology for the industrial sector, building and construction, irrigation and water supply, certain of the social services (notably medicine), and even the provision of simple consumer goods and services. Again, there must be a balance between properly focused and controlled research and ongoing pilot schemes and evaluation efforts.

But what of the present? One must be wary of the adviser who surveys the African scene and simply concludes that the answer is to have *more* skilled manpower or higher standards or more research or more capital, or more of whatever it is he is surveying the shortage of. He must be pressed to advise on the suitability of the uses to which available resources are at present being put and on the sequence of steps to be taken to reach his prescribed targets. Someone somewhere must also be weighing the needs in each sector before the recommendations for any are acted upon. (Planning ministries are, of course, intended to perform this function but are not always able to.) Great harm has been done by doctors, educators, agricultural scientists, industrial engineers (dare I add statisticians and economists?)—all pushing their own "requirements" upon African governments. What can be done in the research and extension sphere without waiting for any more outside support?

Much might be done both to rationalize present research and to disseminate existing knowledge more effectively. Efforts in both research and extension are often too thinly spread. There almost certainly exists a "threshold" size below which returns in any one sphere are negligible. The degree of focus is usually too broad. This factor is related to size; threshold size is smaller if the focus is narrower. As a start, existing national research programs should be studied with the aim of improving the return from present research inputs.

Education. Recent evidence that protein malnutrition in infancy permanently impairs mental development suggests that the most productive investment in African education today may have nothing whatever to do with school systems. The development and/or dissemination of acceptable protein foodstuffs may have a much greater productive payoff in the rural areas than the half-baked primary "education" which is today dispensed to a tiny minority of rural children, usually for only a year or two each. Again, the children of the poor are more likely to approach their capacity for self-fulfillment and human satisfaction from adequate nutrition than from schooling which primarily "teach[es] the schooled the superiority of the better schooled." [23]

What can be done with the inherited colonial systems of educational institutions? Since "orthodox" administrators and educators, "trained in a mould cast over a hundred years ago" (Pearson Report, p. 200) are still the only readily available kind for African school systems, it will prove extraordinarily slow and difficult to effect any meaningful changes within them. The direction of change must, however, be clear.

Increased emphasis on and rewards (material and non-material) for technical skills must be the cornerstone of the reformed system. But this changed emphasis, which now is fast becoming part of the conventional wisdom of African education, is only the beginning of the edifice. There is a great temptation to erect more technically oriented educational structures which are as unsuitable as those they replace; the new university faculties of agriculture, engineering, and medicine in Africa show it.

One does not reorient a nation's skills and outlooks simply by shifting the composition of the university curriculum which caters to a miniscule percentage of the "student" population. Manpower planning has devoted far more attention to top-level education than to the rest of the system. Any increased scientific orientation of education must begin in the primary schools and extend through all the subsequent levels.[24] For this to occur it is necessary to have teachers trained in the new mold, and this will take time. Meanwhile, agricultural, veterinary, medical, and other technical officers—most of whom are already engaged heavily in adult education—could be utilized more in the school system, providing instruction and facts to teachers and to students. Schoolteachers and students, for their part, could do more for the rural development effort themselves.

The highest returns (in the sense of discounted present value) from educational inputs undoubtedly come from adult education—where it is effectively offered. At present this is mainly conducted outside the formal education system by extension officers, community development officers, and the like. Most observers feel that their performance leaves much to be desired—the field level officers often lack suitable (not necessarily high-level) training, receive relatively low incomes and low prestige, lack incentives for more effective performance, and consequently suffer from low morale. Improvement of rural adult education and stimulation of action based on it are among the most important of development objectives, but they are usually in the hands of agricultural ministries which were constructed for other (administrative) purposes. It may be necessary to break out of civil service procedures before rural development can be pushed as effectively as it needs to be. Restructured incentive systems, greater concentration of efforts, freedom from topheavy bureaucratic structures, and increased flexibility and responsiveness to local initiatives at the field level are among the potential advantages of creating semi-autonomous rural extension and development bodies.[25]

Facile generalizations are sometimes heard about the hopelessness of changing the ways of the old and the consequent need to work with the young through the school system. It is worth recalling that there are large numbers of adults under thirty-five, who grew up during the struggle for independence or after and who are very much part of the "youth" of the nation. Neither must one forget that, quantitatively, the most important teaching in the field of agriculture is that conducted by parents for the benefit of their children.

Efforts to train and motivate educators of adults should in most places now claim higher priority than those directed at the education of the young. In addition, the schools could provide valuable increased inputs through pilot and experimental plots, self-help construction and clearing activities, and even direct extension efforts. The practical experience gained by students and teachers in these ventures would constitute important learning in itself and should also dampen elitist tendencies. The schools must be thought of and developed as integral parts of the rural development teams in the districts rather than as escape hatches for a fortunate few from the "idiocy of rural life." A practical and more scientific direction is bound to emerge spontaneously from such reorientation.

There is a danger that the educational institutions, techniques, and assumptions of Europe and North America will now be transferred in the technical fields as they previously were in the liberal arts and law. Faculties of agriculture should test innovations not in environments resembling the temperate-zone family farm, complete with cleared, square, one-crop plots and tractors, but in those of the African smallholder. The emphasis should be not so much on the frontiers of pure agronomic research as on the application of scientific methods to the solution of the practical problems of raising and ensuring smallholder yields. Similarly, medical schools should emphasize preventive medicine, public health, and family planning to a much greater extent than do conventional European schools.

In all these technical fields the greatest need is not for the "degree-holder" but for the medium-level skilled worker who can carry his knowledge to the districts for unsupervised application. The opportunity cost of doctors and modern hospitals, however soul-satisfying they may be, is very high: 50 rural dispensaries for one urban hospital, 100 medical assistants and midwives per medical doctor, are conservative estimates of the tradeoffs. Africa must avoid the training, at home or abroad, of cadres of specialists catering only to the few while the masses remain unserved. If the recipients of such training do not actually join the "brain drain," they are likely to become "second-rate teachers of pretentious subjects" in the capital city.[26] In its Appendix, the Pearson Report calls for the training, in Africa, of the "highest-level scientists" to conduct problem-oriented research and build relevant training institutions (p. 276). It is unfortunate that the phrasing appears to back the production of expensive and sophisticated degree holders.

Nor is formal schooling, even in medium-level technical subjects, necessarily the most suitable educational approach. Throughout Africa there have been difficulties in finding jobs for graduates of new technical and vocational schools. Employers frequently prefer to train their own workers because it is cheaper and because the training is more directly productive. Apprentice systems in traditional industries still play an important role and could perhaps be built upon.[27]

The process of building educational institutions is not so advanced that undesirable trends of this kind cannot still be arrested. The 1970's, during which Africanization of educational systems is likely to be completed and consolidated, are crucial. Vested educational interests can develop during this decade which would take generations to dislodge.

Industrialization and Integration

In Africa, as elsewhere, great stress is given to industrialization, the key symbol of structural change in a developing society. But this continent still has a smaller proportion of its economic activity in the industrial sector than in any other. While the economic, social, and political problems of urbanization are already upon Africa, many of those which usually accompany industrialization can still be avoided.

Industrialization *need* not follow the well-traveled Latin American path from import substitution to inefficiency, stagnation, and total failure to alleviate the rising unemployment. Poor countries embarking upon import-substitution industrialization have, in the past, not discriminated adequately among industrial projects, presumably because of their determination to achieve structural change. They have encouraged, or at least approved, industrial schemes in which the net foreign exchange savings was too small, the employment generated too low, the inefficiency tolerated too high, the technique inappropriate, and the learning or other external effects nonexistent. Since the typical African economy is smaller than the typical Latin American one, the possibilities for rational import-substitution projects will be exhausted sooner in the industrialization process. Latin-style mistakes have already been made in Africa, many at the insistence of foreign suppliers and investors, but sounding the alarm now can still prevent far more. African states must distinguish good projects from bad ones, they must know when to stop the import-substitution drive, and they must extract maximum gains from every project (good or bad). Institutions and decision-making procedures must be created and personnel trained to service the needs of African governments in this respect.

The "easy" consumer goods import-substitution possibilities will have been exhausted in most of tropical Africa by the end of the 1970's, if not sooner. The production of *simple* capital goods and other inputs is another possible avenue which should be pursued. But for small economies, industrial development must soon become a matter of export performance. Economic integration within Africa will help (Kenya exports about half of her gross manufacturing output to her partners), but sales to world markets must also be contemplated if recent rates of industrial growth are to be maintained into the late 1970's and the 1980's. Most African states have preferential access to European or British markets for many manufactured goods and thereby enjoy substantial effective protection from potential competitors in Asia and Latin America. There are reasons for concern about these special trade relations with Europe, but if they are to be negotiated, full advantage should be taken of them quickly. Very little has been. It is unlikely that small African states will soon go very far through converting their suboptimal-scale and protected import-substituting industries into effective exporters to non-African markets. But industrial centers which are based originally on import substitution, not individual industries, *can* be reoriented toward exports. New alternatives must be studied, technical advice provided, and incentives created for exporting activities.

Generally speaking, African tariff systems betray the same bias toward import substitution (particularly with respect to consumer goods) as do Latin American ones, and there is every indication that currency overvaluation will soon be as prevalent in Africa as elsewhere. The arguments for the use (whether conscious or not) of these policy instruments must be heard afresh in the African context. Currency overvaluation and bias against manufacturing for export should be less attractive where the losers therefrom are not land-owning oligarchies but small-holder farmers; where the income distribution issue is primarily a matter of reducing rural/urban and skilled/unskilled income differentials; where the need for export performance is more compelling because of smaller size; and where the share of total world supplies of individual commodities is smaller and the potential for terms of trade gains from overvaluation consequently less. (The last can, in any case, be handled better by commodity-specific domestic tax and price policies. Most African countries already have Marketing Boards ideally suited to this sort of operation.) It should not require re-emphasizing that the African scarcity of skills will increase the difficulties of maintaining an overvalued currency through controls.

What possibilities might there be for manufactured exports? First, there are the obvious processing possibilities for commodities now exported in their primary states. Although the possibilities for adding value through processing are not at present always great and are further held down by the escalated tariffs of major importers, these can be exploited more fully. Once developed world processors have been displaced and the pressures for their protection removed, the returns to the producing nations will be increased. More fundamentally, however, one could begin to think in terms of particular industrial *processes,* perhaps using imported inputs, which might lend themselves to African production for export. These will have to require little skilled manpower, which is Africa's scarcest input; use materials that are relatively cheap to transport or available locally; and make extensive use of unskilled labor. (With respect to the last, the real wage must be held down if African labor-intensive processes are to compete with those of Asia.) Industrial research and promotion activities must be reoriented to the consideration of such export possibilities.

Industrialization possibilities would be greatly assisted by the development of intra-African economic cooperation. Economic integration is nowhere as important as it is in Africa where national markets are exceptionally small.[28] Yet, despite the repeated recommendations from analysts and commentators, the political power of the pan-African ideal, and the encouragement from the United Nations Economic Commission for Africa, experience with African integration arrangements has been disappointing. There are no doubt many explanations for this, most of them having to do with the difficulty of achieving equity in the distribution of benefits and costs among member states. One fundamental cause of international disagreement is that too much has usually been attempted at once. It should not be necessary to produce at one stroke an all-encompassing common market complete with coordinated industrial planning. Suggestions as to the first steps are conspicuously absent from most general treatises on the need for integration except, perhaps, for the advocacy of regional approaches. For instance, it should be far easier to work out reciprocal tariff concessions on a product-by-product basis than to eliminate all duties and achieve a uniform external tariff simultaneously. Surely, if such agreements can be reached between African states and Europe, they can be achieved within Africa. An immediate (if largely symbolic) gesture would be, as suggested earlier, the extension of the preferential tariff rates granted to the EEC by EEC Associated States to the rest of Africa (if not the Third World). More significant, agreements for reciprocal preferences and credits, intra-product specialization, joint public industrial ventures, and the like, should be sought among African states. Improved internal transport systems—without which the agreements may be meaningless—should be jointly planned and, as soon as possible, constructed.

Other areas of cooperation such as payments unions or reserve pools, international development banks, coordinated international commodity marketing, utilities and transport facilities, insurance, applied research, river basin development, tourism development, and unified dealings with foreign corporations are often feasible without many of the difficulties other forms of integration encounter. There are already many examples of such cooperative agreements in Africa, but they could be multiplied between now and 1980. These efforts and institutions are most likely to be productive if their objectives are fairly *specific,* and if they consciously seek to economize on scarce skilled manpower. In the past the institutional mechanisms for general intra-African cooperation have frequently tended to siphon off scarce talents for meaningless busywork.

Planning and Decision Making

Experience with economic planning in Africa has been a good deal more successful than that with economic plans. It is important to understand the distinction, although not too many non-economist commentators draw it. While the elaborate national plans, usually written by foreigners, have usually been forgotten soon after their production and have had limited effect upon subsequent government investment allocations and policies, there *has* been steady improvement in the quality of economic decision making. Planning ministries, planning units in executive ministries, economic research institutes, and statistical offices have sprung up throughout Africa during the last decade to produce important increases in the quantity and quality of data, much more sophisticated evaluations of policy alternatives, and greater coordination of government development efforts. All this is not to say that there is not a lot left to be done. Of course there is, but there is a much clearer conception of what *needs* to be done than there was a decade ago. It is now widely recognized, at least among professional economists, that coordinated long-term planning and constant evaluation must be part of the normal functioning of government rather than a periodic exercise for the purpose of writing a plan document. The most important subsequent steps in this area are probably educational and organizational.

Education of *all* government servants and politicians as to the purposes and possibilities of planning still needs doing. But, for the present, cadres of planning economists must be provided. The training of African general economic advisers and specialist planners for agriculture, transport, and manpower has not progressed rapidly enough. Expatriate planners have paid very little attention to the needs of African personnel who will carry on the tasks when the foreigners leave; the economics courses offered in African universities have too often been of very limited relevance to government needs. During the 1970's more pertinent training must be provided, primarily in Africa, for African planners and economists. Because of the sensitivity of these key government positions, this training must be a matter of the very highest priority.

The organization of planning, decision making, and evaluation is an area in which experiment will continue. At the center, attention must constantly be given to the most productive allocation of available planners, the most suitable ministerial division of responsibilities, the creation of new coordinating committees or other institutions where required, and so forth.

More important still, however, is the whole area of center-periphery relations. Local councils, provincial, state or regional administrations, and field officers of central institutions (government, party, or whatever) must somehow be brought into planning and decision making more effectively than they are at present. In the recent past the need was to build a national identity, which required national planning, and, therefore, the emphasis was very much on the center. The point has now been reached in most African states where, in the interests of efficiency and political necessity, thought may have to be directed to moving some of the decision making and financial power *away* from the center. The specific forms of such decentralization will obviously depend on the particular circumstance, but states as different as Tanzania, Zambia, Ghana, and Nigeria are already seeing this need. Decentralization of decision-making authority and of some financial powers (in some instances, perhaps, to non-governmental bodies—cooperatives, credit unions, improvement associations) may do a lot for the citizen's sense of involvement with publicly directed development efforts and thus for that elusive "quality of life" to which reference was made earlier.

W. Arthur Lewis has emphasized the political need for a system which provides for the achievement of central consensus among the various ethnic groups which make up most African states.[29] The need for a degree of consensus is clear, but the appropriate degree and the particular instruments for its attainment are less obvious; one hesitates to offer generalizations suitable for application to every context. Decentralization, however, has the obvious advantage of reducing the number of questions about which a difficult consensus must be reached.

These are all aspects of a much broader politico-economic problem —that of making the public sector function efficiently. Most African states place heavy development responsibilities on government and parastatal bodies. These must not be permitted to degenerate into inefficient backwaters of political patronage, bureaucratic inertia, or worse. It is the planners' responsibility to avert that possibility. During the 1970's some of the public service traditions and practices which are still malleable may begin to harden into established custom. This challenge to the planners is, therefore, of crucial importance. The development of smoothly running, politically responsive, and efficient systems for decision making, forward planning, information collection and evaluation, not merely with respect to state activities but with respect to the entire economy, must be their paramount objective. That this objective does not necessarily have anything to do with plan preparation is a lesson which has been learnt in some African states but not all.

One final point should be made in connection with this discussion of economic planning and decision making. Tropical Africa is the most aid-dependent part of the Third World—that is, an unusually high proportion of its total income is obtained from official foreign assistance. This is, perhaps, inevitable given its low material levels of living and its colonial history. Its relative dependence upon foreign assistance is likely to diminish as its own development efforts grow. There exists some risk that in the meantime an "aid mentality," analogous to the "export mentality" formerly found in some small Latin American states, will inhibit the development of the tough development-oriented social reforms and economic policies which are necessary if independently based and meaningful progress is to be achieved. Each African state must, therefore, make its plans, wherever possible, in such a way as not to prejudice the success of its overall development effort should the expected resources flow from abroad not materialize. This is easier said than done, but formulating the objective in this way may contribute to the development of more truly self-reliant development strategies.

CHAPTER TWO

THE DEVELOPMENT
SECTORS

The Debate

As the participants joined more deeply in the debate on growth and structural change, they found themselves confronted, again and again, with a set of obstructions which tend, in this last third of the twentieth century, to turn the process of development from dynamic forward movement into a vicious circle or, worse, a downward spiral.

The first spin is given by the surge of population. It washes away any possibility of full rural employment and spills into mass migrations to the cities. There it swirls over existing urban structures, habits, and skills, leaving behind a rising pool of citizens who are either miserably underemployed or altogether workless. These marginal men, on the farms or in the cities, are too poor to create a dynamic domestic market. Yet their consumption, however pitiful, laps away the margins for local saving. Meanwhile, the sheer pressure of their existence and of their movements—from the *minifundia* they erode and then leave to the megalopolises they create and swamp—deepens the world's environmental crisis and threatens to make the increasingly urban world of tomorrow a place of inhuman habitation and squalor.

All these facts and risks are in some measure part of an interlocking crisis. All the different streams of pressure unite to form the flood. Successful development consists precisely in damming back the freshets and producing not an uncontrollable inundation but separate and manageable heads of energy. Successful family planning is one such control

—well publicized but still ominously short of answers. The "Green Revolution" of rising productivity in agriculture is another—provided it does not simply lower employment on the land still further and channel the benefits into an elite too narrow to provide any breakthrough to a mass market for foodstuffs. Accelerated industrialization is part of the solution, especially if labor-intensive technologies are consciously sought and used. Education, by training young people in adaptable skills and attitudes, could create a mass of citizens able to respond to new opportunities. Planned decentralization of urban growth with regional markets linked to the needs of the "Green Revolution" could greatly expand local unskilled employment by way of massive construction of new urban centers and structures. Even the search for a better environment could help to break the vicious circle if a proper understanding of ecology were to reinforce productivity on the farms and underpin a sane urban policy.

In short, over the next three decades the developing world is threatened, as a result of the interconnection of all its crises, with the risk of continuing, "obdurate underdevelopment." Yet there are hopeful pointers toward a strategy of escape. In this chapter, we give extensive quotations from Conference papers on these specific issues.

Population

WITH EXTRACTS FROM

Population Programmes and Social and Economic Development

BY T. K. RUPRECHT AND CARL WAHREN

Discussion centered on the *Report on Population* issued, in February, 1970, by the Organisation for Economic Cooperation and Development (OECD) Development Centre.* The starting point was, inevitably, the

* This draft report was kindly made available by OECD as one of the working papers of the Conference. The printed version is now available as T. K. Ruprecht and Carl Wahren, *Population Programmes and Social and Economic Development* (Paris: OECD Development Centre, OECD, 1970). Quotations reprinted with permission of the publisher.

completely unprecedented character of today's growth in population, and its entirely new impact upon problems of development. As the OECD Report puts it:

"The point that population growth rates of the magnitude of 2% to 3.5% per year are unprecedented historically needs to be appreciated. World population grew very slowly in the interval A.D. 1–1750. It required more than a thousand years to double compared to the 35 years it takes at 2.0% rate. It is not possible to determine exactly the date when the rate accelerated, but by 1750, population was growing at approximately 0.5% per year, a rate that yields a doubling time of some 150 years. . . . During the eighteenth and early nineteenth centuries . . . the upturn for Europe shows an acceleration to 0.9% in the decade 1820–30 . . . and finally a reacceleration to the neighborhood of 1.0% for the period 1880–1910. . . .

"The only historical cases in which population grew in now developed countries at rates comparable to the current situation were in the open countries of migratory settlement, the United States, Canada, Australia and New Zealand. Here, rates of population growth close to 3.0% were obtained. The experience of these countries, however, has limited current relevance even for today's open countries which have large potential agricultural resources. This limited relevance is due to the fact that the population dynamics of natural and migratory increase are very different. This difference is especially obvious in relation to age structure which is weighted toward the younger ages under conditions of rapid natural increase and toward the middle, productive ages under conditions of migratory increase because of the predominance of adult migrants.

"The conclusion which follows is that the underdeveloped countries today are facing their development task under demographic conditions which are substantially different from those which prevailed in the great majority of the now developed countries. It is our opinion that this difference is not merely a difference in degree but a difference in kind. This point may be seen by a comparison between the historical European and the current situation in the time required to double the population. The maximum European rate of 1.1% was capable of doubling the population in 61.2 years. The maximum individual country rate of 1.4% could double it in 49.9 years. The commonly experienced rate in the underdeveloped countries of 3% doubles the population in only 23.5 years. These are differences of 2 to 3 times. Furthermore, a reduction of 0.5% points from the maximum European rate of 1.5% extends the doubling time by 23.1 years (from 46.6 to 69.7 years) while a similar reduction from 3.0% to 2.5% stretches the doubling time by only 4.6 years. This is a difference of 5 times. . . .

"A final aspect of the relevance of historical demographic experience may be seen from a comparison between the timing of economic development and the period of most rapid population increase. Considerable diversity in economic and social development is apparent in the European case as well as in the current situation for the underdeveloped countries. It appears that over the nineteenth century, Western European countries evidenced growth rates in per capita income which ranged from rates as high as 3.0% per year in Germany 1875–1890 to as low as 1.5% in Sweden 1870–1880 and 1.0% or less in Italy 1860–1890. Differences in literacy levels are also apparent as are dissimilarities in economic structure. Regarding the latter point it may be noted that in 1870 the percentage employed in agriculture was 19 in Great Britain, 43 in France, and 62 in Italy. While these dissimilarities existed, it is clear that by the time population growth reached its maximum rate after 1880, the level of economic, social, and political development was considerably more advanced than is the case in most underdeveloped countries today."

Against such a background, development is, no doubt, possible but dreadfully hampered. The OECD Report summarizes the problem in this way:

"Theoretical and empirical analyses show that fertility reduction is not a prerequisite for economic development and that constant high fertility is not an absolute barrier. These studies demonstrate, however, that the changes in economic growth parameters, which are required to offset the disadvantage of constant fertility and rapid population growth, increase significantly the difficulty of the development task. A reduction in fertility can make an important contribution to development, especially in the longer run period after 15–20 years. . . .

"Because the effects of a demographic event are not fully worked out for very long periods, often exceeding 50 years, long lead times are required in population policy. Satisfactory current levels of economic performance cannot, therefore, be used as criteria for ruling out the existence of a 'population problem.' . . .

"The argument that larger populations are desirable as a means of increasing the size of the domestic market is inadequate since it neglects the very important per capita income dimension. It is found that a slowing of the population growth rate produces a more developed economic structure in that the agricultural sector is relatively smaller and the industrial and transportation and communication sectors are relatively larger. One importance of this is that it is these latter sectors which are most characterized by economies of size, or the economic advantages associated with large markets and, therefore, large-scale production.

"The conclusion also emerges that the education problems, as the economic development problems, cannot be eliminated by a reduction in fertility, but can be made substantially easier. Considerable improvement can be received in exchange for moderated rates of population expansion. Similar statements are valid for health and housing."

No one quarreled with the analysis. Few questioned the need to increase international assistance to policies for population control—although, as has already been mentioned, it was felt that assistance could be both more effective and acceptable if it occurred within a framework of concern for the welfare of the whole family. Equally, neither the OECD Report nor the participants felt that a real breakthrough in persuasion and technique had yet occurred. The Report gives this warning:

"In attempting to gauge the future contribution of family planning as currently conceived, organised and carried out, it is important to realise first that the only cases where family planning programs can be shown to have had an apparent impact on the birth rate are those countries, such as Taiwan, Korea, Hong Kong, and Singapore, where they were established in a situation in which a downward trend in fertility had already begun. Thus, it seems that *where family planning programs have been successful, they have been so only in special and uncommon circumstances.* Second, even in these "successful" programs the age and parity distribution of acceptors is such as to indicate that family planning is used by couples who already have large families and may, therefore, be highly sensitive to incremental births. For example, in Korea, only 27% of women accepting an I.U.D. had less than 3 living children and 32% had 5 or more. Thirdly, it appears that in many cases there are significant numbers of contraceptive users prior to the beginning of national programs although the form of contraceptive practice is often inefficient and unsatisfactory, e.g., in Ceylon 41% had practised family planning before their loop acceptance, but 31% of these used abstinence, and in Taiwan, K.A.P. (Knowledge, Attitude and Practice) sample survey statistics indicate that in 1965, essentially before the program, 22.8% were currently using contraception and 26.6% had ever used it."

Unemployment

WITH EXTRACTS FROM

Unemployment and Underemployment in the Developing World

BY ERIK THORBECKE

The pressures of unprecedented rates of population growth make themselves felt at every one of the critical turning points or "dangerous corners" of development. Uncontrollable urban migrations, increasing numbers of illiterates, strains on savings, a deteriorating environment— all these are steadily aggravated by the inexorable rise in population. But the immediate and most critical consequence is the growth of unemployment.

The debate on unemployment was based upon Erik Thorbecke's paper, "Unemployment and Underemployment in the Developing World," and took as its point of departure his estimates of the scale of the problem. The first was a rate of growth of the labor force of the developing countries which is double that of the developed world. In fact, "in the post World War II period . . . while the growth rate of the labor force dropped slightly in the developed countries from 1.1% per annum to 1% between 1950–65 . . . the corresponding rate rose from 1.7% to 2.2% annually in the developing world. . . ." This average masks a number of areas where the growth is even more formidable. According to recent OECD figures,[1] the rate of increase in the 1970's will be 2.8% in Southwest Asia, 2.6% in North Africa, and over 3% in Central and Tropical South America.

If one takes unemployment in the classical sense of workers looking for jobs at going rates, there is little doubt, in spite of a relative lack of reliable statistics, that unemployment is already very high. To quote Dr. Thorbecke:

"Available census figures based on the 1960's for Africa and the Middle East show unemployment rates of between 9% and 11% of the labor force for Algeria, Morocco, Ghana (urban areas), and Iran; while survey data indicate unemployment rates ranging from 4% in Tangier, to 13% in the large towns of Nigeria, and 20% in Abidjan (Ivory Coast). With respect to Latin America, census data show unemployment rates ranging all the way from a hard-to-believe 1.5% in Guatemala to slightly above 10% in Panama, Uruguay, Venezuela, and Barbados; survey data, on the other hand, reveal substantially higher unemployment rates with the majority falling between 10% and 20% of the labor force. Finally, the unemployment rates derived from survey data in Asia range from about 3% for the urban areas of Thailand to about 10% in Singapore, Ceylon, and India."

Moreover, the evidence, such as it is, strongly supports the supposition that unemployment is generally growing worse. In particular, an Organization of American States (OAS) study covering all Latin America [2] shows the total number of unemployed rising from 2.9 million in 1950 to 8.8 million in 1965 and the unemployment rate from 5.6% to 11.1% of the labor force over the same period.

But formal unemployment statistics do not reveal the full problem. It is not simply one of workers looking for jobs but of the many who work only part time or who do not seek work at all because it is simply not available. Again, hard statistics are not readily available for mea-

TABLE 1.   ESTIMATED "UNEMPLOYMENT EQUIVALENT" IN
LATIN AMERICA, 1960, BY ECONOMIC SECTOR

	% of Total Labor Force	Unemployment Equivalent (% of sector)	Proportion of Unemployment	
			% of Total Labor Force	% of Total Unemployment
Agriculture, forestry,				
hunting, and fishing	47.0	32.6	15.3	59.5
Mining	1.8	19.0	0.3	1.2
Manufacturing	13.2	16.7	2.2	8.6
Construction *	3.9	6.4	0.2	0.8
Electricity, gas,				
and water	3.9	2.0	0.1	0.4
Transportation and				
communication †	5.7			
Commerce and finance	6.9	19.0	1.3	5.1
Services	17.5		6.3	24.5
Total	99.9		25.7	100.1

* Visible unemployment only; tentative because of limited data.
† Not analyzed, for lack of data.
Source: Organization of American States, The Unemployment Problem in Latin America (October, 1969).

suring what would happen if all other things were equal. Evidence as well as common sense, however, suggests high and rising rates of under-employment.

"If a broader definition than involuntary unemployment is used such as the ratio of the number of available but unused labor hours to the total available labor hours—which in a way would measure both open unemployment and underemployment—the magnitude and thus the seriousness of the problem are magnified. Such studies have been done in a number of countries, and at least for one continent (Latin America), revealing 'unemployment equivalent' rates ranging all the way from 20% to over 50%. Table 1 shows the overall estimated 'unemployment equivalent' in Latin America for 1960 broken down by economic sector. According to these figures more than one-fourth of the total labor force was unemployed in the above sense. Alternatively, the extent of labor underutilization in 1960 was equivalent to some 17 to 18 million workers being completely unemployed (in other words, 25.7% of the total labor force). There is every reason to believe that the corresponding 'unemployment equivalent' would be substantially higher in 1970.

"Since the great bulk of the labor force is employed in agriculture in the developing world—ranging from 45% to 80% in the great majority of the less developed countries—it is, of course, to be expected that the greatest underutilization of labor would occur in that sector. Table 1 confirms this phenomenon for Latin America by revealing that almost one-third of the labor resources were unemployed in agriculture, which represented about 60% of total Latin American unemployment. It is likely that the degree of underutilization of labor in agriculture in many parts of Asia and Africa would tend to be as high as in Latin America, if not higher. In addition, since a larger proportion of the labor force is engaged in agricultural pursuits in Asia and Africa than in Latin America, the share of agricultural unemployment to total unemployment (according to the unemployment equivalent concept) is likely to be even higher than the 60% figure applying to Latin America. In any case, the last column of Table 1 probably reflects fairly accurately the relative importance of the degree of labor underutilization, by economic sectors, prevailing in many developing countries—60% in agriculture and about 25% in services. In contrast, census and survey information based on open involuntary unemployment, in the narrow classical sense, tends to indicate that practically all the existing unemployment is centered on the urban areas as opposed to the rural areas. . . .

"A trend which is integrally related to the unemployment problem is the increasing rural-urban migration. This trend is reflected in a number of developing countries by urban growth rates of population which are about three times higher than the corresponding rural growth rates. It can be hypothesized that this migration is a symptom of the unemployment problem at least to the extent that one of its major causes is the push factor of very low income levels and high rates of labor underutilization in the rural areas. It is true that the high wage rates prevailing in urban activities and the availability of certain types of services in the cities as opposed to the country exert a pull factor on the migrants as well. In some cases the underemployed migrants are converted into open unemployed but much more typically . . . end up as underemployed service workers (shoe shiners, street vendors, part-time gardeners, domestic servants, and the like). One could argue that traditional agriculture in the country and traditional services in the cities are the residual claimants, or rather outlets, for that part of the labor force which cannot be absorbed in the other sectors.

"A final phenomenon which is directly affected by the increasing unemployment level in the developing world is the increasing inequality in the income distribution, both on personal and regional bases. . . ."

In the discussions, no one questioned these trends. Nor was there much dispute over Dr. Thorbecke's analysis of the causes of this deepening employment crisis.

"Perhaps the first and foremost contributing factor is the continuing acceleration in the growth rates of population and labor force which has occurred in the developing world since the end of the Second World War. It is, of course, true that an increase in the supply of labor can be a strong positive force in economic growth and development if the new entrants in the labor force can be productively absorbed. Unfortunately the potential for absorption is quite limited. . . .

"A second factor, which has been well described and documented in many countries, is the whole set of biases and distortions affecting factor prices. The result of these distortions was to reduce the price of capital below its equilibrium level (its marginal value product) while forcing the price of labor above its equilibrium. Such biases in factor prices can and often did lead to the adoption of more capital-intensive techniques to take advantage of the relatively cheap factor of production (capital) and save on the relatively more expensive one (labor).

"A number of policy measures undertaken in developing countries had the impact of reducing the cost of capital: the maintenance of overvalued exchange rates, industrial promotion laws and regulations, and subsidized interest rates. . . .

"Among the elements which tended to push the cost of labor above its equilibrium level are minimum wage legislation, social welfare benefits and policies, and the influence of some labor unions. In general, the intended effect of these factors appears to have been the achievement of a more equitable income distribution. In fact, however, it is likely that the benefits achieved in terms of higher wages and better social security benefits for the workers were more than offset by an increase in both absolute and relative underemployment and unemployment. The direct effects of these distortions affected primarily the modern sector; indirectly, however, they greatly reinforced the discrimination against agriculture in favor of industrialization.

"In the late 1940's and throughout the 1950's, it was widely believed that industrialization was the unique key to development and that the industrial sector, as the advanced sector, would pull with it the backward agricultural sector. More specifically, industry, as a leading sector, would be a source of alternative employment opportunities to the rural population. The tendency was to equate the modern sector with high productivity of investment and thus direct the bulk of investment to industry and industrial infrastructure. As the conceptual framework used by economists and policy makers moved from the simple one-sector (Harrod-Domar) model to a two-sector model, the latter continued to assign to subsistence agriculture an essentially passive role as a potential source of 'unlimited labor' and 'agricultural surplus' for the rest of the economy. A popular policy prescription to encourage the transfer of labor and of the agricultural surplus was to turn the terms-of-trade against agriculture. . . .

"In addition to the artificial distortions mentioned above, the main policy instruments which were used to promote industrialization were a high level of protection to foster domestic industries, an unbalanced public investment program favoring the modern sector, and turning the terms-of-trade in favor of industry. In a nutshell, these policies led to the creation of many relatively inefficient industries producing import substitutes (which in some cases resulted in negative value-added, expressed at world prices) and the stagnation, and sometimes even strangulation, of agricultural output. Furthermore, even though manufacturing output (valued at domestic prices) was growing at relatively high rates in many developing countries, the capacity of that sector to absorb labor proved extremely limited—the elasticity of output with respect to labor being often of the order of three.

"Related to the industrialization trend was the inward rather than outward-looking approach to international trade. Many developing countries concentrated on import substitution rather than export promotion. . . .

"Artificial distortions affecting factor prices encouraged the adoption of a relatively capital-intensive (labor-saving) technology. In addition, it is important to note that in many activities the range of available technologies is largely based on the conditions prevailing in the developed countries. Much of that technology originated in the industrialized countries and therefore tends to fit the resource endowments and factor prices of these countries. It has also been argued that the range within which labor and capital can be substituted for each other in developing countries is very narrow. There is some evidence, however, that the options open to these countries are somewhat greater than appears on the surface. Technologies of different vintage exist in advanced countries, some of which may be appropriate to the requirements of the developing world. A counter-argument, however, is that reliance on techniques which are becoming obsolete in industrialized countries (for example, use of second-hand capital equipment) is likely to cause serious difficulties in terms of maintenance, availability of parts, and overall servicing of that equipment in the future. There appears to be a large potential scope for designing and implementing 'intermediate technology' befitting the conditions prevailing in developing countries. In fact, it is still largely a virgin territory for both engineers and economists.

"In addition to the above factors which encourage the adoption of relatively capital-intensive techniques, there is a substantial amount of evidence that labor productivity increases over time at a high rate in a number of advanced sectors such as industry, transportation, and banking. . . .

"A final phenomenon which has been suggested as contributing to the unemployment problem is the scarcity of high-level manpower. It has been argued that the scarcity of skilled workers encourages the use of more capital-intensive techniques which in general require a lower level of labor skill (labor-intensive methods often require highly trained workers who may simply not be available). . . ."

The participants, on the whole, agreed with Dr. Thorbecke's conclusions—that a 6% rate of growth, however essential as one element in policy, would not of itself defuse the deepening employment crisis and that, in addition, the need would be to put the greatest emphasis on population planning, accelerate rural development on a labor-intensive basis, invent and apply new labor-intensive technologies in industry, carry through large-scale public works in both the rural and the urban sector (construction is a suitably high provider of manual and relatively unskilled jobs) and, on the part of the developed nations, hasten the dismantling of protection against labor-intensive manufactures such as textiles, apparel, and footwear and labor-intensive primary materials such as sugar.

Some participants went so far as to suggest the need for direct controls over migration to slow down the hopeless silting up of unemployed migrants in the cities. And even those who believed such controls to be politically impossible and socially undesirable were left with some sense of hopelessness when faced with Dr. Thorbecke's final calculations which suggest that, given a continuation of present levels of population growth and the same ratio of employment to the work force, only in parts of South America and Africa would a 6% rate of growth be sufficient to absorb the available work force by 1980. Elsewhere the needed rate is higher—8.4% in West Asia, 6.6% in East Asia, 6.6% again in Central America.

Education

WITH EXTRACTS FROM

Education for Development

BY PETER WILLIAMS

Against the developing world's background of rising unemployment and profound dislocations of the traditional social order, most participants were well aware of the critical nature of the educational problem in development. Much of the likely opportunities for work would still be in the rural sector. Yet that sector could be changing rapidly under the impact of new technologies. In the cities, modern industrial jobs, dependent upon very specific skills, are not likely to expand as rapidly as the manpower available for urban work. Capacities for venturesome adaptation and for self-employment can be at least as important as more formal skills. Above all, the ability to cope with existence and escape complete disorientation in a world whose whole roof of tradition has fallen in may be the most significant of all the needed new cultural capacities.

In this context many participants felt strongly that it would be wholly stultifying to allow the technical skills implied by the pursuit of economic growth rates to overlay the need for full human development. In the words of Peter Williams' paper, "Education for Development":

" 'Development' is a broad enough concept. It is only when it is narrowed to mean 'economic growth rates of 6% to 7%' and when other policies, institutions, and actions are made subservient to this narrower objective that the aim becomes suspect. The development economist will protest that this is a caricature of what he believes about the nature of man and the purpose of development; he will argue that 6% growth is merely a convenient shorthand to describe the achievement of a fuller and better life for millions of individuals. Nevertheless, there is a great danger of being bewitched by this shorthand into a confusion of thought which can lead to the exaltation of the means to an end in itself. Adequate financial returns become a substitute for a fuller life and 'manpower resources' displace human beings. This may lead on to the proposition that education in developing countries should be strictly utilitarian in function, concentrating on the production of useful technical *skills,* while the inculcation of *values* through philosophy and culture should be assigned an insignificant place in the curriculum. . . .

"Although social and political objectives inevitably seem less clear-cut than economic criteria, rational planning of the education system in the light of the objectives chosen is equally necessary when wider objectives are sought. The most appropriate educational structure for any particular society will reflect its stage of economic and educational development and no global prescription can be made to suit all. However, the attachment of greater weight to social policy considerations may lead in the direction of relatively more emphasis than an economist might be prepared to accord on the potential value of primary education in the process of development. This emphasis finds support from the

'Fundamental Human Rights' school of thought as well as from educationalists concerned with the enlargement of the pool of talent from which students at higher levels can be drawn.

"These particular arguments are less compelling to me than the consideration that widespread education at primary level widens participation in modern (or hopefully modern) institutions. Development policies which involve only a handful of secondary school and university graduates operating "modern" production units have not so far been conspicuously successful in increasing human welfare, even where they have been associated with impressive economic growth rates. What is needed are economic and other policies which seek growth through harnessing the energy and invoking the enthusiasm of the mass of the people in town and countryside. Wider opportunities for the right kind of primary education (as well as for adult education) would form logical parts of this strategy. This is not always a particularly popular viewpoint among the more politically articulate members of society, who already have no difficulty in getting primary education for their children, but now demand an expansion of secondary schools and universities.

"These upper stages of education are indeed crucial for providing the leadership and organization of the development effort as well as producing the quality teachers essential for sound primary school development. It is at these upper levels that consideration of the *type* of education—general or vocational, specialized or unspecialized—becomes more important because of the high cost involved and the more obvious waste when the products of such courses cannot be productively employed. The complaint is often voiced that at these higher levels education in developing countries tends to be too academic and general and that more specialized vocational training is called for. Careful distinctions need to be made if this kind of discussion is not to become hopelessly confused. Much academic education is sterile precisely because it is *not* general but is narrow and specialized, developing little else than the memory and not serving at all to enlarge the understanding or the physical, emotional, and moral capacities of the receiver. Conversely, vocational education *need* not be specialized. Where training is given by an employer in a work situation, it may be appropriate and profitable to make it highly specific to the task in hand. This type of training is now receiving higher priority, and the encouragement of in-service training with appropriate apprenticeship arrangements, supported perhaps by training levies on employing firms, is attracting greater interest in much of the third world. . . .

"Many, perhaps most, developing countries are not, however, at the stage where employment opportunities of a specialized nature are sufficiently plentiful to justify large-scale establishment of institutions and courses to give a very specific training. The division of labor in these countries has not gone sufficiently far. Many school and college graduates will consequently have to be self-employed, or, if employed, will work in small-scale establishments where versatility and a wide range of skills will be the best asset. For these people the most useful education will be a broad and general one, which does not mean it must be biased in the direction of the humanities rather than science and technology. But a narrow scientific or technical training may be as inappropriate to the real needs of a developing country as a narrow academic education and has the disadvantage of being considerably more expensive. There have been countless examples from all three developing continents of the premature establishment of specialized technical courses whose graduates have not subsequently been able to find jobs.

"This point is only too well understood by the recipients of education, the students, whose preference for general and academic courses has too often been misunderstood as prejudice borne not of realism but of purely prestige considerations. In fact, their motives may be more rational and more complicated than is often allowed by their critics. There are countless examples in the developing world of agriculture and engineering courses, particularly at the technician level, which are under-enrolled. Pressure from parents, students, and teachers has forced many secondary schools with an initially vocational orientation into an increasingly academic mold. When this reluctance on the part of individuals really does stem from ignorance of actual employment opportunities, it may be overcome through improved information to the schools about the changing pattern of employment opportunities, for students do not in practice shun manual or technically oriented courses where these obviously lead to remunerative jobs. But at other times it is not so much a case of *wrong* perceptions by the student and his parents, but of perceptions *different* from those of the planner. The government from its standpoint may see that employment problems are looming for secondary school or university graduates, while the size of the technical cadres in the country is small and skills are being imported. There may accordingly be an attempt to shift the emphasis to vocational courses in the schools. But the individual student (and his parents) are quite unwilling to be regarded as fodder for the fulfillment of some abstract plan. He notices that the courses lead to only one or two types of specialized job and thus seem risky in a rapidly changing employment market, that salaries for these grades are often low, that the courses are mostly specialized dead-end courses which offer little opportunity for further advancement either academically or professionally, that the exhorters and preachers (who abound in developing and developed countries alike) always seem to be telling *somebody else's* children that they should be dirtying their hands or returning to the land. Their own children never seem to receive this advice. The courses and jobs have little prestige—is this the cause or the effect of the failure of the brightest students to enter them?

"These conflicting attitudes and interests of students and parents on the one hand and policy makers on the other deserve far more attention. Education is not something applied to an inert mass—other people's children—to promote development; it is an activity from which many participants each seek their own satisfactions and it performs different functions for each. A major challenge of our time is to try to harmonize the perceptions of the different groups involved in educational development. Certainly parents and children must revise their ideas about the true prospects of school- and college-leavers at each level in an age of educational inflation. But the policy makers themselves should try to understand *why* students persist in individual choices that may seem irrational to the planner. . . .

"Even when all the possible improvements to the curriculum and structure of education systems have been considered, one is still forced back to the conclusion that the schools on their own can assist but not effect development. The teacher and the school are only one of a host of influences on the growing child, and the best education will find it difficult to withstand a hostile social and economic environment in which economic opportunity is lacking and satisfying participation in the work of building a modern community is impossible. The potential contribution of education can only come to fruition when certain other conditions external to the school are met. In a purely economic context classical economists remind us that 'land' and 'capital' are as necessary as 'labor' for economic growth and one might add that appropriate economic organization is also essential. It should be possible to form a much livelier and better endowed school-leaver if appropriate reforms are made in school administration, the curriculum, and teacher training, but the obstacles to productive employment will remain. At fourteen or sixteen a child is not physically mature; he has no training or experience, no capital or land; and he is often dependent on his family for providing these in a situation where the very role of a minor acting as entrepreneur or farmer may be quite unacceptable socially. Moreover, rural life with its lack of modern amenities is scarcely appealing. It is not just obstinacy and unrealism that stand in the way of Back to the Land appeals. The environment must change as well as the education system if the two are to interact in a productive way."

The Green Revolution

WITH EXTRACTS FROM

The Green Revolution, Rural Employment, and the Urban Crisis

BY LESTER BROWN

AND

Socio-economic Aspects of the Green Revolution

BY V. G. RASTYANNIKOV

The breakthrough to new techniques in agriculture—the so-called Green Revolution—can provide a clear way out of the vicious circles of "obdurate underdevelopment." Rising productivity on the farms can yield margins for reinvestment, possibilities of rural employment, improvements in country living standards, and conceivably a check to uncontrolled and premature migration away from the farms. Some of the underlying reasons for optimism are made clear in Lester Brown's paper, "The Green Revolution, Rural Employment, and the Urban Crisis": *

"The impact of the new seeds on production levels is a result of their prairie-fire-like spread wherever conditions are suited to their use. Their widespread adoption in turn relates to their remarkable capacity for doubling yields of the varieties they replace. Both the wheats, developed in Mexico by the Rockefeller Foundation, and the rices, developed by Ford and Rockefeller jointly in the Philippines, are of short stature. It is their short, stiff straw, enabling them to respond to up to 120 pounds of nitrogen per acre, which distinguishes them from the traditional thin-strawed varieties which begin lodging (falling down) at about 40 pounds of nitrogen.

"In addition to their exceptional yield capacity, the new seeds mature earlier and adapt to a much wider range of latitudinal and seasonal variations than do indigenous varieties. By maturing in 120 days instead of the 150 to 180 days required for the varieties they replace, the new rices open up new opportunities for multiple cropping.

"Countries traditionally in food deficit are now using the new seeds and becoming self-sufficient, some actually generating exportable surpluses. The Philippines, the first country to use the new rices on a commercial basis, has ended half a century of dependence on rice imports, becoming a net exporter. Pakistan, as recently as 1968 the second-ranking recipient of United States food aid, has sharply reduced its dependence on food imports and is expected to be self-sufficient in both wheat and rice in 1970. Food imports into India are now less than one-half those of the food crisis years of 1966 and 1967.

"Gains in cereal production in countries where the new seeds have been successfully introduced are without precedent. Pakistan increased its wheat harvest 60% between 1967 and 1969. India upped its wheat harvest by one-half from 1965 to 1969. Ceylon's rice harvest increased 34% in two years. Annual increases in wheat yields per acre on the

* Most of the data and many of the ideas in this paper are from Mr. Brown's book, *Seeds of Change: The Green Revolution and International Development in the 1970's* (New York: Praeger Publishers, 1970).

Indian subcontinent following introduction of the Mexican wheats were double those for corn in the United States following the introduction of hybrids a generation ago.

"Spread of the new seeds in Asia has been rapid, going from 200 acres in 1964/65 (mostly for trial and experimental purposes) to 34 million acres in 1968/69.

"Outside Asia, the new seeds were introduced more recently. In North Africa, planting of the new wheats has been limited largely to Tunisia and Morocco, although small quantities were introduced into Algeria and Libya in 1969. The new wheats now cover virtually all the wheat land in Mexico, where they were originally developed. Neither the wheats nor rices, however, have made much progress in South America."

"The principal constraint on the spread of the new seeds is water. The new wheats can realize their full yield potential only under irrigated conditions; the new rices, all short-strawed, require careful water control, a condition prevailing on only a minor portion of the rice land in Asia where most of the rice is grown under conditions of natural flooding.

However, the benign possibilities of the Green Revolution cannot be left to chance. Its impact on employment and on rural social structures can work for good or evil. On these points, V. G. Rastyannikov issued a comprehensive warning in his paper "Socio-economic Aspects of the Green Revolution."

"*Polarization.* Within the present agrarian framework, large segments of the working farmer group (or stratum) are often deprived of critical preconditions for dynamic development. They have no savings at all, and their economy is a semitraditional, subsistence one. [The paper's estimate is that an average of two-thirds of Asian farm land is in subsistence farming.] On the other hand, the large producers, among whom the highest positions are occupied by big landowners on the way to become capitalists, are much more prepared to 'accept' the Green Revolution immediately, and many facts show that it is really this narrow stratum which at present appropriates the major fruits of the 'new agricultural strategy.'

"Yet the social consequences of such a process are opposed to the genuine achievement of a consolidated transition of agriculture to an intensive stage of development. The rural elite, which is closely inter-linked with precapitalist forms of activity (rack-renting tenancies, and growing concentration of money-lending capital), cuts off by these ac-tivities the lower, major strata of producers from any possibilities of normal development. Moreover, it is the rural elite, including large semifeudal landowners, who manage to utilize in their favor the major part of the state investments directed into agriculture to develop inten-sive production. In Pakistan during the Third Five Year Plan period (1965/66–1970/71), the state allocated from its budget revenues a huge sum—about Rs. 1.5 billion—for one purpose only, to subsidize the difference between the market price and the distribution price of modern inputs and machines (fertilizers, tractors, and the like). How-ever, 'the entire rural income generated by agricultural subsidies and outlays has gone to a small number of big landlords.'[3]

"Their number is small. In West Pakistan, according to the Agri-cultural Census of 1960, they directly farm—in farms of over 60 hectares—only 10% of the land. Of the 58% of the land farmed by small farmers who work with less than 10 hectares, nearly half is held under share cropping arrangements which take up to 50% of the gross output. Moreover, one of the most dramatic current consequences of the Green Revolution is to stimulate a more intensive process of ex-propriation in the vast sector of working cultivators.

"As Indira Gandhi, the Prime Minister of India, reminded the Conference of Chief Ministers, in November, 1969: 'In spite of legal protection to the tenants, they have been dispossessed of their lands by the money-lenders and others. In most cases the landlords were them-selves money-lenders who, lured by high profits in scientific farming, took over land and downgraded the tenants to the position of share-croppers and the latter to landless labor.'[4] In other words, each step by the rural elite on the way to agricultural 'progress' is connected with a depressive effect on the majority of farmers; so the progress of the elite is realized to a great extent at the expense of a regression in the other segments of the agricultural economy. . . ."

"*Investment.* The transition from the traditional technological base to modern technology and expertise in agriculture considerably raises capital requirements. In fact, as recent trends show, since the mid-60's, the increased availability of modern inputs, accompanied by an increase in the utilization of irrigation potential, has led to a continuing growth in the rate of productive capital accumulation in the agricultural sector. Moreover, urged on by the food crisis, the planning authorities in some Asian countries strive to shift the center of gravity of the developmental programs more toward the development of the agricultural sector and toward industries catering to it. These are now allocated a relatively larger share of the national investment. For example, in India the share of capital outlays for agriculture, cooperation and community development, and major irrigation amounted in 1966/67 and 1967/68 to 21% and 23% respectively of the total, as against 20% in the Third Plan period (1961/62–1965/66).

"Nevertheless, the capital investments needed for laying the foundations for intensive agriculture are tremendous. According to the calculations made by a group of American experts, in order that the developing countries of the world may do no more than double agricultural production by the year 1985, a sum of about $32 billion must be invested in the production of modern agricultural means of production. This calculation, incidentally, more or less omits the capital needed for mechanization. . . . [5]

"In a multistructural agrarian economy, the Green Revolution, once started, increases the process of income polarization in rural areas by sharply increasing the incomes of the wealthiest groups. Hence a problem arises. Through what mechanism can a part of the enlarged incomes, especially those going to the topmost rural groups, be preempted for the purpose of accelerated national economic growth and, in agriculture, for the growth of the *whole* productive sector, not simply a separate segment of it? The outmoded land taxation system, even though supplemented on the statute books by an agricultural income tax, cannot achieve this aim. In fact, in India in the financial year 1968/69 the agricultural income tax made up only 7.8% of the total direct agricultural taxes, and in West Pakistan, even less—1.5%.[6] It is worth noting that in the developing Asian countries it is the rural elite, the large landowners, who bear the minimal burden on taxes as compared to all other well-to-do and richer groups liable to taxation of incomes. According to conservative estimate, in India in 1968/69 the rural groups with incomes of Rs. 4,800 and more were expected to pay only 0.63% of their incomes in tax.[7]

"The real paradox is that the rural elite not only is the main beneficiary of the Green Revolution but manages to load the major burden of investment on intensive agricultural development onto other strata of society, first and foremost onto peasant producers (mainly through the system of indirect taxation). Meanwhile, the excessive incomes of the large farmers are too often utilized, not for enlarged production, but for various forms of parasitic enrichment (speculation, money-lending, and so forth). So the experience of developing Asian countries testifies that a taxation mechanism which would effectively work in the teeth of opposition from rural elites is yet to be created."

"Employment. A shift to intensive agriculture is fraught with serious consequences for the growing labor force. According to various estimates, in developing Asia, even under the present 'traditional' technical basis of farming, the rate of underemployment in terms of man-day units amounts to one-fourth and more of the total agricultural labor force. In the initial stages, which are primarily confined to the application of fertilizers, use of higher-yielding varieties of seeds, and water management—in other words, labor-intensive methods—the Green Revolution tends to draw in an additional labor force, including newcomers. But this development is possible only to a certain limit. Moreover, in a number of countries, a shift toward intensive agriculture is accompanied from the very beginning by an intensive process of labor-saving mechanization which spreads under present conditions almost exclusively through larger holdings. For example, in Turkey the tractor pool numbered 44,000 units in 1956 and 55,000 in 1965; in 1967 it increased to 75,000 machines [8] and now, according to an unofficial estimate, the number of tractors used in agriculture is close to 100,000 units. In India only 31,000 tractors were in use in 1961 and 54,000 in 1966. However, by the beginning of 1970 the number of tractors worked on farms may rise to 100,000. In a single year, 1969, about 29,000 tractors were to be assembled in India and imported from abroad. At present, one estimate suggests that tractors work more than half the wheat area planted in high-yielding varieties.[9]

"This inevitably leads to a reduction of labor requirements, without much possibility of the absorption of the displaced by other sectors. For instance, in the Punjab (Pakistan), according to the farmers' evidence, as a result of an increase in the number of tractors, the amount of labor required had been reduced by about 50% per unit of land as compared to the period before mechanization (from eight to four persons per 40 hectares of farm land). Using these figures as a basis for their calculations, S. R. Rose and E. H. Clark established that, provided full-tractor mechanization covers the total area in farms of 10 hectares and more in West Pakistan by 1985, 600,000 to 700,000 laborers will be displaced on this sector (i.e., 16% to 19% of the net increase in the agricultural labor force in West Pakistan). If, therefore, we are to appreciate the actual trends in growth of nonagricultural employment, 'the conclusion one must arrive at is that a large part of the increase in the labor force would be left in the countryside without adequate employment, and that mechanization would worsen the situation that would otherwise prevail.' [10]

"Thus the agrarian overpopulation would pile up still further, would be concentrated on the poorest, smallest farms which are already oversaturated with surplus labor. That is one reason—among many—why, in the initial stages, stable and sustained economic growth in intensive agriculture must be spread much more evenly. Smaller cultivators must be drawn together through different forms of organization (cooperation, etc.) and provided with conditions and means for investment, marketing, and so forth. This policy involves more risk and requires more effort and capital expenditure on the part of government. But it is absolutely essential if the Green Revolution is to be a success without large and drastic consequences for the employment situation. . . ."

Dr. Brown takes a rather more optimistic view of the employment possibilities, yet he, too, agrees on the critical need to avoid premature or unsuitable mechanization. He quotes a report from the AID mission in New Delhi on the effect of the new wheats on employment: "The Green Revolution has definitely been employment-creating. In the Punjab (state in northern India) there have been serious labor shortages during the April-June period when wheat is harvested, threshed, marketed, and the summer crop is sown. Wage rates (non-agricultural) have risen as high as $2.00 to $3.25 per day. Agricultural labor rates have also risen. Mechanization is increasing rapidly, largely because of the labor shortages." [11]

Dr. Brown further observes:

"This conclusion is borne out by experience in such countries as Taiwan and Japan, where, as agriculture modernized, labor requirements increased. Japanese and Taiwanese farmers now invest about 170 man-days in the production and harvesting of an acre of rice, as compared with 120 man-days in India and 100 in the Philippines. But while more labor is required per acre in Japan and Taiwan, less labor is required per ton of grain. Available data suggest that a similar situation obtains in Turkey, India, and Pakistan, where labor used per ton of the new cereals averages perhaps 20% less than with traditional varieties.

"As wages rise, and as the new seeds make agriculture more profitable, mechanization becomes increasingly attractive. Perhaps the most immediate issue of the agricultural revolution is whether mechanization will come so fast as to displace large numbers of farm laborers and thereby measurably worsen conditions in the cities. If mechanization proceeds so rapidly that millions are forced to join the army of unemployed in the countryside, or to migrate to cities not prepared to receive such an influx, the agricultural revolution could become a curse rather than a blessing.

"Perhaps the most striking illustration of farm mechanization without regard for the social consequences is the mechanization of cotton picking in the United States. Mechanical cotton picking spread very rapidly during the years following World War II, until virtually all cotton was being harvested mechanically. The principal reason that blacks had been brought from Africa to the United States—to pick cotton—suddenly vanished. Employment on farms on the Mississippi delta declined nearly 90% over the two-decade span from 1940 to 1960. For hundreds of thousands of blacks there was no alternative to migration to the urban areas of the North—Cleveland, Watts, Newark, Detroit, Harlem, and Chicago. Culturally, socially, and vocationally, they were unprepared for urban living. Confined to their black ghettoes and unable to find work, they became alienated, bitter and resentful. These feelings intensified, eventually reaching the explosive point. Scarcely a city in the United States escaped their wrath. A feeling that they had been denied a rightful share of the economic opportunities and material abundance of the society of which they were ostensibly a part, combined with a feeling that they had little to lose, triggered the explosion.

"The parallels between this movement of rural people, unprepared for urban living, into urban areas unprepared for them in the United States and the massive rural-urban migration in prospect in the poor countries are disturbing. The ingredients for creating a social tinderbox, susceptible to ignition by the smallest spark, are present in both situations. It is for this reason that poor countries must make conscious efforts to mechanize selectively, so as to expand rural employment rather than diminish it."

Dr. Brown further points out that the potentially beneficial effects of the Green Revolution also depend upon the trading policies of the developed nations:

"A rise in the demand for export depends upon gaining access to the highly protected grain markets of the rich countries, particularly Japan and Western Europe. As the roster of poor countries with exportable surpluses of wheat, rice, and feed grains lengthens, there will be increasingly strong political pressures on rich countries to open their markets to fair competition.

"But the record of the 1960's has been one of increasing protectionism and increasingly distorted production patterns. The share of the world's food supply contributed by high-cost, inefficient producers has increased rapidly, and often at the expense of the more efficient producers. Europe, insisting on growing more and more of its own food, regardless of the cost to its consumers or to producers elsewhere, has accumulated burdensome surpluses of cereals and dairy products and is approaching a crisis unless it adjusts its agricultural policies.

"In 1969 West Germany was imposing an import duty of 76% on wheat. Its duties on imported feed grains ranged from 73% for corn, to 83% for barley. It is not surprising that European cereal prices are nearly double world market levels, or that the German livestock producer pays almost exactly twice as much for feed grains as his American or Canadian counterpart.

"Expensive as feed grains are under the Common Market's agricultural policy, European dairy farmers still find it profitable to convert them into butter. With the support price for butter at nearly one dollar a pound, these farmers have produced a surplus of 660 million pounds, a veritable mountain of butter!

"France's exportable surplus of four and one-half million tons of barley had to be marketed outside the Common Market with an enormous subsidy. It exported soft wheats in 1969 with an export subsidy roughly equal to the world market value of the wheat. If Pakistan's effort to export soft wheats in the early 1970's materializes and becomes a matter of competing subsidies between the French and Pakistani treasuries, there can be little doubt of the outcome.

"It can be argued, although not very persuasively, that one of the luxuries the rich can afford is inefficiency, even on the scale represented by current agricultural policies in Europe and Japan. The poor countries can support no such luxury. They must have a rational system of trade in farm products through which they can hope to earn more of their way in the world.

"But when surpluses from the rich countries are dumped on the world market at a price well below the cost of production, the poor countries are deprived of this opportunity. As long as the poor countries were mostly food aid recipients, agricultural import policies of the industrial countries were not a major concern. But now that more and more poor countries are developing an exportable surplus of one or more cereals, this becomes a central issue. The Green Revolution is altering the context in which the debate on agricultural policies in the rich countries takes place, making it an aid as well as a trade issue.

"The pending saturation of the world rice market is a case in point. During 1967 and early 1968, the world rice price reached $200 a ton, nearly double that prevailing during the early 1960's, triggering a global production response. With the introduction and rapid spread of the high-yielding rices, many poor countries, once rich importers, such as the Philippines and Pakistan, are generating exportable surpluses. Coming at a time when import needs of traditional importers (Ceylon, Malaysia, and India) are declining, prices are sliding, and even at reduced prices markets cannot always be found.

"While the poor countries were developing their new-found capacity to export, Japan, traditionally the leading world rice importer, was raising its internal rice support price until by 1969 it was nearly triple the world market level. As a result of this policy, Japan became self-sufficient in rice. It today has a record 5.6 million tons of rice in surplus stocks. The Japanese rice market, once open to imports from

East Asia, is closed to the outside world today. But rice is the lifeblood of most Asian economies. Should the bottom fall out of the rice market, poor countries traditionally exporting rice, as well as those with new-found technologies and exportable surpluses, would suffer greatly. Foreign exchange earnings would decline, rural unemployment would rise, and the flow to the cities would accelerate.

"The alternative, of course, would be for Japan, currently the most serious violator of the laws of comparative advantage of any cereal producing country, to reverse the recent trend in rice prices and resume its traditional role as a rice importer. Every million tons of rice imported by Japan from Southeast Asia would create something like a half million man-years of rural employment in this region. . . .

"As the gravity of the urban crisis in the poor countries begins to unfold in the 1970's, the world will be forced to take inventory of means whereby rural employment can be expanded in the poor countries. When it does, sugar is certain to join cereals at the top of the list. There are few products in which the poor man living in the tropical or sub-tropical regions has such a striking and unquestionable competitive advantage. Sugar produced from sugar beets in the temperate regions costs between six and nine cents a pound to produce—while that produced from sugar cane costs only two to three cents. If economics alone prevailed, there would be little if any beet sugar produced; virtually all the world's sugar would come from cane produced in the poor countries. With the breakthrough in cereal production, land is being released for other crops including, of course, sugar cane.

"At present, the global pattern of sugar production is grossly distorted to the detriment of both consumers in the rich countries and producers, or potential producers, in the poor countries. The United States produces some 60% of its needs, up sharply from a decade ago. Several European countries are now self-sufficient, relying entirely on the highly protected production of sugar beets. The world sugar economy is desperately in need of overhauling, bringing it more in line with present-day realities. A restructuring of the world pattern of sugar production could contribute far more to the economic progress of the poor countries than much of the foreign aid they receive."

Urbanization

WITH EXTRACTS FROM

Housing, Building and Planning in the Second United Nations Development Decade

AND

Urban Growth and Politics in Developing Nations

BY JOAN NELSON

The Conference discussions took as their point of departure the analysis of urban growth in the context of modern development put forward in the United Nations report, *Housing, Building and Planning in the Second United Nations Development Decade*: *

"If the concept of urbanization is to be regarded as a key index of development it must be reconsidered. The central paradox to be explained is the coexistence of a high level of urbanization and a low level of income or what has been called 'rapid urbanization in a context of obdurate underdevelopment.' [12] In the nineteenth century, urbanization coincided with and was apparently a contributing cause of rising income and pragmatically successful modernization. Since, one hundred years later, this is no longer the case, it is necessary to discover what factors have changed and where the wealth-creating circuits of successful development have broken down.

"Four major differences between the move towards an urban society in the nineteenth and in the twentieth century dominate all other local, regional or cultural disparities. The first is the degree to which large cities in the present century have grown up in the developing continents *ahead* of any systematic movement towards modernization. These cities were, in the main, transmission centers for the dispatch of primary materials from local mines and plantations back to Europe and North

* United Nations, Economic and Social Council, *Housing, Building and Planning in the Second United Nations Development Decade* (E/C. 6/90),

America and in return for the receipt and distribution of Western manufactures.

"The economic and political climate was colonialistic. Rio de Janeiro, Buenos Aires, Bombay, Calcutta, Shanghai, on a much more modest scale, Dakar, Lagos, Dar-es-Salaam were all cities looking outward to the markets of the world, to the global exchange of primary for industrial products. They did not grow up, like the cities of Europe and North America, in the wake of local diversification and sustained development. They were, in a real sense, larger than and ahead of the economy sustaining them. It is significant that in 1920, Latin America had as large a proportion of its urban population in cities of over 500,000 as had Europe after a century of full-scale modernization. Today the proportion is actually 10% higher and in sixteen out of the twenty republics more than half the urban population lives in the capital city which in most cases is also the economic and industrial center. . . .

"The second difference is rooted in an explosive growth of population which in its turn follows from the conquest of major epidemics and the grosser forms of contamination ahead of a full-scale diversification of the economy. . . .

"The numbers of those born in the cities are not reduced by cholera and typhus as in the past. And the countryside cannot absorb a rural increase which, between 1920 and 1960, added over half a billion to the rural population, all but 56 million of them in the developing continents. The urban areas expand inexorably—from 68 million to 320 million in the last forty years, with the big cities of over 500,000 inhabitants accounting for nearly half the increase.

"These two pressures for the expansion of urban areas, the pre-existence of 'export cities' and the sheer scale of population growth, appear to have occurred almost independently of basic changes in economic structure. This likelihood is borne out by a closer examination of the directly productive sectors in the different countries. A third divergence from the record of the already developed States now emerges. Broadly speaking, the decisive changes in agricultural structure, productivity and food production which created a vital surplus above subsistence level and preceded the growth of industrial cities in the United Kingdom, in Europe and America and later in Japan, have not yet occurred on a sufficient scale in the developing countries. . . . There is little repetition of Japan's beneficent spiral at the turn of the century by which the farmer, free of feudal dues and doubling his productivity, paid the land tax which helped to finance industry, grew the food that fed the cities and then purchased back from them the bicycles and sewing machines of the new industrial era . . .

"This failure in the rural areas is one strand in the fourth complex of reasons which help to explain why today's developing States cannot easily follow the successful patterns of earlier development. Consideration of a number of developed countries in their earlier stages of development and the percentages of their working force engaged in manufacturing and a comparison of this level with their degree of urbanization, makes clear in every case that the percentage of people living in cities was much lower than that of the working force in industry. In France in 1856, for instance, 29% of the workers were already in manufacturing, but only 10.7% of the population lived in cities. The percentages for Norway in 1890 were 22% and 13.8%, for Sweden in the same year, 22% and 10.8%, for Switzerland in 1888, with its remarkable achievement of cantonal decentralization, 45% in manufacturing and only 13.2% in cities. In other words, a strong thrust in secondary production in a large range of industrial activities in which the output per worker was steadily rising and adding to the available surplus, preceded the growth of a large urban population. The men moving out of agriculture as its productivity rose and its need for labor declined moved into other jobs and, in large measure, into more productive ones.

"The picture in the developing areas today is almost exactly the contrary. In virtually every case, urban population as a percentage of total population greatly exceeds the percentage of the working force in industry. In the United Arab Republic in 1960, 16% of the people already lived in urban areas. The proportion of workers in manufacturing was under 10%. In Tunisia in 1956, the proportion in cities was one percentage point higher while only 6.8% of the working force was engaged in industry. In Asia the situation is similar: 11.9% of Pakistan was urbanized in 1961 but only 6.2% of the workers were in manufacturing. Malaya in 1957 offered a more radical divergence: 22.7% in towns, 6.9% in industry. In the same year, South Korea had roughly the same percentage in industry and over 29% in cities. Only India and Ceylon deviated from the pattern since in the early 1950s only a couple of percentage points separated the two ratios: 11.2% urban and 9.4% industrial in the case of Ceylon, 11.9% urban and 10.7% industrial for India.

"The most extreme contrasts are to be found in Latin America, the continent whose nations have striven hard and long for modernization. In every Latin American republic, urbanization has shot ahead of industrialization. In Brazil, the proportion of city dwellers reached 28% in 1960 but the percentage of the work force in manufacturing was still below 10%. In Chile, a decade earlier, the proportions were 42.5% urban and only 16.9% industrial. Colombia follows, at the same period, with a remarkable 45.8% of the people urbanized and only 9.9% of the workers in industry. In Venezuela, as the 1960s began, the extreme contrast was reached, with 47.2% of the people in cities and only 8.8% of the labor force in manufacturing."

The UN Report's conclusion is that this background of growing worklessness within an alien urban environment is likely to be a deepening cause of disruption:

"The cities are already in crisis as they expand, each year, by two and three times the national level. The situation is inconceivable ten years from now when eighteen cities in Latin America will have passed the million mark, when Lima will have over 3 million inhabitants, Caracas 4 million, Bogota 5 million, São Paulo 7 million, Buenos Aires 9 million. It is hard also to imagine how India will cope with such cities as Bombay and Calcutta where densities of population are already double that of such developed cities as Chicago, and which threaten to grow to 20 and 30 million by the end of the century. . . . Calcutta is by far the most turbulent of India's great cities. The 70% of families living in one room and the unrecorded numbers of pavement dwellers account for at least part of the endemic unrest."

Professor Joan Nelson, in her paper *Urban Growth and Politics in Developing Nations,* disputes the linkage between migration, unemployment, and political instability suggested in the UN report. She argues that lower-middle-class groups and the intelligentsia, rather than low-income rural-to-urban migrants or the urban poor in general, are primarily responsible for urban unrest.

"First, where nations are already somewhat urbanized, many migrants into the largest cities come from smaller towns rather than the country. This reflects the well-documented pattern of step-wise migration. In Santiago de Chile, Rio, and São Paulo, for example, almost two-thirds of migrants do not come directly from rural areas. Even in India, a quarter of the migrants to Bombay in the mid-1950's were urban in origin, and almost half of Delhi's newcomers came from other cities.[13]

"Second, many of the rural migrants have had some prior exposure to urban influences. Survey evidence indicates that a disproportionate number come from villages or locations fairly near cities.[14] Many have visited city friends or relatives one or more times before migrating. Moreover, most migrants are young adults. There is reason to believe that many have better education and training than the average in their places of origin. . . .

"Surveys also show that very few migrants arrive in the great cities aimless, friendless, and penniless. Of those surveyed in several Latin American cities 70% to 90% knew friends or relatives in the city when they arrived, and received some help in finding a place to live and a job. . . .[15]

"That most migrants have contacts in the city is reflected in the otherwise surprising survey finding that, at least in several major South American cities, migrants who seek jobs find them within a matter of days or weeks.[16] Moreover, data from a number of cities (including Bogota, Santiago de Chile, Calcutta, Delhi, Bombay, Madras, Baroda, Hyderabad, Poona, and Karachi) indicate lower rates of open unemployment among migrants (excluding refugees) than among native urbanites.[17] Age structure may account for part of the difference, since more of the natives are in the under-twenty-five age bracket, which suffers universally from disproportionately high rates of unemployment. . . .

"I do not mean to suggest that life is rosy for new migrants. The unskilled and uneducated in particular face difficult problems of survival and adjustment. But the crucial question is whether the newcomers themselves are disappointed and frustrated by what they find in the city. On this point the survey evidence is fairly extensive, and data from many cities, geographic regions, and types of settlements concur: an overwhelming majority of migrants find their situation an improvement over rural conditions.

"Their satisfaction is in part relative to conditions in their place of origin. To illustrate: a sample of low-income migrants in Buenos Aires felt that their former housing had been better. But over half the sample had come from large towns. On a cross-national scale their standards were probably quite high. By contrast, 75% of squatters in Asima, a fringe settlement outside of Baghdad almost entirely settled by rural migrants, viewed their reed-matting shacks with mud-plaster roofs and sparsely scattered outdoor taps as an improvement over their previous accommodations.[18]

"Migrants' sense of gain is also based, in part, on hope for the future. People who move to the city are convinced that they or their children will have more opportunity for education and upward mobility than they would have in rural areas or small towns—a judgment with which few could quarrel, however slim the chances of advancement in the city."

In the debate participants tended to agree on both the relative speed of urban job-getting and the present political passivity of the poorest city-dwellers. The worries were for future employment as numbers continue to rise inexorably. This in turn was felt likely to produce deepening contrasts of affluence and misery in the cities which, in turn, would radicalize student opinion and stimulate revolutionary middle-class leadership. Professor Nelson examined these possibilities and suggested that they point, among other things, to the need not for "crash" programs of urban improvement but for sustained policies to upgrade existing settlements:

"To argue that the swelling urban masses are not likely to be major sources of political instability in the 1970s is not to predict a placid urban scene. The cities will continue to be the strongholds of the opposition, the spawning ground for extremist movements, and the site of nonviolent and violent strikes and demonstrations. They are also the home of virtually all institutions of higher education, industrial establishments, and the middle class in general. . . .

"But it is worth noting that the issues which concern them are only in part traceable to the pressures of rapid urbanization. The housing squeeze, a serious cause of discontent for skilled labor and white-collar groups, is indeed related to rapid urban growth. Hopelessly overcrowded public transportation and public schools undoubtedly intensify middle-class preferences for owning a car and sending their children to private schools. But they would probably want to do so even if urban conditions were much better than they are. Students often demonstrate against increases in bus fares, but this is hardly their central concern. Other salient issues—openings and scholarships in universities, the organization of the universities, opportunities for white-collar and professional employment, taxation levels, foreign private investment and its role in the economy, and national prestige on the international scene—are related indirectly or not at all to urbanization.

"To summarize: rapid urbanization unquestionably causes staggering physical, economic, and human problems. Cities are undeniably the locus of political opposition, and often also centers of extremism and violence. Moreover, urban instability may well increase during the 1970's. But the pattern of urbanization without concomitant industrialization is not the major cause of the instability. Therefore, policies designed to cope with urban problems, whatever their urgency on economic and welfare grounds, will do little to alleviate instability in the cities. That objective must be pursued through other policies and programs directed to improving the relationship of education to the economy and to the other issues which move labor, students, and middle-class groups to political action.

"These conclusions suggest a second, perhaps more helpful, implication for planning and policy. In a number of countries low-cost urban housing programs, policies for dealing with squatter settlements, and other aspects of urban policy have had a sporadic, stop-start, inconsistent character. This has reflected uncertainty as to how to cope with truly staggering problems, but also has resulted from periodic surges of concern about political instability. Many of the 'crash' programs have been ill-conceived and poorly executed, thereby wasting scarce resources and contributing to cynicism among the poor and defeatism among the affluent. The recognition that the urban poor are unlikely to be politically explosive would help make possible less vacillating policies and a longer time-frame for planning. It is to be hoped that the growing pressure of urban problems is itself sufficient to sustain an appropriate sense of urgency, without the additional but distorting impetus of fear."

The UN Report also seeks to go beyond the issue of urban employment, stressing the need to link urban strategies with the wider pattern of development, particularly with regional development closely linked to agriculture:

"A regional pattern of urban growth automatically lessens the dominance of the old 'export cities.' It thrusts development back into the hinterland and diversifies the system of transport and communications which tends, particularly in Africa and Latin America, to run down to the coasts without lateral connections and to make access to Europe or North America easier and cheaper than to the backlands at home. . . .

"The link between agricultural modernization and regional urban development is . . . clear. In fact, the two are very largely interdependent despite the difficulty of finding such a relationship in the data of agriculture or of urbanization. Over the next two decades the technical revolution in farming will, if it is fully financed and supported, be able to produce the indispensable surplus in agriculture. Essentially, its purpose is to modernize the inputs into farming—improved seed, fertilizers, power, machines—and to dispatch the outputs to the commercial sector. Both these processes take place on too large a scale for their organization to be confined to the village level. Yet the major city or cities are often too remote. London was not the spur to Britain's critical agricultural revolution in the eighteenth century. All over the country, small market centers with their new Georgian town halls, corn exchanges and modest country banks, were the symbol of growth and affluence. At a comparable period in American development, the emergence of the Middle West as the greatest corn-producing region of the nation went together with a vigorous and diversified expansion of market and service towns.

"Today, agricultural operations and opportunities are more complex. Increased quantities of fertilizer, tubewells, gasoline, machines and repair services cannot be provided simply on a farm-size, retail basis. Local wholesaling centers are needed. Credit operations require regional banks, co-operatives, inter-village administration, extension services and regional offices; rural education must be backed up with high schools, training colleges and research stations. Certain forms of food processing, as carried out in mills and freezing and canning factories, for instance, can be performed efficiently by medium-scale enterprise and there is evidence to suggest that effective storage—a critical factor which could in some countries add up to 20% to the grain harvest—can be arranged with the lowest overhead costs at the wholesale, regional town level. Without this urban infrastructure, the agricultural revolution will itself be slowed down.

"Although further research is still required, and, in fact, being undertaken on this matter, the relationship of rural development in service centers and the heavier types of urbanization has been under study by the United Nations Research Institute for Social Development. An examination of experience in Bulgaria, where it is an avowed aim to avoid congestion of economic activities and concentration of population in a few large towns, has led to the designation of a limited number of localities as 'service centers' in which carefully selected socio-cultural equipment has been provided, and industry of specific size and characteristics will be located. Comparable efforts in France have gradually focused on building up regional capitals as 'poles of growth.' Selected examples of national urbanization policy such as these could be described in greater detail to illustrate both the comprehensive nature of such programmes, which embrace the rural exodus as well as alternative patterns of urbanization, and their relative feasibility and practical success.

"Many factors must be taken into account in the system of regional capitals if the objectives of national development and social change are to be met. Transport links, the fertility of local soils, administrative divisions, and historical tradition normally combine to give one town or another a wider range of attractions. The kind of points system used to grade communities in the Kenya plan, with given weights for accessibility, existence of facilities, traditional markets and so forth, could be used to work out the most suitable distribution. Redistribution has been achieved in some lands and is thus possible. The essential is to plan for a regional infrastructure of towns with the same farsighted attention to detail now given to the preparation of transportation grids or power systems, and to see all of these—towns, power and communication systems—as the essential underpinning of agricultural growth. . . .

"Two issues can be distinguished: on the one hand, an urban strategy for the future and its impact upon employment; on the other, policies designed to meet the needs of urban societies that already exist and are in a critical state. The two separate approaches have this in common: the very great importance for investment and for employment of the construction industry. Buildings, including housing, can equal 50% of a country's fixed investment. This sector is a large employer of labour, particularly of relatively unskilled labour. There is also the likelihood that house-building and home-ownership, in large cities and small, act as a potent mobilizer of savings and hence of productive investment.

"It is one thing to think of housing in welfare terms and to speak of the annual need for 24 million dwelling units as though these were huge benefits to be doled out from the wealth accumulated by productive enterprise in other sectors of the national economy. The problem then seems insuperable. But houses for which people will work and save are simply another highly attractive consumer durable. The stimulus their construction gives to other industries, such as local raw materials, building components, drainpipes, water faucets, tiles and glass, is just as valid for growth as the stimulus given by many other types of industry. It is an essential complement of these other industries. The links between housing construction and the rest of the economy can be wider and stimulate an even greater range of activity. Above all, much of the work is at present labour-intensive and may be kept so. Indeed, housing construction tends to be the first and easiest industry for the rural migrant to enter."

Environment

WITH EXTRACTS FROM

Environment

BY MAX NICHOLSON

It is relatively easy to see the place, in a total development strategy, of such facets of policy as family planning, expanded employment possibilities, increased productivity on the farms, controlled urbanism, and a modern approach to education. It is not so easy, above all in developing lands, to imagine the role of ecological planning. For one thing, the widespread awareness of the problem is relatively new.

Max Nicholson presented the problem to the Conference in his paper, "Environment." Only as the 1970's begin has public opinion begun to realize that the planetary environment, the "biosphere," is not "static and passive, inexhaustibly productive in the face of ignorant and injurious practices and relatively invulnerable as a permanent asset." Only now are the developed nations beginning, tardily, to count the cost of using the "biosphere" as a dump for the leavings of the "technosphere," that part of the environment which is man-made and increasingly dominated by man's scientific and technological inventions.

This definition of the "technosphere," however, underlines the ecological dilemma for developing peoples. They may be impressed by the evidence of the damage done by irresponsible technology. They may share developed peoples' revulsion when the oceans, far from being at their task "of pure ablution round earth's human shores," degrade the beaches with the filth of oil and garbage. They may question the models of full development which, by way of uncontrollable technology, gadgetry, and urban agglomerations, submit human beings to every form of pollution—of noise, of air, of sight, of smell. Yet is there not a risk that, in opting for ecological control at this stage, they may slow down their own development?

This is, in part, an argument of power—to pull more nearly level with the achievements of the wealthy states. But it is even more an anguished response to the ineluctable pressures of rising population. Without quick decisions how can the multitudes be fed and housed and employed? This is why Mr. Nicholson puts such stress on population control—to allow a breathing space for developing governments to take a more informed and cautious look at technological man's impact upon his own resources and environment.

But, with or without successful family planning, the problem has still to be faced. Mr. Nicholson illustrates the degree to which ecological considerations can radically affect not only problems of amenity but the actual profitability and running costs of both industrial and agricultural projects.

"An incorrect choice of site for a development project often occurs when land reasonably suited to several alternative uses is allocated to one which could equally be satisfied elsewhere and thus made unavailable for another for which its advantages are unique. The erection of a factory on a coastline with greater earning capacity for tourism or housing construction on a rich deposit of minerals are simple examples. Only land capability classification can minimize such mistakes. A more obscure and more common category consists of sites which, although not entirely unsuitable for the desired development, are only able to sustain it without injury if given more continuous, more skilled, and often more expensive maintenance than was foreseen or can be assured. Such sites often display run-down or damaged facilities which are blamed on poor maintenance when the fault should actually be assigned to unrealistic site selection, often based on insufficient environmental knowledge.

"A more subtle category consists of sites unnecessarily used for a purpose which could have been just as well met by adapting another site in the same area to multipurpose use and thus increasing the resources of disposable land. For example, a large void excavated for opencast or strip mining can become a water-supply reservoir, and perhaps also serve certain recreational needs, if a combined design is planned in advance. . . .

"There has been a massive worldwide loss of land owing to unsound practices of pastoralism. On many wild areas cropping of wild herbivores can yield more protein than their attempted replacement by domesticated livestock, although the scope for such cropping and the drawing of appropriate ecological lines between the two await the funding of more research. Closely related and vastly extensive problems are created by burning and deforestation, often stimulated by the displacement of tribes from more favorable lands claimed by development projects. In certain cases the resulting loss of water yields has terminated local cultivation and even deprived cities of natural water supplies. Where new reservoirs have been constructed in forested uplands, advantage has been taken of construction roads by local people who strip the tree cover. This opens the slopes to rapid erosion and has been known to silt up a reservoir to such an extent as to write off a substantial part of its rated capacity. The extent to which current development generates indirect repercussions on "waste" lands, which may be needed for development later on, or throws open hitherto unused lands to destructive practices is one of the gravest unfaced problems of present policies. All unused land should be conserved as a bank for the future, and any access fortuitously provided to it should be carefully controlled.

"The needs of long-term development call for a worldwide survey of existing, threatened and potential erosion and for the adoption of plans which will end the insane wastefulness of permitting fertile top-soils and water-yielding catchments to be converted into bare sterile surfaces producing nothing except occasional devastating floods."

Mr. Nicholson's chief recommendation, in the present stage of en-vironmental knowledge—a recommendation widely supported at the debate—is that governments and international agencies should give en-vironmental needs their proper weight in planning.

"A useful approach . . . takes the form of a Chart of Human Impacts on the environment, ranging from land reclamation, drainage and dam-building through forestry, agriculture, mineral extraction and fisheries and water abstraction to construction on the land for various purposes and to the use of the land for various activities such as recrea-tion and tourism, ending up with withholding the land from use, for example, in wilderness areas.

"It is possible to list every relevant activity or operation, showing the area or land-type which it affects, its incidence in time, space and degree, the nature of the effects, the main interested parties and typical examples which have occurred and been documented as showing the analysis of the problem, and some possible lines of treatment. Such a chart was constructed for Great Britain in 1963 within less than four months of part-time work by a small team; [19] it could and should be done for any territory affected by large-scale developments to provide a check and guidelines for action.

"A particular value of [this] . . . is that [it] facilitate[s] the fore-casting, analysis and appropriate treatment of environmental issues even by executives and specialists totally unfamiliar with such questions. At present, many of those taking decisions on land use and land manage-ment do not know where to seek advice before it is too late. As a result, there has been a widespread failure to commission surveys and re-searches which could indicate how to diagnose and treat chronic prob-lems such as deforestation, over-grazing, destructive burning, and the triggering off of erosion and siltation. Certain countries, such as Tunisia, have had maps prepared indicating areas of actual and potential soil erosion. In Tunisia it was recognized in 1964 by the Secretariat au Plan et á l'Economie Nationale that sound economic planning in rural areas called for the systematic presentation of key ecological factors in the form of photo-ecological maps on a fairly large scale (basically 1:200,000) accompanied by explanatory handbooks." [20]

To make this new ecological approach effective Mr. Nicholson recommends a very large increase in the training of competent experts in ecology and the social sciences.

"It is clear that the world needs a small network of international ecological stations to do for the various great biomes (such as tundra, grassland, desert, tropical savanna, tropical forest, and coniferous forest) what leading marine stations such as Naples and Woods Hole have long since done for the oceans. Efforts currently being made to establish the nucleus of this essential research network are crippled by the total absence of effective interest and support on the part of the United Nations agencies and of most of the great foundations.

"Furthermore, it is now practicable to cover the earth with a series of key stations where most ecologically significant conditions are adequately recorded on a standard basis and changes regularly monitored on land safeguarded against change of use in the permanent interests of science and development. It is one of the objects of the International Biological Program to create the necessary conditions for such a network and to bring a nucleus of it into operation, with the backing of an international data bank and processing center using modern computer facilities. . . .

"Another urgent need is to create in the main agencies concerned with development small liaison points to bridge the gap between the conduct of surveys and decision making (usually regardless of environmental factors) and the available expertise, varying from instance to instance, which needs to be harnessed into teamwork. Economics, engineering, agricultural and other forms of expertise are already admitted to the magic circle but not ecology and other environmental professions." [21]

CHAPTER THREE

TRADE AND LIQUIDITY

The Debate

THE INTERNATIONAL CONTEXT

The starting point for the Conference debate on trade and liquidity, investment, and aid was, inevitably, the world market system as it actually operates today. Orthodox analysis holds that the developed nations grew by seeking maximum productivity within an Adam Smithian world where a creative and efficient division of labor is achieved by pursuing comparative advantage both nationally and internationally. Therefore, the traditionalists say, today's developing nations can follow the same route, with due attention to price and efficiency; like Canada or Sweden, they can move from primary exports to import substitution and on to the export of manufactures within a conveniently expanding network of international commerce and exchange.

But this view of the development process is based on a number of assumptions. The first is historical continuity in developmental experience—Western Europe and America yesterday; Japan, Mexico, Southern Europe, the Soviet bloc today; and you, the developing nations, tomorrow, all hastening over the same route to the final felicity of full-scale development.

The second assumption is that both the local and the international markets, with their price signals registering the realities of demand and supply, will provide the best guide to the development process, since what cannot be produced and sold at a profit provides no margin for reinvestment and rising productivity.

The third assumption is that the world market is, on the whole, a fluid place in which goods, capital, manpower, and ideas can move freely to achieve the optimum "mix" of factors of production and, hence, the optimum growth of real resources.

But, as most participants tended to agree, the first and second assumptions depend mainly on the third; and that is simply a myth. It is a myth first of all because of the world's wholly irrational division into supposedly sovereign states. These may include a whole world, like China, or be no more than a faint appendage to a mineral deposit, like Mauretania or Gabon. But each claims the right to make what it can of "comparative advantage." As a system they pose, in the words of Harry G. Johnson, the fundamental problem of "reconciling the traditional and anachronistic conception of the 'isolated state' with the economic—and political—facts of a rapidly integrating world in which there is increasing mobility of goods, capital, labor (at least educated labor), and knowledge. In the long run, we shall have to become one world politically as well as economically." (See "The Multinational Corporation as an Agency of Economic Development" in chapter 4.)

Professor Johnson's parenthesis—"at least educated labor"— points to the second element of myth. Today's migration policies, by which developed nations draw in the educated brainpower of the Third World and close their doors to the unskilled, are simply one part of the world's general imbalance of power and opportunity.

It is necessary to insist a little on the issue of increasing imbalance, even though its relevance to domestic transformation has already been stressed in the previous chapters. It dominated the whole debate. For some, the fact of an unbalanced world economy was seen simply as current reality, the world as Western man's hard effort and technological drive have fashioned it. They did not deny the remarkable lopsidedness of the international market's division of wealth, investment, commerce, services, and research. In each case, at least 80% of the world's resources are controlled by the 20% of its people who live in already developed lands. But they argued that the division simply represents the pattern of progress, intellectual capacity, dedicated effort, and attention to comparative advantage which has brought some nations to modernization ahead of others. It is now up to the laggards to follow the same route, and, encouragingly enough, countries such as Taiwan and Korea and Greece are showing every sign of succeeding.

Especially in the New York discussions, participants from government and business, aware of the pressure of decision making amid the daily realities of the current world, tended to see existing conditions as "normal," either requiring no more than relatively small readjustments or certain to resist any change at all. From this perspective the proposals of the Pearson Report could already be judged to be on the radical side. Moreover, some argued that any more basic reforms would be self-defeating since they would contravene the underlying economic conditions of operating a successful market system.

It is hardly necessary to underline the gap between these views and those of the more radical participants. For them the "realist" attitude, compounded of historical self-satisfaction and dubious economic orthodoxy, simply disregards other realities that lie deeper than the present surface of international relations. They argue that the Western powers secured their domination not by the laws of the market but by a particular sequence of world conquest and land occupation. They secured their 80% control in the eighteenth and nineteenth centuries and then constructed a theory of the world market based upon their "right" to send their capital and their goods wherever they chose—the free trade argument—which was precisely designed to keep that control by inhibiting the development of anyone else. Within their own economies, this devotion to the market was not so apparent. America, Germany, and Japan all developed behind whatever protective controls seemed to be required by self-interest. It was the defenseless colonial world that had to carry the full brunt of free trade with its *assumption* of comparative advantage and its *reality* of the advantage operating only in favor of the powerful and developed.

At the Conference the radical critics were even prepared to doubt whether the developed nations could be genuinely ignorant of these disproportions in power or of the degree to which they operate against the interests of the Third World. "Look at the historical record," they said, in effect. "The Japanese knew what they were doing when they excluded European traders in the seventeenth century. You Americans broke with Britain to escape from its restrictive trade system in the eighteenth. The Russians went their own way in 1928. In each case, they were acting to protect their own ability to develop. You cannot construct a true partnership between unequals. When you talk of partnership, we still see domination, the continuance of a near-colonial relationship which you consider ended simply because your analysis of colonialism excludes most of its economic and social substratum. What you call an open international economic system is still, in the main, the reflection of your moment of historical conquest, of the rules you drew up and imposed when, briefly, your interests organized the world."

This, then, was the division of opinion in the debates at Williamsburg and, still more vividly, at New York. To those participants who did not question or saw no hope of modifying the status quo, the proposals of the Pearson Report already go much further than realism would suggest. At the other end of the spectrum, the radical critics, mostly younger participants from both developed and developing states, derived their argument precisely from the "unreformability" of the whole system. They called for a "clean break"—cutting off trade; rejecting aid; building closed, planned, development regions in which power, policy, and resources would be under authentic local control. Between these two outer limits the majority moved toward a center point, more radical than the Pearson Report, less uncompromising than the outlook of the radicals—in short, the views ultimately brought together in the Columbia Declaration.

INTERNATIONAL TRADE

The discussions on growth and structural change in developing countries had already established the critical role played by exports in making possible a sustained expansion in the local industrial sector. The starting point of the debate on international trade was, therefore, the degree to which the present structure of the world market, with the overwhelming predominance of its developed members, does or does not give the less developed states scope for rapid growth.

Some participants followed W. Arthur Lewis in stressing the phenominal postwar growth in world trade—an expansion of never less than 7% a year, rising at times to a remarkable 15%. How could one speak of lack of scope against such a background? Many participants, however, argued that most of the advantage had, in fact, flowed to the already developed states. The share of the less developed nations in world trade, although larger in absolute terms, had in fact fallen relatively from 34% in 1950 to 22% by 1965. In the crucial area of manufactured exports, it still amounted to less than 10%, and much of this was provided by such wholly atypical economies as that of Hong Kong. Take oil away and even the primary sector looks much less flourishing.

One explanation—which secured considerable agreement—followed the analysis of secular changes in the pattern of Atlantic demand put forward by Ragnar Nurkse and applied in detail to Latin America by Raúl Prebisch. In the developed world, a lower growth of population has been coupled with a scientific revolution which permits better use of resources and encourages the invention of substitutes. This combination has tended to reduce the thrust of demand for many primary products. In the developing lands, on the contrary, the need for industrial imports is not only a precondition of industrialization. The need increases sharply during the period of early import substitution. The papers of both Stanislaw Wellisz (see Chapter 1) and Paul Streeten and Akbar Noman (in this chapter) brought out this dependence very clearly in the case of the largest underdeveloped area—the Indian subcontinent. Thus, the competitive balance is almost wholly on the side of the industrial exporters, and one reason for the tendency of the terms of trade to turn against developing lands is simply that they are always selling in a buyer's market. Local gains in productivity and efficiency (for instance, Ghana's doubling of its cocoa crop in the early 1960's through the use of better plants and pesticides) are simply passed on to the rich states as a result of the lower prices that are paid to the local producer.

At the same time, developing states have to buy in a seller's market, often at an inflation-induced rate. Gains in the efficiency of the product can offset this to some extent. Yet, insofar as efficiency in capital goods can take the form of making possible further economies in the use of labor, it may not be a form of "efficiency" for which developing states are very anxious to pay.

The central point of difficulty lies in the balance of bargaining power in a market governed by such very different elasticities of demand. As Reginald Green put it in a statement to the Conference:

[for the developing nations] the basic problem . . . is one of income elasticities. . . . Exports are dominantly made up of products with income elasticities greater than unity and imports of manufactures with income elasticities greater than unity. Therefore, taking the *tiers monde* as a whole, exports can be expected to rise by less than industrial [developed] economy product and imports to rise faster than developing economy product. If industrial economy growth averages 6% and population increase 2%, then its imports from the *tiers monde* may grow by 4% to 5% a year, ignoring price changes. That rate would allow a 2% to 4% growth rate for the *tiers monde* economies consistent with external balance, assuming net capital inflows (after current servicing including dividends and capital repayment or repatriation) rose at the same rate. (The actual net capital flow picture is much worse.) In this highly simplified analysis lies the case of the bleak prospects for free trade leading to development in the latter half of the twentieth century except for industrial economies which—by definition—are already classifiable as reasonably developed.

This basic view of the difficulty was generally accepted, although a number of participants, particularly in New York, felt that it took too pessimistic a view of what a developing nation could itself do to diversify and increase its exports, once it had made export promotion a central policy. Pakistan, Colombia, Korea, and Taiwan were cited as examples of successful growers and diversifiers. To this, some critics replied that, to judge by past behavior, more success on these lines would simply impel developed states toward even more active policies of self-protection.

At this point the debate reached the crux of the argument between the majority and the minority who, on the whole, think that the present international economy is working reasonably well and that any tampering with it could prove unproductive. But what kind of normality have you in mind? asked the majority. If it includes, as you say it does, free flows of resources, guided by profitability and comparative advantage, then you must admit that it is largely fiction. You do not yourselves practice this orthodoxy. Free trade simply yields to national self-interest.

The manifold instances of this self-interest were thoroughly aired during the debate. Critics of the present system pointed out on what scale and over how many different fields discrimination could be said to exercise a dominant influence. In the case of agricultural products, they cited Europe's excise duties on coffee, cocoa, and tea. They described Atlantic "free trade" monstrosities, such as subsidized exports of uncompetitive beet sugar, which, on one calculation, cost the developing world a billion dollars a year. On the side of manufactures, they brought up the Atlantic tariff structure which has had a built-in bias against manufactured imports, and which now, as a result of the Kennedy Round, works with particular hardship in the case of primary producers beginning to process their own materials. (The Kennedy Round, it will be recalled, introduced all but zero tariffs for most manufactures except those based on the intensive use of labor or raw materials—in other words, precisely those manufactures that are most interesting to the developing world.) They cited the bias in market organization, for instance, the total domination of developed nations in all service industries and the persistence of regional economic organizations (such as the European Common Market's association with Africa) which freezes the dependence of the less developed members.

Even theory did not escape. How but by unconscious discrimination can one explain the curious convolutions of trade orthodoxy which allow tariff protection for infant industries, yet frown on export subsidies or multiple exchange rates? These, as Professor Streeten and Mr. Noman pointed out in their paper, could have the same effect with infinitely less damaging impact on the local price level.

From all this, a large majority drew the conclusion that developing states have little hope of breaking through to industrialization and full development by way of so-called free trade in the world market. Only if special measures for trade expansion are adopted, will they be able to achieve the growth in exports they require for any rapid breakthrough to industrial growth and modernization.

In this, of course, there was no quarrel with the proposals of the Pearson Report. Its trade recommendations are clearly radical, quite possibly too radical for orthodox opinion. They include the abolition of excise and import duties on non-competing products important to developing lands, an organized effort to allot developing countries a firm share in the growth of the industrial powers' domestic demand, support for commodity agreements, an end to quotas, general non-reciprocal preferences for the manufactured exports of developing lands, and a variety of measures to increase trade within the Third World—for instance, mutual preferences, a clearing agreement backed by the International Monetary Fund, and a preliminary untying of aid in favor of developing suppliers (Pearson Report, p. 97).

Clearly these recommendations, if carried through, would genuinely widen the developing nations' access to developed markets. The proposals would considerably reduce the unequal bargaining power of the developing nations, give reasonable hope that exports could become a genuine means of growth, and restore some reality to the concept of "comparative advantage." In fact, the quarrel of the Conference majority—if it was a quarrel—was not so much with these proposals as with the Report's underplaying of the difficulty of securing them. Some argued that a little more might have been said about the extraordinary blandness of the developed states' pursuit of self-interest. They talk seriously of comparative advantage, of the risks of domestic inflation, of the dangers of ever-rising costs of living. And, as James Mirrlees pointed out in his paper, "in a sane world, the developed countries would be searching the world for the cheapest sources of imports." (See "The Terms of Trade," in this chapter.)

But are they in fact out scouring the planet for cheaper goods, for supplies which would lighten the housewives' burden? On the contrary, it is precisely food, textiles, clothes, and shoes which appear on every list of restrictions and quotas. Developing countries are solemnly told to set up funds to diversify production away from sugar and groundnuts and coffee and tea. But the funds and levies and subsidies in the industrial countries are designed to diversify agriculture *into* such uncompetitive products as rice and beet. The response to pressure from cheap foreign textiles is not a phased withdrawal, *à la* Massachusetts, from this low-profit, low-wage industry into more efficient alternatives. The cry is for still further protection. And these are but the most blatant examples of a "heads I win, tails you lose" method of playing the game of international trade.

However, as André Philip pointed out, the reason for this stubborn twisting of the rules lies in the political impossibility of accepting the full consequences of free trade without radical readjustments within even the most competitive and industrialized economies. "The modern class struggle, the deep conflict of interests, is not between the Third World countries and capitalist firms, which will always be able to dispose of their equipment, but between the developing countries and the craftsmen, peasants, and industrial workers who in our countries represent the marginal undertakings and would be eliminated by competition from the underdeveloped countries."

True free trade cannot protect the marginal man, whether he is in a declining industry in a developed country or caught in the preindustrial stage of a developing economy. Policies are required to safeguard and develop the interests of both, and this can be done only by *joint* approaches in which policy changes in developed and developing countries are geared to one another so that the clash of interest is reduced to a minimum and planned growth quickly absorbs the unavoidable shocks of change. To quote Mr. Philip again:

This means that [commercial] aid to the Third World is impossible in the context of a liberal economic policy. There can be no question of speedily abolishing quotas and customs dues, for this would lead to violent revolt from the producers in the industrialized countries. Adjustment can be made only in the context of a generalized system of preferences, retaining barriers against exports, particularly agricultural products, from other industrialized countries but guaranteeing to the Third World countries only, by long-term agreements at stabilized prices, entry to our markets for an increasing proportion of the growth of our consumption in each main category or sector. This calls in the industrialized countries for a long-term plan, structural reforms, and financial compensation, within the framework of an agreed economic policy which will insure the regular growth of national product.

Little on this scale of elaboration is hinted at in the Pearson Report. Perhaps, therefore, one could best sum up the chief Conference criticism of the Report's proposals on trade by saying that they underestimate the need for a really far-reaching joint approach to the reform of the whole context of international trade. They also do little to suggest the extreme political difficulty of securing it.

This, in turn, set the direction of the radicals' attack. What, they argued, could be more naive, more irrationally optimistic, than to suppose such a degree of self-reformation to be possible among the powerful and the rich? At present, it should be recognized that the trend is in the other direction—toward more rigid quotas, greater protection in the developed states, more uneconomic competition offered by their subsidized primary exports. Moreover, even if they were readier to practice a less biased version of "free trade," it would still present acute dangers to the developing world. To increase the dependence of their economies on the rhythm of growth in developed states may not have had disastrous consequences in the long boom of the 1950's and 1960's. But will developed economies have the wit to sustain 5% to 6% growth through what promises to be the more difficult decade of the 1970's? Are the

1920's and the 1930's to be dismissed as unrepeatable? If not, how can developing states avoid the blizzard?

Most radical of all was the criticism outlined in Samir Amin's paper (see Chapter 5) and supported by a number of other participants. He asked, in essence, if the developing states would have any long-term interest in moving into the labor-intensive industries as the developed world moved out of them? In his own words:

We are at present undergoing a large-scale scientific and technical revolution; the industries of the future (automation, electronics, atomic energy, and space exploration) are based on the relatively massive employment of skilled labor as opposed to the "classical" concept of industry based on the large-scale employment of unskilled labor. A new form of international specialization would arise, reserving the advanced industries for the center, freeing it from the unrewarding tasks of "classical" industry and assigning these to the peripheral areas. This would step up development at the center and accentuate the gap between it and the peripheral areas.

This, in short, was the core of the radical attack. The developing nations cannot allow themselves to continue as "hewers of wood and drawers of water" for the industrialized economies. They must break their shackles. They must establish their own large, planned development areas, build up their own capital, trade on their own terms, band with fellow producers to secure monopoly prices where they are strong enough to do so, withhold their supplies where boycotts are effective, and systematically redirect their own trade to their developing neighbors. The paradigm for the Third World is not Canada, not Sweden, not Korea, not Taiwan. It is Japan turning out the Europeans, or Soviet Russia turning out the capitalists. Any other policy, the radicals insisted, simply implies continuing indefinitely the old colonial bonds.

THE PROBLEM OF LIQUIDITY

The unfavorable competitive position of the developing countries in world trade is, inevitably, reflected in the inadequacy of their reserves. As the Pearson Report points out, reserves in the 1960's have generally fallen very sharply since the boom days of World War II and the Korean War (see particularly Table 3–3, p. 70 of the Report). Many developing countries are operating on reserves that do not represent much more than the equivalent of two months' imports and that may be reduced by price fluctuations which can vary by as much as 15% in a single year. As Professor Streeten and Mr. Noman's paper made clear, this is a crippling inhibition on governments attempting to plan for growth and modernization.

As an important element in this basic trade-induced stringency, we should not forget "invisibles," since virtually 90% of the services required in commerce are provided by developed countries. Indeed, Laurence Whitehead estimated that payments on services from Latin America in the 1960's comfortably exceeded any figure for aid. (See "The Aid Relationship in Latin America" in this chapter.) Now it is true that one rising source of invisible earnings—tourism—is not a monopoly of the wealthy world. The Honourable Philip Ndegwa had reminded the Conference of its importance in the African context (see Chapter 1). Certainly it helps a number of Latin American countries, notably Mexico, to take pressure off the balance of payments. Indeed, Hollis B. Chenery suggested in his paper (see Chapter 1) that, for some areas, a healthy income from tourism might permit a country to bypass the early phase of specializing on primary exports and move more directly to industrialization. However, most participants felt that it could not satisfactorily offset the drain from the rest of the service industries. Moreover, in many countries the whole apparatus of tourism—hotels, tours, travel—is foreign-owned.

The balance of payments is also directly affected by the growing weight of debt. As the Pearson Report points out, the external public debt of developing lands grew from some $20 billion in 1961 to nearly $50 billion in 1968. In some of the largest countries, debt service already absorbs more than 15% of annual export earnings. To this must be added repayments on private investment which, in the case of the larger Latin American countries, puts the percentage up above 25%. All in all it is a gloomy picture, particularly in Latin America. It will be gloomier still if further sharp declines in concessionary finance become the pattern of the 1970's.

The proposals of the Pearson Commissioners have little to say directly on the issue of liquidity, although they support such existing initiatives as the schemes developed both in the IMF and the World Bank to offset fluctuations in export earnings. They also suggest that financial assistance should be given to regional development banks and payments unions whose tasks include the encouragement of local trade. Moreover, they ask whether alternative financing should not be provided when limits are set—as they must be set—to the all but uncontrollable growth of high-cost export credits which have nearly quadrupled in the 1960's. But the chief emphasis is on the handling of debt. Here governments are encouraged to use aid as a form of debt relief, negotiating new loans to pay off old ones and limiting all future assistance loans to an interest rate of no more than 2% with a maturity of twenty-five to forty years and a grace period of seven to ten years.

Once again, the Conference did not quarrel with the Report's proposals. On the contrary, they were accepted as a healthy advance. But the same desire emerged to go further than the Report. There was also the same uneasiness about the degree to which the solutions proposed depend on the good will and good sense of the already rich. Here the concept of "automaticity" began to appear in the dialogue. Would it not be possible, in some degree, to withdraw development finance from the political vagaries of annual parliamentary debate, and might not assistance to liquidity be a sensible place to begin? For instance, could not debt repayments be placed for a time in a revolving fund from which new assistance would be made available? The Pearson Report, incidentally, suggests that such a device might be used to subsidize interest payments made by developing nations. Could the pressure on the reserves be reduced by the understanding that aid given in kind—including tied aid—should be repaid in goods or local currency? Above all—and this point finally dominated the discussions on liquidity—might not a direct link be established between any future creation of Special Drawing Rights and the Third World's need for development finance? After all, the developed nations had just voted an annual $3.5 billion of new monetary resources into existence "out of thin air." Only they had voted themselves into nearly three-quarters of them. Could not a more equitable distribution be established for the future? Robert Triffin developed this issue with the statement "Development and Special Drawing Rights" (printed later in this chapter).

On this central issue of the link between SDRs and development finance, opinion followed the usual divisions of the Conference. Some participants were concerned over what they felt to be a careless invitation to continuous inflation and a dangerous lack of control over monetary expansion. If SDRs were detached from the authority of the financially orthodox, might they not lose their essential quality of acceptability as reserves? Then they would help no one—neither poor nor rich.

In his speech to the Conference, Pierre-Paul Schweitzer, managing director of the IMF, did not take up this point directly. But he stressed the indirect link between the creation of the SDRs and the hope of making more aid available to development. He said that the rich nations now had less excuse for ungenerous behavior:

Industrial countries will be enabled, through the assurances of adequate reserves, to maintain appropriate levels of economic activity and more adequate flows of capital to the developing world. Any threat of reserve stringency in the industrial countries would be likely to lead to policies aimed at restraining capital exports and depressing the demand for imports, with consequent adverse effects on the terms and volume of trade of the primary producing countries. The flow of SDRs should make it more acceptable for larger surplus countries to suffer a reduction in their current account surpluses and thus minimize the burden of adjustment on the developing countries. In this way, these countries can be insulated from the adverse effects of the measures which are so necessary to curb inflation in the industrial countries at the present time.

The bulk of Conference opinion, however, firmly supported the concept of an SDR link to development aid, possibly through the International Development Agency, certainly through multilateral channels. Moreover, there was a measure of general uneasiness about the implications of the rich nations awarding themselves the lion's share of any newly created wealth. On the issue of inflation—which was not taken up in the discussion to any very great degree—at least some of the participants wondered whether warnings of its risks, without mention of the $180 million a year spent on that most inflationary of all activities, war, might not represent a somewhat restricted view of the real origins of pressure.

The Terms of Trade:
Pearson on Trade Policy, Debt, and Liquidity

BY JAMES A. MIRRLEES

Most of us can agree that trading opportunities between developed and developing countries invite further exploitation. Most of us would like to see the people of the developing countries obtain the major share of benefits arising from such exploitation. The developed countries can gain too: there is an important sense in which they can benefit, as a whole, from making fuller use of the products of developing countries. Reductions in taxes, tariffs, quotas, and other restrictions on imports from developing countries can benefit developed and developing countries alike. It is to be expected, therefore, that the Pearson Commission's recommendations should emphasize these opportunities for encouraging and expanding trade (Pearson Report, p. 97). The essential point is that the developing countries can gain—and some of them can gain substantially—from improvements in the terms on which they can trade with the developed countries.

These major arguments for trade expansion do not always play a large part in the management of international trade and finance. Short-term problems cannot be ignored. Indeed, the Commissioners show concern at recurring balance of payments crises, which, on both sides, appear to discourage the expansion of trade and reduction of protection.[1] They also devote some attention to the medium-term problem of fluctuations in export prices and foreign exchange earnings, which have often excited strong feelings, and balance of payments crises.

This paper is an attempt to see what kinds of policies follow from general economic principles, so as to place the Pearson Commission's recommendations in perspective, and to identify the proposals that deserve most emphatic support in the long run. The three main sections are devoted to short-term crises, measures for stabilizing incomes, and trade policy. Finally, the main shortcomings of attempts to help development through trade are mentioned.

The importance to the developing countries of trade policy has frequently been exaggerated, but it is far from negligible. These opportunities should not, in the general concern for direct assistance and capital flows, be neglected.

CRISES

A "balance of payments crisis" occurs when there is substantial undesired borrowing from abroad, or running down of reserves by the government, or extensive underutilization of capacity (without which a large inflow of capital or reduction in reserves would be necessary). Such a crisis is a signal for action of some kind—if possible. Action might be taken in advance, so that "crises" never occur. But that action could be just as damaging as action taken after the actual crisis. For example, one of the ways in which the developed countries adjust their balance of payments is by varying the degree of protection.[2] By this means some avoid crises, but they—and other countries—may suffer as much as if they allowed crises to happen occasionally.

The main problem, then, is the adjustment mechanisms that are used to avoid crises. So long as deflation, protection, and diminished growth play a considerable role in the adjustments, the developing countries will be worse off than under a system in which liquidity and exchange rate (or money wage) variations take the strain. This is not the place to discuss whether such a superior system of international exchange can be devised and established. But we should consider how the developing countries might benefit from it.

In the first place, countries that are not troubled by the balance of payments might be more willing to commit themselves to aid. Casual inspection of the data suggests that countries which care less about the balance of payments have increased their aid fastest. Growth seems to have the same effect.

Second, the cost of trade liberalization would be less if its impact on the balance of payments could be neglected. It is tempting to suppose that all aid could then be untied. But tying is a way of subsidizing particular domestic industries: the motives for tying would be somewhat weakened, but certainly not eliminated.

Third, more rapid growth by the industrial countries—if that would indeed follow from a new system of international exchange—might benefit the developing countries by increasing demand for their products.

Each of these possibilities deserves a slightly skeptical look. There is no obvious reason why increased aid or freeing of trade should bring about a balance of payments deficit for the developed countries as a whole, provided that the developing countries take measures to avoid balance of payments surplus. I think they can generally be trusted to do that—to spend the aid or increased earnings from trade. The problem is that unilateral action by a single developed country may cause it balance of payments difficulties. May it not be possible to devise a scheme to remove that problem, in advance of a complete reform of international exchange adjustment procedures? For example, automatic increase of International Monetary Fund (IMF) drawing rights, corresponding to proven deterioration of the balance of payments arising from aid increases or liberalization of imports from developing countries, would go far to remove the difficulty. Such a scheme, like any proposal for increased drawing rights, implies that some countries may have to bear part of the cost—at least temporarily—of expenditures undertaken by others. But liability under the scheme could be limited, say to 0.5% or less of GNP per year, with fixed repayment obligations. In any case, the proposal is designed to encourage general liberalization, so that the final effect on any particular country's balance of payments would probably be small. If the balance of payments problem is thought to be a serious one, limited schemes of this kind deserve consideration.

It is hard to assess precisely the possible effect on the growth of the industrial economies of improvements in exchange arrangements. But the probable increase in exports arising from such additional growth during the next decade must be rather small. The benefits to the developing countries from the increased exports would be even less important. Large increases in demand would be necessary before the developing countries reaped any large advantage, if the prices paid by the developed countries for these exports do little more than cover the cost of producing them. ("Cost" has to be defined carefully: an appropriate measure of social cost is what I have in mind. There is room for dispute about the social cost of primary commodities, particularly of the labor inputs required. I would want to beware of undervaluing these labor inputs.)

While protection often increases the prices of exports above their costs, subsidies are also common in the developing countries. It would be rash to guess that these countries have much to gain from marginal increases in exports, at existing prices. On the other hand, in the long run, the benefits from rapid world growth may be substantial, particularly for countries that are endowed with fixed supplies of valuable land or mineral resources. Meanwhile, more is to be expected from the increased generosity that growth might encourage.

Probably the developing countries have more to gain from improving the management of their own crises. The treatment of these crises is, to some extent, in the hands of aid-giving countries and agencies. The methods used for controlling these crises and, even more important, the criteria used in assessing them, are basic to the "development partnership."

Usually crises show up in the balance of payments, just as they do for developed countries. It does not follow that "shortage of foreign exchange" is necessarily the cause, or that devaluation is necessarily the solution. This is not to say that classically overvalued currencies do not occur. Many of the developing countries have had money wage rates rising rapidly while keeping the exchange rate fixed. Some have been content with unnecessary unemployment and, having no very serious balance of payments difficulties, failed to devalue. In other cases, a crisis has occurred where wage rates (in real terms) cannot be reduced for any length of time. Then acceptance of reality, not devaluation, is likely to be a more sensible policy.

The point I have in mind is well known. A balance of payments deficit occurs when total expenditure—consumption and investment, public and private, domestic and foreign demands—exceeds the value of sales by more than the net amount that the government willingly allows to be borrowed from abroad. Consider the following (simplified) special circumstances under which such a crisis can happen:

1. There is excess productive capacity in the economy, but domestic demand tends to prefer foreign sources of supply. Domestic industry is "not competitive enough." The value of sales can be increased by reducing costs, particularly the cost of employing labor (provided the economy is producing commodities that are sufficiently ready substitutes for foreign-produced commodities). It looks as though devaluation would be effective.

2. There is no excess productive capacity, but the government would prefer lower public expenditure or greater taxation, having

avoided them merely to maintain full-capacity working of the economy. This is basically the same case as the previous one. The desired changes in fiscal policy, combined with devaluation, seem to be appropriate. Expenditure will be reduced and switched to domestic producers to the extent necessary.

3. There is no excess productive capacity. The government does not want to reduce public expenditure, and it cannot, or believes it cannot, reduce private expenditure by increased taxation or otherwise. In particular, the real expenditure of wage earners cannot be reduced by means of devaluation; they will achieve compensating money-wage increases rapidly. There may or may not be inflation. But, in a sense, demand is excessive.

4. There is excess productive capacity and unemployment of labor, but increased production would increase expenditure (on current inputs and through the expenditure of newly employed labor) by as much as sales. Demands cannot be reduced.

The last two cases are not uncharacteristic. In the last case, the production-encouraging policy of devaluation is not appropriate under the stated conditions. Nor is it made appropriate in case (3) by first reducing expenditure; that will cure the deficit, although it will cause unemployment.

In fact, of course, expenditures can be reduced in these latter cases —and if no external help is available, they have to be. They can be reduced by bringing about unemployment in the more remunerative occupations. Since policies designed to achieve this end also reduce production and sales, total production—the total income of the economy— may have to be reduced by much more than the balance of payments deficit. Although there may be dispute whether it is ever true, in the relevant sense, that other expenditure-reducing policies—taxation of the middle classes, or even industrial workers—are impossible, it must be agreed that, even in an ideally operated economy, laborers have to consume in order to work, and to some extent it is desirable that they should consume well in order to work well. In low-income economies, these constraints may be very important. At the same time, depending upon the political system, higher incomes for certain groups may be a condition for their cooperation in or support of the economy and policy of the country: tax collectors must be well paid to reduce corruption, doctors to reduce migration, workers to reduce industrial disruption. While external pressure to increase taxation is most desirable, I am persuaded that there are genuine constraints, which must be very difficult for developing governments to deal with.

When that is true, the crisis can only be avoided, in the short run, by reduction in expenditure: civil servants dismissed, factories shut down. Devaluation may not achieve that end and is unlikely to do it efficiently. What has to be done in a crisis is to change production (and incomes) in the economy so as to be consistent with the real constraints —including the given flow of external capital—and to organize it in the "best" way consistent with these constraints. Devaluation may be appropriate in the first two cases because it helps to change production activities (and consumption decisions) in the desirable direction. The purpose of devaluation is to reduce the prices of domestic resources relative to foreign goods; if the value of domestic resources is already correctly reflected in relative prices, devaluation is beside the point. The existence of a balance of payments deficit is not necessarily an indication that domestic resources are overvalued. Cases (3) and (4) are examples of that. When industry, and therefore industrial labor, is overprotected—which seems to have happened quite often, as the Commission recognizes (Pearson Report, p. 37)—devaluation would be quite wrong (except as part of a general reform of trade taxes and subsidies); employment has to be discouraged, not encouraged.

The proper assessment of a crisis is rather hard, since it is equivalent to a determination of the optimum use of existing resources for the country in question. In general, we must expect a crisis to indicate that the productive ability of the country—its true income—has, for some reason, turned out to be substantially less than had been hoped. A serious fall in the price of a major export crop may force the government to cut its expenditure; or industrial projects may turn out to be less productive than had been predicted; or a bad harvest may lead the government to divert expenditure from capital goods to food imports. Whenever the government is slow or reluctant to recognize the fact that income has fallen, a crisis will emerge. Fiercely protective measures may be adopted, which can be effective only by reducing the total expenditure of those who purchase the taxed commodities, or by forcing the reduced employment that has become necessary. Such increased trade restriction may well have undesirable long-term effects.

Any action the developed countries then take should be such as to encourage a realistic assessment of the situation and to discourage undesirable protective measures. Is there any case for special aid to a country in such a position? In that there is a downward fluctuation in the country's "true" income, I believe there is a strong case for special help. But one would not like to see the additional aid being used as a means to avoid the adjustments whose necessity has become apparent. No one benefits if aid is used to finance inputs into factories that have turned out to be hopelessly inefficient, or to feed their laborers when they would be better employed digging irrigation ditches. A crisis offers a strong incentive to reconsider economic decisions. The incentive should not be blunted. At the same time, reconsideration takes time, and too rapid adjustment has costs: short-term liquidity could be of great value. There is no obvious reason why the availability of such liquidity—the IMF is the obvious source—should be conditional upon "good behavior." There is, after all, no guarantee that the IMF will be capable of the complex economic audit that is necessary to determine which policies would make sense. But the liquidity can properly be expensive. Better by far to have strict repayment provisions for the loan, well-defined conditions for the right to a loan (depending on total outstanding short-term debt, and a generous definition of allowable circumstances), and strong penalties for default. The developing countries would surely prefer such arrangements.

I conclude, then, that short-term liquidity rights should be as automatic as possible in a crisis *for a short period only,* but that a full-scale *economic audit* may then be required, and that further allocations of aid ought to be determined in the light of it. The economic audit has to consider the system of economic decision making, and the extent to which the crisis has been the result of mismanagement rather than unpredictable adverse circumstances. This brings us up against the problem that criteria for economic audit are by no means fully agreed upon, and that particular reports and even general principles are usually not subject to (professional) public discussion.

The Pearson Commission recognizes the importance of such audits but conceives of them rather as annual reviews. Its treatment of the principles on which they should be based seems to me inadequate and, as far as it goes, misguided. "Financial independence" is seen as the aim: most developing countries could achieve that rather rapidly—at a cost. Must the ratio of imports to exports always fall? How will they measure saving? Exactly how do they want aid-givers to react to the estimates of saving/income and export/import ratios? What about the efficient use of resources? Determination to create savings is important and should be encouraged, no doubt. The quality of decision making, the accounting and management procedures, the use of controls and prices and taxes are at least as important, probably more so. There will be no easy "consensus" among economists or officials. But the case for an agency or commission to set down guide lines, principles, and criteria, and to discuss them publicly is surely extremely strong. While the World Bank has, in the past, done some good work in assessing programs and prospects, a wider and more systematic debate is required. Otherwise, crises are too likely to be treated like acute illnesses, when the patient must accept the all-knowing doctor's view of the correct treatment: the country must adopt the current "establishment" view, whatever that may be, even if it is inconsistent with the aims of its people.

Finally, it is worth remarking that crises are made more likely when adjustment of current policies is difficult: when capital equipment is highly specific, say, or foreign exchange reserves are very low. Shortage of reserves is particularly important; presumably many of the developing countries ought to have more. Can a country that builds up its foreign exchange reserves be sure of getting as much aid as one whose reserves are almost exhausted? On the whole, it is probably better that the reserves should be available to a country, rather than owned by it —provided that it has automatic rights to these funds in crisis conditions.

FLUCTUATIONS

Fluctuations in the national income may or may not be accompanied by balance of payments crises. If a bad harvest reduces private incomes by as much as it reduces production, expenditure may also be reduced, and no deficit arise. It can be very serious for all that. No particular virtue attaches to a government that chooses famine rather than deficit.

It is reasonable that a country should want to smooth out fluctuations in its income by some means or other. Even the inhabitants of relatively well-off countries may suffer quite seriously from reductions in income. This will be so whether the reduction arises from a fall in the prices received for exports, a monsoon failure, a fall in capital imports, or government mismanagement. Fluctuations can be ameliorated by: (1) spreading the fluctuations throughout the economy, so that the burden does not fall mainly on particular groups; (2) reducing investment expenditure in bad years, so as to maintain an even growth in consumption; (3) borrowing from abroad in bad years, paying back in good, or building up reserves.

The burden of fluctuations in export prices can be spread by means of price-support policies; for example, the producer could be paid at a price that is the average of prices during the last five years. Then the fluctuations in government income must be offset by variations in taxation. Harvest fluctuations can, at least in theory, be dealt with by some form of agricultural insurance.

The use of offsetting fluctuations in investment expenditure may not commend itself very readily; it may be too difficult to affect decisions to start investment projects quickly enough, and too costly to impose later delays. But there is always a case for considering the possibility: one should sometimes see "disastrous cutbacks in investment" as a sensible way of getting the future to pay for a rather unlucky present. When most controllable investment projects are financed by aid, there is no advantage in the method, of course.

While some developing countries have occasionally suffered very severe fluctuations, there are few where fluctuations of total income have been regularly very violent. If measures for spreading the burden among groups and over time had been effective, these fluctuations might not merit much attention, as against the prospects for growth.[3] But concern about fluctuations in the world prices of primary commodities persists, and the Commission gives its blessing to "well-conceived" buffer stock schemes, as well as to schemes for supplementary finance in cases of unexpected and sustained shortfalls in export earnings (Pearson Report, p. 97). I believe that the latter recommendation merits more support than the former.

Buffer stocks are, on the face of it, a waste of resources—except that they may replace stocks previously held by producers or consumers. Since stabilization of prices is sought, it must be presumed that an increase in total stocks of the commodity is wanted. Could not the same ends be achieved without this useless store of commodities? The obvious way is by paying a stabilized price to the producers, while allowing the market price to continue to fluctuate; this would be possible if finance were available. Would such a scheme be a worthwhile investment for the developing countries? (If not, they would be better off with an alternative form of aid.) In other words, would the developing countries benefit if, by some means, they insured one another against fluctuations in these export prices? I think they probably would. The difficulty is to find good rules for determining the prices to be paid to the producing countries. The buffet stock has similar problems, however, and reduces the risks of buyers without being paid for the service.

A simpler solution—although not an easy one to achieve—might be a scheme that "insures" against below-trend fluctuations in national income. The difficulties of such a scheme are fairly obvious: agreed assessments of the prospects of different countries cannot be obtained, and as a result it might be impossible to agree on terms. Another possibility is more inviting. The developed countries, being so rich, can bear risk with less cost to themselves than can the developing countries. It would be reasonable for them to bear the risks represented by fluctuations in the incomes of the developing countries. If they did so for many countries simultaneously, they would, in effect, be providing the desired insurance. They could take part of the risk upon themselves by appropriate arrangements for debt repayment. At present the developed countries and multilateral agencies lend at fixed interest. It should not matter much to them in which years interest payments and loan repayments are made, so long as they are not, on average, postponed beyond the presently agreed schedules; especially if fluctuations in different economies do not entirely coincide.

The Commission shows some interest in the "Bisque scheme," under which the borrower has the right to make a number of postponements of repayments, but it expresses faith that "other methods we have recommended will go a long way toward meeting short-term difficulties" (Pearson Report, p. 159). I am not persuaded that it goes far enough in its other recommendations, but a "Bisque clause" does have serious disadvantages. The advantages of the scheme could be obtained by relating repayments and interest payments automatically to the performance of the economy.

Many schemes of this kind can be devised. Payments by the debtor can be related to the outstanding amount of the debt, so that, in a year of average performance, a country that has been doing well previously and, therefore, has a lower debt than was expected pays less than one that has been doing rather badly. Then there are various ways of measuring the performance of a country. The natural one for this purpose is the growth rate of GNP. The first argument in its favor is that low or negative growth is precisely the contingency that the country should be "insured" against.[4] The second argument is that the growth rate is something that most governments have a strong interest in increasing. Reduction of the GNP is not a price worth paying for the right to postpone loan repayments (which will, therefore, be increased in the future, too).[5] Statistical techniques for measuring the constant price growth rate of GNP vary in quality and reliability. In a number of cases figures are not available. But, in general, there is no obvious difficulty. The donor—or, better, an independent agency for economic audit—would estimate the expected rate of growth of the borrowing country. The rules for repayments would then be determined, so as to allow for automatic overpayments and underpayments, depending upon the vicissitudes of the borrowing country.[6]

It should be emphasized that this scheme is designed to take from the developing countries a burden which imposes genuine suffering (fluctuations in incomes, whether arising from external or internal causes) and impose these fluctuations on the donor countries, who would feel them much less. The *aggregate* fluctuations in the incomes of the developing countries are, after all, rather small.

There is a good case for developing more flexible arrangements of this kind and using them, both when fixing the contractual arrangements for new loans and in the thorough rescheduling of debt which the Commission would like to see. If the "need" for repeated reschedulings is to be avoided, it will surely be necessary to build in some kind of automatic flexibility. The large debts owed by many of the developing countries provide an opportunity for creating this kind of flexibility as a means of relieving them of the worst part of their uncertainties.

TRADE

The most important of the Commission's recommendations in the field of trade are those whose aim is to improve the prices the developing countries can receive for their products and to remove restrictions on their access to certain markets. It should not be forgotten that the untying of aid is also a way of improving their terms of trade, the potential gains from which are probably comparable to those from the Commission's other recommendations.

One may guess that the chief reasons for the perpetuation of tariffs and other trade restrictions are: concern about the balance of payments; their possible value as bargaining weapons in negotiating tariff reductions by other countries; and the desire to help certain industries within the protecting country. With suitable arrangements, selective concessions, applying to the exports of developing countries, need not make the bankers' ulcers worse. Selectivity in trade concessions is a way of getting around the second point, too. The Commission recommends the elimination, as soon as possible, of restrictions and taxes on noncompeting imports, but it recognizes the attachment of governments to the protection of particular industries, especially agriculture.

In a sane world, the developed countries would be searching the globe for the cheapest sources of imports and eagerly arranging for the contraction of their own least efficient industries. A sensible buyer pays no more than he need: that is the case for freer trade, regardless of the gains to the developing countries, which are an added bonus. At the same time, legitimate ends are served by protection (sometimes at least); what is at issue is the extent to which they should be served by protection, and whether they could not be served better in other ways.

A few principles can be suggested. There are often costs associated with the contraction of an industry: employees have to look for jobs elsewhere, and they may suffer a loss in income, perhaps premature retirement, certainly a cost of moving, of building up a new life. The first principle is that the developed countries should continue, more actively than now, to seek ways of adequately compensating for these costs, so that they may be properly assessed and *incurred as soon as it pays to do so*. Second, where the costs arise from the decline of employment in a region, it makes more sense to subsidize labor in that region than to subsidize industries that happen to be concentrated there now.

Even if more intelligent ways of dealing with the real problem are found, it may still be true that certain industries are less inefficient than they appear to be. Rigid wage structures, which may have desirable effects on income distribution, make some labor appear more costly to the employer than it is to the economy. Then subsidy is reasonable, and the developing countries, correspondingly, find the market less easy than it might be. But there is no reason for such differences to last for decades.

On the face of it, everyone would gain if the principle were adopted that employment in any production activity where, in the absence of government interference, imports from the developing countries would bring about a substantial reduction in employment, should be allowed to fall by at least a certain proportion each year—3% would be a minimum figure. The experience of some of Britain's "declining industries" is indicated in Table 1.

It is hard to see exactly how one would define a satisfactory commitment to employment reduction. Yet a general obligation to prepare plans seems rather weak. The important point is that a gradual—as opposed to a sudden—reduction must be recognized as a legitimate aim, perhaps the only legitimate reason for restrictions on imports from developing countries, and that the rate of expansion of these imports should be regulated by the relevant effects (in general, changes in employment, but other effects must sometimes be allowed for). It is clear how the developing countries and purchasers in the developed country would gain. Employees in the industry would also gain from a regular and predictable decline. There are few areas in which helping the developing countries would do the people of the developed countries so much good.

TABLE 1. DECLINING EMPLOYMENT IN THREE BRITISH INDUSTRIES, 1956–1965

	Employment		
	1956	1965	Average Annual
	(in thousands)		Decrease
Coal mining	781	560	3.8%
Textiles	935	780	2.0
Agriculture	1,032	842	2.3

Source: Great Britain, Ministry of Labour, Statistics on Incomes, Prices, Employment and Production (H.M.S.O., 1966), with adjustments for comparability.

It may be argued that there are other reasons for preserving an industry: first, that foreign sources of supply are more uncertain; second, that current costs are not necessarily a good guide to the prospects of an industry that has suffered the indignities of a declining reputation. I find neither very persuasive; the second line of argument removes the grounds for all decision and leaves the country doing everything, to no one's advantage. The first argument is more appealing and, in some cases, very strong. But we should be slow to exaggerate the costs of uncertainties. If a country directs its purchases to the sources of supply that seem likely, on average, to be the cheapest, even quite large fluctuations in the prices from each may become, in the aggregate, quite small in relation to the probable benefits. The fact that the international terms of trade are "outside our control" and at the mercy of the inexplicable vagaries of foreign rains and revolutions should not hide the uncertainties that somehow creep out from under the controls the developed countries apply to themselves.

The appendix to this paper gives some projections of future exports. A number of features stand out. If the future does develop this way, manufactures will, by the end of the seventies, already occupy a large place in the exports of developing countries. In some of the non-oil-producing countries, they appear to be becoming really important already. Also, these figures represent a very great diversity among countries: oil producers continue to have extremely good prospects; in aggregate, the others do not in these projections achieve the rate suggested by the Commission, which wants the value of exports to double in a decade. Some countries, particularly those with no foothold on manufacturing and its markets, have very poor prospects.

Such figures have to be interpreted carefully. Obviously one would not suppose that, because a certain pattern of growth rates seems likely, everyone must search very hard for markets in the direction of most rapid expansion (or in the stagnant sectors either); no more should one suppose that the most promising direction for exhortation, investment, and subsidy is exports, just because exports will probably grow less rapidly than one would like. On the whole, the Commission has avoided such traps.[7] But figures of this kind do remind one that the developing countries are unlikely to be able to expand their exports of manufactured and processed goods fast enough during the next decade for a doubling in the real value of their export earnings. No substantial growth in earnings from agricultural exports and raw materials can, after all, be expected; indeed, exports in these areas were probably above trend in 1967.

One must, therefore, avoid the common mistake of regarding foreign exchange "requirements" as, somehow, fixed. In the past, perhaps, protectionist policies have made it seem that output expansion requires, as a necessary condition, import expansion at a corresponding rate. Attempts to substitute for imports, often by encouraging inefficient domestic industries, may have tended to discredit import-substitution policies as such. It does not follow that the developing countries have to stagnate if they find that world demand for primary commodities grows slowly and expansion of manufactured exports is expensive. Growth is made more difficult, though, and aid all the more valuable.

We have to recognize that a substantial part of the growth in manufactured and processed exports, which is bound to be large during the seventies, will represent payments for imported capital goods, raw materials, and replacements, and for domestic raw materials that could have been exported instead. Agricultural exports usually represent a much larger proportion of the country's own labor and other resources. The relative importance of industrial exports is therefore less—sometimes much less—than it seems. But, in the long run, they are very important, and, furthermore, the opportunities for expanding them should be great. In a few countries, manufactured exports are beginning to emerge from their infancy. Even more important, the developing countries now have the opportunity of making their investment decisions much more carefully and intelligently than in the past; better project selection can mean lower costs, a larger proportion of domestic value added in the exports. There are fields of manufacturing—textiles, sporting goods, bicycles, certain kinds of machinery, and so on—in which developing countries can be very successful economically, and on which they would be wise to concentrate, expanding capacity very rapidly if the markets can be found. Resources spent on finding markets for proven economical production may often have much better returns than resources spent on uneconomical diversification of industry.

During the next decade, however, the major part of the gains to developing countries from international trade must come through export of primary commodities. In that field, as a general rule, they should be looking not so much for expanding markets as for good prices. They should also be trying to get revenue through commodity taxes—commodity taxes imposed on purchases by the developed countries. We in the industrial countries cannot reasonably ask the developing countries to regard the losses we sustain as a result of paying higher prices for the commodities they sell us as particularly serious. We should not regard them as serious ourselves.

It follows that, ideally, the developing countries should be administering a system of taxes on their trade with the developed countries; and there is no moral reason why these taxes should not be adjusted to maximize the net revenue of the developing countries—that is, the revenue from export sales less production costs on the margin. Commodities in relatively inelastic demand would be taxed heavily (as would imports in relatively inelastic supply—if there were any). The objections to such a scheme are, I suppose, that the developed countries might turn nasty, and that the developing countries would find it hard to administer.

It is not clear to me that the second argument is a very strong one. In outline, the scheme would provide for an authority to fix certain tax rates, to be levied by all developing countries on their sales to all developed countries.[8] The tax revenue would go to the government of the country from which the goods were sold. It might be desirable to allow for revenue transfers from one country to another on account of re-exports and the import content of exports, but the details should not present insuperable difficulty. The administering agency would be charged with the task of determining the appropriate tax rates, on the basis of the usual guides—statistics and trial-and-error. The principles are well known to economists from optimum tariff theory:[9] so long as producing countries are receiving a price (p), net of the tax, the tax rate (t) should be set so as to maximize $td\ (p + t)$, where d is demand for the commodity.[10] The agency, unlike commodity agreements, could allow for interaction between the demands for different commodities—like jute and kenaf, and coffee and tea.

The advantage of having a central agency fix the tax rates uniformly is that the allocation of production among countries is then left to the economic decisions of the different countries—so avoiding difficult, and almost certainly unproductive, negotiations among countries on production quotas. Agreement to avoid subsidies to domestic producers (in the long run) should be easier to obtain. Experience suggests that prices could be a much more effective guide to production decisions in this area than quotas, which tend merely to preserve inefficient producers.

The real difficulty is that such a scheme would hurt consumers in the developed countries, who would, naturally enough, prefer to give resources to the developing countries, rather than to have them taken from them, especially if the gifts might be less costly and would continue for only a limited period of time. Quite apart from the very serious dangers of retaliation against the developing countries, it might be possible to insist on the General Agreement for Tariffs and Trade (GATT) principles. But the scheme is a system of export taxes for the benefit of development and, as such, should be allowable. Commodity schemes with similar effect exist. Also, the general degree of trade taxation (i.e., of protection) might not be much greater than at present if large reductions were made in import tariffs by the developing countries. These import tariffs may even now have some (probably small) effect on the export prices of primary commodities; but they are certainly not designed to exploit the opportunities of export trade in the most effective manner. As a whole, the developing countries would surely benefit from a shift to export taxation.

Another advantage of schemes of this kind is that they generate government revenue. It is a disadvantage of most proposals for expanding or improving trade opportunities that they will result in increased incomes mainly for private producers, who may choose to spend most of the additional income. It is generally assumed, and this is a position with which I agree, that savings in the developing countries should be increased. Aid can increase savings (although it often does not); better trade will do so only insofar as it generates saving or tax income out of the additional earnings. In principle, a commodity tax scheme increases savings to the extent that it increases export earnings and moves resources out of primary production; the tax makes these net gains available to the government automatically.

No doubt the time is not ripe for such grandiose conceptions. Harry G. Johnson, who seems to be sympathetic, believes that it would be unacceptable.[11] The first step is to estimate the potential gains to the developing countries. There is considerable uncertainty, but the gains are surely substantial. The fact that it requires more-or-less unilateral action by the developing countries is a point in its favor. If they were seen to be ready to operate such a scheme, and the potential effects were well known, it would at least be a powerful bargaining consideration. Those of us who want to see resources transferred to the developing countries should strongly support any moves in this direction.

THE WIDER SETTING

The developing countries have much to gain from trade. We know surprisingly little about the amount. Neither "export earnings" nor "foreign exchange requirements" are remotely satisfactory figures on which to pin analysis and prediction, because, for example, of the substantial foreign exchange cost of exports. But it should be widely agreed that progress toward liberalization will help, provided the developing countries pay due attention to the relevant prices in their choice of development plans and exert influence on private investment decisions. Nevertheless, there are two major areas of concern to which most trade-easing proposals can contribute little:

1. As I have just argued, trade expansion can do little to help savings, except insofar as any income increase is saved.

2. The distribution of gains from trade improvements, as from trade, is ill related to the needs of the countries.

The second point merits action. The Pearson Commission has drawn attention once again to the inequities and absurdities in the distribution of aid. Unfortunately, the various trade policy changes that it recommends—and also the various suggestions I have made in this paper—distribute their gains in a way that no one would deliberately choose. Since, on the whole, the poorest countries—particularly India and Pakistan—transform less of their national products through trade than do richer, smaller countries, improvements in the trade environment will help those least who need help most. This is not at all an argument against such policies, but it suggests a most important point: that aid should offset the inequities of these other aiding policies. The need for some such offset is recognized by the Commission (Pearson Report,

p. 227), but its only relevant recommendation can achieve relatively little in this direction. The Commissioners—with the exception of Professor Robert E. Marjolin—missed another opportunity for improving allocation when they recommended uniform interest rates for all countries (Pearson Report, p. 164).[12] This is a problem that will need careful and continual attention; I would like to see it play a significant role in the discussions of aid-giving criteria and the principles of economic audit. It is surely most desirable that the distribution of aid should, as much as possible, compensate for the effects of developments that favor some countries but not others.

SUMMARY

1. Some facilities for borrowing in a crisis should be automatic, and a crisis should be an occasion for a special economic audit to determine the future course of assistance.

2. Fluctuations in the incomes of developing countries are best dealt with by "insurance," a burden which should not be very large in the aggregate and could be partly borne by the developed countries if loan contracts were so arranged as to schedule repayments predominantly for good years.

3. Growing access of the developing countries' export commodities to the markets of developed countries should be governed by the rate at which employment in the competing domestic industry falls.

4. Consideration should be given to schemes designed to impose taxes on certain exports of the developing countries, the revenue to go to the governments of these countries.

5. Aid allocation should attempt to offset the necessarily inequitable distribution of the gains from developing trade.

Of these, the value of the potential gains from (4) must be much greater than that from any of the others, or from the Pearson Commission's recommendations in this area, at least during the seventies. In the long run, free access to the markets of the industrial countries must be quite valuable. No doubt the present value of relaxing many of the existing aid restrictions is very large. But in the next decade—and beyond that—aid will be enormously desirable and likely to provide more than improved trade policies can.

TABLE 2.   EXPORTS OF DEVELOPING COUNTRIES PROJECTED TO 1980

	1962	1967	Annual Growth Rate	1980 (billions of dollars)
	(billions of dollars)			
Food	7.03	8.50	1.5%	10.2
Raw materials	4.47	4.95	0.5	5.3
Base metals	1.24	2.21	7.0	5.1
Manufactures	1.48	3.11	13.0	15.2
Sub total	14.22	18.77	(5.0)	35.8
Fuels	5.97	9.70	11.0	32.1
Total	20.19	28.47	(7.0)	67.9

Source: United Nations, U.N. Statistical Yearbook 1966 (New York), and G.A.T.T. International Trade, 1966 and 1967.

APPENDIX. A BACK-OF-THE ENVELOPE CALCULATION OF
EXPORT PROSPECTS

In Table 2, I have projected the figures for 1967 for the main exports of the developing countries to the developed countries (excluding the centrally planned economies) forward to 1980 using constant percentage growth rates for each of the five main categories. In each case, it seemed more sensible to project value figures rather than volume figures, partly because there might have been price trends (although in fact these are not very obvious), partly because in such a case as base metals, prices and volume are closely linked. The growth rates used for food, raw materials, and fuels are trends roughly fitted to data for the years 1950–67. For manufactures, I have used the actual growth rate between 1959 and 1967, for base metals the actual growth rate between 1953 and 1967. Export earnings figures for 1962 are given for comparison. The percentage growth rates of the aggregates, shown in parentheses, are derived from the aggregates.

It is interesting to note that export earnings from fuels have shown an amazingly constant growth rate, so that, despite unease, it seems reasonable to project it into the future. Exports of manufactures have also shown very steady growth recently, but they too are concentrated in a few exporting countries. Base metals show quite large fluctuations, and even larger price fluctuations, but no clear trend. Food exports look quite cyclical, with 1967 at the top of a cycle. If one ignored other evidence, one would assume that food exports were above trend in 1967, perhaps by $0.5 billion; base metals are surely above trend in that year, too. But neither of these adjustments makes much of a difference to the final picture.

Finally, it will be noticed that further projection into the eighties would be rather dramatic. But continued growth of manufactured exports at 13% per annum is harder to expect, despite the experience of Japan.

Trade and Liquidity: The Indian Subcontinent

BY PAUL STREETEN AND AKBAR NOMAN

Men of good will face a dilemma in the present aid crisis. On the one hand, it is evident that there is no correlation between the amount of aid per head received and the economic growth of the recipient. All sorts of reasons or excuses can be advanced to explain or to explain away this (to the aid lobby) unpalatable fact, but it remains an awkward fact. On the other hand, it is surely a basic creed, not only of economics but of common sense, that if aid, defined as the provision of additional resources, is used effectively, it must lead to greater production than would have been possible without it. And if economic growth is desired, greater production can be allocated to yield more growth.

The conflict between the (nonconclusive) evidence of absence of a relationship between aid and development (as measured by growth rates) and the logical force of the proposition that more means more, can be used as a challenge to developers to ensure the effective use of aid.

In the conventional gap analysis domestic saving is added to foreign saving to give the total resources available for investment, which, in turn, determine the addition to national income and therefore the

We gratefully acknowledge help from the World Bank, from Mrs. Frances Stewart, Mr. Deepak Lal, and Mr. Vijay Joshi. They are in no way responsible for the facts, figures, or views presented in this paper.

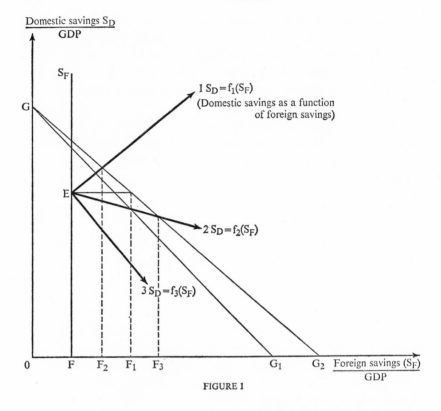

FIGURE 1

growth rate. In Figure 1 the line GG_1 shows alternative combinations of foreign and domestic savings rates required for a growth rate of, say, 6%, on the assumption that they are, dollar for dollar, perfectly substitutable. The line will have a slope of -1, cutting the two axes at angles of 45 degrees. If foreign funds show a tendency to flow into projects with higher capital/output ratios than domestic funds, the line will be flatter, like GG_2. If, on the other hand, recipients are fonder of capital-intensive projects (like moving capital cities or constructing large steel plants) which are resisted by donors, the line will be steeper. If we start from a point E, a crude gap analyst might say that foreign savings must rise by FF_1 in order to achieve 6% growth; in other words the vertical line EF, showing the amount of aid supplied, must shift to the right to point F_1.

But domestic savings are not independent of foreign savings, though the precise nature of the dependence is not altogether clear. The relationship may be as pictured in the three S_D functions: [1]

1. The domestic savings rate might rise with a higher foreign savings rate if the country generates higher savings rates out of the higher incomes made possible by aid or if it responds to "performance criteria," as in line 1;

2. It may fall, but less steeply than the growth line, as in line 2;

3. It may fall more steeply than the growth line, as in line 3.

If the domestic savings rate rises as the foreign savings rate rises, the gap will be smaller, only FF_2. This could be the result of greater private and public efforts, or simply of the higher incomes generated by foreign savings. If the domestic savings rate falls, a *sufficient* increase in foreign savings to F_3 will still achieve 6%, but it will be more than is suggested by the crude gap, because domestic slackening has to be offset. But if the situation is as in line 3, additional foreign savings can only make the growth prospect worse, and the way to achieve 6% may be to *reduce* foreign funds and increase domestic savings.

The supply of foreign savings may, in turn, be a function of domestic savings (when performance criteria are applied seriously). In this case the EF line will be positively sloped and the equilibrium point of intersection E can be shifted to the target rate of growth only through bargaining and agreed changes determining the behavior of the curves.

This formal presentation may clarify one aspect of the dispute between the aid and the anti-aid lobby,[3] even though it is grossly oversimplified and exceedingly crude. Foreign savings must be scrutinized for the terms on which it is supplied. Domestic savings should be an expression which is intended to cover all, and only, developmental expenditure, which includes a good deal of what is normally classified as consumption (health, nutrition, education) and excludes resources saved and invested in projects which make no contribution to development. Growth rates are imperfect and misleading indexes of development. Capital/output ratios have limited value. And so on. But the lack of a relationship between aid and growth remains even if we count aid net of repayments or in terms of the grant element and if we use any other development indicator, such as greater equality, more employment, proportion of the labor force in industry, etc.[3]

The point which the diagram makes is that special attention must be paid to the *net* contribution of aid to development, allowing for a relaxation or an increase of domestic efforts, both private and public, including changes in attitudes and institutions.

While the relation between aid and growth is tenuous, the Pearson Report says that there is "a close link between growth and import capacity . . . all the fast growers in the developing world received substantial amounts of foreign financing of all kinds . . ." (p. 50). Since the argument is that there is no relation between aid and growth and a strong relation between import capacity and growth, we must conclude that there is no relation between import capacity and aid. The Pearson Report does not make it clear what items are intended to be covered by import capacity. A link between import capacity and aid does not reveal which is cause and which effect, or whether there is mutual causation or whether both are effects of a third factor. Fast growth could lead to high rates of growth of exports and could attract foreign capital, thereby raising import capacity; or import capacity might provide the foreign exchange which is used to promote growth; or both causal links might be at work; or entrepreneurial ability or high investment might cause both. Unless we know the direction of the causal link, no conclusions can be drawn for aid policy. Many of the criticisms which we have made of the resource gap apply, *mutatis mutandi,* to the trade gap.

The trade (or foreign exchange) gap assumes, misleadingly, that aid, trade, and private foreign investment are substitutes in the provision of finance for development. But this is not so. First, aid on concessionary terms provides additional resources; trade and private finance do not, in themselves, do so. Aid and private finance provide additional resources *now;* trade does not. Trade converts domestic into foreign resources and may thereby raise national income. It is remunerative if the alternative domestic employment of the resources absorbed in exports shows lower productivity. The second difference is that trade raises incomes and domestic savings, and, therefore, reduces foreign exchange requirements below what they would have been, had the same amount been received through aid. An increase in trade therefore removes the basis on which the gap is calculated. Third, the effects of trade, aid, and private foreign investment on skills and technical knowl-

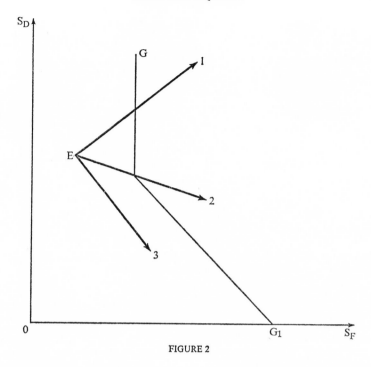

FIGURE 2

edge are different. Only if imports are required in fixed proportions in the production of national output and cannot be supplied from domestic resources can a situation arise as pictured in Figure 2, where E shows the amount of foreign exchange available and the distance from GG_1 shows the dominant trade gap. It can be seen that a reduction in domestic savings in response to an inflow of foreign savings now *may not* affect the trade gap or again it *may*, depending on the location of point E and the slope of the function.[4]

For the purpose of the subsequent calculations we have made the assumption that imports are required in fixed proportions to production. This is a gross oversimplification.

We have interpreted the task of our paper as the provision of an estimate of the import capacity, or the import requirements, of India and Pakistan in the seventies. There are two ways of setting about this. We may begin with the Pearson target of 6% growth and trace the implications of this target for import requirements. Allowance has to be made for reduced dependence on food imports and increased industrial import substitution. We then estimate likely trends in exports, again allowing for growth of home demand for exportables and the institutional prerequisites of exporting. The difference between export earnings from visible and invisible trade and import requirements (derived from the target), plus debt service and divided payments, plus desired accumulation of foreign exchange reserves, yields the foreign exchange (or trade) gap. The other way of approaching the matter is to forecast feasible growth of exports, taking both supply and demand into account, to guess at the net foreign aid available (after deduction of debt service payments), and to derive a feasible growth rate of national income from the import capacity thus calculated. We have used both approaches, according to the requirements of the argument, but mainly the first.

INDIA

The Draft Fourth Five Year Plan 1969/70–1974/75 (DFP) sets a target growth rate of 5.5% per year in the aggregate, which is raised to 6% for the Fifth Plan. The targets of the two plans together come very near the average Pearson target of 6% for the Third World. The target for the Fourth Plan is based on growth rates of 5% for agricultural output, 7% for exports, and a decline in net aid to about half its current level. Complete elimination of foreign aid is envisaged for the year 1978/79.

The agricultural growth rate is rather high, compared with the longer trend rather than with the short period since the disaster years 1965–67. It presupposes an exceptionally low incremental capital/ output ratio (ICOR) in agriculture of around 1.7. If this optimism for agriculture turns out to be unjustified, not only will it be impossible to maintain price stability, but lower agricultural incomes will reduce savings, investment, and exports; they will increase imports and hence reduce the capacity to finance growth. Taking the period 1967/68, the last year for which the DFP gives figures, to 1980/81, India will have a surplus of visible and invisible export earnings over import expenditure after 1978/79. A very high marginal savings rate (MSR) of 28% and an annual increase of investment by 10% are assumed. Exports should grow at 7% and non-food imports at 5% per year. Food imports should be eliminated altogether during the Fourth Plan.

TABLE 1.   ESTIMATES OF EXPORTS BY MAJOR
GROUPS, 1968/69 TO 1980/81

Group of Commodities	1967/68	1968/69	1973/74	1978/79	1980/81	Annual Rate of Growth (%) 1968/69 to 1980/81
		Rs. crores (ten million Rupee units)				
Agriculture and allied products	445	475	667	910	1,024	6.6
Tea	180	180	205	228	240	2.5
All other products	265	295	462	682	784	8.5
Minerals	119	130	193	273	315	7.7
Iron ore	75	86	145	215	252	9.4
Manufactures	581	675	959	1,365	1,566	7.3
Cotton textiles and jute manufactures	294	276	336	369	384	2.8
All other manufactures	287	399	623	996	1,182	9.5
Other exports—unspecified	54	60	81	102	115	5.6
Total exports	1,199	1,340	1,900	2,650	3,020	7.0

Source: Government of India, Planning Commission, *Fourth Five Year Plan 1969/74 (Draft)* (New Delhi, 1969), p. 40.

With intensive import substitution in industry, reduced reliance on food imports, and the phasing out of aid, non-food imports are projected to increase over the decade by 5% per year. The main additional imports will be products for which India lacks indigenous resources or economic substitutes.

Foreign exchange requirements are projected to be Rs. 34,000 million in 1980/81, including interest and dividends. This compares with Rs. 23,750 million in 1967/68. Without aid, this sum would have to be earned by exports and private capital inflow. Exports will have to grow at 7% per year throughout the decade.

The commodity pattern projected by the DFP is shown in Table 1. The growth of traditional exports (tea, jute manufactures, cotton textiles) is anticipated to be slow. Growth is concentrated on metal and metal manufactures (including machinery, equipment, and engineering goods), iron ore, chemicals, and allied products. With world demand for the products expanding as it has in the past, India's prospects are good, if she can produce and deliver.

India's exports have changed direction sharply in the sixties away from Britain and the Commonwealth. The United States is now India's largest market (19% of total exports in 1966/67), with Eastern Europe and the Soviet Union (17%), and Britain (17%) next in line, followed by the European Common Market (9%) and Japan (8%).

The questions are whether the markets of the sixties will remain buoyant in the seventies and whether the trade agreements with Eastern Europe offer the best opportunities to earn foreign exchange for India. Re-exports by socialist countries of Indian goods for convertible western currencies mean that India forgoes these earnings. On the other hand, the security offered by long-term agreements to sell her products may be worth sacrificing some convertible foreign exchange.

While the DFP is consistent with the Pearson target of growth, some of its assumptions are very optimistic. It is worth examining the results of less optimistic forecasts. For this purpose, we rely on six assumptions:

1. Net domestic product growth at 6% per year from the base year 1967/68.

2. Three alternative marginal savings rates: 28% (the DFP rate), 25% and 22%. Even the 25% and the 22% rates would be a great improvement on past performance. Average savings rates in the sixties moved between 8% and 11% of Net National Product. Marginal rates rarely exceeded 10% and were negative after 1965/66.

3. An incremental capital/output ratio (ICOR) of 2.8 for the period 1967/68 to 1973/74 and 3.0 thereafter. This is much larger than the DFP's ratio of 2.0 for the period 1969/70 to 1973/74 and 2.4 thereafter. Professor Minhas has shown that the low aggregate ICOR is largely the result of a very low ICOR for agriculture,[5] and that inventory investment is apparently neglected. Not that these ICOR calculations are very useful guides to forecasts, but, for what they are worth, past experience of rising ICORs over the three Plan periods does not support the exceedingly optimistic estimate.

4. Two alternative projections for exports of goods and services: the DFP's 7% per year, and a more moderate 5%. Even this represents

an improvement over past growth: 1950–67, 1.8% per annum; 1960–66, 2.9%; 1966–67, 2.3%; 1967–68, 8.7%.[6]

5. The DFP's estimate of growth of non-food imports of 5% per year could easily be too low. More imports are also required if we replace the DFP's growth rate of 5.5% of total income by the Pearson target of 6%. Food grain imports are assumed to be eliminated during the Fourth Plan or, if not eliminated, financed by PL 480 and therefore not to impose a foreign exchange cost. The annual average growth rate of commodity imports has been: 1950–67, 4.7%; 1960–66, 2.7%; 1966–67, 2.9%; 1967–68, 10.6%.[7]

6. Debt service rising to $650 million in 1973/74 and $720 million by 1975/76.

The results of these figures and our alternate assumptions are shown in Tables 2 and 3.

It must be concluded that only by a whole series of very fortunate outcomes with respect to both savings and trade can India achieve 5.5% or, a fortiori, 6% annual growth in the seventies, while pursuing "self-reliant growth with stability," as interpreted in the DFP.

The Indians have, in the past, consistently underestimated the time within which dependence on foreign aid will cease. Once again, self-reliance is postulated for the end of the Fifth Plan in 1978/79, when it is envisaged that aid will be eliminated. Over the Fourth Plan, net aid is to be reduced to about half in 1973/74. While aid has its costs, it also bestows benefits, and while it is accompanied by uncertainties, relinquishing aid creates new uncertainties. It would have been more rational to map out differing development strategies, based on differing aid assumptions.

We have seen that the Draft Plan sets up very ambitious targets. Over a quarter of the rise in income would have to be saved to hit the savings target. The Plan thus contains high income projections, combined with high marginal savings requirements. Much of this relies on a heroic strengthening of fiscal policy. These high expectations of growth, combined with the high investment ratios and greatly increased tax collections to maintain financial stability, are accompanied by reduced reliance on foreign aid. According to the Plan, net foreign aid requirements for the next five years would be about $2.3 billion, or about 8% of total planned investment.

TABLE 2.   PROJECTIONS FOR INDIA (*millions of dollars*)*

	1967/68	1973/74	1975/76	1980/81
1. Net Domestic Product				
at market prices	40,890	57,860	65,030	86,820
2. Investment (net)	4,330	9,720	11,700	15,630
3. Savings				
A. 28% marginal savings rate	3,290	8,030	9,970	15,970
B. 25% marginal savings rate	3,290	7,530	9,320	14,770
C. 22% marginal savings rate	3,290	7,020	8,600	13,390
4. Savings gap				
A. (2 − 3A)	1,040	1,690	1,730	−340
B. (2 − 3B)	1,040	2,190	2,380	860
C. (2 − 3C)	1,040	2,700	3,100	2,240
5. Imports of goods and services †	2,417	3,620	4,180	5,850
6. Exports of goods and services				
D. 7% p.a. growth rate	2,053	3,080	3,520	4,930
E. 5% p.a. growth rate	2,053	2,730	3,000	3,810
7. Export-import gap				
D. (5 − 6D)	364	540	660	920
E. (5 − 6E)	364	890	1,180	2,040
8. Debt servicing	444	650	720	
9. Foreign exchange gap				
D. (7D + 8)	1,084	1,190	1,380	
E. (7E + 8)	1,084	1,540	1,900	
As a percentage of NDP				
10. Savings				
A. 3A as a % of 1	8.0	13.9	15.3	18.4
B. 3B as a % of 1	8.0	13.0	14.3	17.0
C. 3C as a % of 1	8.0	12.1	13.2	15.4
11. Investment (2 as a % of 1)	10.6	16.8	18.0	18.0

* 1967/68 rupees converted at $1 = Rs. 7.5.

† Excludes food imports.

Note: The foreign exchange gap in the base year 1967/68 does not add up to the export-import gap plus debt servicing because of exclusion of food imports which are assumed to be eliminated before 1973/74.

For the purposes of comparison we present in Table 3 the long-term projections of the Fourth Draft Plan converted into dollars.

There is a substantial reduction in the planned ratio of imports to industrial production. Reduced dependence on foreign trade is thus envisaged to replace aid. These policies are understandable in the light of past uncertainties, restrictions, and limitations of foreign aid. But the

TABLE 3. PROJECTIONS OF THE DRAFT FOURTH FIVE YEAR
PLAN, 1967/68 TO 1980/81 (*millions of dollars at* 1967/68 *prices*)

	1967/68	*1973/74*	*1978/79*	*1980/81*
1. Net Domestic Product				
at market prices	40,890	56,320	76,370	85,920
2. Net imports of goods & services	1,040	400	−200	−400
3. Net investment	4,330	7,070	11,500	13,670
4. Savings (= 3 − 2)	3,290	6,670	11,700	14,070

Source: Government of India, Planning Commission, *Fourth Five Year Plan
1969–74 (Draft)* (New Delhi, 1969).
Note: The estimate of net imports in 1973/74 in this table allows for possible
slippage in export promotion and import substitution implied in the detailed projections.

planned aid requirements seem much too low. The Indians may well be
realistic in drastically lowering aid requirements, although the investment and growth targets, as well as the attainment of financial stability,
seem very ambitious in the light of this. One can make out a strong case
for a modest plan, with heavy emphasis on agriculture, where relatively
high returns can be reaped from small outlays of foreign exchange and
where expenditure gives rise to low demands on foreign exchange. There
could be a second, enlarged plan, which could be activated if more aid
became available: an optimistic contingency plan.

The need to raise the volume, ease the terms, and reduce the tying
of aid is undiminished either by the low Indian estimates ($400 million
net per year) or by the low aid utilization in 1968/69. Aid receipts fell
from over $1 billion in 1967/68 to only about $600 million in 1968/69.
This drastic fall was the result of a recession and a very slow revival of
investment. Relatively low levels of past aid are reflected in a low level
of investment and development, and the slowing down of development
accounts for the low aid utilization. If one assumes acceleration of investment and economic growth, a substantially larger sum of aid (such
as restoration of the $1 billion net per year) could be used productively.

Debt service is estimated at $548 million in 1969/70 and $560
million in 1970/71. If new aid is given on very soft terms, debt service
may rise to $610–$650 million by 1973/74, depending on the level of

new aid. If new aid were to be stabilized at around $1 billion per year, gross aid disbursements would have to rise to an annual level of $1.6 billion within the next five years and this would have to be almost entirely non-food aid. It must be admitted that the omens are not good.

Food aid constituted about one-third of gross aid in recent years. On the assumption that food grain production will grow, as planned, at 4.5% per annum, India's dependence on food imports will be first reduced and later eliminated. The decrease in food aid, which had been so readily absorbed while food was short, will present problems of adjustment in the balance of payments and in the transfer of aid when its composition is changed. If the increase of non-food imports is to be absorbed, India has to generate a sufficiently large deficit in her balance of payments. While this would be socially beneficial and accelerate growth, it necessitates the politically difficult policies of reducing protection and freeing imports. Equally, donors would have to take certain actions to effect the transfer. A high proportion of non-project aid, an easing of terms, and reduced tying would be important components of such a policy.

The danger of over-optimistic planning can be seen in the need for the imposition of controls over domestic finance to avoid foreign exchange crises. These take the form of restrictions on investment (which tends to have a higher import content than consumption) and on imports. These measures in turn limit efficiency, cost reductions, and export growth. The vicious circle of controls, higher costs, reduced competitiveness, and more controls is thus perpetuated. Overpessimistic planning has, of course, its own dangers. The solution of the dilemma is a series of rolling plans, based on alternative assumptions, so that maximum flexibility is preserved.

We conclude that there are many and serious obstacles to the transfer of a larger quantity of aid of a better quality than is envisaged in the Draft Fourth Plan; however, this is an essential condition for the ambitious targets of this Plan. If the planners' pessimism or pride or submissiveness to pressure groups with regard to aid turns out to be justified, it is difficult to see how their optimism with regard to investment and growth can also be justified. It looks as if two disparate components of two contingency plans had been combined, to get the best of two incompatible worlds.

PAKISTAN

Pakistan's Third Five Year Plan is in its last year. The Fourth
Plan, 1970/71–1974/75, has not yet been published. We therefore do
not have a recent blueprint of Pakistan's development strategy for the
seventies, as we have for India. Although the Third Plan contained long-
term projections to 1985, the economic situation and the political climate on the eve of the Fourth Plan are quite different from those envisaged when the Third Plan was drawn up.

The perspective plan foresaw an average annual GNP growth rate
of 7.2% over the period 1965–85. Over that twenty-year period, agriculture was projected to grow at 5.6% and the manufacturing sector at
10.2% per year. The elimination of foreign assistance was another objective of the plan. For this purpose exports were projected to increase
at about 8% and imports at about 4.2% per annum. External resources
would decline from Rs. 3,690 million (8.1% of GNP) in 1965 to Rs.
2,500 million (1.9% of GNP) in 1980, and Rs. 2,000 million (1.1% of
GNP) in 1985. Thus, despite the explicit statement of the objective,
foreign assistance is not quite eliminated by 1985. Furthermore, the
perspective plan estimates net inflow (exclusive of debt service). It does
not specify the date by which foreign assistance is to be entirely eliminated.

However, the Third Pakistan Plan was revised in its second year,
and, although most of its main targets were left substantially unaltered,
the revised strategy had far-reaching implications for long-term growth.
It attempted to "secure the desired acceleration in the growth of the
economy with lower levels of total investment . . . by concentrating on
agriculture, by a fuller utilization of installed capacity and by postponing
or reducing import intensive or capital intensive development." [8] The
growth rate of GNP is likely to average 5.5%–6% per year over the
Third Plan period; not much short of the 6.5% plan target. However,
expansion of productive capacity will fall significantly short of the original plan expectations. Furthermore, about half the increase in GNP is
estimated to have originated in the service sector. The economic significance of the increase in income is somewhat ambiguous.

Therefore, we cannot use the document as a source for the design
of a realistic strategy for the seventies. The Third Plan has not yet fully

TABLE 4. DISTRIBUTION OF FOREIGN EXCHANGE
EARNINGS, 1951/52 TO 1967/68

	1951/52	1954/55	1959/60	1964/65	1967/68
Primary raw materials	89%	88%	63%	53%	42%
Manufactured goods	1	3	25	29	37
Invisibles	10	9	12	18	21
Total	100	100	100	100	100

Sources: Government of Pakistan, Planning Commission, *The Third Five Year Plan,* abridged ed. (Karachi: June, 1968), p. 5; 1967/68 percentages calculated from Government of Pakistan, *Pakistan Economic Survey 1968/69* (Karachi, 1969).

run its course, and many aspects of that Plan period cannot yet be definitively evaluated.

Pakistan's export performance is a feature of the Third Plan period which is clearly encouraging, even though export earnings are expected to be slightly less than the Plan target. In contrast with the stagnant fifties, the Second Plan period witnessed export receipts more than twice the Plan estimate. This led to a bold export earnings target of 9.5% average growth over the Third Plan period. Foreign exchange receipts are likely to average about 8% yearly growth.

Over the period 1951/52–1967/68 the composition of Pakistan's foreign exchange earnings underwent a considerable change (Table 4). Pakistan has been fairly successful in diversifying her exports. The export bonus scheme, fiscal concessions, and other export incentive schemes have contributed to the annual compound growth of manufactured exports at a rate of 15% during the period 1960–67. In effect, Pakistan operates multiple exchange rates, thus offsetting the overvalued official exchange rate. This has enabled her manufactured exports to compete with some success in the world market. However, there is more doubt about the efficiency of the export-promotion measures in terms of the *net* foreign exchange earnings (gross export earnings less their direct and indirect import content). This also has obvious implications for allocation since foreign exchange saving or earning capacity is an important investment criterion. The cost of export diversification may well have been very high.[9] As in the past, the main impetus to future growth of exports is likely to come from manufactures and invisibles. The speed at which production capacity can be expanded has been and remains the principal determinant of production and exports of jute manufactures. Miscellaneous manufactures have accounted for 25%–30% of manufactured exports and 12%–15% of merchandise exports in recent years. Their share is likely to increase in the future. Exports of cotton manufactures, invisibles, and raw jute in 1967/68 already exceeded the 1969/70 target.

However, Pakistan may well experience "teething problems" in the production and export of heavy, more complex manufactures,[10] and the long-term prospects of raw jute exports are rather poor. On the other hand, there is the possibility that Pakistan will become a growing exporter of food grains in the seventies.

Exports to socialist countries have generally grown faster than total exports. Export receipts under bilateral agreements with them have risen from an insignificant share of total export receipts in 1964/65 to more than one-tenth in 1967/68. Bilateral exports have been concentrated on the traditional exports of raw jute, raw cotton, and rice. Moreover, manufactured goods have found an important outlet in bilateral trade.

Pakistan's exports have changed direction away from Western Europe (from 39.6% of total exports in 1959/60 to 32.5% in 1967/68), and above all from the United Kingdom (17.6% to 12.7%), and toward Eastern Europe and the Soviet Union (4.5% to 8.3%) and the Middle East (5.0% to 11.0%). However, the United Kingdom has remained the largest country market and Western Europe the largest regional market. The relative importance of the United States was the same in 1967/68 as in 1959/60 (about 9%). The fall in the share of exports to Asia (30.3% to 26.0%) largely reflected the disruption of trade with India.

Pakistan's share of world exports declined from about 0.8% in 1950 to about 0.31% in 1960 and has remained virtually unchanged between 1960 and 1968. (At 0.3% Pakistan's 1968 share compares with Hong Kong's 0.73%.)

We have suggested that the rather optimistic long-term projections contained in the original Third Plan have lost credibility through the events of the last few years. Our own projections are crude and tentative, more in the nature of prognoses, based on different specified hypotheses, than of predictions or prophecies. Their tentative and hypothetical nature cannot be overemphasised.

We make the following five sets of assumptions:

1. GNP increase of 6% per year from the base year 1967/68.

2. Foreign exchange earnings expansion of 8% per year (their recent rate).

3. Two alternative marginal rates of savings, 22% and 25%. This compares with the prospective Plan's projections of a 25% marginal savings rate over the period 1970–75, rising to 28% in 1975–80.

Pakistan's saving performance so far gives little indication of a clear and distinct trend, as is evident from the following figures:

	At constant 1959/60 prices			At current prices
	1949/50–1954/55	1954/55–1959/60	1959/60–1964/65	1959/60–1964/65
Marginal rate of savings	17.9	–2.7	13	22

Government of Pakistan, Planning Commission, *Outline of the Third Five Year Plan* (Karachi, 1964), p. 7; Government of Pakistan, Planning Commission, *The Third Five Year Plan* (Karachi, 1965), p. 22; and United Nations, Economic Commission for Asia and the Far East Feasible Growth and Trade Gap Projections in the ECAFE *Region* Development Programming Technique, no. 7 (E/CN. 11/844 Bangkok, 1968), p. 7.

(Any detailed analysis of Pakistan's savings performance is very difficult. Conceptual differences and ambiguities do not wholly explain the bewildering discrepancies and inconsistencies in savings data for Pakistan. It is only a slight exaggeration to say that there are as many estimates of the savings rate as there are sources.) Over the period 1964/65–1967/68, the marginal savings rate is estimated to be lower than the average savings rate. Thus gross savings as a percentage of GNP at market prices has been declining, from just short of 13% in 1964/65 [11] to between 9% and 10% in the subsequent three years.

4. Three alternative growth rates for total foreign exchange pay-

ments on goods, services, and debt servicing: 9% per year, 8%, and 7%.

The assumptions underlying the projections of foreign exchange payments are probably the most arbitrary. Imports during the Third Plan period are estimated to have been considerably less than Plan expectations as a result of aid falling short of Plan projections. At the same time, the reduction of development imports was higher than plan projections due to larger defense and food imports. Furthermore, although receipts of external assistance were considerably below Plan expectations, debt servicing payments exceeded Plan estimates because terms of aid were harder than expected.

The postponement of import-intensive investment during the Third Plan period is likely to increase future import requirements for a given growth rate of GNP. Moreover, debt servicing is expected to impose a growing burden in the seventies. One offsetting factor is the likelihood that food imports will be eliminated.

The difficulties of making import projections are aggravated by the poor quality of import statistics. The differences between the State Bank data and those of the Central Statistical Office are larger than can be explained by the normal leads and lags. Differences in coverage also account for part of the discrepancy, though again it is doubtful whether they explain all.

During the Second Plan period total imports and payments expanded at the annual rate of 15.8%. In the past the average annual growth rate of imports has been: 1950–67, 6.5%; 1960–66, 5.5%; 1966–67, 22.3%; 1967–68, −9.5%.[12]

5. Gross capital-output ratio (gross fixed capital formation plus inventory investment in a year, divided by additional GNP in the next year) of 4.0. This may well be an underestimate as the postponement of capital-intensive investment in the Revised Plan and the slow expansion of productive capacity will raise the capital coefficient in the future.[13] The inherent limitations of the concept of capital/output ratio make any attempt at a precise estimate futile.

In the *Outline of the Third Five Year Plan* the Planning Commission projected a gross capital/output ratio of 3.5 for the Fourth Plan (1970–75) and 3.6 for the Fifth Plan (1975–80). Subsequently, the long-term projections in the *Third Five Year Plan* reduced the gross

TABLE 5.　CAPITAL/OUTPUT RATIO OF PAKISTAN

	1951–55 (Actual)	1955–60 (Actual)	1961–65 (Pro-jected)	1966–70 (Pro-jected)	1971–75 (Pro-jected)	1975–80 (Pro-jected)	1980–85 (Pro-jected)
Capital/output ratio:							
net	1.6	2.0	2.1	2.5	2.7	3.0	3.0
gross	2.7	3.5	3.2	3.4	3.6	4.1	4.3

Source: Mahbub ul Haq, *The Strategy of Economic Planning* (Karachi: Pakistan Branch, Oxford University Press, 1963), p. 68.

capital/output ratio to 2.9 [14] (assuming no time lag between investment and output).

Another extrapolation of the capital-output ratio is presented in Table 5. The projections resulting from assumptions 1 to 5 are presented in Table 6.

On our assumptions it seems that Pakistan will need substantial and growing amounts of capital imports in the seventies if she is to meet the Pearson growth target.

Pakistan's receipts of external financial assistance in the first four years of the Third Plan have fallen far short of expectation. Commitments were assumed to run at an average annual level of $580 million. Actually, they came to $483 million—17% below the estimate. Against estimated disbursements of $620 million a year, only $462 million were in fact disbursed, about one-fourth less. An even tighter situation prevailed over the first three years of the Plan period when commitments and disbursements were 20% and 30% below Plan estimates. This shortfall in aid was one reason for the revision of the original Plan strategy.

As a result of a larger share of export credits (which became a major form of financing the Third Plan) and generally harder terms of official assistance, debt service rose much more rapidly than projected, amounting on average to about $125 million a year. By 1968/69 the debt service ratio had risen close to 20%.

Some of the issues raised in discussing India's aid requirements are also relevant to Pakistan's future, although Pakistan has received nearly

TABLE 6.   PROJECTIONS FOR PAKISTAN (*millions of dollars*)*

	1967/68	*1973/74*	*1975/76*	*1980/81*
1. GNP at market prices	14,070	19,910	22,370	29,870
2. Investment (gross)	2,060	4,780	5,360	7,160
3. Gross savings				
A. 25% marginal savings rate	1,340	2,800	3,420	5,290
B. 22% marginal savings rate	1,340	2,630	3,170	4,820
4. Savings gap				
A. (2 − 3A)	720	1,980	1,940	1,870
B. (2 − 3B)	720	2,150	2,190	2,340
5. Foreign exchange earnings	770	1,220	1,420	2,090
6. Foreign exchange payments †				
C. Grow at 9%	1,280	2,140	2,540	3,910
D. Grow at 8%	1,280	2,030	2,370	3,480
E. Grow at 7%	1,280	1,920	2,200	3,080
7. Foreign exchange gap				
C. (5 − 6C)	510	920	1,120	1,820
D. (5 − 6D)	510	810	950	1,390
E. (5 − 6E)	510	700	780	990
8. Gross capital/output ratio		4.0	4.0	4.0
9. Growth rate of foreign exchange				
earnings		8.0%	8.0%	8.0%
As Percentage of GNP				
10. Gross investment (2 as a % of 1)	14.6	24.0	24.0	24.0
11. Gross Savings				
A. (3A as a % of 1)	9.5	14.1	15.3	17.6
B. (3B as a % of 1)	9.5	13.2	14.2	16.1

* 1967/68 rupees converted at $1 = Rs. 4.76.
† Excludes PL 480 and Indus Basin imports.

twice as much aid per head as India. There is the same need to raise the volume, ease the terms, and reduce the tying of aid to procurement, projects, and commodities. The possibility of self-sufficiency in food grains and the decline in food aid present similar political problems of adjustment in the balance of payments toward absorption of non-food items (however beneficial these would be to the economy as a whole) and, for donors, of increasing the transfer of products which are not in surplus in their own countries. The growth of exports of manufactures may run into protectionist barriers put up by industrial countries and the growth of food exports against demand limitations. A rise in private foreign investment is likely to impose a growing foreign exchange burden. The role of the international corporation, both in investment and in promoting manufactured exports, will become more important. But it is hard to see how, even with growing foreign investment and trade opportunities, Pakistan can achieve 6% growth without large amounts of aid.

LIQUIDITY

Few things are so good for the balance of payments in the short run as a dose of deflation. Britain and India share the experience of enjoying dramatic improvements in their balances after a period of recession. In India the change from 1967 to 1968 showed an improvement of $483 million and, even after substantial repayments to the International Monetary Fund, led to the rebuilding of depleted exchange reserves. For Pakistan, too, 1967/68 brought an improvement in the balance of payments and an addition to reserves.

What will happen as India steps up her development expenditure, utilizes industrial capacity more fully, and is called upon to service the rising foreign debt? We have concluded that the DFP is oversanguine in respect to savings and foreign trade. But even if the assumptions, the coefficients, and the resulting projections were approximately right, things may go wrong for a while.

The way to meet unfavorable short-term events is to use reserves. Reserves can take the form of unused industrial capacity, of inventories, and, for our purposes, of foreign exchange. In the past, it has been a characteristic feature of developing India that it was short of *needed* reserves and was therefore often forced to maintain *unwanted* reserves (e.g. of industrial capacity). The argument that foreign exchange reserves have low or no yields and that a developing country cannot afford to hold assets in such a "wasteful" form has by now worn thin. It is now realized that, while reserves appear to have low yields compared with productive investment, the disruption to the economy caused by being caught short of reserves imposes costs which are much higher than the forgone earnings. The alternative measures which have to be employed, like deflation or quantitative import restrictions, may impose higher costs on the economy than the lost earnings from holding foreign exchange reserves. The substantial, but not clearly visible, benefits of reserves consist in the ability to avoid these costs. Furthermore, poor countries are liable to have less easy and rapid access to cheap foreign credit. It is for these reasons that India and Pakistan need higher reserves in relation to imports (or any other index of need) than they have had in the past.

India's quota in the IMF is $750 million, which is 3.53% of total quotas. Special Drawing Rights (SDRs) are to be created at the rate of $3.5 billion in the first year (1970) and $3 billion in each of the two subsequent years. India's share of these will be $124 million in the first year (an increase of 14.4% over 1969 reserves) and $106 million in the two subsequent years (12.3% increase), altogether $336 million. This represents 4.9% of her imports.

Pakistan's IMF quota is $188 million. Pakistan will receive $31 million SDRs in the first year (10% increase over 1969 reserves) and $27 million in the two subsequent years (9% increase), giving a total of $85 million. This represents 3.1% of her 1968 imports.[15] Tables 7 and 8 show the historical record.

The optimum ratio of reserves to imports is difficult to determine, but it is easy to see that, whatever the optimum ratio, the two countries are below it. The creation of SDRs will keep step with the growing value of world trade, but additional strengthening of reserves is needed. No allowance is normally made in trade gap calculations for the need to build up reserves. Much of what counts as import capacity could not be used for this purpose: tied loans, exports to Eastern European countries, and earnings in blocked currencies are of no use, except to the extent that expenditure switching is possible. It is only the export earnings of convertible currencies which can be used directly.

The argument so far has been conducted on the tacit assumption of fixed exchange rates. Targets and gap projections tend to be formulated in a price-less world. The neglect of price variations by planners is matched by the reluctance of monetary authorities to change the parity of the exchange rate. The bias built into the politics of many countries against changes in parities of their exchange rates has meant that the potential degree of flexibility provided by the IMF has not been fully used. Governments have thus deprived themselves of at least one instrument of policy in the attempt to reconcile internal and external policy objectives. The results have been restrictionism, protectionism, and, in

TABLE 7. TOTAL RESERVES,* 1959–1969 (millions of dollars)

	1959	1960	1961	1962	1963	1964	1965	1966	1967		1968				1969		
									III	IV	I	II	III	IV	I	June	July
India	814	670	665	512	607	498	599	608	579	662	718	720	754	682	769	856	—
Pakistan	302	317	277	280	308	244	221	200	171	161	183	195	203	252	306	316	300

* Gold + IMF reserve position + foreign exchange.
Source: International Monetary Fund, International Financial Statistics, September, 1969.

TABLE 8. INTERNATIONAL LIQUIDITY POSITION* 1960 AND 1968 (millions of dollars)

	Liquidity Position		Change in Reserves	Imports		Ratio of Reserves to Annual Imports (percent)	
	1960	1968		1960	1968	1960	1968
	(1)	(2)	(3) (2 − 1)	(4)	(5)	(6)	(7)
India	670	682	12	2327	2510	28.8	27.2
Pakistan	317	252	−65	654	996	48.5	25.3

* Gold + IMF reserve position + foreign exchange at end of the year.
Sources: International Monetary Fund, International Financial Statistics, September, 1969; and United Nations, Conference on Trade and Development, Handbook of International Trade and Development Statistics, 1969 (TD/STAT/2).

some cases, inhibitions of growth, with detrimental effects on the flow of trade and capital to the developing countries.

The present mood is more receptive to policies of limited exchange rate flexibility, whether in the form of a crawling peg, a widened band, a combination of the two, or managed floating rates.

From the point of view of our present investigation, two questions arise:

1. How would any proposed changes in exchange rate arrangements affect, directly and indirectly, the development prospects of India and Pakistan?

2. What would be the implications of such arrangements for the policies to be pursued by India and Pakistan? Should they be adopted or adapted, or are quite different arrangements appropriate?

If greater flexibility liberalizes trade, capital, and aid policies in the West, this will benefit India and Pakistan. This benefit, indeed, is one of the most powerful reasons for the adoption of such arrangements in the West. But the more direct effects of frequent small changes in the relative values of major currencies are more difficult to predict. One must ask how they affect the value of sterling reserves, the burden of debt service, the terms of trade, and the ability to pursue stabilization and adjustment policies.

The increased difficulties of managing asset holdings whose relative values are uncertain constitute a strong argument for a generally acceptable international reserve asset. SDRs are a step in the right direction, and the adoption of limited exchange rate flexibility is a strong argument for a more rapid move in this direction. The real burden of debt service would also vary with fluctuations in the relative value of the currency.

Terms of trade problems arise if, say, tea and jute are largely sold in London where their prices are determined, while imports come from America. If India's and Pakistan's rates are pegged to sterling, dollar prices of exports fall, while dollar prices of imports rise. Much will depend upon the geographical pattern of trade, and the way in which prices are determined. In view of the small (though growing) importance of foreign trade, the small (though possibly frequent) changes in exchange rates, and the possibility of using the London forward exchange market, the effects of limited flexibility in the West on India and Pakistan are likely to be, on balance, favorable and will not present the difficulties which they might present to small developing countries. To the extent that flexible rates of the value of their own currencies are useful to India and Pakistan, a move in this direction by the West will also help them.

The second question relates to the appropriate currency arrangements for India and Pakistan. It will be generally conceded that limited exchange rate flexibility can make only a small contribution to the more deep-seated problems of poverty, structural change, and development.

One method of adjusting the persistent tendency of import requirements to outpace export earnings of India and Pakistan is the adoption of a dual exchange rate: one fixed and higher (more units of foreign currency for one unit of domestic currency) for traditional primary exports and essential imports such as certain capital goods, industrial raw materials, and food; the other lower (fewer units of foreign currency for one unit of domestic currency) and possibly floating or frequently adjusted, for new, especially manufactured, infant-industry exports and inessential or less essential imports. The low rate might be left to equilibrate the forces of supply and demand and might rise as exports earnings from manufactures rise with growing competitiveness.

The case for a dual rate rests on certain peculiarities of the economies of India and Pakistan. It is well known that manufactured import substitutes will normally have to face the initially high costs of infant industries. Cost ratios between manufacturing and agricultural production will be less favorable than they will be after economies of scale have been established and industrial attitudes and aptitudes created. If protective devices are adopted in an attempt to bring internal price ratios in line with internal cost ratios, the size of the market will be restricted and incentives to raise efficiency will be blunted. This will result in further claims for protection. Even apart from these cost-raising and efficiency-reducing tendencies, the attempt to set up import-saving industries will raise, for a period, import requirements relative to export capacity, so import substitution has to be accompanied, initially, by higher rather than lower foreign exchange expenditure. This tendency will be aggravated and prolonged if the protective devices raise costs and discourage efficiency. Since import substitution was embarked upon in order to save foreign exchange, it is frustrating to find that it appears to be self-defeating. This frustration often manifests itself in an accentuation of nationalistic and autarkic measures.

To avoid these results, the need to increase exports has been stressed. But if these consist of manufactured products, the common difficulty, as with manufactured import substitutes, is that such activities are conducted at too high a cost to be competitive with the established manufacturing exports of advanced industrial countries. The commonly advocated remedy—a depreciation of the exchange rate—does not solve the problem. The traditional exports of primary products will tend to be in inelastic supply in the short run (and demand will be inelastic in the long run for large countries like India and Pakistan), and depreciation, unaccompanied by an increase in export taxes, will inflate prices and incomes in this sector. This may be justified if expansion of production or re-equipment and modernization are wanted. But world demand is normally not such as to warrant export expansion of primary products. The inflation of the incomes of the primary exporters following devaluation will raise their demand for food and may, in some cases, reduce its supply (for example by the transfer of land from food to jute production). In addition to this, the higher domestic costs of imports, many of which form industrial inputs, which result from devaluation, and the resulting wage-cost inflation, will soon tend to wipe out the cost advantages gained by devaluation. Conventional anti-inflationary policies of restriction of domestic demand cannot tackle this type of inflation. If pursued vigorously enough, they create unemployment without touching the imported inflation in the traditional export sector and lead to the coexistence of unemployment and inflation.

The appropriate solution is to apply different remedies to staple exports, the prices of which are largely determined by world demand, and to manufactured exports, whose prices are determined by costs of production. This can be done in three ways: a system of dual exchange rates, indirect taxes and subsidies, or centralized marketing.

By employment of a dual exchange rate export prices could be rendered competitive, while inflation of incomes of the growers of primary products would be avoided.[16] This would also prevent the inflation from being communicated to the prices of home-produced food and to industrial wages and thus avoid the danger of wiping out the benefits of exchange rate depreciation.

A purist might argue that multiple rates should be chosen so as to reap the maximum benefits for the nation of different demand and supply inelasticities. But, quite apart from the rules of the IMF and possible foreign retaliation, it would not be desirable to proliferate the number of exchange rates because avoidance and evasion would be made easier, particularly as the dual rate can be supplemented by a system of indirect taxes and subsidies.

While the high rate would be chosen for primary export commodities, the low rate, which could be more flexible and allowed to float, would apply to all those imports which do not qualify for a currency allocation at the official rate. Importers would obtain an import license by purchasing the necessary amount of foreign exchange. The range of goods which would be covered by this rate could be varied by the government from time to time, and the free rate could thereby be influenced. Manufacturers unwilling to shoulder the risks of the variable rate would be able to buy foreign exchange forward. The government may have to set up a purchasing agency or a marketing board in order to ensure that the foreign exchange proceeds of the primary exports are surrendered at the official rate. To avoid foreign exchange allocations for the specified imports being used for other purposes, the government could ask for advance deposits in local currency.

Against the advantages of a system of dual exchange rates must be set at least two disadvantages.[17] If they were designed to stimulate manufacturing, the stimulus to manufacturing industries would not be uniform but would favor those making plentiful use of the imports allowed in at low prices. Thus, if all primary products were allowed into the country at the favorable rate chosen for "essentials," oil refineries, for example, would benefit; cotton spinning would be favored compared with weaving and clothing. If capital goods were permitted at the low rate, this would give an undesirable encouragement to capital-intensive methods of production. Exports using much of the favored imports would be favored and might lead to negative value added. On the other hand, to keep the price of imported food (which will be diminishing in importance) low will favor labor-using industries and this will be desirable. A second possible objection is that dual exchange rates, which permit imports of food and raw materials at low prices, discourage the local production of these goods, unless special measures are taken to subsidize local producers, for example by a system of deficiency payments. It has been argued that domestic agricultural production should not be penalized in this way. But we have seen that food imports will be of decreasing importance. The case for a dual rate on the import side is probably weaker than on the side of exports.

The increased competitiveness of manufactured exports derived from a lowering of prices to foreign buyers achieved in this manner has a number of additional advantages. If the low rate is allowed to float and thus to equilibrate the demand for and the supply of non-essential imports with the demand for and the supply of manufactured exports, the discount of the floating rate (the premium on buying foreign exchange over the official rate) will reflect the balance between the demand for inessential imports and the supply and the competitiveness of manufactured exports. The lower the rate, the greater the encouragement to exports. If the response is an increase in the supply of exports, this will tend to reduce the discount and bring the two rates nearer together.

Such a system would also meet a number of difficulties which arise from the different levels of development at which different developing countries find themselves. Differences among less developed countries, which have tended to increase in the last few years, can present problems similar in nature to those between less developed and developed countries. A system of simple preferences for manufactured imports, without a number of safeguards for the least developed, may simply award the lion's share of the markets to those less developed countries already more advanced and therefore least in need of assistance.

A system of dual rates, with one rate floating to equilibrate the demand for foreign exchange for less essential imports with the supply of foreign exchange earned by manufacturing exports, would automatically adjust the handicap to the level of industrialization. The least developed countries at the earliest stage of industrialization would enjoy the greatest price advantages for manufactured exports, while those whose cost conditions approximate those of the industrial countries would find their discount dwindling away.

In addition, it would encourage trade between developing countries without, once again, jeopardizing the chances of the least developed countries of participating in industrialization. It is a common failing of schemes of regional integration among developing countries that some member countries not only fail to share in the benefits of industrialization but are deprived of the opportunities which protection would have given them. The proposed system would combine the benefits of regional integration in South and Southeast Asia with those of participation in the industrialization process by the least developed and would thus remove what has been a main obstacle to plans of integration among countries in the region. While it is not normal to assume exchange rate flexibility between members of a union, it might overcome some of the present obstacles.

A system of indirect taxes and subsidies can be used to achieve the same effects as a dual exchange rate, although it may be more difficult to administer. Traditional exports and inessential imports are taxed, and the tax revenue is used to subsidize manufacturing exports and essential imports.

Finally, the same objective can be achieved by a national central marketing agency which buys primary products at low prices and sells them at higher prices in world markets. The agency would need to have the right of monopoly purchase from the farmers. The agency might also provide other services to the farmers. The case for such marketing agencies is stronger, the more important it is to fix different prices for different primary exports, and the weaker the case for permitting imports in at a high rate.

The infant industry argument, often interpreted to justify protection, can be interpreted as an argument for subsidies or for dual exchange rates. Although both protection and subsidies tend to bring nearer together the price ratio between manufactures and primary products and their cost ratio, protection does it by raising the prices of manufactures, while subsidies and dual rates do it by lowering their costs.

Both India and Pakistan, through their export bonus and import entitlement schemes, through a system of indirect taxes and subsidies, and through other regulations and controls, are in fact employing a system of de facto multiple exchange rates. Our proposal is to simplify this complex administrative apparatus and to replace it by a system of dual rates, possibly modified by indirect taxes and subsidies. The establishment of dual exchange rates has been called a wrong step in the right direction. This is to damn with pained phrase. If the above arguments are accepted, the verdict would have to be revised.

Our conclusions on international liquidity and monetary arrangements are these:

1. India and Pakistan will have to give high priority to rebuilding their foreign exchange reserves. SDRs and larger quotas will help but can make only a small contribution in the near future. The two countries *need* additional reserves and there is *little evidence* to suggest that they are *unwilling* or *incapable* of holding them (i.e. reconstituting them over a period of years). Conditional liquidity in the form of IMF drawings represents a line of defense, but it ought to complement more adequate *unconditional* liquidity.

2. A move toward limited exchange rate flexibility among the advanced industrial countries is likely to benefit India and Pakistan, although it presents them with some difficult choices with regard to portfolio management of their liquid international assets and with regard to the pegging of their own exchange rates. Much more thought should be given to the repercussions of limited flexibility among industrial countries on the development prospects of developing countries.

3. Limited flexibility has not much to offer to exchange rate management of India and Pakistan, but the advantages and drawbacks of dual exchange rates and other forms of monetary and price management are worth exploring more fully.

The Trade and Aid Relationship in Latin America
BY LAURENCE WHITEHEAD

HOW LARGE A FLOW OF RESOURCES?

Compare the following statements (and note that the first two are from the same source):

1. [There has been] a transfer of resources on an unprecedented scale from richer to poorer countries . . . By 1961, almost $8 billion, or nearly 1% of the GNP of the high-income, non-Communist nations was flowing into low-income nations . . . by 1968 it had reached a total of $12.8 billion in public and private resources . . . [Pearson Report, p. 3]

2. It is not uncommon to hear the total flow of resources to developing countries referred to as something which the rich countries "give" to the poor. Nothing could be further from the truth . . . only Official Development Assistance should be designated as "aid" . . . The share of grants in official

development assistance has declined from 87% in 1961 to 63% in 1968. Moreover, official lending . . . also generates a considerable reverse flow to the developed countries in the form of interest payments. If such income on *past* loans is subtracted [from the figure for total net flow of resources of $12.8 billion] . . . the remainder in 1968 amounted to only about $6.3 billion . . . By comparison, in that year the same DAC countries spent $35 billion on liquor and $15 billion on cigarettes. [Pearson Report, pp. 139–40]

3. The post-war average [of the flow of resources based on balance of payment figures] claimed by the developed countries has been $1.9 billion and claimed by the underdeveloped countries only $900 million.[1] [Wendell C. Gordon]

4. A large and swelling flood of resources contributes to this progress [in the Western hemisphere]. In four years the United States alone has contributed almost $4½ billion in grants, in loans, in goods, and in expert assistance. The nations of Latin America have channeled $22–24 billion into development. And more than an extra billion has come from other countries and international agencies . . . In the last year and a half we have loaned over $847 million—and that is almost $150 million more than was loaned in the entire two full preceding years combined . . .[2] [President Lyndon B. Johnson, 1965]

5. [From the time I became President] I have accelerated America's contribution to the hemisphere. . . . We raised the total flow of funds. For the three years 1961 to 1964, it ran about $3,700 million. From 1964, 1965, 1966, that $3,700 million was raised to about $5,000 million.[3] [President Johnson, 1967]

In the last two passages quoted, Johnson's figures include flows of private capital, which, as the Pearson Report (p. 139) points out, "have no more the character of 'aid' when they flow to developing countries than when they flow between developed countries." Net *official* bilateral assistance from the United States to Latin America and the Caribbean came to a total of about $1.7 billion for the three years 1964–66. Even if all net official multilateral assistance is attributed to the United States, the total would still only be $2.5 billion—only half the sum Johnson claimed to be "contributing to the hemisphere." (See Table 28 of the Pearson Report, p. 394.)

From these quotations, it is obvious that the total of "aid" can be calculated in about as many ways as there are calculators. It is not my purpose here to analyze which method is correct (for example, Gordon's figures can be roughly reconciled with the second set of those from the Pearson Report [4] if one uses the same group of countries and the same

TABLE 1. THE FLOW OF RESOURCES INTO LATIN
AMERICA, 1946–65 (*billions of dollars*)

	Latin American Region	Underdeveloped Countries as a Whole
Net transfer payments (public and private)	+ 2.4	+ 20.6
Net capital movement (public and private)	+ 17.2	+ 39.6
Net investment income (public and private)	− 24.0	− 42.8
Gordon's "Effective Aid Financing"	− $ 4.4	+ $17.5

Source: Wendell Gordon, "Has Foreign Aid Been Overstated?" *Inter-American Economic Affairs* 21, no. 4 (Spring, 1968), p. 12.

Note: On these figures the donors would be wiser to leave private capital flows out of account when speaking of their "contribution to development." Of course, this method of calculating is as open to debate as the OECD figures it is challenging, and many people would reject Gordon's expression "effective aid financing" as an accurate label for the calculation he has done. But similar objections in the opposite direction could be directed at the calculation of the so-called "net flow of financial resources."

definition of "effective aid financing"). The point is simply to explain how the developed countries may be congratulating themselves on their generosity while the recipients may be making alternative and less flattering calculations.

The Balance of Payments Record

Rather than debate definitions, I prefer to present the United Nations Economic Commission for Latin America (ECLA) breakdown of Latin America's balance of payments (see Table 2) so that we can see the relative contributions of different flows to the continent's capacity to import. After all, the purpose of "aid financing" or "flows of resources," however defined, is supposed to be to enable less developed countries to import more than they otherwise could, so that they can invest more. If this is the correct view, then action that affects any item on the balance of payments may be relevant to "aiding growth," whether or not the item is normally included in calculations of "aid."

TABLE 2.   LATIN AMERICA'S BALANCE OF PAYMENTS, 1960–67,
CUMULATIVE TOTALS (*billions of dollars*)

	I *19 Republics* *and ex-British territories)* *(excluding Cuba,*	*II* *18 Republics* *(Column I* *excluding Venezuela)*
1. *Balance of Payments on Current Account*		
Exports 75.0		
Imports 63.5		
i Merchandise balance	+11.5	—
ii Balance of freight, insurance, and travel	− 6.0	—
iii Balance of trade (i + ii)	+ 5.5	− 2.1
iv Net interest on foreign loans	− 3.4	− 3.2
v Net profit on foreign investments	− 9.6	− 4.7
vi Net private transfers	− 0.3	+ 0.4
Balance on Current Account (iii − [iv + v + vi])	− 7.8	− 9.6
2. *Balance of Payments on Capital Account*		
i Net official transfer payments	+ 1.1	+ 1.1
ii Net long term public loans	+ 3.0	+ 2.9
iii Net long-term private loans	+ 2.8	+ 2.7
iv Net foreign direct investment	+ 3.2	+ 3.4
v Other autonomous capital movements (i.e., domestic capital and short-term liabilities)	+ 0.0	+ 1.1
vi Net movement of autonomous capital ([i + ii + iii + iv] − v)	+10.1	+11.3
vii Net compensatory capital movements	+ 0.1	+ 0.2
viii Errors and omissions	− 2.4	− 1.9
Balance on Capital Account (vi − viii)	+ 7.8	+ 9.6

Source: United Nations, Economic Commission for Latin America, *Economic Survey of Latin America,* Vol. 12, 1967 (E/CN.12/808), Santiago, Chile, pp. 80, 90, 94–95. Supplemented from International Monetary Fund, *Balance of Payments Yearbook,* Vol. 20 (Washington, D.C., 1966–67).

Note: It is best to separate the case of Venezuela from the other eighteen republics since it has a very large balance of trade surplus and is not a recipient of aid.

Balance of Trade. The first thing we can see from Table 2 is that merchandise exports from Latin America exceeded imports by a large margin—$11.5 billion more goods were exported from the nineteen republics than they imported over the period 1960–67. However, the overwhelming bulk of Latin America's trade is shipped by foreign ships, mostly in the fleets of the developed countries, and is insured with companies in the developed countries; these services cost no less than $6 billion.[5]

Even allowing for this massive outflow for services, the balance of trade for the nineteen republics was still a surplus of $5.5 billion. In other words, they exported about 7% more goods and services than they imported. When Venezuela is removed from the calculation, there is a small deficit; the remaining eighteen republics imported about 3% more than they exported. So a small amount of capital inflow might be needed to finance these extra imports. But these modest requirements could be offset by the huge Venezuelan surplus. If other things were equal, Latin America could have imported $5.5 billion more capital goods to increase its development, paid for entirely out of export proceeds, without receiving any aid or foreign investments or contracting any foreign debts.

Balance on Current Account. But of course other things were not equal. By the time the Alliance for Progress began, Latin America had already amassed large debts with the developed countries. Foreign companies owned many of the more profitable enterprises. In the period 1960–67 ("the greatest period of forward movement, progress, and fruitful change" as Lyndon Johnson called it),[6] the nineteen republics had to pay $13 billion to the developed countries in interest on these foreign debts and in profit. (This compares with a cumulative total of $14 billion spent on this account in the period 1946–60.) If such an outflow had gone to purchase needed imports, Latin America's total volume of imports would have risen over 20%. But it flowed out to investors and bankers of the developed countries, largely to service obligations incurred before the "vast cooperative effort." Once this outflow is taken into account, the respectable balance of trade surplus is wiped out. Thus, the area managed to combine exporting $5.5 billion more than it imported with a current account deficit exceeding 10% of exports.

As usual, Venezuela may be considered atypical. Over half the profit outflow was from Venezuela—$4.9 billion. But the remaining eighteen republics were required to pay $7.9 billion in interest and profits to foreign creditors. Thus, for these eighteen republics the deficit on current account was almost five times as much as the deficit on the balance of trade—a total of $9.6 billion.

Net Movements of Autonomous Capital. Because of foreign obligations accumulated before 1960 Latin America had a large current account deficit. Therefore, it needed to incur more foreign obligations which will require huge expenditures on servicing. It is true that some of these capital inflows were provided on generous terms and some were grants, so, although they imply obligations regarding internal politics, behavior in international organizations, and various other political actions, at least they do not imply very heavy financial obligations. Their net benefit to the balance of payments may not be very large if they are tied; the obligation to pay interest or profits to foreign creditors may be replaced by the obligation to buy imports from the nearest and perhaps most expensive market. However, these "artificial" capital inflows are not that large in proportion to the deficit they must fill. Net official transfer payments received by the nineteen republics (cumulated 1960–67) amounted to only $1.1 billion compared with the current account deficit of $7.8 billion. Net long-term public loans added another $3 billion, but not all of these were on soft terms (for example, this figure includes Mexican government securities floated on European capital markets). Even if we could consider the full $4.1 billion capital inflow as "aid," it would still be insufficient to offset the $6 billion Latin America spends on shipping, insurance, and the like, let alone the $13 billion outflow of profits and interest.

The $6 billion in foreign private loans and foreign direct private investment was more important than these capital inflows from official sources. Private capital flows take place in pursuit of economic advantage and cannot be regarded as "aid" in any meaningful sense. The indirect effects of private foreign investment will be considered later. But just in terms of the size of the "flow of resources," new inflows of private capital are more than offset by profit outflow on past investment.

Errors and Omissions. This $2.4 billion needs explaining, since it is twice the amount donated by developed countries to the area ("net official transfer payments" in Table 2). In theory one expects errors and omissions to occur with equal frequency in both directions, so that over an eight-year period they should more or less net out. But Latin America's errors and omissions do not cancel out; on the contrary, they appear as a large drain on the continent's resources, and they seem to be growing over time. They added to a $0.43 billion outflow in 1946–50, $0.45 billion in 1951–55, $2.1 billion in 1956–60, and $1.5 billion in 1961–65.

A large percentage of these errors and omissions appear to represent unauthorized outflows of private capital from the area—most of it owned by Latin American citizens. ECLA, in attempting to estimate the full extent of private domestic capital outflow from Latin America, did its calculations by adding two-thirds of the "errors and omissions" to the recorded outflow. Its report continues:

The net outflow of private domestic capital from Latin America, registered or unregistered, can be roughly estimated at an aggregate of 5,000 million dollars [1946–62], of which 3,000 million was sent out in the decade 1951–60 and more than 1,000 million in 1961 and 1962. It has represented approximately 30 percent of the total inflow of all forms of foreign capital into the region for the post-war period (1946–62).[7]

Over the same period official donations to Latin American governments reached only $1 billion, one-fifth of the private domestic capital leaving the continent. It seems that the governments of the developed countries might make a more significant contribution to Latin America's capacity to import if they helped register, control, and, if possible, discourage this outflow than if they doubled their grants. Such policies would be a useful supplement to increased aid, if not an alternative to it.

When aid statistics are seen in this context of the over-all balance of payments, it becomes apparent that aid is a relatively minor item. If the objective is to raise Latin America's capacity to pay for capital imports, one method would be to raise net official payments or net long-term public loans. But clearly, a very substantial rise would be needed to have any significant impact—and the benefits could easily be wiped out, for example by a rise in shipping rates or by an increase in "errors and omissions."

ECLA calculates what it calls the "net contribution to external purchasing power" made by foreign capital flows—aid, investment, and

TABLE 3.   FOREIGN CAPITAL FLOWS TO LATIN AMERICA, 1960–66
(*billions of dollars*)

	19 Republics	18 Republics (excluding Venezuela)
1960	+0.4	+1.1
1961	+0.3	+1.1
1962	+0.1	+1.1
1963	−0.1	+0.7
1964	+0.2	+0.9
1965	−0.8	−0.2
1966	−0.4	+0.2

Source: United Nations, Economic Commission for Latin America, *Economic Survey of Latin America*, Vol. 12, 1967 (E/CN.12/808), Santiago, Chile, 1968.

autonomous and compensatory loans, offset by profits, interest payments, and amortization. This concept seems to me the most appropriate if we want to measure the real "flow of resources" to less developed areas.

ECLA comments ". . . the aggregate flow of autonomous and compensatory foreign capital made a positive, although sharply declining, contribution to the capacity to import up to 1962. In the following years, with the exception of 1964, the position was reversed, and negative figures of about $820 million and $350 million were shown in 1965 and 1966 respectively, so that imports in those years were curtailed by the same amounts." [8]

Of course, the picture would look more favorable if Venezuela was excluded, but there remains a declining trend in "flow of resources" to the eighteen other republics, as Table 3 shows.

On the other hand, these figures only show the "flow of resources" by foreign capital; the picture would look worse if we could include the substantial outflow of domestic capital from the region, which also affects its capacity to import.

Now, using this concept of "flow of resources," and assuming the same objective of raising capacity to pay for capital imports, the same end might be better achieved by efforts to influence items of the accounts other than the aid figures. For example, a "partnership in development" between rich and poor countries might do better to stimulate shipping and insurance industries in the developing countries, or, at least, to eliminate monopolistic pricing of existing shipping conferences. Better still would be a concerted attempt to discourage profit repatriation from the less developed countries. The cooperation of developed countries might enable developing countries to tax more heavily those enterprises that repatriate more of their profits. If this seems utopian, one could at least ask developed countries to cooperate with those less developed countries that seek to reduce monopolistic profiteering by adopting appropriate tax policies, anti-trust measures, or nationalization. (This follows naturally from the Pearson Report analysis (p. 10) that "where monopoly profits are being earned [by foreign companies] the proper remedy would be to reduce tariffs, take action against specific monopoly practices, renegotiate concession agreements, or initiate competitive enterprise." Developed countries do not always favor such policies.)

From this viewpoint, Latin America would clearly do better if it were allowed to halt interest and profit payments on past capital movements, even though this meant losing all foreseeable future inflows of foreign capital. It would need an implausibly large increase in these inflows to make them more attractive than this hypothetical alternative. The governments of the developed countries would presumably want to compensate the private interests affected; that might be the most effective form of aid they could give.

Conclusion

Clearly there is considerable room for honest differences of opinion about what should properly be described as a "flow of resources" from developed to underdeveloped countries. The net flow of official grants and loans from rich to poor countries is an important positive transfer which the Pearson Commission is understandably anxious to increase. But the "flow of resources" cannot simply refer to this one item. For, if we use the term in this way, we are forced to admit that what we are calling a "positive flow of resources" can coexist with a situation where a poor country needs to export twice as much to the rich country as it can import from it. Surely the term must be reserved for situations in which the aggregate capital inflow net of interest and profit repatriation enables the recipient country to import more goods and services than it exports. A reverse situation must deserve the label "negative flow of resources."

Of course, some components of this flow which are consciously budgeted by the governments of developed countries may be separated for the purpose of analysis. They may even be labeled "aid," although one might object that the term implies that the recipient is obtaining something below cost and should therefore be grateful.

But when such calculations are made, they must not be used dishonestly. We have heard a lot of rhetoric about "unprecedented transfer of resources" and "great adventure." No doubt the donor governments, only conscious of taxpayers' resistance to aid programs, feel they are making an unprecedented effort. But the process cannot be viewed solely from the angle of the donor governments. For the recipient governments the perspective is different. Latin American governments find themselves needing to export more than they import, to run up foreign debts, and to run their economic (and political) policy to the satisfaction of foreign investors,[9] simply to pay off the profits and interest on their past debts. Furthermore, an increase in "aid" may not raise the capacity to import at all, if, at the same time, developments elsewhere, themselves the results of increased aid, tend to produce rising outflows under such headings as "transport and insurance," "profits and interest payments," and "errors and omissions."

TRENDS IN INTEREST AND PROFIT OUTFLOW

Public Indebtedness

At the end of 1950, the cumulative external public debt of the nineteen Latin American republics stood at $2.2 billion. It rose to $4.0 billion in 1955, $6.6 billion in 1960, and $8.9 billion in 1962.[10] More recent figures are provided by the Pearson Report, which shows a larger figure because it includes Guyana, Jamaica, and Trinidad and Tobago. The external public debt of these twenty-two countries rose from $10.2 billion at the end of 1962 to $12.2 billion in 1965, $14.5 billion in 1967, and $14.8 billion by June 30, 1968. (Pearson Report, p. 371) The public indebtedness of Latin America grew more slowly than that of any other part of the Third World in the 1960s, but even so it was rising in proportion to the area's GNP. External public debt of the nineteen republics rose from 5.7% of their GNP in 1950 to 8.5% in 1960 and about 10.7% by 1965. On the historical record, such loans appear to resemble addictive rather than curative drugs. Extrapolating the trend we can guess that public debt may well now be about 14% of Latin America's GNP, and by 1980 it could easily be approaching 20%. The extent to which this would impede economic growth of the area depends on the terms of the loans provided. But even on generous terms, the accumulation of such a large volume of debt, in relation to resources, would represent a potentially huge obligation. Even with very generous repayment terms the temptation to default would be rather considerable. The question therefore arises whether a rising ratio of indebtedness is a necessary aspect of aid policy for the seventies.

Direct Foreign Investment

A full account of long-term external obligations ought also to include the balance of private transactions. Portfolio capital is relatively unimportant (less than 15%) so I shall concentrate on direct foreign investment. The Pearson Report (pp. 371 and 376) shows that whereas only 31.4% of the Third World's public debt was incurred by Latin American countries in 1966, the continent received 52.3% of the developed countries' direct foreign investment. This total investment of $15.7 billion was allocated as follows: $5.3 billion in manufacturing, $4.9 billion in oil, $1.7 billion in mining and smelting, and no less than $3.8 billion in "other" branches (which includes the growing number of foreign-owned supermarkets, banks, hotels, and also the traditional foreign investments in plantation land, shipping, and the like). Another source shows the regional breakdown of this investment—with Venezuela receiving almost one-third of the total, and Argentina and Brazil between them receiving fully another third.[11]

Slightly less than two-thirds of this direct foreign investment was by United States companies ($9.8 billion in 1966), and it was highly concentrated. ECLA states that "at the end of 1950, for instance, some 300 large United States companies, each having assets of $50 million or more, owned over 90% of all United States direct investments in Latin America."[12] (Direct investment is defined as a situation in which United States ownership in the enterprise is at least 10%.) They consider that this concentration has probably increased since then.

ECLA figures, brought up to date by my own estimates, show that the average rate of return on United States investments in Latin America fell sharply in the second half of the fifties (principally because the profit

TABLE 4. ESTIMATED PERCENTAGE OF RETURN ON U.S. DIRECT
INVESTMENTS IN LATIN AMERICA

	1951–55	1956–60	1961–65	1966–68
Mining and smelting	9.2%	11.0%	15.0%	22.6%
Petroleum	29.5	18.1	15.5	16.2
Manufacturing	12.0	9.0	9.1	9.4
Other	9.4	8.0	8.4	7.1
All	15.0	10.9	11.9	12.4

Sources: United Nations, Economic Commission for Latin America, *External Financing in Latin America* (E/CN.12/649), New York, 1965, for the period 1951–60. Subsequent years calculated from U.S., Department of Commerce, *Survey of Current Business* annual reviews of foreign investment. (Book value of investment. Net earnings after local taxes.)

margin on Venezuela petrol investments was sharply reduced by the revolution of 1958), but has gradually risen since, to about 12.4% in 1968. Despite this improved profit situation very little new capital was attracted in, and the great bulk of the profits obtained by foreign investors was not ploughed back but repatriated to the parent company. For example, between 1960 and 1968 the total earnings of United States direct investments in Latin America were $9.9 billion, according to the U.S. Department of Commerce. No less than $7.7 billion was repatriated to the United States. Of course, if the case of Venezuela were treated separately, the picture would be slightly less startling, but even in the rest of Latin America most profits earned by American companies flow out of the country.

It is very difficult to make reliable estimates of changes in the volume of foreign investment in Latin America over time. I estimate that direct foreign investment fell from 18.8% of Latin America's GNP in 1950, to 16.3% in 1960, and 13.3% in 1965. This almost certainly exaggerates the trend. For example, Mexican laws now require in many sectors at least 51% ownership by Mexican nationals. Statistics of foreign investment in Mexico therefore underestimate the real amount of foreign control over the economy, since Mexican owners of some enterprises are often merely nominees for foreign investors. To this extent foreign investment may be keeping pace with the growth of Latin America's GNP and some of the capital outflow I have identified as coming from domestic Latin American enterprises may really be coming from foreign-controlled companies disguised as national concerns. On such shaky evidence I hesitate to make any prediction about the future growth of foreign investment, particularly since current nationalizations are likely to affect the business climate, and the relative attractiveness of Latin America depends not only on conditions in the area but also on the alternatives available elsewhere.

However, at existing rates of return, and in the present political climate, it seems impossible for Latin America to bid large amounts of capital away from the alternative opportunities available in many industrial countries. Certainly there was a period when generous terms *did* attract a fair amount of capital, but few governments are able to continue offering such terms indefinitely. Once foreign investments have become substantial, any political instability or decline in generosity to foreign investors produces a turnaround. The milking of established investments becomes the prevailing pattern. In these circumstances it may be difficult to attract more foreign investment without establishing authoritarian regimes, pursuing inflexibly orthodox economic policies, and offering huge incentives to foreign companies. Many Latin American regimes have gone a long way in this direction, but most have not, apparently, gone far enough to achieve success. Mr. Nixon, Mr. Rockefeller, and Mr. Pearson appear to recommend even greater efforts in the same direction, but prevailing opinion in Latin America, as expressed at Viña del Mar and by the recent spate of nationalizations, suggests a preference for another alternative. Instead of attracting new foreign investment, the costs of existing investment may be curtailed.

Trends in the Balance of Payments Costs

We have seen that public external obligations are rising fast, while private obligations have probably remained static or even declined slightly in proportion to Latin America's GNP. But the ratio of these obligations to GNP represents only a theoretical and long-term claim on the area's resources. It is the servicing of these obligations that presents the immediate problem. The Pearson Commission has analyzed this servicing problem, showing that the terms of official aid loans have hardened in the sixties, and recommending a new standard for acceptable loan terms.

TABLE 5. INVESTMENT INCOME AS A PERCENTAGE OF EARNINGS
ON CURRENT ACCOUNT

	1946–50	1951–55	1956–60	1961–65	1966–67
19 Republics					
Direct Investment Income	10.0%	10.6%	11.3%	10.8%	10.9%
Interest	1.6	1.2	2.0	3.8	4.3
All Investment Income	11.6	11.8	13.3	14.6	15.2
18 Republics					
Direct Investment Income	5.6%	5.7%	5.6%	6.5%	6.8%
Interest	1.9	1.5	2.7	4.8	5.2
All Investment Income	7.5	7.2	8.3	11.3	12.0

Sources: United Nations, Economic Commission for Latin America, *External Financing in Latin America* (E/CN.12/649), New York, 1965, p. 64. Figures for 1961–67 calculated from ECLA, *Survey of Latin America*, Vol. 11, 1966 (E/CN.12/767 Rev. 1), (New York, 1968), pp. 68–71, and ECLA, *Economic Survey of Latin America*, Vol. 12, 1967 (E/CN.12/808), Santiago, Chile, 1968, pp. 63, 94–95.

Table 5 shows investment outflow as a percentage of Latin America's earnings on current account. From 1946–50 to 1966–67 investment outflow rose from 11.6% of current account earnings to 15.2%. Most of this increased burden on export earnings can be traced to the growth of interest payments, reflecting both the rapid rise of public indebtedness and the hardening of terms. Profit outflow in the same period remained fairly steady at between 10% and 11% of Latin America's current account earnings. However, if we exclude Venezuela, where the profit outflow of the oil companies has been sharply cut back, we find that for the remaining eighteen republics profit outflow has also been a rising proportion of current account earnings.

It is difficult to project these figures into the future. On one hand, we may hope that Latin America's export earnings will rise faster in the next decade. Additionally, the volume of direct foreign investment is difficult to predict, the rate of return is liable to considerable fluctuations, and the proportion of profits reinvested may be quite sensitive to policy changes. On the other hand, a further rise in public debt can be predicted with some confidence. If this is accompanied by a further hardening of terms on which loans are granted, as much as 7% or even 8% of current account earnings might need to be earmarked for interest payments by 1980. However, if the Commission's recommendation (that no future loans should carry more than a 2% interest rate) were immediately implemented, then, even with increasing indebtedness and the present rate of growth of exports, interest payments would probably not rise much above their present proportions—at least not unless better loan terms resulted in a greatly accelerated growth of indebtedness.

In other words, even if the Commission's proposals are immediately and fully implemented, throughout the next decade we can expect the nineteen republics to continue paying approximately 15% of their foreign exchange earnings as profits and interest on their foreign obligations. If the Commission proves over-optimistic—either about the rate of growth of exports or the improvements in loan terms that are forthcoming—investment income could rise to as much as 20% of foreign exchange earnings by 1980.

It could be objected that this discussion of balance of payments costs of private investment is one-sided. So far I have simply regarded profit outflow as a negative item in the calculations of "flow of resources," and a growing levy on export earnings. The Pearson Report itself condemns attempts to measure the balance of payments impact of foreign investment simply by comparing "new capital inflow" with the total profits of the accumulated foreign investment in the country. It may be that foreign investment has created a large export sector to offset the burden of profit outflow and thereby made possible the servicing of this burden. Furthermore, foreign investments may generate large tax incomes to finance development expenditure, and they provide access to the latest advances in technology. (See Pearson Report, pp. 100–101.)

If we include all these indirect effects, it may well be true that a country will grow faster receiving some foreign investment than not receiving any. But the question Latin America faces now is not this. Rather, given the growing burden of past foreign investment and the scarcity of new investment funds on acceptable terms, will the continent now grow faster by trying to attract still more investment or by curtailing the costs of existing investments?

Let us reconsider foreign investment in this light. There is an immediate and certain burden of profit outflow to service past investments. To offset it, there is the possible benefit of new capital inflow, and a possible contribution to export capacity or import substitution by these new foreign enterprises. Thus, where the profit burden is already very heavy and the prospects of offsetting benefits seem very uncertain, the balance of payments situation may still justify expropriation or nationalization.

There are some indirect benefits, but also perhaps some disadvantages. Sometimes the indirect effects reinforce the direct effects in the sense of justifying expropriation. Albert Hirschman has recently argued that the most important effects of foreign investment in Latin America are indirect, and that *at the present stage* they are increasingly negative. "If this is so," he concludes, "then the climate for foreign investment ought to turn from attractive at an early stage of development to much less inviting in some middle stretch—in which most of Latin America finds itself in the present time." [13]

So, because of both economic reasons and current political trends in the area, we cannot confine our analysis to the possible benefits of increased aid and private investment. We must consider what policies the developed countries should adopt if confronted by expropriation and default.

Expropriation and Default

The Latin American republics have a long history of political independence; default is not unthinkable for several have defaulted in the past. When export earnings slumped in the depression, it became totally impossible to service accumulated debts. Chile's servicing obligations amounted to 103% of her export earnings in 1932; for Bolivia the figure was 50%; and for Brazil in 1933 it was 45%. [14]

Since 1945 hardly any country has defaulted on its obligations, other than those which have become Communist. The international agencies exercise fairly effective discipline, and countries on the verge of default have been able to reschedule their debts instead. (The Pearson Report summarizes the record on pages 383–84.) But in Latin America there have been numerous conflicts with private foreign investors. In 1969–70 Peru and Bolivia nationalized foreign oil companies without paying any compensation. Clearly a policy for aiding less developed countries needs to establish an attitude in the face of these tendencies.

Bronfenbrenner has bluntly stated the case:

The issue . . . is not whether confiscation can be justified by some accepted or conventional occidental standard of morals or propriety, but merely whether it brings the pragmatic results desired, namely economic development without sacrifice to the scale of living of the mass of the population. It will be our contention that confiscation has done so, is doing so, and will continue to do so, by shifting income to developmental investment from capitalists' consumption, from transfer abroad, and from unproductive "investment" like luxury housing. Therein lies the appeal of confiscation, although it is argued persuasively on the other side in developed countries that these accomplishments require totalitarian dictatorship for their realisation, and that development is not worth this price.[15]

Perhaps this account assumes too readily that confiscation will be accompanied by other policies conducive to economic development. Bolivia, for example, nationalized Standard Oil in 1937, the major tin companies in 1952, and Gulf Oil in 1969, without any of these measures bringing "the pragmatic results desired" so far. On the other hand, a great deal of capital is currently being transferred from Latin America which could otherwise be devoted to productive investment. It is not at all clear that continued respect for existing obligations will bring a sufficient inflow of new capital to compensate for such losses. Not only are private investors very hesitant, but the 1970 United States Foreign Aid Bill is the lowest since the program began, and Latin America is a low priority. The political costs of confiscation depend on how violently the developed countries react to it.

Therefore Bronfenbrenner's recommendations still appear relevant to contemporary "aid" policies in Latin America:

1. Diplomatic relations with confiscating governments should not be broken off.

2. No more favorable treatment should be demanded for Western nationals in the event of confiscation than is given to citizens of the confiscating country . . .

3. Domestic compensation for victims of foreign expropriation should neither be promised nor ruled out wholesale. Amounts to be paid should be estimated on the merits of individual cases, with consideration for (a) the manner in which the property was acquired, (b) the historical and reproduction costs of the assets confiscated, (c) the record of the claimants' relations with the people and government of the confiscating country prior to confiscation, and (d) the returns already paid prior to confiscation.[16]

The same principles can be extended to public indebtedness. If large new loans on generous terms are not available, a government may be justified in defaulting. When this happens, it must naturally debar the country concerned from future credit, but there should be no automatic imposition of further penalties. These may only force the country into a siege-like economic strategy, as with Cuba. In some circumstances the quiet acceptance of expropriation and default may be the greatest contribution the developed countries can make to the welfare of the less developed. Perhaps the real turning point in aid to Latin America in the sixties has been the failure to invoke the "Hickenlooper Amendment" against Peru in retaliation for its virtual expropriation of the International Petroleum Corporation.

THE EFFECTS OF INCREASED "AID"

The case for confiscation and default will be weaker if the Pearson Commission recommendations come into effect and the volume of credit is stepped up and the terms are eased. In that case, the foreign exchange costs of investment outflow may be more than offset by the inflow of new capital. The moment for default would be postponed, although the eventual scale of default would quite possibly be even greater in the end. Only if aid has a direct and powerful effect on the growth rate will increased aid now reduce the pressures to default later. But the Pearson Report (p. 49) states quite clearly that "the correlation between the amounts of aid received in the past decade, and the growth performance is very weak." Unless we can find good reasons for expecting a change in the future, even the full implementation of the Pearson Commission's proposals would not really remove the temptation to expropriation and default.

Possible Explanations

It could be argued that aid really does increase growth and that those countries that received most aid were most in need of it—without aid their growth record would have been even worse. Even if this argument could be proved, the correct conclusion would be to investigate why some countries grow faster even without much aid. The correct policy might be to effect changes on other fronts rather than increase the amount of aid. In the absence of other changes, the present levels of assistance are not inducing sufficient growth to permit independence from aid at any foreseeable time in the future. In these circumstances, to rely on "more of the same" to accelerate self-sustaining growth appears to be an act of faith

Recently Keith Griffin has volunteered some suggestions why there is no association between aid and growth. Of course, unless one argues that aid is the *major* determinant of growth, one should not expect a strong positive association between these two variables. But it is interesting that, using data from twelve Latin American republics, 1957–64, Griffin found a loose *negative* association. He went on to suggest some reasons why such a result might be expected.

Aid may produce a shift toward less efficient use of capital—data for twelve Latin American countries show that the capital/output ratio varies positively with the amount of aid received. More important, additional foreign resources, provided through aid, permit an increased level of activity, but it would be very rash to assume that all this extra activity is increased investment. Aid should also permit some increases in domestic consumption, in which case the increase in foreign savings may be offset by some reduction in domestic savings. He found that in Colombia, 1950–63, "for every dollar of foreign aid received, domestic savings declined by about eighty-four cents." [17] Finally, foreign aid usually carries with it the obligation to offer favorable conditions to foreign private investors. Griffin is concerned that this strategy impedes the emergence of a strong domestic entrepreneurial class or of a cohesive developmental ideology. He cites the case of Mexico after the nationalization of foreign oil companies in 1938, where a foreign boycott and domestic mobilization of the masses paved the way for subsequent growth.

My discussion of Latin America's capital flows suggests a possible additional argument: aid inflows are related to the favorable treatment of foreign investors, but they cannot secure such favorable treatment as to attract substantial private capital away from Europe, Canada, and so on, into Latin America. The treatment is just favorable enough to permit unrestricted outflow of private domestic and foreign capital and profits. Furthermore, aid flows to individual countries tend to increase in times of political instability, when future development gains have to be sacrificed to immediate political necessities. Therefore, to some extent, aid inflows may foreshadow a decline in growth rather than be the cause of it. But, in periods of uncertainty, by bolstering regimes committed to free movements of capital, the positive effects of public capital inflows on growth may be offset by the negative effects of profit repatriation and private capital outflow.[18] Indeed full convertibility is normally a *sine qua non* for the receipt of aid.

Griffin's argument tends to imply that growth would be accelerated to the extent that aid was curtailed. My argument, by contrast, implies that growth would be accelerated to the extent that private capital outflow was curtailed. Instead of arguing for the reduction of aid, I argue for a changed strategy of aid-giving. We should cooperate with those countries that try to stem the outflow of private capital, by whatever means seem most appropriate in the circumstances. Sometimes it may be by nationalization, sometimes by tax measures, sometimes (although not very often) simply by foreign exchange controls, and sometimes by measures promoting the local reinvestment of profits. Griffin objects that this last solution "would lead to the denationalization of existing nationally owned industries, to a rapid rise in foreign owned enterprises relative to domestically owned firms, and to even larger profit repatriation at a later stage." [19] The first two objections are irrelevant to the question of growth (although not to the question of kind of society). The third objection should be tackled when the situation arises. If all other methods of stemming the outflow of private capital prove impractical, Latin American governments may secure greater growth by confiscating both domestic and foreign accumulations of private capital.

The argument is not that only Communist regimes should receive aid. It is simply that, if developed countries want to accelerate the rate of growth of the less developed (rather than merely to keep them as political and economic client-states), they should cooperate with efforts to stem the outflow of private capital. If a sovereign state decides the only effective way to achieve this end is to abrogate the rights of private property, then those genuinely in favor of development should try to restrain the developed countries from excessive and damaging retaliation.

CONCLUSION

1. The real "flow of resources" from developed to less developed countries has frequently been exaggerated. A more realistic account of total transactions should be provided. Grants or loans that carry with

them direct obligations to acts of violence at home or abroad should be called aid-bribes, or preferably be discontinued.

2. Latin American countries should be encouraged to develop their own merchant marines and insurance facilities, whenever these would be broadly competitive.[20]

3. Developed countries should cooperate with efforts by less developed countries to stem the outflow of private capital, whether foreign or domestic. The utmost restraint should be exercised in dealing with cases of nationalization or expropriation.

4. Public loans may be offered on more generous terms and administered through multilateral agencies. But to be effective it is more important that they no longer be associated with concessionary terms for private capital. It may sometimes be sound policy for less developed countries to default, in which case they will inevitably be debarred from further credit, but additional sanctions should be avoided.

5. Efforts should be made to minimize the indirect costs of aid—both indirect financial costs and the effects on local enterprise. Among other things, the emoluments of foreign experts could be drastically reduced.

Even if all these measures were fully implemented, they would not be sufficient to guarantee rapidly accelerated growth, but they would leave the Latin American republics freer to grow fast.

How realistic a list is this? Items 1 and 5 are relatively moderate measures, which might be acceptable to the developed countries and would be marginal improvements. Item 2 might raise more difficulties, but at least some steps could be taken in this direction. The chief difficulties are likely to arise over points 3 and 4, where private enterprise and market discipline may seem threatened. There are those who believe that the developed capitalist countries will go to any lengths to maintain private foreign investment and external debt servicing. In fact the choice is not necessarily so stark as that. "Chileanization" may become more acceptable, if it is seen as the only alternative to nationalization; debt rescheduling terms become easier the greater the felt danger of default. Perhaps if overseas investments cause enough friction, the United States government might even adopt Hirschman's scheme for an Inter-American Divestment Corporation. But these solutions will be powerfully resisted in the developed countries, except for rather brief periods when the triumph of a worse alternative seems particularly imminent (as when the Alliance for Progress was founded in 1961), or when a major failure of foreign policy produces a temporary reluctance to risk further entanglements (as the Vietnam war has sheltered the Peruvians and Bolivians). We cannot focus our attention exclusively on these episodes of generosity and assume that there normally exists a broad harmony of interests between developed and developing countries. Those in the developed countries concerned with the progress of the Third World must be willing to fight against exploitative tendencies at home.

Development and Special Drawing Rights: A Statement

BY ROBERT TRIFFIN

The Pearson Report is indeed a model of brevity on the relationship between development and liquidity. All I could discover on this subject was a single paragraph of about half a page (p. 225). Even this paragraph is mostly descriptive and factual. Its only concrete suggestions are contained in two sentences and are not even mentioned in the specific recommendations listed in conclusion. They are:

1. "But when the scale of the issue of SDR's has been decided on appropriate grounds, there are strong reasons of simplicity and equity for the developed countries to relinquish a part of their quota of the new reserve medium in favor of the less developed countries.

2. "IDA may be a channel by which the contribution of the resources to development could be assured, and proposals for making use of this channel in this way are worthy of study." (Pearson Report, p. 225)

I cannot but feel that this is a meager crop, and an extraordinarily timid and inadequate treatment of a vital issue. One might argue that political realism dictated such modesty on the part of the Commission. Yet the elected representatives of one of the major donor countries showed much more daring and courage than the Commission. The Joint Economic Subcommittee of the United States Congress on International Exchange and Payments, after extensive hearings, has come out repeatedly in favor of linking SDR's and development assistance. Its last report on the subject recommended to the Annual Meeting of the IMF and the World Bank the following resolution:

"Resolved, that the Executive Directors of the International Monetary Fund and the International Bank for Reconstruction and Development promptly consider an amendment to the IMF Article of Agreement, supplementing the Special Drawing Rights amendment ratified on July 28, 1969, whereby those IMF members who have previously contributed to the International Development Association would direct that 25 per cent of their Special Drawing Rights allocations be retained by the IMF to finance expanded IDA development assistance."

I certainly feel that this would be at least—to use a time-hallowed formula—"a step in the right direction." Eventually, it should go much further: all—and not only 25%—of the SDR allocation should be earmarked for *collectively agreed purposes,* rather than, as now, for arbitrary distribution to all IMF members in support of whatever *national* policies they are currently following, which may, at times, be totally contrary to the views and interests of the world community, and even to those of the major contributors to the SDR system.

My views on this are well known, and I have summarized them as forcefully as I could before the Congressional Subcommittee referred to above. (See particularly its *Hearings* of May 28, 1969.)

While recognizing the immense and path-breaking program initiated by the SDR Agreement, I submitted that its arbitrary method of allocation was:

(1) *Morally repugnant:* distributing two-thirds or more of the SDR's as near-gifts or soft loans to the richer countries in the world;

(2) *Economically absurd:* distributing them as manna from heaven in support of disruptive, as well as of cooperative, national policies;

(3) *Politically unviable (fortunately):* because major net lenders could not agree indefinitely to sign such blank checks financing policies in which they have no voice and with which they may thoroughly disagree.

The only moral, economic, and political long-run solution is that *collectively created* SDR's should be put at the service of *collectively agreed* policies, development financing being at least one of the latter. The lending power conferred to the IMF by the willingness of its members to accept SDR's as part and parcel of their monetary reserves should be used by the IMF to finance such jointly agreed policies, e.g. through the purchase of development obligations from the World Bank, the IDA, etc.

Far from being a radical innovation, such a procedure would bar a radical, but retrogressive, innovation in world monetary arrangements. It would retain a traditional link between reserve accumulation and development financing, rather than break that link as envisaged under the present system of SDR allocation. The accumulation of sterling balances as reserves by foreign central banks traditionally helped Britain finance a larger amount of capital exports particularly to less developed countries than it could have sustained otherwise. The same was true of the dollar balances accumulated, in the same way, by foreign central banks, and particularly by the surplus countries of continental Europe since the end of World War II. We would have been unable to finance as large an amount of foreign aid and capital exports if surplus countries had cashed their dollar reserves for gold. In essence, the willingness of foreign monetary authorities to accumulate large reserves in the form of sterling and dollar balances enhances the ability of London and New York to provide long-term financing for economic development, private and official, to the countries of the Third World.

The basic assumption underlying the creation of SDR's, that they will have to substitute gradually, but increasingly, in the future for reserve currencies in development financing, should certainly not suffer as a consequence of this shift. What would be revolutionary, but in a retrogressive direction, would be to terminate a "link" which has always existed in the past between the creation of fiduciary reserves and development financing.

Throughout history reserves have always had to be either earned or borrowed, and this latter method of reserves accumulation—or reconstitution—was normally and more appropriately used by the developing countries rather than by the highly developed and capitalized ones. These normally *earned* their reserves by transferring to other countries more goods and services than they absorbed from them; i.e. by contributing to foreign economic development.

The SDR agreement would enable them to accumulate reserves without having to earn them. They would get each year, under the present Agreement, more than $2 billion of reserves, and probably much more in the course of time, without having to contribute a cent to development financing.

My own long-term proposal would be to increase reserve creation by securing agreement from all countries to accumulate an agreed portion of their reserve in the form of deposits with the Fund. This would enlarge the lending capacity of the Fund, but the Fund would not necessarily use this lending capacity to the full. It would do so to the extent required to assure a reasonable growth rate of reserves (probably 4% to 5% a year on the average) in the light of generalized inflationary or deflationary pressures on the world economy. It could even be limited by treaty to the average rate of increase regarded as desirable, larger increases requiring more than a simple majority vote.

The $3 billion—roughly—of new reserves that the Fund should be called upon to create annually under such a formula would be used to finance *collectively agreed* objectives. Financial assistance to developing countries would come under this category and could be extended, for the most part, through the intermediary of specialized institutions such as IDA or the World Bank. The Fund would buy the obligations of such institutions, enabling them to enlarge their operations. The developing countries would increase, thereby, their next expenditures abroad, leading to a corresponding growth of *earned* reserves by the countries in surplus, i.e. by those that contribute real resources to economic development.

This would not be enough to satisfy all the needs of the so-called Third World, but $2 to $3 billion a year is not to be sneezed at, and would be far better employed in this way than through any alternative method of reserves increases now in sight.

CHAPTER FOUR

PRIVATE INVESTMENT

The Debate

The Pearson Commission's proposals for private investment are directed toward improving the climate for investment and smoothing out some of the difficulties which arise in what is, politically, an increasingly sensitive area. The Report affirms that private investment can be a genuine spur to local development. It can bring in otherwise unobtainable technology and managerial experience. It can engage in local training at all levels. It can provide employment and stimulate local habits of saving and investment. It can, by increasing local efficiency and diversifying local production, save imports and increase exports. These indirect effects must, the Report suggests, be added to the advantage of the direct inflow of foreign exchange.

True, the overall flow of direct investment is still not much higher than that of the 1950's—about $2.7 billion a year. The distribution of the benefits is also uneven. Half of all private, direct investment in developing lands is in minerals, 40% in oil alone. Half of the cumulative total is accounted for by Latin America.

One can argue that the sharp rise in portfolio investment helps to offset the low direct flow. It had grown from just under $200 million a year in the early 1960's to over a billion dollars in 1968. But successful bond issues are usually confined to the more promising states. Countries with per capita incomes of less than $100 attract not much more than 12% of private investment, direct or indirect. In fact, it is neither a major spur nor a major problem in the poorest lands—unless, as in Gabon or Kuwait or Mauretania, there is virtually nothing else. But then, of course, such countries are no longer "poor" on a per capita basis, however backward in every other respect.

But, all in all, the benefits of private investment are judged to be substantial. They do not replace the need for concessional assistance. But they reinforce the public effort. So the Report recommends that the local environment for domestic and foreign private investment be improved and made more stabile, that the reinvestment of profits and the sale of equity to local purchasers be encouraged, that such agencies as the International Finance Corporation assist the governments in developing nations to assess foreign initiatives and to negotiate agreements, and that they generally make expert advice available on industrial policy.

In the Conference debates on private investment, opinion divided as on other topics. Particularly in the New York sessions, the Pearson Report's proposals raised no difficulty for those who spoke from a background of administration and management of international capital. These participants pointed out that one of the main aims of modern foreign investors is to project "a good corporate image" in the host country. The old buccaneering days when traders "followed the flag" (or, as often, took it along with them) are over now. Developing countries enjoy political independence. They can strike their own bargains. All that is required is a proper recognition of the just needs of private enterprise—security to repatriate profits, security against arbitrary or uncompensated nationalization, security against xenophobic forms of discrimination, and so forth. Provide the right climate and the capital can flow in, to the benefit of investing firms and receiving states.

The central body of opinion at the Conference took a more discriminating line. One could call them "show me" supporters of private investment. They did not deny its capacity to transfer technological skills and stimulate local production. But they did suggest a long hard look at the price tag. As Laurence Whitehead's paper had pointed out (see Chapter 3), the return payments for foreign investment may well exceed new sums flowing in, thus adding to the pressures on the balance of payments. Both Paul Streeten and Michael Kidron disputed the indirect benefits postulated in the Pearson Report since such benefits flow from any form of investment, local or foreign, and, in any case, can be assumed only if the foreign investment diverts no local resources from other uses, pulls no potential exports into local processing, and stimulates no otherwise avoidable imports. Specific calculations might show foreign investment to be as likely to increase the problem of foreign exchange as to lighten it—save perhaps in oil states so lacking in other activities that the whole stimulus to larger exports can be attributed to the single major industry.

Even obvious "benefits"—the reinvestment of profits or the introduction of otherwise unavailable technology or technical assistance from outside agencies in working out the investment bargain—aroused some skepticism. Might there not be danger in a reinvestment rate which steadily increased foreign control of the new industrial sector? Would the new technology match with local levels of need and training, or would it perpetuate the division between elite sectors and the often unemployed, unskilled masses? In any case, was the wholly owned subsidiary the only possible route to advanced technology? Might it not also be secured by methods which entail a less heavy future financial outflow—by management agreements coupled with transfer of techniques, by joint ventures, by large local minority or majority holdings? And, in the matter of technical assistance, The Honorable Mohamed Diawara, minister of planning for the Ivory Coast, reminded other participants that, in former periods, private enterprise came in and made its own technical decisions, profits, or mistakes. So it carried its own burdens. Today, however sophisticated the technical advice given by outside organizations, it could be wrong. Then it would involve local governments in expensive mistakes, in which case "the state has no recourse to an appeal procedure against the firm of consultants or those who loaned the funds and if the state does not pay—on the grounds that it was misled—the world will be outraged by this breach, and, by way of example only, the World Bank will refuse any new loan because there is litigation."

Behind virtually all the reservations which found expression in the debates there lay not so much doubts about the economic advantages of private investment as about its social and political drawbacks. Above all, there were doubts in that most sensitive of areas, the post-colonial achievement of sovereignty, where the risk was felt to be loss of independence, loss of control. For this reason, the role of the new multinational corporations as instruments of development was intensely debated.

Some shared Harry G. Johnson's belief that they represent potential instruments of economic growth and unification on a worldwide scale, beyond the irrationalities of national boundaries. (See "The Multinational Corporation as an Agency of International Development" in this chapter.) Judd Polk, reminding the Conference of the astonishing growth of the American giants—their overseas output is now, at $200 billion, equal to 20% of the United States GNP—argued that "investment abroad is clearly in the direction of the better international use of resources induced by the real pull of higher marginal yields." Might not the multinational corporations do for a world economy what the big American corporations did for the United States at the turn of the century—create a vast, unified market in which specialization, the division of labor, comparative advantage, and the highest productivity are produced by an "optimum mix" of the factors of production?

At this point the debate plunged straight back to the center of the Conference's main division—those who accepted the existing world economy as normal, and those who saw it as neocolonial, based on domination by the rich and exploitation of the poor. If circumstances are held to be normal, this dependence (or domination) can be described as an optimum mix of factors of production. From the neocolonial angle of vision, it becomes the "specialization" of the poor in providing unworked materials and unskilled labor while the rich—nations, firms, multinational corporations, individuals—provide the investment, the management, the technology, and the research, and in return engross the whole profit. The bargain is altogether too uneven and has increasing political implications. Just as Populism in the Western United States was the response to Eastern domination at the turn of the century, so, today, a new "populism" could easily sweep the developing world.

This, indeed, *was* the response of the radical minority, and for them the only sane solution was an end to further private investment, expropriation of existing enterprises, and the creation of local, self-reliant industry with whatever technical assistance can be secured entirely without strings.

The middle ground of the Conference was occupied by those who, on the whole, agreed with the arguments developed both by Professor

Streeten and by Albert O. Hirschman. (See "How to Divest in Latin America and Why" in this chapter.) Private investment is valuable. It does provide indispensable technological imports. But it can be too powerful and it can stay too long. The solution lies in institutional inventiveness—in devising new frameworks for private investment which capture the advantages and eliminate the risks. Orderly forms of transfer to local ownership, possibly by way of an International Divestment Corporation, could be the answer in some cases. A new statute of internationalization might be required for the new planetary corporations. But one thing seemed clear. Any arrangement perpetuating the total dependence of the poorer countries, however realistic it may seem in terms of today, would be unlikely to survive the "populist" explosions of tomorrow.

The Multi-National Corporation
as an Agency of Economic Development:
Some Exploratory Observations

BY HARRY G. JOHNSON

During the past twenty years or so the large multinational corporation —and primarily the international company based in the United States— has emerged as a potent agent of economic transformation and development, not only in the more laggard "developed" countries but also in the developing countries of the world. Both economic theory and economic policy have been slow in recognizing this phenomenon, which has excited a mixed reaction of welcome to the increased efficiency brought about by foreign direct investment in a country, and of dislike and fear of what is seen as the growth of foreign economic power over the country's destiny. Thus far, in the developed countries, welcome for solid economic advantages has dominated xenophobia, in practice if not always in political pronouncements, though such books as Jean-Jacques Servan-Schreiber's *Le Défi Américain* testify to public concern in Europe, while "American domination" is a perennial worry in Canada.

In the developing countries, the "crisis of aid" with which the Pearson Commission was concerned has made it necessary to take a strongly positive view of what the multinational corporation can contribute to the promotion of economic development, and to look to private foreign investment as an important element in the development process. While the Pearson Report calls for a substantial increase in both the overall total of aid as now conventionally defined and the proportion and total of official aid, contemporary political circumstances make it extremely unlikely that official aid will increase on the scale recommended. It is more likely that official aid will decline, even in absolute real terms, and that increasing emphasis will come to be placed on preferential trading arrangements and on increasing private foreign investment. This prospect makes it necessary to consider the scope for and limitations of the promotion of economic development by private foreign investment, and, more specifically, by direct investment by the multinational corporation.

Heretofore, development promotion has been considered a major responsibility of government, requiring extensive economic planning and at least some degree of effective government intervention in and control over the private sector of the economy, including the activities of foreign corporations. The planning approach to economic development, supported by official foreign aid, has not worked noticeably well in the past, as the Pearson Report documents. This is the major reason why the foreign aid required to support the continuation of that approach is unlikely to be forthcoming in the future, and why the emphasis in development policy is likely to shift toward increased reliance on private competitive forces.

Such a shift of emphasis will, if it is to work effectively to promote development, require fundamental changes of attitude in the developing countries. The multinational corporation is not, like government, able to tax the public to obtain resources to be spent on what are considered politically desirable types of development. Instead, the corporation is constrained by the need for profitability and motivated by the objective of making profits. And a profit-motivated development process will be different in character from a development process planned and controlled by politicians and bureaucrats.

In particular, such a development process is likely to conflict sharply with mounting concern about social justice in the distribution of income. "Social justice" requires the redistribution of income from those who are capable of producing it to those who are not; the best hope is that the latter will eventually become capable of rendering an adequate contribution to the productive process. Profit-motivated development, by contrast, entails rewarding those capable of productive contribution to the extent of that contribution, as a means of stimulating the development of further productive potential.

In concrete terms, reliance on direct foreign investment to promote development is likely to mean highly uneven development, at least with respect to the direct impact of development. There are two reasons for this. The first is that large-scale, direct foreign investment by the multinational corporation is not characteristic of industry in general but instead tends to be confined to industries engaged in the extraction and marketing of natural resources, and to a miscellaneous collection of industries that can be loosely and variously described as "science-based," "technology-intensive," or "characterized by product differentiation." Thus development based on such investment is likely to be highly selective as among industrial sectors. The same phenomenon can, of course, be observed in the advanced countries, where the corporate sector tends to lead the other sectors in efficiency and productivity. The second reason is inherent in the nature of the corporation, as a profit-seeking enterprise, and especially the corporation that undertakes direct foreign investment.

The corporation's concern in establishing branch operations in a particular developing economy is not to promote the development of that economy according to any political conception of what development is, but to make satisfactory profits for its management and shareholders. Its capacity to make profits derives essentially from its possession of productive knowledge, which includes management methods and marketing skills as well as production technology. It has no commercial interest in diffusing its knowledge to potential native competitors, nor has it any interest in investing more than it has to in acquiring knowledge of local conditions and investigating ways of adapting its own productive knowledge to local factor/price ratios and market conditions. Its purpose is not to transform the economy by exploiting its potentialities (especially its human potentialities) for development, but to exploit the existing situation to its own profit by utilization of the knowledge it already possesses, at minimum cost to itself of adaptation and adjustment. The corporation cannot be expected to invest in the development of new technologies appropriate to the typical situation in developing countries of scarcity of capital and abundance of unskilled, uneducated, illiterate labor and in the mass training of blue-collar, white-collar, and especially executive native personnel. It already has at its disposal an effective technology appropriate to the abundance of capital and skilled labor in the developed countries, as well as access to the capital and skilled-labor markets in the developed countries. Hence it will invest in technological research on the adaptation of its technology and in the development of local labor skills only to the extent that such investment holds a clear prospect of profit.

While the multinational firm has an incentive to invest in the transformation of the local economy only to the extent that such investment promises greater profits, the incentive may nevertheless be sufficient to induce a substantial contribution to development. Two particular incentives are especially important in this connection. First, labor skills imported from the developed countries are likely to be extremely expensive in comparison with the cost of training local labor, especially as the cost of training is largely either the labor-time of teachers or the labor-time of students, both of which are infinitely cheaper in poor countries than in rich ones. Hence, the foreign company will have a large profit incentive to train a native staff rather than import foreign labor.

Second, given the complex input-output relations characteristic of modern industry and the dependence of profitable utilization of the product on the knowledge of the user, the firm may have a substantial incentive to invest in the diffusion of productive knowledge in two directions: to the local suppliers of inputs needed in its production process, and for which it demands quality standards superior to the customary standards of those industries; and to local customers who may have to be taught the technology of using the firm's products effectively.

These two incentives can be simply illustrated by reference to two examples related to the improvement of agricultural production: firms interested in the distribution and sale of canned foods have a strong commercial interest in teaching farmers to produce a high-quality, standardized product as efficiently as possible; firms that produce fertilizers, farm machinery, and other agricultural inputs have a strong commercial interest in teaching farmers how to use these inputs efficiently to increase their farming profits.

These incentives are important aspects of the potential role of direct foreign investment as an agency for the promotion of economic development. Self-interest and the private profit motive can serve the social interest, and they may do so more effectively than governmental activities (such as agricultural research stations) that are nominally directed at the social interest but not subjected to the hard test of generating visible profits.

Still, the implication is that the main contribution of direct foreign investment to development will be highly specific and very uneven in its incidence. In particular, the direct and visible impact is likely to be the training of a relatively small number of native employees for jobs on the factory floor and in the company offices, and the creation of a relatively tiny elite of higher-income people in a general environment of low income and heavy unemployment. Any more general influence in promoting development will have to stem, on the one hand, from the exemplary value for local enterprises of the existence of efficient, well-managed, science-based subsidiary firms, and their production of skilled native workers and executives who can be attracted into native enterprises, and, on the other hand, from the ability of the state to use corporate and income taxes levied on foreign firms and their employees to finance education and other developmental expenditures.

Although these more general influences on the promotion of development are incidental to the corporation's own purposes, they may be quite significant. The second influence is particularly worth stressing, since critics of direct foreign investment generally fail to recognize the indirect contribution to general social purposes that the foreign corporation makes through the taxes it pays on its profits. The almost universal existence of double-taxation agreements means that a developing nation acquires the right to the tax revenue from foreign capital and from the application of foreign knowledge, at the expense of the government and taxpayers of the country in which the parent company is domiciled. Moreover, the source of revenue is easy to identify and tax, whereas developing countries typically find it difficult to tax local sources of revenue effectively. The revenue-generating possibilities of the foreign corporation provide some offset to the uneven and selective direct contribution to the promotion of development.

It is worth noting, in this connection, that the limitations on the potentialities of foreign direct investment as an agent of economic growth derive in part from social considerations that are generally accepted as just by well-intentioned people but in fact serve to inhibit the development process. These are the considerations that sanction both the legitimacy of trade union organization as a means of obtaining "a fair rate for the job" and the desirability of legislation directed at ensuring "fair" wages and working conditions in industry.

Foreign firms are excessively sensitive to local demands for "decent" wages and working conditions, and for pay comparable to that earned by similar workers and executives in the advanced countries. This sensitivity is reinforced by the fact that skilled and educated people are more mobile internationally than unskilled and uneducated people, as a result of the discrimination in immigration laws in the advanced countries in favor of talented immigrants as against the unskilled run-of-the-mill. But the effect of the social insistence on the payment of "fair" wages is to overprice the labor in question in relation to its social opportunity cost, hence inhibiting development by taxing the corporation with the obligation to pay unnecessarily high wages and to discourage efforts to develop more unskilled-labor-intensive methods of production.

This is a fundamental point about the development process that is too little appreciated. Human societies are essentially conservative. They resist change until it has occurred and then attempt to capture and institutionalize the benefits of change within the traditional framework of social relationships. By so doing, they inhibit change itself, in the name of social responsibility. To the extent it complies with these social processes, the multinational corporation cooperates in the social attempt to prevent economic change and to stop economic growth from taking place.

Increasing reliance on the multinational corporation as an agency for promoting economic development is likely to exacerbate problems that have already appeared in the relations between the nation-state as a powerful political entity with a bordered geographical domain and the multinational corporation as a powerful economic entity with an unbordered world market domain. Those problems appear as a conflict between the sovereignty of the national state and the economic liberty of the large firm, or as a conflict between the claims to sovereignty of different national states. (Specifically this arises between the headquarters nation of the investing corporation and the nation within whose borders the investment occurs.) The former conflict involves a clash between the nation-state's politically derived ideas of what development consists of and how corporations should behave and the corporation's own concepts of how it should behave as a profit-seeking enterprise operating in a particular political environment. The latter conflict involves a clash between the claims of nations to exercise sovereignty. This clash arises because nations claim sovereignty both over all activities within their territorial borders, whether of citizens or of foreign residents, and over all activities of citizens whether conducted within their borders or not; it focuses on the extraterritorial exercise of national power. Both conflicts involve the overlapping of domains and the dispute of rival sovereignties inherent in this overlapping. They can be resolved, in the long run, only by a formal or informal division of powers such as prevails in a federal state. At the present time, these conflicts are, and for some time ahead will be, aggravated by two factors.

The first factor is the philosophy of authoritarian nationalism, which has been the unhappy legacy of European political philosophy to the contemporary world accepted automatically by European thinkers who nevertheless regard themselves as socialists and progressives. This political philosophy is aped without second thought by developing country thinkers who in turn regard themselves as anti-imperialists and radicals. This philosophy generates two blindly emotional attitudes unhelpful to rational understanding—deep suspicion of the profit motive and the market system, and unquestioning belief in the superiority of the political over the economic process in the selection of economic decision makers and the formulation of economic decisions. Both attitudes irrationally favor the claims of national sovereignty over the claims of corporate enterprise. However, the nation-state is territorially limited and the corporation is not. Additionally, competition among nation-states for the economic favors of the corporation and the xenophobic character of the nation-state itself will prevent the formation of a conspiracy or cartel of nation-states to exploit the economic potentialities of the international corporation in the service of national power. Therefore, the long-run trend will be toward the dwindling of the power of the national state relative to the corporation. To survive as an effective influence, the political process will have to move in the direction of world government. The Pearson Commission's recommendations for changes designed to increase the power of the World Bank are unconsciously aimed in that direction.

The second factor is inherent in the dominance of American-based corporations among the multinational corporations. This dominance has two important implications. The first is that, rightly or not—and usually wrongly—such corporations will be regarded with suspicion as political agents of the United States government, rather than as instruments through which shareholders (who may be of all nationalities) are seeking to maximize their profits. The second stems from the special nature of the relationship—ideologically if not always in practice—between business and government in the United States. The American version of free enterprise (more accurately, the mixed economy)—reinforced by the gigantic size of the United States economy—entails a greater independence of business in relation to government, and, correspondingly, a greater necessity that political control over corporate activity be exercised by law and in the open, rather than covertly by conspiracy and back-scratching among specialized members of a recognized and homogeneous political, economic, and cultural national elite, than is characteristic of most other countries.

Hence conflicts between the political interests of the government of a nation and the economic interests of an American corporation investing in it, and between the political interests of the United States government and the political interests of other national governments in the foreign activities of American-based corporations, are likely to be more apparent and provocative of public discussion than is the case for relations between governments and multinational corporations of other nationalities. Relations between other governments and their multinational corporations, with respect to the foreign operations of the latter, command less public attention. In the long run, again, the problems of national sovereignty over the multinational corporation and of conflicting national sovereignties with respect to its foreign operations will have to be resolved by some sort of international agreement on a code of company and governmental conduct; but first it will be necessary to reconcile the conflict between American and other views on the proper relation between the corporate enterprise and national government.

Judging by past experience, political criticism of the local activities of a multinational corporation are likely to comprehend every major aspect of its operations and to involve, for the most part, rather naive and economically debatable assumptions about what the corporation should be doing in the national interests of the country.

Furthermore, the critics rarely if ever realize that the policies which they would like to impose on the foreign corporation may involve substantial costs through reduced efficiency (which will be borne by the domestic consumers of the corporation's products, not the corporation's shareholders), or may channel income to favored groups of citizens without promoting development, or may simply be unreasonable, given the constraints imposed on the corporation by other governmental policies.

One frequent criticism of the foreign corporation concerns its alleged "discrimination" against the employment of natives as skilled workers and executives. As already mentioned, the corporation has cost-incentives to employ qualified local people rather than import labor; reliance on imported personnel, therefore, presumably reflects a scarcity of qualified local talent. Insistence that foreign corporations employ more natives involves burdening the enterprise (and hence ultimately the domestic purchasers of its products) with the costs of either training local talent to the required standard or paying them wages and salaries in excess of their value to the enterprise.

Another similar criticism concerns the insistence of many corporations on retaining complete ownership of the local affiliate, whereas the critics assert that local capital should be allowed to participate in the equity. In some cases, this amounts to a claim that native capitalists should have the right to acquire equity in successful enterprises, including part ownership of the knowledge it has built up by past investment, at bargain prices—a right not generally conceded by native capitalists to one another. In other cases, the claim ignores the fact that share ownership conveys the right of access to information about the company's operations, information which could be exploited to found rival enterprises based on stolen knowledge. This claim also ignores the fact that share ownership carries a voice in decision making which might be used to disrupt the integration of the corporation's overall operations.

Foreign corporations are frequently criticized for purchasing a high proportion of their production inputs from their parent or other foreign countries. Insistence on purchase of a high proportion of inputs from local sources, though intended to diffuse development and to encourage industrialization, may, in fact, burden consumers with excess-cost and inferior products, inhibit the achievement of scale economies by the company, and dissipate scarce local entrepreneurial talent into inefficient and socially unproductive supplies enterprises. The corporation is very likely to have a more accurate judgment of the local industrial sector's comparative advantages and disadvantages than do the country's civil servants, and an observed preference on its part for imported inputs may well reflect that knowledge. It is important to remember that the high productivity of the modern corporation is achieved largely through specialization on its own small part of the production process, made possible by its ability to rely on the quality and reliable flow of inputs purchased from its specialist suppliers. Forcing the corporation to develop the capacities of local suppliers may be putting it into a new kind of business for which it is not organizationally and technically equipped.

In all of these criticisms there is an evident element of confusion in understanding the role and incentives of the corporation, and of government. The role of the corporation is to minimize cost by obtaining its human, material, and knowledge inputs from the cheapest possible source. The role of government is to use the monopoly revenue it derives from its control of the tax system and the power it derives from its legal authority to re-allocate resources in an economically inefficient fashion to serve politically determined ends—and primarily to purchase political support for itself.

Conflicts between governments over the multinational corporation center on the issue of extraterritoriality—specifically, the application of American anti-trust and "trading with the enemy" laws to the trade of foreign subsidiaries of American-based companies with other foreign countries, and the application of American balance of payments policies to the financial operations of such subsidiaries. In this context it should be noted that United States policies are more visible than those of other countries but are not necessarily more reprehensible purely on that account. The fundamental issue is the dual claim of the national state to sovereignty over both all residents and all citizens. This issue necessarily brings national states into conflict with one another and should be seen, not in terms of the traditional categories of "American imperialism," "colonialism," and so forth, but in terms of a more general and fundamental problem of reconciling the traditional and anachronistic conception of the "isolated state" with the economic—and political—facts of a rapidly integrating world in which there is increasing mobility of goods, capital, labor (at least educated labor), and knowledge. In the long run, we shall have to become one world, politically as well as economically.

How to Divest in Latin America, and Why

BY ALBERT O. HIRSCHMAN

The dispute between Peru and the United States over the expropriation of the International Petroleum Company is only one of a monotonously long list of incidents and conflicts which call into serious question the wisdom of present institutional arrangements concerning private international investment. This paper will discuss the principal weaknesses of these arrangements, with particular emphasis on political economy rather than on economics proper, and will then survey a number of ways in which current institutions and practices could be restructured. It is written against the backdrop of rising nationalism and militancy in the developing countries, particularly in Latin America, and of an astounding complacency, inertia, and lack of institutional imagination on the part of the rich countries.

The basic position adopted here with respect to foreign private investment is that it shares to a very high degree the ambiguity of most human inventions and institutions: it has considerable potential for both good and evil. On the one hand, there are the celebrated and undoubted contributions of private international investment to development: the bringing in of capital, entrepreneurship, technology, management and other skills, and of international market connections, all of which are

This paper originally appeared, in a slightly longer form, as Essays in International Finance No. 76, published by the International Finance Section, Princeton University, November, 1969. Reprinted by kind permission of publisher and author.

either wholly lacking in the poor countries, or are in inadequate supply given the opportunities and programs for economic development. On the other hand, foreign investment brings not only the dangers of economic plunder and political domination which are the stock-in-trade of the various theories of imperialism, but a number of other, more subtle, yet serious effects and side-effects which can handicap the development efforts of countries placing prolonged and substantial reliance on private investment from abroad. The picture that has sometimes been painted of the career of foreign investment is that at one time, long ago, the negative aspects predominated: there was sheer exploitation of human and natural resources as well as crude power play in the early free-wheeling days, when capital followed the flag or was, on the contrary, the "cat's paw of empire"; but this unfortunate phase has been outgrown, so it is widely thought, with decolonization, with the worldwide assertion of national sovereign states and their taxing powers, and with the desire, on the part of modern foreign investors, to perform as "good corporate citizens" of the host country and as "partners in progress." Unfortunately, this edifying story of human progress is incomplete and one-sided. It can, in fact, be argued that certain negative aspects of foreign investment do not only continue to coexist with the positive ones, but typically tend to predominate over them as development proceeds, at least up to some point. These are the just-mentioned "more subtle" effects and side-effects that will now be briefly explained.

PRIVATE FOREIGN INVESTMENT—AN INCREASINGLY MIXED BLESSING

The positive contribution of foreign investment to an economy can be of various kinds. In the first place, it can supply one of several *missing* factors of production (capital, entrepreneurship, management, and so forth), factors, that is, which are simply and indisputably not to be found in the country receiving the investment. This is the situation often prevailing in the earliest stages of development of a poor country. More generally, foreign investment can make it possible for output to increase sharply, because it provides the recipient economy with a larger *quantity* of comparatively scarce (if not entirely missing) inputs.

Another contribution of foreign investment, conspicuous in relations among advanced industrial countries and inviting often a two-way flow, is of a rather different nature: it can have a teaching function and serve to improve the *quality* of the local factors of production. By on-the-spot example and through competitive pressures, foreign investment can act as a spur to the general efficiency of local enterprise. This effect is likely to be particularly important in economic sectors which are sheltered from the competition of merchandise imports from abroad. Such sectors (services, industries with strong locational advantages) appear to expand rapidly at advanced stages of economic development. If foreign investment is successful in enhancing the quality of local enterprise, then its inflow will be providentially self-limiting: once the local business community achieves greater efficiency, there will be fewer openings for the demonstration of superior foreign techniques, management, and know-how. But what if local businessmen, faced with overwhelming advantages of their foreign competitors, do not respond with adequate vigor and, instead, deteriorate further or sell out? This is, of course, the nub of recent European fears of the "American challenge." I cannot deal here with this problem, but the fact that it exists has interesting implications for the topic at hand.

If foreign investment can fail to improve and may even harm the *quality* of local factors of production, then the question arises whether it may also, under certain circumstances, lead to a decrease in the *quantity* of local inputs available to an economy. In other words, could the inflow of foreign investment stunt what might otherwise be vigorous local development of the so-called missing or scarce factors of production?

This question has been little discussed. (Important exceptions are the article by J. Knapp "Capital Exports and Growth," and a paper by Felipe Pazos.) [1] The reason for the neglect lies in the intellectual tradition which treats international investment under the rubric "export of capital." As long as one thinks in terms of this single factor of production being exported to a capital-poor country, it is natural to view it as highly complementary to various local factors—such as natural resources and labor—that are available in abundance and are only waiting to be combined with the "missing factor" to yield large additional outputs. But, for a long time now, foreign investors have prided themselves on contributing "not just capital," but a whole bundle of other valuable inputs. In counterpart to these claims, however, the doubt might have arisen that some components of the bundle will no longer be purely complementary to local factors, but will be competitive with them and could cause them to wither or retard and even prevent their growth.

The possibility, and indeed likelihood, that international *trade* will lead to the shrinkage and possibly to the disappearance of certain lines of local production as a result of cheaper imports has been at the root of international trade theory since Adam Smith and Ricardo. This effect of trade has been celebrated by free traders through such terms as "international specialization" and "efficient reallocation of resources." The opponents of free trade have often pointed out that for a variety of reasons it is imprudent and harmful for a country to become specialized along certain product lines in accordance with the dictates of comparative advantage. Whatever the merit of these critical arguments, they would certainly acquire overwhelming weight if the question arose whether a country should allow itself to become specialized not just along certain commodity lines, but along factor-of-production lines. Very few countries would ever consciously wish to specialize in unskilled labor, while foreigners with a comparative advantage in entrepreneurship, management, skilled labor, and capital took over these functions, replacing inferior "local talent." But this is precisely the direction in which events can move when international investment, proudly bringing in its bundle of factors, has unimpeded access to developing countries. (In the fine paradoxical formulation of Felipe Pazos: "The main weakness of direct investment as a development agent is a consequence of the complete character of its contribution." [2])

The displacement of local factors and stunting of local abilities which can occur in the wake of international investment is sometimes absolute, as when local banks or businesses are bought out by foreign capital; this has in fact been happening recently with increasing frequency in Latin America. But the more common and perhaps more dangerous, because less noticeable, stunting effect is relative to what might have happened in the absence of the investment.

As already mentioned, foreign investment can be at its creative best by bringing in "missing" factors of production, complementary to those available locally, in the early stages of development of a poor country. The possibility that it will play a stunting role arises later on, when the poor country has begun to generate, to a large extent no doubt because of the prior injection of foreign investment, its own entrepreneurs, technicians, and savers and could now do even more along these lines if it were not for the institutional inertia that makes for a continued importing of so-called scarce factors of production which have become potentially dispensable. It is, of course, exceedingly difficult to judge at what point in time foreign investment changes in this fashion from a stimulant of development into a retarding influence, particularly since during the latter stage its contribution is still ostensibly positive—for example, the foreign capital that comes in is visible and measurable, in contrast to the domestic capital that might have been generated in its stead. One can never be certain, moreover, that restrictions against foreign investment will in fact call forth the local entrepreneurial, managerial, technological, and saving performances which are believed to be held back and waiting in the wings to take over from the foreign investors. Nevertheless, a considerable body of evidence, brought forth less by design than by accidents such as wars, depressions, nationalist expropriations, and international sanctions, suggests strongly that, after an initial period of development, the domestic supply of routinely imported factors of production is far more elastic than is ever suspected under business-as-usual conditions. If this is so, then the "climate for foreign investment" ought to turn from attractive at an early stage of development to much less inviting in some middle stretch—in which most of Latin America finds itself at the present time.

The preceding argument is the principal economic reason for anticipating increasing conflict between the goals of national development and the foreign-investment community, even after the latter has thoroughly purged itself of the excesses that marred its early career. The argument is strengthened by related considerations pertaining to economic policy-making, a "factor of production" not often taken into account by economists, but which nevertheless has an essential role to play. In the course of industrialization, resources for complementary investment in education and overhead capital must be generated through taxation, the opening up of new domestic and foreign markets must be made attractive, institutions hampering growth must be reformed, and powerful social groups that are antagonistic to development must be neutralized. The achievement of these tasks is considerably facilitated if the new industrialists are able to speak with a strong, influential, and even militant voice. But the emergence of such a voice is most unlikely if a large portion of the more dynamic new industries is in foreign hands. This is a somewhat novel reproach to foreign capital, which has normally been taken to task for being unduly interfering, wire-pulling, and domineering. Whatever the truth about these accusations in the past, the principal failing of the managers of today's foreign-held branch plants and subsidiaries may well be the opposite. Given their position as "guests" in a "host country," their behavior is far too restrained and inhibited. The trouble with the foreign investor may well be not that he is so meddlesome, but that he is so mousy! It is the foreign investor's mousiness which deprives the policy makers of the guidance, pressures, and support they badly need to push through critically required development decisions and policies amid a welter of conflicting and antagonistic interests.

The situation is in fact even worse. Not only does policy making fail to be invigorated by the influence normally emanating from a strong, confident, and assertive group of industrialists; more directly, the presence of a strong foreign element in the dynamically expanding sectors of the economy is likely to have a debilitating and corroding effect on the rationality of official economic policy-making for development. For, when newly arising investment opportunities are largely or predominantly seized upon by foreign firms, the national policy makers face in effect a dilemma: more development means at the same time less autonomy. In a situation in which many key points of the economy are occupied by foreigners while economic policy is made by nationals it is only too likely that these nationals will not excel in "rational" policy-making for economic development, for a good portion of the fruits of such rationality would accrue to non-nationals and would strengthen their position.[3] On the other hand, the role and importance of national economic policy-making for development increases steadily as the array of available policy instruments widens, and as more group demands are articulated. Hence the *scope* for "irrationality" actually expands as development gains momentum. That its *incidence* increases also could probably be demonstrated by a historical survey of tax, exchange-rate, utility-rate and similar policies that were aimed directly or indirectly at "squeezing" or administering pin pricks to the foreigner, but managed, at the same time, to slow down economic growth.

The preceding pages have said next to nothing about the direct cost to the capital-importing country of private international investment nor about the related question of the balance of payments drain such investment may occasion. While these matters have long been vigorously debated, with the critics charging exploitation and the defenders denying it, the outcome of the discussion seems to me highly inconclusive. Moreover, undue fascination with the dollar-and-cents aspects of international investment has led to the neglect of the topics here considered, which, I submit, raise issues of at least equal importance and suggest a simple conclusion: strictly from the point of view of development, private foreign investment is a mixed blessing, and the mixture is likely to become more noxious at the intermediate stage of development which characterizes much of present-day Latin America.

Hence, if the broadly conceived national interest of the United States is served by the development of Latin America, then this interest enters into conflict with a continuing expansion and even with the maintenance of the present position of private investors from the United States. Purely political arguments lend strong support to this proposition. Internal disputes over the appropriate treatment of the foreign investor have gravely weakened, or helped to topple, some of the more progressive and democratic governments which have held power in recent years in such countries as Brazil, Chile, and Peru. Frictions between private investors from the United States and host governments have an inevitable repercussion on United States–Latin American relations. In a number of cases such disputes have been responsible for a wholly disproportionate deterioration of bilateral relations. The continued presence and expansion of our private-investment position and our insistence on a "favorable investment climate" decisively undermined, from the outset, the credibility of our Alliance for Progress proposals. Land reform and income redistribution through taxation are so obviously incompatible, in the short run, with the maintenance of a favorable investment climate for private capital that insistence on both could only be interpreted to signify that we did not really mean those fine phrases about achieving social justice through land and tax reform.

If these political arguments are added to those pertaining to economics and political economy, one thing becomes clear: a policy of selective liquidation and withdrawal of foreign private investment is in the best mutual interests of Latin America and the United States. Such a policy can be selective with respect to countries and to economic sectors and it ought to be combined with a policy of encouraging new capital outflows, also on a selective basis and with some safeguards.

THE "LOST ART" OF LIQUIDATING AND NATIONALIZING
FOREIGN INVESTMENTS

Before the possible elements of such a policy are examined, it is worth noting that liquidation of foreign investment has frequently happened in the history of capital movements. But, as a result of convergent developments, such liquidation has strangely become a lost art. Worse, this art has not been properly recorded by economic historians. In part, this is so because economic historians, like both the advocates of foreign investment and its critics, have been far more interested in the tides of capital flow than in its occasional ebbs. Moreover, the tides have been more regular and easier to detect and measure.

Some of the "mechanisms" which in the past permitted partial liquidation of foreign investment have been the unintended side effects of such large-scale, sporadic, and wholly unedifying happenings as wars and depressions. The two World Wars led to a substantial decline in both the absolute and the relative importance of foreign investment in the national economies of Latin America. In the first place, with most Latin American countries joining the Allies, German investments, a not unimportant portion of the total (think of all those prosperous breweries!), were expropriated. Secondly, the British were forced in both World Wars to liquidate a good portion of their security holdings, in order to pay for vitally needed food, materials, and munitions. Some of these securities were acquired by the citizens of the countries for which they had originally been issued. Thirdly, Latin American countries acquired large holdings of gold and foreign currencies during the wars, as they continued to export their primary products, but were unable to obtain industrial goods from the belligerents. These accumulated holdings made it possible for them to buy out some foreign investments in the immediate postwar period. The most conspicuous, but by no means the only, instance of this sort of operation was the purchase from their British shareholders of the Argentine railways by the Perón government in 1946. Finally, the wars led to a complete interruption of capital inflow. Since, at the same time, Latin America's industrial growth was strongly stimulated, the relative importance of activities controlled by foreign capital declined substantially.

The depressions which periodically afflicted the centers of capitalist development until the Second World War had similar results. Again, capital inflow would stop for a while during periods in which the Latin American economies frequently received growth impulses because, with foreign-exchange receipts low, imports had to be throttled, giving domestic industrial production a fillip. Moreover, when overextended corporations based in the United States and Europe fell on hard times, a sound management reaction was frequently to retrench and consolidate. In the process, foreign branch plants and subsidiaries were sold off to local buyers, a process which has been well documented in the case of American investments in Canada during the depression of the thirties.[4] Sometimes, especially in the case of European firms, these transfers took the form of ownership and control passing into the hands of the parent company's local managers who, while of foreign origin, would eventually become integrated into the local economy. Finally, of course, there were cases of outright bankruptcy and forced liquidation.

The quantitative importance of these various factors remains to be established. But, in the aggregate, they must have had a substantial limiting effect on the foreign-investment position in Latin America during the first half of the twentieth century.

Actually, a less cruel mechanism permitting the nationalization of foreign investment was also at work before the "good old days" of portfolio investment had been eclipsed by direct investment. While those days were of course by no means wholly good, portfolio investment, which took primarily the form of fixed-interest bond issues, did have several advantages for the capital-importing country. Among these, the lower cost and the existence of a termination date have been mentioned most frequently. There is, however, one further property of portfolio investment which is of particular interest in the context of the present essay. This is the fact that nationalization of portfolio investment could take place at the option of the borrowing country and its citizens, who were free to purchase in the international capital markets securities that were originally issued and underwritten in London or Paris. I have collected (and hope eventually to publish) considerable evidence that these so-called "repurchases" of securities by nationals of the borrowing countries took place on a large scale in such countries as the United States, Italy, Spain, Sweden, and Japan in the late nineteenth and early twentieth centuries. They also occurred in much poorer countries, such as Brazil, and were in general so widespread that the phenomenon is referred to in one source as "the well-known *Heimweh* [homesickness] of oversea issued securities." [5] As a result of this *Heimweh,* then, an increasing portion of maturing bond issues often came to be owned by the nationals of the borrowing country, so that payment at maturity did not occasion any balance-of-payments problem.

This is not the place to speculate on the reasons for which the bonds issued abroad became so often a preferred medium of investment for national capitalists; suffice it to say that patriotism or nationalism on the part of local investors probably had little if anything to do with it. Whatever the reason, it appears that international investment, as formerly practiced, permitted the gradual transfer, via anonymous market transactions, of foreign-held assets to nationals, entirely in accordance with the capabilities and wishes of the borrowing country's own savers.

Today's arrangements are totally different, of course. Transfer to local ownership and control of foreign-held subsidiaries requires either an initiative on the part of the parent company or a decision to expropriate on the part of the host government. A valuable mechanism of smooth, gradual, and peaceful transfer has become lost in the shuffle from portfolio to direct investment.

Up to this point, it has been established (1) that progressive liquidation and nationalization of foreign private investments is likely to become desirable in the course of economic development, and (2) that mechanisms to this end functioned, if unwittingly and irregularly, in the nineteenth and through the first half of the twentieth century, but have no longer been available over the past twenty-five years or so.

The purpose of recalling these mechanisms was to sharpen our institutional imagination and perception for substitute mechanisms which it may be desirable to put into place at the present time. An open and far-ranging discussion of various possible alternatives is obviously desirable. The following pages are meant as a contribution to such a discussion, rather than as a fixed set of proposals. . . .

An Inter-American Divestment Corporation

In the light of the above considerations, partial liquidation of *existing* foreign investments in Latin America is outstandingly important. The book value of direct investments by the United States in Latin America amounted to $11.9 billion at the end of 1967, while the annual outflow of fresh capital from the United States (outside of reinvested profits) never reached $500 million during the past five years, even on a gross basis. The steady increase in book values is, moreover, due more to the reinvestment of profits than to fresh funds newly invested. In other words, if the quantitative and qualitative role of foreign-controlled enterprise in Latin America is judged to be excessive, something must be done about the existing foreign firms operating in the area, rather than only about those that may conceivably establish operations there in the future.

Vital as it is, this subject has received much less attention than the desirable regime for new foreign investments. It is of course the politically most delicate part of the operation here contemplated. Also, from the economic point of view, the use of any capital and, worse, foreign-exchange resources for the purchase of property rights over assets already located and functioning within the territories of the developing countries seems perverse to those who remain basically convinced that the pace of economic development is conditioned on little else than the availability of capital and foreign exchange. Those who are not so convinced and who take seriously the economic and political arguments developed earlier would see nothing fatally wrong in allocating a portion of the country's savings and foreign-exchange resources to the purchase of foreign investments already in their midst. From the purely financial point of view, moreover, expenditure of foreign exchange for the purchase of existing foreign assets could in a number of cases be preferable to the indefinite servicing of these assets (depending on one's estimate of the applicable discount rate and of future earnings and remittance patterns). The trouble is that the recipient countries do not generally have the financial resources to seize these opportunities nor have they in fact been able to borrow or to use aid funds for this purpose. Moreover, even when local resources are available there may be difficulties in bringing seller and buyer together, because the foreign owners may be ready to sell at a time when the local investors are not quite ready to purchase or because the two parties have difficulty in agreeing on the value of the assets to be transferred, without a mutually trusted third party.

A need exists, then, for a financial intermediary, an agency, that is, which has resources of its own enabling it to acquire foreign-owned assets and to hold them until such time as it can place them with local investors. Dr. Raúl Prebisch earlier this year proposed that such an agency should be established within the Inter-American Development Bank.[6] This course may well be preferable, because of the special urgency of the Latin American situation, to a suggestion I made as early as 1961, but with total lack of success, to the International Finance Corporation (IFC) that it devote a portion of its resources to this task.

The proposed agency—I shall call it the Inter-American Divestment Corporation—would engage in several distinct types of operations. In some cases it could limit its role to that of arbitrator and guarantor. As just noted, it could help set the fair price of the assets to be transferred from the foreign to the domestic owners and, if payment is to be made over a period of years, it could guarantee the debtor's obligation and, to some extent perhaps, the convertibility of his currency into that of the creditor. One can imagine situations in which the purchaser would have to be granted longer terms than can or should be imposed on the seller, as is common in some agrarian-reform operations. In this case, the Corporation would need to supply funds of its own to bridge the gap between the two sets of credit terms. The most usual type of operation would presumably consist in the outright acquisition by the Corporation of a controlling block of shares of the firm to be divested, without any fixed schedule of repurchase by local investors.

As in any foreign aid project, some contribution should be forthcoming from the local government as an earnest that it judges the particular divestment to be important enough for it to commit some resources of its own. As the Divestment Corporation acquires experience, it should be able to attract additional resources from the private-investment-banking community, much as is done by the IFC in connection with new ventures.

Which foreign-owned firms should be eligible for divestment assistance on the part of the Corporation? In deciding this crucial matter, the Corporation should probably take its principal cues from the governments of the host countries. Just as the doctor asks the patient where it hurts, so the Corporation could periodically inquire among governments which are the firms where foreign ownership is felt to be irksome. In many cases there will be a history of conflict which will clearly point to the main trouble spots. One can also easily imagine situations in which governments are reluctant to point a finger at specific firms. For this and other reasons, it should be possible for private parties in the host country, for the foreign investors, and for the Corporation itself to take the initiative in the divestment process which, in the end, will require the agreement of the host government as long as it is expected to contribute some of its own resources to each divestment operation.

An interesting question arises with respect to the eventual disposition of the equity which will be acquired by the Corporation. One objection will surely be levied against the operation: Is it really desirable to transfer presently foreign-owned firms to local ownership when the new owners cannot but be drawn from the very small clique of already too powerfully entrenched local capitalists? History issues a warning here, for this very sort of thing happened in the second half of the nineteenth century when liberal parties came to power in a number of Latin American countries. The newly installed, anti-clerical governments expropriated the sizable lands owned by the Catholic Church—and then proceeded to sell them at bargain prices to the landed elite. As a result, the concentration of landholdings became far more pronounced.

At the present time, the weight of concern over a similar development in case of nationalization of foreign investment varies no doubt from country to country, as well as from industry to industry within each country. Moreover, the Corporation could make a deliberate attempt to broaden the basis of industrial ownership when it sells its portfolio. This should, in fact, be one of its principal functions. If foreign-owned assets were to be sold directly to local investors, it would be impossible not to sell to the few and the powerful. But, if an intermediary stands ready to hold the divested assets for some time, the outcome may be quite different. One attractive possibility is that the agency would sell, on the installment plan, a substantial portion, and perhaps a majority, of the equity of the erstwhile foreign firms to white- and blue-collar workers, with first choice being given to those who are employed in such firms. This would be a method of tapping entirely new sources of capital

formation. Moreover, in this manner, the liquidation of foreign ownership would become the occasion for effectuating, by the same stroke, a
more equitable distribution of income and wealth within the host country. As in the case of the Mexican *ejido,* special safeguards may then
have to be established to protect the new asset-holders against the
temptation to sell out right away.

Those who have stressed the advantage of a late start have usually
had in mind the technological windfalls accruing to the newcomers and
their freedom from a declining industrial plant based on some previous
but now passé phase of industrial expansion. For various reasons, these
advantages have been more in evidence for Germany and Japan than for
countries whose industrialization was much more tardy; but the latter
could perhaps attempt some social leapfrogging, as, for example, in the
manner just indicated.

It is quite conceivable, moreover, that the foreign investors themselves would take a more benign view of divestment if they knew that
their assets were to be transferred to their workers and employees rather
than to their local competitors or to some public agency.

The projected divestment operations via a financial intermediary
could be made to serve another objective that is particularly important
within the present Latin American setting. It could help create financial
and, hence, managerial ties among firms located in several Latin American countries. In this form a foundation would be laid for truly Latin
American multinational corporations. The absence of such corporations,
combined with the ever alert presence throughout Latin America of
United States-controlled multinational corporations, accounts for much
of the timidity with which Latin Americans have moved so far in the
direction of a Common Market. Thus, the proposed divestment, combined with a measure of "Latinamericanization," rather than mere nationalization, of the divested enterprises could impart a much needed
momentum to the integration movement.

By now, I hope to have convinced the reader that it is worthwhile
to raise funds for the Corporation. In part, such funds should simply
be taken from the general pool of foreign aid monies. For the reasons
indicated, the use of aid funds for this purpose could be eminently "productive," using this term in a wide and realistic meaning. The question
what fraction of the total should be allocated to this purpose is no doubt

difficult to resolve; but it is not more so than many other allocation decisions that are constantly made in practice without the guidance of availability of precise "cost-effectiveness" criteria.

Nevertheless, the nature of the proposed operation may point to special sources of finance that are not available for other purposes, so that the Corporation would not have to compete for general-purpose aid funds. A first thought that comes to mind in this connection is that the opposition in the United States Congress to appropriations for foreign aid is now motivated, to an increasing extent, by apprehension over the way in which aid and its administration makes for uncontrollable and possibly escalating involvements by the United States in foreign countries. A program of financial assistance which would have disengagement as its principal objective might therefore gather more public support at this point than the conventional aid program. In fact, if such a program were presented separately from conventional aid, a new political coalition might get behind it so that in the political sense the funds accruing for our purpose could become truly additional. Appropriation for the Corporation might also have other appeals. Aid for divestment is unexceptionable from the points of view of both balance of payments and inflationary impacts. The dollars disbursed by the agency would immediately return in full to the divesting country, such as the United States, but they would not enter directly into that country's spending stream.

The program may be opposed on the ground that the taxpayer of the United States should not be asked to "bail out" its corporations that have engaged in foreign operations at their own risk. In reply it may be argued that a large part of the risk of recent foreign investments has already been taken over by the taxpayer, through the investment guaranty program. Moreover, the Divestment Corporation should be in a good position to minimize the "bail-out" aspect of its operations: one of its principal tasks would be to negotiate a fair price for the assets and to convince the foreign investors that are being bought out to accept deferred payment for a substantial portion of their claim.

In a search for special sources of finance, it is natural to eye those parties which stand to gain from the proposed operations. The beneficiaries, in a sense, are the foreign investors themselves. In the first place, they will receive a valuable new option—to sell out at a fair price —as a result of the contemplated arrangements. The proposed agency would in effect administer a program whose purpose is to *prevent* the confiscation of foreign-held assets by timely transfers of these assets. Obviously not all foreign-owned firms will be able to exercise the option. But the orderly liquidation of foreign ownership in the cases where it is particularly objectionable to the host country cannot help but be a boon to the remaining foreign-controlled firms. The presence in a country of foreign interests that are felt as irritants poses a danger for the prosperity and, indeed, the life of *all* foreign firms, no matter how constructive and popular they may be. Hence a contribution from all corporations with foreign assets can be justified. As long as firms are willing to pay a premium which insures them against the risks of actual confiscation, there is no reason why they should not contribute something toward a program which materially decreases these risks.

Another possible source of special finance for the divestment agency should be briefly mentioned. The agency may well be the ideal beneficiary of the much discussed "link" between the new monetary reserves created as a result of the Rio Agreement (the Special Drawing Rights) and the developing countries. The principal objection against any such link has been that the reserve creation should not become a mechanism for effecting permanent transfers of real resources from one set of countries to another. This objection would be largely met if the industrial countries used part of their allocation of Special Drawing Rights for the subscription of capital or bond issues of the Divestment Corporation. The partial use of the new reserves for the repatriation of foreign-held assets could not have an adverse effect on the intended increase in world liquidity, for the simple reason that this use, unlike others that have been proposed, would not entail any real transfer of goods and services.

Built-in Divestment—a Garland of Schemes

Considering the mass of foreign investment, the Divestment Corporation will be able to operate only on a highly selective, *ad hoc* basis. The question arises, therefore, whether the institutional framework within which foreign investment is conducted should be modified with a view toward building into it a mechanism making for eventual divestment. This question is best discussed in considering desirable regimes for *new* investments. Whether any such regime could or should be extended to existing foreign-owned firms can be considered subsequently.

The topic has given rise to a considerable literature and to several proposals. For example, the desirability for foreign capital to become associated with local capital in joint ventures has been exhaustively canvassed. Whatever the merits of this device, its usefulness is now recognized to be limited. In many situations, particularly those involving the transfer of new and complex technology, complete foreign control and ownership is said to be required or desirable at the outset. For this reason, increased attention has been given—by such authors as Paul Rosenstein-Rodan, Paul Streeten, and Raymond Vernon—to the possibility of a gradual transfer of all or the majority of the new firm's capital to local ownership, in accordance with a fixed schedule.

This is a fruitful idea which should be spelled out in full institutional detail. Consideration should, for example, be given to the granting of fiscal incentives to firms electing this option. In the capital-exporting countries, the parent company committing itself to gradual divestment of its foreign assets over a stated number of years could be given a credit against its income tax liability for some portion of its foreign capital outlays; alternatively or additionally, the firm could be exempted from all capital gains taxation on profits made in selling its foreign assets to local investors. The capital-importing country could facilitate divestment by allowing the foreign-owned company to pay income taxes in stock in lieu of cash. Such an arrangement would probably have to be restricted to economic sectors in which foreign enterprise is not competing with domestic enterprises. Where there is actual or potential competition, the arrangement would give an unfair cash-flow advantage to the foreign firm.

Gradual divestment over a given number of years normally means expenditure of scarce foreign exchange. It also requires the finding of local partners. The difficulties here are, first, that such partners are not always easy to come by. It would be necessary to designate some public agency of the host country, perhaps acting in cooperation with the Inter-American Divestment Corporation, as a residual buyer of the stock to be transferred from the original owners in accordance with a fixed schedule and a prearranged price formula. Another drawback of a direct sale of assets from the foreign owners to nationals has already been mentioned. The local buyers that would be found most readily may not be the most desirable, if advantage is to be taken of the unique opportunity afforded by divestment for diffusing ownership more widely than before.

Finally, in most situations, there will be a need to agree on a "fair price" of the assets: the potential for conflict over this issue is almost as great as that over the actual presence of foreign investment.

These problems of a scheduled gradual sale of equity from foreigners to nationals point toward a simpler and more radical arrangement: namely, that a firm established with foreign capital be given a term of x years, at the end of which all or the major portion of foreign ownership would simply be vacated, without any compensation. Some of the ideas already discussed in connection with the Divestment Corporation can be utilized in deciding on the parties on which ownership should be bestowed at the end of the term. Up to a certain percentage, the foreign owners could distribute the stock directly to their employees and workers, or to their favorite local charity or foundation, and another portion would be handed over to the Inter-American Divestment Corporation for the purpose of fostering industrial integration. The new owners would be free to negotiate a management contract with the former owner-operators.

Arrangements which set a time limit on ownership have long existed in concession contracts. The major drawback of such arrangements has also long been known: they encourage early depletion and discourage keeping up with technical progress during the years immediately prior to expiration. In manufacturing, the former danger would be rather smaller than in mining, and the latter would be reduced if the divesting firm is scheduled to maintain a minority equity position and is interested in a continuing relationship with its erstwhile foreign branch through management contracts and other technical assistance services. Also, if the foreign owners know that they will be handing a substantial portion of the equity over to their workers and employees or to their favorite charity or foundation in the host country, they will presumably be more reluctant to squeeze their property dry in the last years than they might be if it were to be handed to the government. Nevertheless, the objection to a fixed termination date is serious enough to prompt consideration of yet another institutional design.

Limiting ownership of a firm to a certain time period, at the end of which that ownership lapses or "expires" automatically, is tantamount to setting a ceiling on the profits the firm can remit to its parent. Why not make explicit this implicit ceiling on profit remittances? Instead of specifying the number of years a firm may remain in foreign hands, it would, in other words, be conceivable to limit the total amount of profits a subsidiary could remit to its parent. This amount would be related to the capital originally committed to the project, as well as to any fresh funds brought in subsequently over and above reinvested profits. Such a regime for divestment would have incentive effects directly opposite to those of the traditional concession. Since the firm can make the pleasure of control and ownership last by remitting as little as possible, that is, by reinvesting all of its profits, the incentive to deplete and milk the subsidiary would be replaced by the incentive to reinvest (on the assumption that management, control, and growth are important motivating forces for the modern corporation).

It may be useful to pick a number for illustrative purposes. Suppose that the ceiling on remittances is 200% of the originally invested capital. This could mean, for example, that a parent company would lose ownership of its subsidiary after it had received a 10% dividend on invested capital for twenty years. The internal rate of return of such a financial result would be just short of 8%. In other words, if a rate higher than 8% were appropriate as a discount rate in the particular environment where the subsidiary operates, a financial situation in which 10% would be earned for twenty years would be superior to one in which 8% would be earned in perpetuity. Hence, the perishable nature of the investment need not impair decisively its rentability, particularly in the frequently encountered situations where the applicable discount rate is fairly high.

Consideration could be given to the question whether, in computing the aggregate "allowable" profit, some discount rate should apply to the dividend remittances themselves. If this were done, payments made at a later date would contribute less heavily to the eventual extinction of ownership than payments made in the first years of the new enterprise and the incentive to postpone and hold down profit remittances might be further strengthened. The arguments against any such complication are: first, that it is a complication; and, second, that the real burden of profit remittances for the host country does not depend so much on the country's national product, which can be expected to be larger in later years, as on its balance of payments, which could well be in a more critical position ten years *after* the initial investment than at the time at which the investment is made.

The last point highlights an important advantage of the scheme under discussion. One of the major complaints with respect to foreign investment has been that because of reinvestment of profits—which in turn are made possible in part through local borrowing—the book value of the foreign-owned firms is likely to grow apace during an initial period, so that eventual dividend remittances may be a multiple of the capital originally brought into the country. While the scheme here discussed encourages reinvestment of profits, it averts the threatening prospect of huge remittances which might be made once the firm's growth slowed down, when they could represent an unacceptable burden for the country's balance of payments.

In all fairness, so it may well be asked, if cumulative profits are subject to a ceiling should they not be granted a floor in compensation? No doubt, such a floor could make the scheme much more attractive to the capital-exporting firms. The floor should obviously be at most 100% of the initially invested capital and probably rather less, so as to preserve an adequate degree of risk. Suppose a payback of 50% of the invested capital is to be guaranteed as a consideration for the 200% ceiling that is imposed on profit remittances. The capital-exporting country could provide such a guarantee simply by permitting the parent company a tax credit against its income tax liability up to 50% of the capital invested. As was pointed out before, such a tax credit may be desirable in any event in order to encourage firms that invest abroad to take advantage of the divestment options.

Once some of the divestment arrangements sketched out here become available for *new* investments, it will be desirable for *existing* investments to be able to participate in them. Existing foreign firms should, of course, be eligible to operate under one of the several divestment options that will be offered to new firms. Once again, fiscal incentives granted by the capital-exporting or capital-importing country, or by both, could be used to make participation attractive. There is no particular difficulty in adapting to existing firms the options calling for gradual sale of equity or for outright divestment after a certain number of years. Problems are more likely to arise with respect to the option

terminating foreign ownership after remittance of profits in some multiple of the originally invested capital. Applying this rule to the original
capital of the existing firms may be too restrictive, yet taking the present
book value as a yardstick may be too generous. Some middle ground
between these two solutions may have to be found.

To what extent would the existence of the Inter-American Divestment Corporation keep existing firms from electing to convert to some
of the automatic divestment procedures here advocated? If a firm could
be sure that it would become an object of the tender mercies of the
Divestment Corporation, it might well prefer that course to any automatic divestment arrangement (other than gradual sale of equity), since
it would be paid for its assets instead of losing them outright after a
certain lapse of time. Actually, this sort of "competition" from the Divestment Corporation is not a serious danger. In the first place, the
Corporation will not have sufficiently large funds to make acquisition a
likely prospect for the average foreign-owned firm. Secondly, given its
limited resources, the Corporation will generally acquire the assets of
existing firms under medium and long-term credit arrangements instead
of paying cash. In these circumstances, foreign firms may often decide
that they can do better under divestment schemes which allow them to
manage their affairs and earn profits for a number of years ahead. . . .

CONCLUSION

Rapid and incomplete as it is, the preceding survey of conceivable
divestment arrangements will have given the reader a sense of the
sizable alteration in the institutional environment for foreign private
investment that is advocated here. Several questions are raised in consequence: (1) what would happen to the outflow of private investment
funds if some of the arrangements spelled out were actually adopted as
national policy by the developing countries of Latin America as well as
by the capital exporters such as the United States? Would that outflow
slow down to a trickle or come to a full stop? And (2) if the latter
occurred would considerable damage be done to economic development
in Latin America?

To answer the last question first, it is my belief that the larger
countries of Latin America are today in a quite favorable bargaining
position to insist on substantial institutional changes of the kind here

indicated. The damage that would be inflicted on them if international capital took offense and stopped flowing to them is no longer what it might have been 100, 50, or even 25 years ago. Most literature and official reports about Latin America stress the continent's continuing poverty and problems. These laments have hidden from view the very real economic progress that has been accomplished over the last twenty-five years. With a per capita income of around $500 and a population of 250 million people, the Latin American continent is now well supplied with both "light" and "basic" industries. Countries such as Brazil, Mexico, and Argentina produce a large and constantly increasing portion of the capital goods needed by their industrial establishment. A boycott of Latin America by international investment capital might reveal the strength and resilience and ability to *fare da sé* in a great number of areas which the Latin American industrial establishment has acquired, in much the same way in which the two World Wars permitted its then fledgling industries to take vigorous steps forward. Perhaps Latin America really needs at this point a sort of "economic equivalent of war," a measure of insulation, that is, from the advanced economies that would permit it fully to deploy the potential for entrepreneurship, skills, and capital formation which it has accumulated over the past twenty-five years of continuing intimate contact. In other words, it is quite conceivable that a temporary suspension of the flow of private capital toward Latin America would be beneficial rather than calamitous for the area's growth. That Latin Americans can afford to make "demands" from a position of strength was perhaps sensed when their official representatives started to speak in quite a new voice to the United States at the Viña del Mar conference of May, 1969.

The question remains whether a boycott by private capital would necessarily result from a Latin American attempt to change the rules by which the game of international investment is being played. This is not at all certain. There are at least some signs that a number of private investors may be willing to operate in a substantially altered institutional environment. In the first place, they know how to bend with the wind—an example is the "Chileanization" of Kennecott and now also of Anaconda. Some farther-sighted corporations in mining and telecommunications are no longer waiting for pressures from the host countries to provide for "-ization" of substantial equity in their concession contracts. A few scattered experiments in divestment are also going forward under the auspices of IFC, ADELA, and of the AID guaranty program. Furthermore, where official ideology proscribes "private ownership of the means of production" altogether, private companies located in Western Europe and the United States have been able to do business via so-called "co-production agreements" through which capital goods, technology, and skills are transferred, with repayment scheduled often in kind, on a medium or long-term basis. As a result, Western business firms find themselves in the ironical position of granting a better deal to their ideological foes than to their friends. Finally, a few small experiments in bringing manufacturing operations into an area and then turning them over to community ownership and control are now being tried out in the United States in some of the black ghettos; corporations such as Xerox and Aerojet have been pioneering in this field.

It may well turn out, then, that the corporation will once again justify its reputation for flexibility. The radical nature of the changes required should nevertheless be clearly visualized. If the corporation is celebrated as an institution, this is so to a large extent because it has permitted business to be carried on *sub specie aeternitatis,* by an organization, that is, whose life span has become as unlimited as that of older permanent institutions such as the nation-state and the church. It is here suggested that, in some of its foreign operations, the corporation ought to institutionalize its own demise. Having achieved deathlessness, it must rediscover how to die.

Putting it less brusquely, the corporation must learn how to plan for selective impermanence. Perhaps it would do so more cheerfully once it realizes that the same need exists increasingly for other institutions proud of their permanence, such as the nation-state. So, why not be a trail blazer?

CHAPTER FIVE

THE AID RELATIONSHIP

The Debate

The core of the Pearson Report is, of course, the proposal for the continuance and expansion of concessionary aid. Its form can be briefly
repeated. The Report recommends a transfer of resources from developed to developing nations equivalent to a minimum of 1% of each
rich country's GNP. Of this, 70% should be in public grants or concessionary loans, 20% of which should be distributed through multilateral channels. In addition, the Report contains a great variety of
suggestions designed to make aid more flexible and efficient—untying
aid, more program assistance, inclusion of local costs in aid allocations,
appropriations covering longer periods, better procedures to plan and
review aid strategies, more emphasis on the efficient coordination of
technical assistance with capital aid.

In the Conference discussions, one common strand of opinion
seemed very largely absent—the opinion of those who argue that capital
assistance distorts price signals, undermines the efficiency of the market
and, as such, hinders growth and development. Even those who felt that
the link between receiving aid and making more rapid economic progress
was largely unproven tended to accept the moral argument that some
transfers have to be made because the rich are rich, the poor poor, and
the gap between them is widening. The "realists" at the Conference confined themselves to warnings that opposition to foreign aid, especially
in the United States, had actually increased since George Woods first

sounded the alarm at Stockholm. In these circumstances, the Commission's proposals—which would bring the flow of resources up from $12.7 billion to $24 billion between 1968 and 1975—were already far beyond any level likely to be achieved. To propose further radical changes would be at best an academic exercise, at worst a demonstration of intellectual futility.

The majority felt, however, that no useful debate could be carried on unless the Report were set in the "real world" context—not the real world of orthodox thinking in which the overwhelming preponderance of the developed nations is taken as immutable and natural, like some medieval hierarchy or self-confident Victorian bourgeoisie—but the "real world" of dynamic, clamorous history in which the revolt of the poor, the radicalization of the masses, and the disenchantment of the young are facts of life in any epoch in which there is a convergence of violent injustice, social disintegration, and radical dissent.

That the radical minority felt this deepening alienation to be at the heart of world society goes without saying. For them, it follows logically from the planetary control exercised by a neocolonialist "establishment," by men and nations trained by history to the habit of domination and unable to see that that phase of history is done. Speaking for several members of this group, Idrian Resnick read a dissenting statement:

The direct consequences of the [Pearson] Commission's recommendations would be to increase the economic and political vulnerability and dependence (not interdependence) of the LDCs [less developed countries] by keeping them politically weak, making their economies increasingly reliant upon assistance and markets in which their individual position as buyers and sellers is weak, and expanding the importance of private investment from multinational corporations. Development will be retarded rather than promoted, even though GDP in poor countries may rise.

The less obvious consequences of pursuing the Pearson pattern of ignoring the messages of the past and the realities of the future, will be to intensify the polarization between the rich and poor, postponing the solution, but thereby increasing the severity and destructiveness of the process by which it is achieved.

Many of the schemes and proposals of the Report and the Conference, while having merit, depend upon voluntary, unilateral decisions on the part of the developed nations. Yet the political imperatives for such fundamental transformations are unmentioned . . .

Given, therefore, the group's sense of the extreme unlikelihood of any creative action by the powerful, they concluded that the developing peoples would have to take their own political measures.

Poor countries should aim at self-reliance (not self-sufficiency). They should structure their economies so as to minimize the impact of influences from the developed world. Thus, while they would not stop trading (and would even expand their trade) with developed countries, they should decrease its importance by extending their trade with Third World countries; export diversification and import substitution should be evaluated primarily in terms of their contributions to self-reliance and only secondarily *vis à vis* their growth return; aid would continue but the consequences of its volatility minimized and its political influence reduced—at the expense of lower rates in growth of GDP, if necessary—by reducing its relative contribution and spreading its sources. . . .

By strengthening various existing regional economic and political institutions and organizations, the LDCs can devise common strategies with which fully to utilize the inherent power of their *collective* position. Among the elements of such a strategy might be the following: (1) the repudiation of high-cost loans or a decision to repay them in local currency or goods excluded from the donor country; (2) planned disruption of raw material supplies, where they are in relatively inelastic demand or produced almost exclusively in the LDCs; (3) discrimination between suppliers of imports where *together* the LDCs are a significant market for commodities; (4) coordinated expropriation of multinational corporations' investments; and (5) coordinated switching of reserves from currency to currency.

But it should not be thought that the radical critique was confined to the dissenting minority. True, the drastic nature of their counterproposals did not command wide support. But they were not alone in their sense of the gap between rich and poor, of history lying with the weight of centuries on the relations between powerful states and those still undeveloped, of a colonial inheritance still to be undone not only politically but economically and socially where the old patterns still prevail. All this was felt widely among the participants and accounted for much of the criticism of the Pearson Report's supposed "overoptimism." As I. G. Patel suggested in his paper:

In many of the non-aligned countries, the acceptance of massive aid was not so much an act of conscious policy as something into which one stumbled in a moment of foreign exchange crisis, something about which powerful political and intellectual groups had a reservation right from the outset.

Suspicions that, at bottom, aid was an instrument of neocolonialism or the cold war in a new guise were easily nourished and fanned in the face of increasing evidence of intervention in matters of internal policies, of open patronizing of particular local leaders, of the gap between the professions and the performance of aid-givers, and, occasionally, of some outrageous lapses in diplomacy. (See "Aid Relationship for the Seventies" in this chapter.)

The Conference as a whole responded with wry amusement to Mahbub ul Haq's analysis of the same malaise.

Mr. Polanski's Dilemma

"One of the major deficiencies of the Pearson Commission Report is that, although it is titled "Partners in Development," it does not really define the emerging relationship between the developing countries and the developed world. I had quite an argument about this with my friend, Mr. Polanski. It all started when Mr. Polanski made a very provocative statement that there never has been, and there never will be, any meaningful partnership or aid relationship between the developed world and the developing countries. Now I simply could not let such a statement go unchallenged, and I argued that this partnership is nothing new and has always existed and will always exist. It existed in the last two centuries in the form of a colonial relationship between equal partners; it exists today in the form of an aid relationship between independent states. Even the terminology has changed only slightly: it was known as "White man's burden" previously; it is known as "debt burden" today. The only thing that might have changed, I conceded, is some impatience in the developed world to terminate this partnership, and this was entirely natural and understandable. When the developed world was on the receiving end of the partnership with its colonies, there was no unseemly haste to end a mutually beneficial relationship. But today, when it is at the giving end, it is naturally slightly impatient that we in the developing countries should grow up and assume our own burdens.

"I also did a neat little exercise to convince Mr. Polanski that this relationship greatly promoted international growth and cooperation. I argued from the experience of India and Pakistan that, when we were associated with Britain in a partnership in the nineteenth century and the British had this slight problem about financing their industrial revolution and their structural transformation, we willingly brought out our gold and our diamonds and our agricultural produce for nominal prices and told them to go ahead and not lose the opportunity for a techno-logical breakthrough. We cheerfully stayed on as an agrarian economy and applauded the industrial strides of our partner. In the modern ter-minology, such a thing will be called a transfer of resources, but the world was such a happy community at that time that we never even dreamed of such terms or asked for performance audits.

"Mr. Polanski, unreasonable as he is, wanted to know the magni-tude of the transfer and I mentioned an off-the-cuff figure of $100 mil-lion—a modest estimate for which I may be disowned by my fellow economists in the sub-continent. I could not confirm to him whether this amount was 1% of our GNP at that time. Anyway, I argued that this amount could be treated as a voluntary loan, at 6% interest, which has been happily multiplying over the years so that it stands at $410 billion today. I also explained to him that, since the amount is multiplying every 12 years, at this stage it is an advantage to leave it with Britain as it will be $820 billion by 1982. We can always draw on this amount whenever we need to finance a bit of our own delayed structural trans-formation. But Polanski, who does not understand the basic principles of sound international finance, kept on insisting that we must call up the loan immediately. I tried to reason that Britain is in no position to pay and, being equal partners, we are in no position to collect. If we insist on quick repayment, the international community may have to do a bailing-out operation. I also told him that in matters like this we ought to be more generous and even write off some of the debt—for instance, we could forget the $10 billion and only ask for the remaining $400 billion.

"But Polanski, I am afraid, remains unconvinced and I am at a loss how to explain to him the inherent logic and strength of our part-nership in development. And, much to my annoyance, I discovered that, when I was not looking, Mr. Polanski had taken away my copy of the Pearson Commission Report and, after the title "Partners in Develop-ment," had added a big question mark (?)."

It was just because so many of the participants accepted the his-torical analogies and recognized the inherited imbalance in the world's

North-South relationship that a majority at the Conference were prepared not only to accept the Pearson Report's recommendations on aid but to question very seriously whether, either in social purpose or political discernment, they go far enough.

The debate took two main lines of criticism. The first was that the Report shows an inadequate appreciation of the extremes of wealth and poverty which, both between and within the nations, are bound to continue and even worsen. The second followed from this. The Report, the critics argued, overlooks the risk that a continued paternalism on the part of the rich and a combination of dependence, inferiority, and a lack of genuine self-determination on the part of the poor would undermine any idea of genuine partnership in development.

The starting point, which was fully discussed in Richard Jolly's paper, "The Aid Relationship" (in this chapter), is the flat prediction that, even with 6% rates of growth, the gap between developed and developing nations, which the Pearson Report describes as "a central issue of our time," will be three or four times wider by the year 2000, when the per capita GDP of developed countries could have passed the $7,000 mark while Asia and Africa will still be at about the $400 level. Moreover, these average figures mask the fact that within the nations perhaps a quarter of the population will have been left behind in the drive for modernization and subsist in conditions which will make present urban ghettoes and rural slums look like model settlements.

The Commission's aim of achieving a 6% rate of growth which would lead to "self-sustaining growth" was not, in itself, rejected. Without expansion, the gap could be wider still. But the majority sought for a more direct approach, socially and politically, to the problem of the world's deepening imbalance. Socially, they proposed an aid policy of a specific income target—not less than $400 a head in all countries by the year 2000—and also specific targets of social progress (for instance, better nutrition for all children, particularly the protein essential to early growth; schooling and housing targets; health standards; and family planning goals). These, it was felt, might be sought with the help of special assistance funds set up for the purpose. The Pearson Report proposes one such special program—for population policy—under the auspices of the World Bank and the World Health Organization. It would probably be more acceptable to sensitive opinion in developing lands if this were part of, or flanked by, complementary funds for housing and education, areas in which the needs for research, experiment, and action are comparably large.

These social needs and pressures reach their height in the countries with per capita incomes of less than $300. Therefore, it was argued, the bulk of direct concessionary aid should be directed to them, serving the double purpose of accelerating the process of transformation and offsetting its harsher effects. Nations at the next stage of growth, while still requiring selective help, would profit more from the achievement of reforms in international trade, leading to greater access to the world market.

The second main issue was, in large measure, a political issue, and it was raised, first by Dr. Jolly, in discussing the concept of "self-sustaining growth." This could mean that at some point round about the year 2000, developing states would be ready to graduate out of dependence into an anarchic world of absolute sovereignty and a jungle-like international economy. Yet if, on that day of nominal "independence," the gap between the poor and the wealthy states were to be as great as, or greater than, today, what sort of independence would they in fact achieve? Would not all the power, all the decision making, all the ultimate influence remain with the giants, reducing the others, however self-sustained their growth, to client status?

To this risk, the tentative, searching reply of the majority at the Conference was to look for a genuine strengthening of the world's international institutions. They stressed the very wide range of political suggestions scattered through the Report, all of which are designed to institutionalize the growing interdependence of all the nations. They would use the purposive and collective pursuit of development as a main means of strengthening and reforming existing international institutions (the Jackson United Nations Capacity Study * was mentioned repeatedly in this context) and creating the new programs and agencies which an emerging world order, based upon mutual adjustment, obligation, and support might be found to require. Only by such a process of internationalization—of policies, of institutions—can a planetary society come

* See United Nations, Development Program, *A Study of the Capacity of the United Nations Development System,* 2 vols. (DP/5), 1969. This study was headed by Sir Robert Jackson and has come to be known as the Jackson Report.

into being within which rich and poor can coexist as citizens, if not with equal wealth, at least with equal rights and in mutual respect.

This larger purpose underlay the Conference's emphasis on all the Commission's proposals for greater multilateral policy and action. Only in a genuinely international framework of consultation and decision making could aid, as Hans Singer put it, "cease to be charity and become the first sketch of a world tax system." Only by securing a number of automatic transfers from rich to poor—through SDRs, through debt redemption funds, through five-year fundings of the IDA—could one avoid imprudent and often wounding political debate. Only by strengthening regional development banks and institutions could the poorer nations emerge as valid partners in the development dialogue. Only by strengthening the efficiency and the coordinating capacity of international institutions could they take over more of the work from the bilateral agencies. Above all, a style, a method in world economic diplomacy, would have to emerge in which the exceptional and often hectic character of aid-giving from rich to poor makes way for a quiet acceptance of living together on a small planet where tolerance, good manners, and the habit of coexistence are the conditions of survival.

The Aid Relationship:
Reflections on the Pearson Report
BY RICHARD JOLLY

A major international document such as the Pearson Report must be judged by two criteria, different from one another yet each closely related to the objectives which the report is designed to serve. First, one must examine how accurately it diagnoses the developmental problems discussed and whether it suggests adequate remedies to deal with them. And second, one must examine how skillfully it presents its message for

I am grateful for comments on an earlier draft of this essay from Dudley Seers, Hans Singer, and Paul Streeten. I have tried to take account of the comments made by participants in the Columbia University Conference on International Economic Development. However, responsibility for the views expressed in this paper is mine alone.

the purpose of influencing the direction, though not necessarily all the details, of public opinion and government policy. In the short run, these two criteria may be in conflict, for a report best designed to influence public opinion and convince policy makers may need an emphasis more optimistic or more pessimistic than the true situation. In the long run, however, the efficacy of the report will depend on how well it fulfills *both* of these criteria.

Some of the tension between these two objectives must have been evident to the Pearson Commissioners, and it certainly affects the opinions of anyone commenting on the report. Clearly, the Pearson Commission has produced a major document which gives the stamp of the personal but distinguished authority of the individual commissioners to a large number of fundamental yet underemphasized facts about development in the modern world: the growing inequality between the rich and the poor countries of the world in terms of income, nutrition, educational opportunity—indeed in terms of almost all the material dimensions of human well-being; the poverty and deprivation of millions of children and adults, primarily but not only in the developing countries; the requirement that countries with low incomes develop rapidly; and the desirability and usefulness of the richer countries playing a bigger and more important part in the process. More important, the Pearson Report makes many major recommendations concerning the necessity for expanded and improved programs of aid and technical assistance and more enlightened policies toward trade, supplementary finance, and debt repayments, to name but a few policy areas requiring substantive modifications. At a time when the general mood in the developed countries favors further reducing aid and disengaging from the development problems of the poor countries, the Pearson Report represents an important landmark. Therefore, those anxious to counteract the mood of withdrawal will hesitate before embarking on major criticism, lest what is intended as constructive comment play into the hands of those who would prefer to obliterate the whole message.

Yet, if one is to evaluate the report objectively, one must record the fact that the Pearson Report, on the whole, leans a long way toward attempting to influence reluctant public opinion in the rich countries by presenting an excessively optimistic view on developmental problems— optimistic in terms of recent development achievements, optimistic in terms of future prospects, and optimistic in its evaluation of world cooperation summarized in the very title *Partners in Development*. There is obviously much truth in all of the claims of this detailed and careful report. The argument of this paper, however, is that more pessimistic conclusions could be drawn from much of the material presented in the Pearson Report and that these conclusions would be nearer the truth than the optimistic ones reached by the Commission.

THE AID OBJECTIVE

The gap between the living standards of different parts of the world is growing more rapidly than ever before. In 1850 the gap in output per capita between rich and poor countries was perhaps $100 or $200. During the next hundred years, this gap increased five or tenfold to about $1,000 in 1950, to $1,500 in 1960, and to over $2,000 in 1970. As is shown in Table 1 based on the projections and assumptions of the Pearson Commission, the gap seems likely to reach $7,000 by the end of this century.[1]

There are several points to be made concerning these figures. First, whatever allowances are made for their unavoidable margins of error, the broad conclusions will not be changed. The absolute gap is large,

TABLE 1.   AVERAGE PER CAPITA GDP BY WORLD REGION (*U.S. dollars at 1960 prices*)

	1950	1960	1967	2000 (estimate)
Developed countries	$1,205	$1,587	$2,042	$7,450
Developing countries				
Africa	95	110	118	430
Latin America	350	433	486	1,770
Asia	80	95	110	400

Source: Figures for 1950–67 from United Nations, Economic Commission for Latin America, *Economic Survey of Latin America* (E/CN.12/825), March 12, 1969; growth rates from Pearson Report, p. 358. Projections for 2000 for the developed countries are a continuation of 1960–67 per capita growth; for the LDC's, 6% growth of GDP plus population estimates given in Pearson Report, p. 56.

Note: Developed countries include North America, Western Europe, Australia, New Zealand, Japan, and South Africa.

has grown immensely, and will grow incomparably more by the end of the century, provided there is no world war. Common to a number of studies, these conclusions are not in serious dispute.

Second, data for individual countries would reveal certain contrasts even more extreme than those shown (others, of course, would be less extreme). And third, inequality *within* many developing countries has been an increasingly serious problem, in large part the result of growing urban unemployment and sluggish rural development. If these facts were included in our data—for instance, by showing separately the average incomes of the bottom quarter of each country's population —some of the gaps would be even greater. By any test, the level of real poverty among the bottom quarter of the population in many developing countries is of serious proportions.

These latter points explain why the absolute "development gap" between countries may be as critical a factor as the relative gap. Poverty among the rich may be a matter of relative income. For the really poor, however, not having bread means not having bread, not merely not having cake. And even for those who are well above the line of "real" poverty, the absolute gap indicates a visible difference in living standards to which the relative gap only indirectly refers. The point is not that one measure of the gap matters and the other does not. Both the relative gap and the absolute gap are significant, and neither should be ignored.

The Pearson Commissioners recognized the fundamental importance of the recent growth and phenomenal size of this enormous disparity between rich and poor. Indeed the very first sentence of their report states that "the widening gap between the developed and developing countries has become a central issue of our time." *Yet under the proposals they put forward, the gap will continue to increase to three or four times its present absolute size by the end of this century.* It may even widen in relative terms. By the end of the century, however, with the gap much wider and with per capita income in a third of the world still less than $400 (compared to about $10,000 in North America), the Report (p. 126) suggests that development aid will "largely have disappeared."

It is difficult to treat as entirely adequate a report which so clearly identifies a central problem but which recommends measures, however welcome they may be, which so signally will fail to remedy the situation which the report diagnoses. The reason for the divergence between diagnosis and suggested cure is basically that, *despite the identification of a major part of the problem as growing inequality between the developed and developing countries,* the analysis of the report rests on the unquestioned assumption that the main purpose of aid is to enable countries to achieve self-sustaining growth. Since self-sustaining growth may in some sense be achieved by most countries by the year 2000, aid can disappear according to the Commissioners, whatever the size of the gap, then or now. In addition, since self-sustaining growth is not explicitly identified with a rate of growth fast enough to narrow the gap (even relatively), the Commission's recommendations allow the gap to persist or widen. Indeed, if one accepts the target of 6% growth, given their projected rates of population increase, the output per capita growth rate of the developing economies will be less over the next two decades than that of industrialized countries. In relative terms the gap will continue to grow, and even if it does not, it will widen in absolute terms to the point where the imbalance in living standards, wealth, and economic power will make today's inequalities look rather modest.

In contrast to the Pearson Commission approach, this continuing gap, not simply the date of attaining self-sufficiency, should set the perspective within which proposals for international development must be viewed. The problem of international development must be seen as a persistent problem of world inequality—the tendency of the rich to grow richer, in part with benefits to the poorer, in part to the disadvantage of the poorer, but on balance very much faster than the poorer. Far from being a short-lived phenomenon, the evidence suggests that this will be a growing characteristic of the coming decades and will exacerbate present tensions to an unprecedented degree. Far from implying that aid will taper off by the end of the century, the widening gap implies that transfers of income and development assistance—whatever form they may take—will be required in much greater amounts.

In addition, more fundamental issues are raised than aid or its equivalent. There must be a complete reconsideration of the world economy, starting with what to the Pearson Commission is fundamental to international development, "the willingness to look at the total economic relationship between developing and industrialized countries" (p. 79). If one takes seriously the grave consequences of a growing

output per capita gap in the coming decades, one must consider afresh
the whole question of the economic objectives of aid and development
assistance policies. At least three broad strategies might be adopted:

(1) To enable developing countries to achieve self-sustaining growth
(2) To diminish inequality between countries
(3) To abolish the extremes of poverty within countries by, for
for example, providing assistance to insure some minimum
standard of living.

Far from being intrinsically unreasonable, the second and third of these
strategies have almost always received important emphasis in the works
of great economists [2] and have been widely adopted as national policy
goals over the last century. Although there are important differences between applying these strategies *within* countries and applying them *between* countries, the differences are manifest mainly in problems of
implementation, not in judging the relevance of the objectives themselves.

The recent emphasis on poverty programs within the developed
countries, particularly the United States, has important implications for
future aid programs. Whatever their other causes, demands to deal with
internal poverty arise in part because the "have-nots" of society have
become more conscious of their situation and more determined to change
it, and in part because the "haves" of society have been growing steadily
richer and are prepared to pay more in response to these demands.
Among both groups, improved communications have led to greater
awareness of the income gap and of the means which already exist to do
something about it. In a less dramatic way, a similar process is also
operating in the world at large, and its impact is likely to grow in the
coming decades. As it does, the priority given to aid to abolish poverty
and to narrow extreme income differentials throughout the world will
increase.

One might ask why, when poverty and inequality are so stressed
as fundamental problems within countries, self-sustaining growth has
become the accepted objective of international aid. The answer to this
question is simply that it has not. Self-sustaining growth may be the
declared objective, but it has certainly not been empirically adopted

with any consistency. Empirical studies of the allocation of aid among developing countries show little correlation between the volume of aid allotted and any variables except size of country and proximity to communist borders. The emphasis on self-sufficiency has been a normative emphasis, particularly of economists. It is an attempt to recommend what ought to happen. It does not determine what does.

Since economists are largely responsible for formulating this aid objective, it may be enlightening to recall the origin of the concept of self-sustaining growth. Its theoretical underpinnings stem from a Harrod-Domar-Lewis-Rostow view of development in which the driving force is capital accumulation, and the main problem is raising the proportion of savings in national income. At a time when "take-off" theory was all the rage, Millikan and Rostow developed their proposals for a new foreign policy within this framework. During the last decade, the emphasis on capital accumulation has greatly diminished as foreign exchange, skill shortages, and organizational difficulties have received more attention. The Pearson Commission attempted to integrate the concept of self-sustaining growth with policies aimed at increasing exports and at increasing each developing state's capacity to substitute domestic production for imports, as well as at raising domestic savings rates. But as the section of the Pearson Report on trade policy makes clear, a country's power of action is often more limited in the field of exports and imports than in the area of domestic savings (pp. 80–98). This may make the path to self-sustaining growth through foreign exchange much less easy and automatic than that through domestic savings.

The idea that at higher income levels growth becomes self-sustaining—the belief underlying self-sustaining theories of aid—is primarily derived from a concentration on domestic marginal savings rates, rather than one on international trade prospects and income elasticities in a world of technological dominance by the richer countries. It is thus not clear why self-sustaining growth was so readily taken by the Pearson Commission as the objective of interstate aid. One suspects that the main reason was the *assumption* that electorates in developed countries would be willing to support an aid program only if, from the start, the termination of the aid program were in sight. With a burst of effort from the donor, with suitable policies from the recipient, and with convenient assumptions about marginal savings rates and incremental capital/output ratios, a developing country could raise savings and investment rates, grow faster, and within four or five planning periods not merely be independent of aid but begin to join other donors in providing aid to relatively less developed countries. The donor country is thus offered an aid rationale which provides a strong incentive for a sustained effort over short-run and medium-run periods with the promise of aid becoming unnecessary in the long run.

But what is the *evidence* that the self-sustaining growth rationale is the one most effective in winning public support for international assistance? It certainly is not the one most used by private aid-giving agencies, agencies which tend to emphasize either the human suffering which accompanies real poverty or the practical and readily appreciable value of specific projects. Provided that the emphasis on poverty does not lead to smug self-satisfaction over what "we" do for "them," the facts of poverty are a large part of the reality of the situation and thus an appropriate point on which to focus. The general point is that assumptions about the public appeal of hypothetical aid objectives are a poor substitute for hard evidence on how best to present the facts and causes of poverty and growing world inequality and how best to win public support for international action to deal with these problems.

To the recipient country, the supposed attractiveness of self-sustaining growth is that "countries do not desire permanent dependence on financial aid, and while private foreign investment always has its role, they want to be able to finance their own progress and not to depend indefinitely upon the sometimes uncertain interest of the wealthy countries. . . . Progress toward self-reliance for all nations will enhance mutual respect and is in the most profound interest of the world community as a whole." (Pearson Report, p. 126) It is questionable, however, whether self-sustaining growth at reasonable rates—leaving aside, for the moment, the possibility of complete economic independence—will be possible in a world divided by an income gap three or four times its present size. In terms of trade, production, technological progress, and skilled worker migration, the dominance of the developed countries' ideas, interests, technology, and economic power will, if present trends continue, be much greater, not smaller. International negotiations between rich and poor countries will take place between parties even more unequal than at present. Perhaps this state of affairs was accepted by the Pearson Commission members who qualified their comment on the disappearance of aid by remarking that "concessional transfers directed to other purposes would doubtless remain" (p. 127). In a world of such divisions, however, concessions—in the sense of agreeing to less than bilateral bargaining on the basis of *individual* national power—will be essential and will have to be institutionalized by multinational arrangements.

This discussion also makes clear an underlying but often unemphasized weakness in the whole notion of self-sustaining growth *at reasonable rates*. At first sight, the choice of self-sustaining growth as an objective appears to avoid the difficult value judgments needed to determine which countries to support and the type and appropriate level of transfers from rich to poor countries. Taking self-sustaining growth as the objective *seems* to lead away from politics and value judgments into technocratic calculations of comparative rates of savings investments, exports, imports, and growth, and the size of the consequent savings and foreign exchange gaps. But what is a *reasonable* self-sustaining rate of growth? The 5% of the First Development Decade? The 6% of the Pearson Report? Or should it be the rate which a country chooses for itself? Or, to be totally circular, should it be that rate at which a country could grow without opening up a foreign exchange or savings gap? What constitutes a reasonable rate of growth cannot be determined without some reference to the size of the income gap between rich and poor countries. And as this gap continues to widen, the range of growth rates which appear reasonable will surely increase.

This phenomenon is already evident in the area of unemployment. In spite of the accelerating growth of national income over the past decade, open urban unemployment, particularly among the young and the uneducated, has grown rapidly in most developing countries, to the point where it has become the major economic problem of the 1970's. It is now calculated that national incomes must increase at rates well above 6% over the next decade to prevent the unemployment position from further deteriorating. In Latin America, for example, they must grow at nearly 7% simply to maintain the present unemployment situation, and at 8% if unemployment is to be reduced to "reasonable" levels by 1990. By 1980, what seems a reasonable rate of growth may have increased even further.[3]

Rising required rates of growth by themselves do not constitute an insuperable barrier to the concept of self-sustaining growth. If the framework of analysis based on self-sustaining growth is accepted, rising growth rates would simply require even higher savings rates (probably leading to a longer period before the inception of self-sustaining growth but not precluding its attainment altogether). However, at this point the whole framework of discussion must be re-examined in light of the question whether the aid relationship between rich and poor countries can be distilled even in principle into a matter of financial transfers to meet savings or investment gaps in order to make possible self-sustaining rates of economic growth.

The inadequacy of this approach to the aid relationship can be shown by referring again to the problem of unemployment. Of the many causes of the unemployment problem, five stand out as fundamental: rapid population growth, halfhearted land reforms, rising urban wage levels, technological advances in capital-intensive techniques, and systematic biases toward capital-intensive methods. All are related to failures of policy and conflicts of interests or objectives within developing countries. But an important cause of each is also the dominating influence of rich-country technology, politics, and economic leadership. In light of the widening gap between rich and poor, most of these factors seem likely to cause productivity per man to rise within the developing countries even faster in the future, leading to yet higher required rates of economic growth if unemployment is to be contained. Clearly, any adequate solution requires substantial change in the whole structure of international influences, not just a move toward self-sustaining growth.

Few persons—and certainly none of the Pearson Commissioners— would disagree with the necessity of a broader approach. The Pearson Commission itself made reference to the much broader aspects of the total relationship between developing and industrialized countries and dealt specifically with numerous important policy alternatives in the fields of trade, private foreign investment, and scientific and technological research within an evolving international framework for development. But if interdependence in this wider sense and in a new international framework is inescapable, and if dependence in other respects will remain, one must wonder whether it is desirable to look to the disappearance of international aid.

THE AID RELATIONSHIP

Viewing the aid relationship against the background of these various considerations, one wonders, in the first place, how long the developed countries can continue to talk optimistically about marginal transfers without facing up to the obvious need to end world poverty. Technically and financially—in terms of economic resources—it would be possible to do so. Socially and politically—in terms of organization—skillful social and human planning would be required in order to tackle the sources of poverty and not simply to disrupt the pattern of life in developing countries with more invasions of rich-country technology. The sooner serious study begins and frank talk is forthcoming to win over public opinion to the real issues, the better off we will be. After all, ending world poverty must be the long-run target.

Second, one realizes that we must take seriously the question of world distribution of income between countries and not only within them. This means not only moving toward some acceptable pattern of world income distribution, but also recognizing that interdependence in the world economy carries the same implication as interdependence within the national economy: namely, that transfers from the rich to the poor are not charitable gifts to be given when the mood of generosity or pity runs high but are just and obligatory payments, a logical and coherent part of an interdependent world economy being managed (however visionary this may seem) in the interests of all. In the year after one-sixth of the people in the world simultaneously watched the first earth man step onto the moon, the concept of using some of the world's resources to eliminate human poverty should not be unrealistic, especially since many more billions of dollars have been spent on war in Vietnam than on all forms of aid to all developing countries.

Third, one sees that we must make very specific decisions concerning what this view of the aid relationship means in terms of an evolving world political structure and administrative organization. It is here that one must refer to the Jackson proposals, which, in this respect, provide a sharp and important contrast with the Pearson Report.[4] The Pearson Report constitutes a soft sell of aid to the enlightened interest of the developed countries. The Jackson Report is a hard-hitting set of proposals for organizational reform within the United Nations. It may be argued that it is unfair to compare the two in this way, since their purposes were different and necessarily implied reports of a different character and at different levels of administrative detail.[5] Nevertheless, one is struck by the operational tone of the Jackson Report compared with the somewhat more formal, almost textbook style of the Pearson Commission Report. This would not matter if each approach led to a discussion of the politics of implementation. But the Pearson Report often stops short of specifics, while the Jackson Report proposes changes in institutional structures which, in fact, hold the promise of much deeper changes in the balance of world power.

In terms of administrative organization, the Jackson proposals prepare the way for a strong and effective international operation designed for a long-term attack on world poverty, an attack not intended to terminate upon the achievement of self-sustaining growth. Major elements of these reforms would make possible greater aid efficiency and much clearer objectives in the operation of development programming. Fundamental to the Jackson approach are proposals for:

(1) The programming of international assistance at the country level, with a much stronger United Nations resident representative playing a central coordinating role;

(2) "Development Cooperation Cycle" comprising all the elements of project formulation, budgeting, implementation, and evaluation within a five-year framework and approved by an international Governing Council; and

(3) Reform at the United Nations headquarters and within its agencies and regional bodies designed to strengthen the international economic system, particularly by laying the foundations for a less bureaucratic organization with a high-level and specially trained career service supported by a strong information network and a revised accounting system; at the political level, the Economic and Social Council of the United Nations is envisaged as the coordinating force overseeing the world attack on poverty and inequality.[6]

All of these proposals are of major and immediate administrative importance. In terms of politics, their significance is that they provide a basis for the shift in the balance of power which a successful effort to end world poverty will require. This point must not be overstated, however. One could well argue that the Jackson proposals do not go far enough to assure long-run institutional reform. But it is difficult to imagine any fundamental change in international aid politics or relationships without these changes as a minimum. Jackson himself hints that his proposals might in time evolve into the beginnings of some form of world government. For those concerned with the long-run solution to the development gap, these political dimensions of the Jackson Report are fundamental and provide the basis upon which the Report must be judged:

(1) Its explicit recognition of a growing international operation within a perspective of increasing interdependence between nations; there certainly must be much stronger international institutions than exist today if inequalities in national power and wealth are to be subject to greater international influence.

(2) Its call for a shift of emphasis within United Nations Development Program operations to the country level, achieved in particular by giving the resident United Nations representative greater power;[7] there is great significance in geographically shifting control for the operation to a location where the governments of the developing countries will have easier access to and greatest opportunity to influence politically—and indeed psychologically—the key organization man and his staff.

(3) Its clear recognition that, for all their inadequacies, the United Nations Development Program and the United Nations Councils are politically representative of developing country interests in a way which the allocation of votes in the World Bank and the International Monetary Fund makes virtually impossible.

At the moment, the second of these dimensions may seem to have less political than administrative importance. Certainly its administrative significance is considerable. The third may seem more a matter of form than of real power. Indeed, the Pearson Report seems to suggest that it may be worth sacrificing these forms in order to give donor countries confidence that they have control over the financing which they provide. But it is precisely at this point of institutional structures that one must not sacrifice long-run advantage for short-run gain. The long-run solution requires a strengthening of those international institutions which have at least some semblance, however slight, of balanced representation of rich and poor. Until these institutions grow to real strength, the chance of changing international policies sufficiently to offset growing world inequalities seems slim indeed.

Aid Relationship for the Seventies
I. G. PATEL

THE SETTING

The Pearson Commission was born out of a sense of crisis and despair about development assistance. From modest beginnings in the early fifties, foreign aid had increased to substantial proportions by the middle of the Development Decade. For the poorer two-thirds of mankind, the decade and a half before the establishment of the Commission was a period of rapid awakening and sizable progress toward modernization and a sense of national identity and purpose. And yet, the concept of international cooperation for building stable and self-reliant societies began to lose its shine before it had gained any widespread currency. Among donors and recipients alike, there was frequent talk of a crisis of confidence and a feeling of disenchantment with foreign aid. It was against this background that a "grand-assize" of internationally eminent persons was summoned to "meet together, study the consequences of twenty years of development assistance, assess the results, clarify the errors and propose the policies which will work better in the future." (Pearson Report, p. vii)

The approach of Mr. Pearson and his colleagues to this challenge

The mood reflected here is that of the author in his personal capacity. While valuable comments from Messrs. S. Guhan, M. R. Shroff, C. S. Swaminathan, R. M. Honavar, A. T. Bambawale, and Alaknanda Patel have been incorporated, the attempt has been essentially to capture a feeling which is neither necessarily shared nor even sustained by them.

is essentially to demonstrate that aid in fact has worked and to prescribe more of the same for the future. With their gaze set firmly toward a better future, the eminent and well-intentioned Commissioners have said all that is desirable in regard to foreign aid. Their Report is a heartwarming document, particularly for the aid advocates whose passion for perfection and sophistication in making recommendations finds a response on almost every page of the document.

But when the initial exhilaration of hearing what one wants to hear is over, one is assailed by doubts. Can it be that the social and political roots of the malaise go much deeper than mere disappointment with the achievements of foreign aid? Is there not a danger here of attempting to cure a mental sickness as if it were a simple case of malnutrition? Granted that, often, the way out of a psychological malady is to set some ambitions to rest, at least for a while, and to focus instead on a few points of healthy endeavor that the mind can more easily fasten on to. Equally, it is all too easy to succumb to the romanticism of "crisis of confidence" or "disenchantment" or even to create one out of what may be no more than, say, the temporary juxtaposition of some rather abrasive but powerful personalities in the constellation of aid. The Commissioners, with their vast experience of human affairs, may well be wise in ignoring the seeming psychosis of aid as either transient or grossly exaggerated and in concentrating instead on what is ideally desirable for world development. But it is at least worth trying to be a little more explicit about the reasons for the sense of crisis in aid and inquiring if a somewhat different emphasis from that of the Commission's would not make for a better prescription in the immediate future.

THE ROOTS OF THE CRISIS

It would be futile to attempt to trace the origin of the crisis in aid to a single or simple source, if only because the aid-giving as well as the aid-receiving countries present a wide diversity of attitudes. Indeed, it is the way these differing attitudes acted and reacted on each other that seems to have led to the escalation of estrangement, and the best way to disentangle the story is to see how the different threads have pulled at each other.

Foreign aid appeared for the first time on the world stage in 1948, as a frank adjunct to the cold war. The simplicity and directness of such an approach to foreign aid, combined with its success in achieving the limited but well-defined objective in Europe, naturally gave it a sanctity which justified wider application. There was at least a pleasing ring to the word "ally," a concreteness in the number of armed divisions created, and a satisfaction of one's sense of tough realism in distinguishing between allies and those who refused to stand up and be counted.

But such a state of affairs was bound to create its own repercussions. Among the poorer countries, they took the shape of an assertion of nonalignment. Perhaps the more interesting reaction was among the aid-giving countries themselves. A hard-headed and frankly political or military approach to aid was bound to stir the liberal conscience. It was some such stirring that had prompted President Truman to try to balance the Marshall Plan with the announcement of the Point Four Program and of support to the Colombo Plan. But, for the major part of the fifties, liberalism was in exile except in Canada; it is not an accident that in the Colombo Plan Canada was perhaps the only country which looked on aid primarily as a matter of promoting development. The role of other Commonwealth countries in the Colombo Plan was then marginal. France had embarked on its own course of winning friends and influencing people. The United States was caught between the cold war philosophy and the nagging of liberals. And the rest were busy rebuilding themselves. The World Bank did its quiet work, but no one thought of identifying it as aid at the time.

Into this situation came India's first foreign exchange crisis, which provided a major point of departure in the history of foreign aid. The Pearson Commission rightly emphasizes that the creation of the Aid India Consortium in 1958 marked an important—indeed the first— landmark in the evolution of a new attitude toward foreign aid. But the claim that it also marked "the development of institutions for mutual cooperation, which now make aid unquestionably more effective than it was when it began" (Pearson Report, p. 128) deserves a closer look as does also the precise nature of the change that took place in the attitude toward foreign aid.

Certainly, the size of India, its commitment to political democracy, and the value of its example to others prompted a response in many quarters when, after successfully implementing its first Plan, it found itself in a serious foreign exchange crisis. In addition to the creation of the Aid India Consortium, the establishment of the U.S. Development Loan Fund in the latter part of the Eisenhower administration and of the International Development Association were, in large part, a response to India's needs. For many influential scholars and politicians in the United States, Canada, Britain, and elsewhere India became the rallying point for a new concept of foreign aid—an essentially humanitarian transfer of resources from the rich to the poor in order to achieve internationally the goals of economic opportunity for all, which had become an accepted part of national objectives in all modern societies. And let it be said without any reservation that the response was unstinting and spontaneous, at least in the initial stages (from 1958 to 1964). What was true of India was even more so for several other countries.

But the relatively liberal phase in foreign aid, which began around 1958, was not free from at least a tinge of cold war politics, and it brought with it its own seeds of contradiction and conflict. A certain distinction between "allies" and "friends," between neighbors and others, became like-minded people and the rest remained and colored the assessment of needs as well as performance. The lip service to democratic values wore thin. Across the simmering continents of Asia, Africa, and Latin America, with their deep discontents and rising social and economic passions and expectations, revolutionary and even self-destructive situations were bound to arise from time to time; they made it difficult to strike consistent attitudes or to project an image of steady and orderly growth all around.

The liberal brings to this untidiness of world events his sense of purpose that often shades off into his own peculiar brand of touchiness. While it is certainly true that it is the strategy of mobilizing larger sums for development assistance, in the teeth of opposition, by exaggerating what it can achieve in the short run and by advancing theories of the big push or the take-off which recoiled on itself to produce the sense of crisis, there is something more to it than that. Most liberals believed in the theories and were anxious to witness dramatic results during their tenure. In large part, the disenchantment was also theirs and not that of others whom they were trying to persuade to part with a little more of their money. Among the liberals many were afraid of being considered soft and were prone to invent their own form of toughness.

They may be in favor of spending more money. But they will insist on performance, they will judge and assess, they will use money as an instrument for bringing about desirable changes in policies abroad and for supporting "right-minded" groups in the struggle for local leadership.

But such a recipe for international intervention or even involvement on an extensive scale cannot suit the realities of the second half of the twentieth century. It is not surprising that it should produce so soon an attitude of mutual distrust and recrimination about foreign aid itself. First and foremost, the donor countries themselves can demonstrate little conviction of their own adherence to the performance criterion. As long as the distribution of aid is governed to an important extent by considerations of political, ideological, geographical, or historical affinity, and as long as nation-states feel compelled to compromise with principles in the midst of a rapidly shifting kaleidoscope of events, it is idle to claim that the distribution of aid is or can be related strictly to performance.

In the absence of such a correlation, the recipient countries are all the more likely to resent an interventionist aid policy. Assessment of relative performance with a view to determining aid shares is also an invitation to the recipient countries to denigrate each others' progress and to provide ammunition to critics of aid for opposing aid to one or the other country. Behind the facade of unity at international gatherings, the developing countries have engaged in a tug-of-war to preserve or augment their particular apportionments of available aid.

There is no doubt that the new style in aid aroused serious resentment in the developing world. In many of the nonaligned countries, the acceptance of massive aid was not so much an act of conscious policy as something into which one stumbled in a moment of foreign exchange crisis, something about which powerful political and intellectual groups had reservations right from the outset. Suspicions that, at bottom, aid was an instrument of neocolonialism or the cold war in a new guise were easily nourished and fanned in the face of increasing evidence of intervention in matters of internal policies, of open patronizing of particular local leaders, of the gap between the professions and the performance of aid-givers, and, occasionally, of some outrageous lapses in diplomacy.

In such an atmosphere, everything assumes a somewhat abnormal

air: the involvement of some United States universities in Pentagon
activities makes most university teachers from the United States suspect
in the eyes of many intellectuals; the willingness of some countries to
let research, intelligence, and aid management get somewhat mixed up
gives foreign aid an altogether new and unpleasant odor. Nor is it impossible to point to instances where the assessment and advice of even
international agencies have been either biased or wrong, thus lending
support to the thesis that insistence on satisfying particular criteria of
performance is yet another guise for promoting ideological conformity
around the world. Recrimination, mistrust, and even open hostility are
further encouraged by the internal power struggles in many developing
countries—and sometimes by the open conflicts between them. One
would not get even a glimpse of the deep undercurrents of feeling set in
motion by what is considered a new landmark in aid history from reading in the Pearson Report the chapters on India and Pakistan, which
seek in the main to prove, with some justification, that the policy of
intervention was not without its rewards. But silence on the hazards
and the costs of such a policy cannot make for an effective salvage
operation.

Among the donors, by the mid-sixties, the advocates of aid as an
instrument of the cold war had little to enthuse them—the cold war had
abated in some areas (though considerably heated up in others), allies
in many cases had turned fickle or frankly opportunistic or were drawn
into a more neutral posture by the pressure of internal or external
events. The liberals were bewildered by the reaction to their well-
intentioned attempts to improve economic performance and disillusioned
about the pace of progress that was possible both in the mobilization of
aid and in the adherence to purely economic objectives even among
those who so badly needed better economic performance. The more
liberal among them turned tougher still, bemoaning the "softness" of
the developing societies to the point where they saw foreign aid as a
crutch to perpetuate this "softness," a sentiment not without its echo
among the poorer countries themselves.

Meanwhile, the impact of the Vietnam war and the coming of the
postwar generation to full manhood were creating an altogether new
situation in the affluent one-third of the world. Somehow, President
Kennedy's Peace Corps soon became *passé*; we have yet to comprehend

what the younger generation in the United States and Europe really think of issues like foreign aid. Having renounced any sense of identity with their own nations, they seem to find it difficult to identify themselves with other nations. To many of them, aid and the desire to shape the policy of others is only an example of the kind of unnecessary and annoying meddlesomeness of the middle-aged which produced Vietnam. The more militant among them perhaps salvage their consciences from the charge of indifference to the plight of the poorer countries by identifying themselves with more militant causes at home or by averring that the solution to the poverty of Asia and Africa lies in revolutionary transformation of their basic social structures. The young being young, perhaps most of them, even today, would be happy to pay their tithes for the development of the poorer two-thirds of the world. But perhaps they would prefer to do so without much fanfare of organizations and reviews and assessments, and certainly without getting involved in having to mete out rewards or punishment. But whatever their present mood, it is quite clear that the destiny of foreign aid and much else besides is now passing into the hands of a generation that seeks to assert its discontinuity with the past without having charted so far its own course of continuity into the future.

The new era in foreign aid which began around 1958 had yet another guiding principle: that the responsibility for giving aid must be shared widely and equitably among the richer countries of the world. There was a desire to rope in more and more countries to the category of donors and to insist on greater harmony in aid terms and a better sharing of the aid burden. While in itself unexceptionable and indeed beneficial to the cause of aid, this process of proliferation brought its own problems of standardization and coordination. Attitudes are bound to differ among any group of donors, and attempts to coax, cajole, or coerce some into doing something generate their own reactions. The attitude toward aid on the part of some donors was frankly commercial; they saw it as an inevitable adjunct to export promotion in an era of tied aid and fierce competition in the supply of capital goods. Together with the harder terms of the loans of some countries, this made aid worth much less than its face value; and since aid was a loan which had to be repaid, it was easy to sneer at it as nothing more than ordinary commercial credit. For those donors whose aims were frankly commercial, the growing burden of repayments on the part of the debtors and the demand to rephase this burden were a signal to cut donor losses by limiting their new commitments. Comparisons about aid burdens are not easy to make in an era of tied aid. Interest rates and maturity periods can be compared, but the cost of tied aid varies so that a country can still claim that if its interest rate is high, its prices are cheaper. At any rate, the diversification of the sources of aid and the emphasis on better sharing and on harmony in aid terms contributed their own share to the air of controversy and despair that surrounded aid toward the middle of the first Development Decade.

To sum up, the crisis in aid was and is an amalgam of many factors and not just a reaction to exaggerated claims made earlier, or the result of any general lack of appreciation of what has already been achieved in the developing world with marginal but crucial external assistance. It had much to do with the hangover of the cold war which still persists. The strident style of performance-oriented aid diplomacy, which smacks of neocolonialism to many in the developing world, did not help either. In a sense, aid is bound to be doubly cursed. But the curse was perhaps heightened by the combination of a number of things including the balance of payments difficulties of some of the rich, the divisions and dissensions among the poor, the sharpening of internal social and political tensions in many parts of the developing world, the revival of political conflicts among some of the new donors, and, above all, the frustrating horrors of Vietnam. Right now, an altogether new variety of retreat from international responsibility seems to be overtaking the young, from which some of the more influential of the older guard are also not immune.

How are we to put a new life into the aid chapter at this stage? What are the errors most particularly to avoid? And where are we to look for a new motivation, a new style, and a better aid relationship? There is no doubt that with all the aid-weariness and the desire to get rid of aid as quickly as possible, and despite all the hankering after revolutionary panaceas, the developing countries can benefit immensely from a net inflow of external resources on concessional terms for many decades to come. There is no doubt either that the richer countries can afford to respond, with profit, to all the suggestions of the Pearson Commission. But equally, aid, however desirable, will continue to generate tensions unless there is a dramatic change in the present relationship between donors and recipients.

THE COMMISSION'S APPROACH

The Commission's basic approach, as already indicated, is one of advancing on all desirable fronts. Its main recommendations, as they relate to the subject matter of this paper, may be paraphrased as follows:

1. It is possible to set most, if not all, developing countries on the path of adequate and self-reliant growth before the end of the century. Inferentially, it is possible also to eliminate the need for aid, if not over the next decade or so, at least over the next three decades.

2. A 6% rate of growth will enable a progressive reduction in the savings and payments gap, and such a rate of growth in the developing countries is feasible if the flow of external resources reaches the magnitude of 1% of the GNP of the wealthier countries by 1975 (and presumably is continued at that level for some years).

3. Since the growth objective cannot be achieved by aid alone and requires hard and protracted effort on the part of the developing countries themselves, "increases in development aid should in the future be closely linked to the economic objectives and the development performance of the aid-receivers." (Pearson Report, p. 17) At the same time, aid-givers should eschew political and nondevelopment objectives.

4. Since performance is not a one-way street, the developing countries are entitled to ask for assurance of definite and long-term commitments of aid. The Commissioners recognize that "there are virtually no facilities for the monitoring of recipients of the aid commitments." (p. 228) But they state that the monitoring and assessment of performance "is best done in a multilateral context in which donors and aid-receivers jointly review the past and plan for the future." (p. 17) Accordingly, the existing consortium technique must be reviewed, extended, and improved upon. There is an expression of hope "that each [consultative] group will increasingly provide for explicit and formal review of *donor* aid policies and procedures" and thus give "recipients an opportunity to monitor donors, and donors to monitor other donors." (p. 130)

5. On the day-to-day administration of aid, since cumbersome procedures "on both sides" often hamper the effective use of aid, "a

meeting of major aid donors and recipients should be held in 1970 to identify major procedural obstacles and means to overcome them." (p. 19)

6. To create a better sense of "partnership in development," there should be "a substantial enlargement of the responsibilities of international organisations" and "a thorough review of their practices and policies." The share of multilateral aid should be raised from its present level of 10% of total official development assistance to a minimum of 20% by 1975. It is worth noting that the Commission's recommendations call for a substantial absolute increase in both bilateral and multilateral aid.

7. "The President of the World Bank should, in the course of 1970, invite the heads of the appropriate organs of the U.N. and other multilateral agencies, as well as representatives of bilateral aid-givers and of developing countries, to a conference to consider the creation of machinery essential to the efficiency and coordination of the international aid system." (p. 22)

In a sense, when so much that is central to the proposed aid relationship is delegated to reviews and consultations yet to be undertaken, it is perhaps premature to subject these recommendations to too severe a scrutiny. But the Development Assistance Committee review of procedures is hardly likely to be more than a routine meeting of a working party or a group of experts. It will be interesting to see what the World Bank really makes out of the proposed conference on aid coordination. Chances are that perhaps not much will happen except larger attendance at the many meetings of consortia, consultative groups, and the like. There is talk of a separate institution or agency to review aid and performance without any direct responsibility for providing or administering aid—separateness itself somehow guaranteeing greater objectivity and influence. If the establishment of such an agency were to lead to a corresponding retrenchment in the activities of the bilateral aid missions, the World Bank, the International Monetary Fund, and the UN family, there would at least be some gain. But that is hardly likely, and even the developing countries may not wish to have just one single court of appeal this side of Heaven.

A certain improvement in the aid relationship, if not in the general aid climate, has been discernible over the past year or two. The real question is whether the Commission's formula of mutual monitoring of performance in multilateral forums is likely to generate a better aid climate without reviving the resentment which led to its appointment. Unfortunately, the concept of a genuine partnership in development somehow lacks credibility. There has never been any real sense of equality between donors and recipients even when they attend the same consortium meetings and sit around the same table in many other forums. For the recipient to be frank about the policies or attitudes of donors in a forum where aid is to be distributed is about as difficult as the proverbial passage of the camel through the eye of a needle. Criticism of donor policies, even when it comes from non-recipients, is seldom answered in the manner in which recipients are obliged to answer the most far-reaching criticism of their own policies. There are obviously two sets of rules. The donors have parliaments and public opinion which reign so supreme that a mere reference to them should silence all criticism, whereas the recipients should obviously be able to manipulate at will their parliaments and public opinion in the interest of appropriate development policies. A mere equality of opportunity in engaging in dialogue cannot establish parity in decision making. Nor can the platonic world of knowledge as a sufficient basis for right conduct be easily summoned into existence. One has only to look at the constitution and functioning of the World Bank and the International Monetary Fund and, by contrast, the persistent refusal to provide any real resources to the UN and its agencies to see how even multilateral institutions have to remain in line with the hard realities of economic and political power. Even when they assess relative needs and performance, they must keep one eye on what is feasible, i.e., palatable to the powers that be.

If the doctrine of mutuality in monitorship or genuine partnership in development is impractical, the insistence on performance as a yardstick for aid lacks both practical conviction and moral appeal. True, aid resources are scarce and must be wisely used. Waste can only recoil on the total effort. But performance—or its cruder side-kick, absorptive capacity, which was once fashionable—puts relatively backward societies at a disadvantage. One has only to attend a conference where African countries are represented to see how deep is the resentment against the approach of giving more to those who have already demonstrated the beneficial use of aid. There is also something awkward about punishing ordinary people for the temporary aberrations of their leaders. Performance for a society can only be judged over the long pull as no society can be free from upsets and stresses and strains from time to time. The task of building societies is more akin to the bringing up of children than to the disciplining of sinners, so a stop-go policy of aid in response to temporary vicissitudes becomes as unfair as it is artificial. The Commissioners rather carefully relate only increases to better performance. But if their intention was to emphasize that all poor countries should continue to receive a reasonable share of aid irrespective of the twist and turn of their fortunes and that only the focus of concentrated spurts in international effort should change from time to time in the light of available opportunities for rapid returns, they fail to say so. And, in matters of this kind, nuance makes all the difference in the world.

Many other comments are possible on the Commission's approach to an appropriate aid relationship. Would it not have been wise, for example, to prescribe goals for the next decade only and leave out speculations about the end of aid? Can the issue of bilateral versus multilateral aid be resolved simply by asking for more of both? If there is aid-weariness and a need to make the aid relationship multilateral, should not the question at least be raised whether an increase in the proportion of multilateral aid of the total would be desirable even if it comes about at the expense of bilateral aid? If the problems of coordination are becoming important, is it not time to advise at least the smaller donors to contract or conclude their bilateral programs by making over their funds to multilateral agencies? No discussion of the aid relationship can be complete without a searching look at the growing aid bureaucracy with its own brand of specialization, vested interests, and tendency to propagate and perpetuate itself. Do we really need a large and specialized cadre of career aid professionals or an increasing number of those who perform development tasks in their own countries to be temporarily seconded to international organizations? Why is it that, when we are dealing with complex and even violent convulsions in the social and political order around the developing world, the arbiters of their performance and prospects are almost invariably drawn from the ranks of the modern know-alls—economists and lawyers? Is experience gained in the richer countries or even in the poorer countries some decades ago such a sure guide as to justify its preponderance in the counsels of our world organizations?

There are no easy answers to these questions. But they are a vital part of any development strategy or aid relationship. The Commission perhaps can be well content with laying down the broad outlines, re-asserting the ideal approach, and reminding us of the basic facts. There is no alternative either to the main thrust of their argument: focus on development as the central objective of aid and a growing sense of partnership in the realization of the objective. But before we take for granted success along the road charted by them, we had better remind ourselves about its intricacies and pitfalls. At any rate, it is worth asking if our next few steps should not be rather carefully and warily chosen till we see a little more of a propitious opening toward the admirable course charted by the Commission.

AN ALTERNATIVE FRAMEWORK

In a fundamental or long-term sense there is, and indeed there can be, no alternative to the Commission's recommendations. It is obviously true that aid levels should increase, aid terms improve, greater regard be paid to purely development objectives, appropriate development poli-cies encouraged, the machinery for co-ordination and evaluation strength-ened, and a franker and freer dialogue initiated among donors and recipients alike. These are endeavors that must persist and that will inevitably hover between different degrees of success from time to time. But there are still questions of immediate priorities and emphasis, of nuance and style—questions as difficult to get hold of as they are vital. Absolute assertions are hardly appropriate in such a complex and emo-tionally charged endeavor. But as a means of inviting debate and dis-cussion, two propositions are worth placing on the table:

1. The whole debate and discussion about foreign aid needs to be carried on for some time in a low key, and the giving and receiving of aid conducted in as quiet and routine a fashion as possible, so as to avoid any more grating on nerves.

2. Among all the possible ways of improving the quality and quantity of aid, the one that deserves most attention is that of imparting a greater sense of continuity or automaticity in aid by exploring some altogether new ways of mobilizing and distributing aid without too scrupulous a regard for theoretical perfection or too much involvement in other countries' affairs.

The style that is most likely to suit the decade of the seventies is not one of intervention or even involvement but of duty done without too much fuss or subsequent bother. The enemy today in the richer countries is not so much disenchantment as indifference. The poorer countries themselves are in a mood to call it a day if aid gives the slightest suspicion of intervention. And it is doubtful if most of the voters in the affluent countries have an appetite for detailed reviews and judgments about distant countries, the inner logic of whose development they neither comprehend nor wish to comprehend. There is sufficient vitality in the developing countries themselves to demand real and rapid performance from their leaders; the advice of others, whether accompanied by aid or not, is more likely to be accepted the more quietly and unconditionally it is given. The donors also are more likely to improve the quality and quantity of their aid the less they are badgered about matching the performance of others or invited to underwrite concrete and specific goals for advancing world development or reducing inequality.

A quiet style in aid would also mean a rough and ready approach to equality of sacrifice in aid and equity in aid distribution. Over time, such kinks tend to get ironed out; it is perhaps better, for the time being, to summon everyone to do his best and to let every developing country share in available aid for some easily acceptable and identifiable objectives such as raising the level of education or health facilities or urban housing or irrigation use or electricity available. Trying to add up everything into tests of performance, growth rates, take-off points, or formulae for equity is perhaps less important than taking up some concrete and urgent universal problems and tackling them as a concrete contribution of the international community. Financing total costs, and not just imports, might provide a welcome departure from looking at aid largely as an instrument of export promotion. Linking aid to projects with a predominantly social rather than economic content might generate more warmth and a broader based appreciation of the benefits of aid. It might even provide a better outlet for the restlessness of the young in the richer countries. When one builds houses and clears slums rather than sets up industries, the points of conflict on issues of economic policy are minimized and the dialogue on overall performance gets automatically divorced from particular acts of assistance.

There are several corollaries to this subdued "aid on long-term trust" approach: it implies an encouragement to internationalization of aid; a curtailment of aid establishments to the minimum; and, perhaps, a greater role financially for a number of specialized agencies rather than concentration of international effort in one or two aggressively development-minded institutions.

What is the guarantee that such an approach will augment the flow of aid or at least prevent a decline? The blunt fact is that there is no such guarantee anyway, and all that one can do is hope for the best. The poorer countries would be well advised to plan on the basis of rather modest levels of aid, treating each increase in the level of aid as something to be subsequently deployed rather than assumed in advance. That way lies less frustration and greater cordiality. And it is at least arguable that a quiet approach, which does not pretend to answer anything more than the satisfaction of some urgent and universally acceptable wants, is as likely to evoke a generous response from the rich as anything else.

Side by side, we can explore some new and imaginative avenues for imparting a greater degree of continuity and automaticity in aid flows, taking them as far as possible out of the annual wrangles for appropriations and even from the "non-decisions" of consultative groups and consortia. The appeal would be on many fronts, each with a recognizable justification of its own. There is reason to believe that even the richer countries would be anxious to trade-off the right (or is it the annoyance) of annual reviews of their own intentions and policies in favor of a longer-term commitment if simultaneously they are released from the constant pressure to do more and better.

It would be idle to pretend that alternatives that are both acceptable and adequate can be easily suggested. But one has to make a choice of where and how one chooses to fight and what rewards one is prepared to treat as a bonus if they happen to come. For example, it would be more important to seek a five-year commitment for the third IDA replenishment than to settle for a three-year replenishment out of fear of sacrificing a better opportunity in the future. Equally, it would be better to settle as best one can this question of IDA replenishment in time rather that to drag out negotiations and create a hiatus as was done on the last occasion. Clearly, those who wish to do better now or later could be invited to make voluntary contributions, and, indeed, there could be a general invitation to everyone to make additional contributions by way of a transfer from their bilateral aid budgets.

The idea of a link with the creation of the Special Drawing Rights of the International Monetary Fund is another device that needs to be seriously pursued. There is considerable appeal all over the world to this suggestion, and it is somehow easy to convince ordinary citizens that if they get something for nothing, they should be willing to share a part of it with less fortunate people. Is it really necessary to go beyond the simple logic that convinces simple people and create difficulties for every solution by a display of our technical virtuosity?

Another promising idea (that has been endorsed in a different context by the Pearson Commission) is to urge a convention whereby all developed countries would agree to put repayments of capital and interest in a separate fund that would be used to make fresh loans. In the long run, this is likely to be much more effective than the present procedures for multilateral debt refinancing, which create problems of their own such as generating a lack of faith in the creditworthiness of the countries concerned and engendering feelings of unfairness among donors by a sort of retrospective equalization of past aid terms. An ordinary citizen or politician is more likely to heed the argument that, even if he is not prepared to vote for more aid, he should not be in a hurry to claim his due from the poorer countries. The simple device of a separate funding of repayments to create a revolving fund for aid can go a long way in imparting greater stability and continuity to aid levels.

Perhaps it is also time to consider raising resources for aid by indirect rather than direct taxation—or at least by specific liens on both direct and indirect taxes for specific purposes. It is at least possible that the world community might readily accept a levy on cigarettes for enabling the World Health Organization to improve the standards of health and hygiene around the world and to alleviate the meanness of urban conglomerations. A levy on liquor could perhaps be appropriately assigned to improvement of education or nutrition.

There is understandable concern that what the poor countries gain in aid is more than offset by deterioration in their terms of trade. World action to stabilize and improve the prices of primary commodities has been singularly tardy. Can it not be that the developing countries would gain more if a part of the high-powered advocacy of aid were devoted to the stabilization and improvement of the terms of trade for primary products? While waiting for more liberal access to rich markets, can we not agree, for example, that a part of the protective duties levied by the rich against the products of the poor should be made over to some international agency for the benefit of diversification of the trade and economies of the developing countries directly affected? Acceptance of such ideas cannot be easy. But it is worth knocking at many doors as there is no knowing when which one will open. The basic advantage of such specific endeavors is that they appeal to the ordinary man's sense of justice and fair play. The more general appeal to man's responsibility to man in a world which is getting more and more interlinked is getting somewhat stale. In the present mood, the international community is more likely to respond to suggestions that embody at least a rough and ready approach of paying a price for particular acts of unfairness or indulgence or of sharing a good fortune for obviously worthwhile purposes.

In conclusion, perhaps it may as well be made clear that this comment seeks to offer a few suggestions, not as a substitute for the Commission's recommendations, but as a supplement to them. The point of departure is essentially one of style and nuance. There is no reason to think that the Commissioners were unaware of much that has been said here or that some of them may not endorse many things that have been advocated here. The Commission was addressing itself mainly to the parliaments and the public in the aid-giving countries; it is natural to assume that the time for making a proposal is hardly the time to dilate on the difficulties of marriage or on the need to take a less romantic view of each other. But this occasion is more like the reunion of an estranged couple. The better course may well be to carry on quietly for some time and build around obvious things like the children and the garden. Meanwhile, it can do no harm to read the old letters again or even to turn the pages of the manual on ideal marriage one read with such avidity not so long ago.

Development and Structural Changes:
African Experience

BY SAMIR AMIN

Somewhere in the Pearson Report, we are pleasantly surprised to learn that the concept of "development" embraces more than mere growth: that development is growth accompanied by structural change (p. 124). This is a truly surprising statement, since nowhere, before or after this passage, does the Commission do anything other than argue strictly in terms of growth. Analysis is therefore necessarily made in terms of distressing poverty. Worse still, by restricting itself to this inadequate conceptual framework, the Report tends to stress insignificant facts, ignore the significant ones, and draw hasty conclusions. This springs from an apparently forced "optimism" that leads it to recommend, for the future, the solutions that have been applied over the last two decades, even though their failure is evident.

According to the Pearson Report, growth in the less developed countries over the last two decades has been relatively rapid—much more rapid, at any rate, than that of the developed countries at a comparable stage in their development. (For example, growth expressed in terms of per capita GDP is higher. Similarly, the investment effort is said to have been much better in the less developed countries over the last twenty years than it was in the developed countries in the nineteenth century.) Acceleration in this growth is said to be hampered by two main obstacles: inadequate growth in exports, and inadequate financial resources. The Report thereupon recommends: a more outward-looking growth orientation (which is advocated explicitly, particularly on pp. 14 and 235), and an increase in aid from the developed countries. The Report then tells us that if these two recommendations can be implemented, then toward the end of the century many of the developing countries will be able to "get off the ground" (pp. 28 and 126). Ob-

Translated from the French, for the Columbia Conference on International Economic Development, by the Translation Bureau, Secretary of State Department, Government of Canada.

viously, this depends on the possibility of simultaneously putting an end to the population increases that currently blunt to a considerable extent the benefits of growth. My intention is to show:

(1) that analysis made in the apparently "common sense" terms of the Pearson Report is superficial and deceptive and suggests ineffectual "solutions" derived from a philosophy of pious wishes.

(2) that this results from the fact that such analysis *fails to take into account the meaning of the structural changes that development demands,* particularly the conditions and limitations of agrarian capitalism, and the dynamics and limitations of outward-looking industrialization based on foreign capital.

(3) that, as a result, the analysis in question denies itself an understanding of the fact that *it is integration into world markets that is the real obstacle to development.*

Although what follows is based largely on African experience, with which I am most familiar, I believe that these conclusions have general validity.

THE FACTS: A HISTORICAL COMPARISON OF GROWTH IN
THIRD WORLD AFRICA WITH THAT OF THE DEVELOPED COUNTRIES

The Pearson Report reminds us that between 1850 and 1950, growth in per capita GDP in the developed world did not exceed 2% to 2.5% per year, with investment roughly 10% of the GDP. The developing countries are already doing better, as shown in Table 1.

Furthermore, in a number of fields that are decisive in the long run, the Report cites favorable performances of the last two decades.

1. In the establishment of essential physical infrastructure, decisive progress has been achieved: electricity consumption increased at the rate of 10.5% annually (11.5% in Africa), compared with 7.7% in the developed countries; steel consumption at the rate of 8.1% (but only 2.1% in Africa), compared with 4.5% in the developed countries; railway freight traffic volume at 4.4% (4.7% in Africa), compared with 1.1% in the developed countries.

2. Decisive progress has also been achieved in the fields of educa-

TABLE 1.   GROWTH, SAVINGS, AND INVESTMENT RATES, 1960–67

	Developed Countries	Less Developed Countries	Africa
GDP	4.8%	5.0%	4.0%
Population	1.2	2.5	(2.4)
Per capita GDP	3.6	2.5	(1.5)
Agricultural production	1.8	2.1	1.4
Industrial production	5.6	7.3	6.0
Export earnings	8.8	6.1	5.4
Domestic savings (% of GDP)	21.7	15.0	13.1
Gross investment (% of GDP)	21.2	17.8	16.7

Source: Based on Pearson Report, pp. 23–53.

tion and health. Growth in primary school enrollment was 6.8% annually (7.8% in Africa), while growth in secondary enrollment was 9.0% (9.4% in Africa), compared with 1.8% and 6.0%, respectively, in the developed countries. Education expenditure in the less developed countries is already 5% of the GDP compared with 7% in the developed countries. Similarly, the number of inhabitants per physician, although a long way from the figure for the developed countries (750 in 1966), improved from 5,100 in 1952 to 3,600 in 1966 (Africa: from 11,800 to 9,200).

3. In the field of efforts to levy taxes, which is said to reflect up-to-date administrative structures and a feeling of national consciousness, seventeen developing countries have already succeeded in collecting more than 20% of the GDP, twenty countries between 15% and 20%, and twenty-nine between 10% and 15%. This is already far better than European performance in the nineteenth century.

This is certainly a very general picture. In the case of Africa, for example, there are wide variations in all these figures: public consumption varies from 5.6% to 21.1% of GDP, capital formation from 6.7% to 45.7%, growth from zero to 10% annually.[1]

This review of the facts is accompanied by the brief statement that between 1880 and 1913 the less developed countries had already experienced the relatively rapid growth that was associated with the major increase in world trade and capital flows at that time. Then, from 1913 to 1950, stagnation set in, we are told, because world trade and capital flow were themselves shackled. But during this period stagnation was characteristic of the entire world (except Russia), the developed countries as much as the others. Beginning in 1950, the resumption of trade and capital flows at an increased pace once again made high growth rates possible both at the center and at the periphery of the world system.

There can be no doubt that the conclusions drawn from these so-called facts are hasty. If they were correct, the gap between the developed and developing countries, in terms of per capita GDP, would have narrowed progressively. The contrary is true: about 1880, the gap was much smaller than it is today. This means that the statement claiming rapid progress achieved between 1880 and 1913 is incorrect. In point of fact, progress in per capita GDP at that time was much less at the periphery than at the center, despite the growth in exports from the periphery and the very rapid influx of foreign capital, and the moderate increase in population growth rate. Why was this? This is the real question, and the Pearson Report does not even ask it. The fact is that this period saw the establishment of the structures of *underdevelopment*. It was these structures that subsequently hindered growth between 1913 and 1950, as much at the periphery as at the center itself. Thus, the 1913–50 period saw the beginning of the contradictions that characterize the Third World of today, especially between the relative stagnation of economic growth and the continuously accelerating rise in population. The reappearance of relatively high growth rates after 1950 is the result of the resumption of growth at the center. For the periphery, this growth took place within the same basic structures of dependence, the structures of the periphery being shaped, at each stage, to reflect the needs of accumulation at the center.[2] The result is that, as in the 1880–1913 period, growth of the periphery *is weaker than at the center* and not stronger as the Report states.

The figures given by Paul Bairoch, shown in Tables 2 and 3, are better supported than those of the Pearson Report.[3]

These figures show that the gap is widening rather than narrowing. The direction of the trend, masked in the Pearson Report, is apparent in the Bairoch figures: the situation at the periphery is deteriorating despite the improved export performance, and despite the "Green

TABLE 2.   GROWTH IN THE THIRD WORLD (*excluding China*)

	1948–54	1954–60	1960–66
GDP	4.7%	4.6%	4.1%
Population	1.8	2.3	2.5
Per capita GDP	2.8	2.3	1.6
Agriculture	3.5	3.4	2.1
Industry	6.2	8.6	8.2
Exports	4.4	3.7	6.1

Source: Paul Bairoch, "Evolution 1960–67 et perspectives à court terme de l'économie du tiers monde" (Seminar at the Vienna Institute for Development and Co-operation, Klagenfurt, June, 1968).

Revolution," the scope and prospects of which are exaggerated in the Report.

Bairoch's figures are largely confirmed in explicit terms by the report of the Economic Commission for Africa, which actually reminds us of the slow rate of growth on the continent, both in the past and at present. From 1860 to 1960, real per capita growth in Africa is said to have been roughly 0.2% annually for twenty-three countries, 1.3% for fourteen countries, and only 1.9% for the five countries that have the highest per capita GDP today (above $250).[4] The ECA report compares these low rates with rates of growth at the center, as shown in Table 4. Neither in Africa nor elsewhere in the Third World is it possible to

TABLE 3.   COMPARATIVE GROWTH, 1954–66

	Less Developed Countries (excluding China)	Developed Western Countries	Eastern Europe
GDP	4.3%	4.4%	7.8%
Population	2.4	1.2	1.4
Per capita GDP	1.9	3.2	6.4
Agriculture	2.7	2.1	4.5
Industry	8.4	5.6	9.3
Exports	4.9	8.1	9.2

Source: Same as Table 2.

TABLE 4.   GROWTH RATES OF DEVELOPED COUNTRIES

Developed Country	Period	Average Annual GDP Growth
Great Britain	1780–1880	1.27%
France	1840–1960	1.72
United States	1840–1960	1.70
Sweden	1860–1960	2.80
Japan	1880–1960	2.60
Russia	1860–1913	1.40
	1913–1960	2.70

Source: United Nations, Economic Commission for Africa, *The Economic Situation in Africa in Recent Years* (E/CN.14/435), January, 1969.

attribute this poor performance to population increase, as the Pearson Report does. This inferiority was already pronounced *before* the qualitative demographic change at the periphery over the last twenty-five years. Growth at the center, on the contrary, was achieved parallel with a large rise in population—not in spite of it, but largely *because* of it.

At the periphery, the earlier stagnation of population growth did nothing to foster development. Nor is there any justification for saying that if population increase were slower, the growth rate of the GDP would become any higher, since the benefits of this would go toward growth of per capita GDP. Much of the growth has been parallel with the rise in population, especially in the very large agricultural sectors where there is no shortage of land. In Black Africa, but also very generally in Latin America and even in Asia (except for certain areas), increases in agrarian population density are always accompanied by increases in productivity, as Ester Boserup has shown.[5]

With regard to recent developments in Africa, a more detailed ECA study provides the figures shown in Table 5. Here again, the GDP growth figure for Africa is lower than the one given in the Pearson Report. This ECA document provides a breakdown of growth by sector and region as shown in Table 6.

For a group of countries representing 22% of the population of Africa, per capita GDP fell between 1960 and 1966, while it increased by more than 2% annually for only a small group representing 27% of

TABLE 5.   COMPARATIVE ANNUAL GROWTH RATES

	1950–1960			1960–1965		
	Africa	Less Developed Countries	Developed Countries	Africa	Less Developed Countries	Developed Countries
GDP	3.1%	4.6%	4.0%	3.4%	4.8%	5.0%
Population	2.5	1.9	1.2	2.3	2.6	1.3
Per capita GDP	0.6	2.7	2.8	1.1	2.2	3.7
Agriculture	—	—	—	1.7	—	2.1
Manufacturing industries	—	—	—	4.4	—	6.1
Public consumption	—	—	—	3.7	—	4.2
Gross capital formation	—	—	—	3.4	—	6.5
Exports	—	—	—	7.6	—	7.2
Imports	—	—	—	3.2	—	7.8

Source: Nazhat Chalaq, "The Structure of African Economy" (mimeo., United Nations, Economic Commission for Africa, n.d.).

TABLE 6.   AFRICAN ANNUAL GROWTH (*by region*)

	North Africa	West Africa	East Africa *	Central Africa	Southern Africa †
Agriculture	0.1%	2.2%	2.7%	0.4%	2.6%
Mining and petroleum	30.4	9.2	1.6	—	3.4
Processing industries	4.9	6.2	6.5	0.6	8.9
Administration	6.9	4.9	2.9	1.2	4.0
GDP	4.1	3.3	3.1	0.3	5.3
Per capita GDP	1.4	1.6	1.4	1.5	3.4

* Including Rhodesia.
† South Africa, Angola, and Mozambique.
Source: Nazhat Chalaq, "The Structure of African Economy" (mimeo., United Nations, Economic Commission for Africa, n.d.).

the population of the continent. For Africa as a whole, with the exception of southern Africa, per capita GDP went from $103 in 1955 to only $112 in 1966.[6]

AGRICULTURAL PROGRESS; THE DYNAMICS AND LIMITATIONS OF AGRARIAN
CAPITALISM IN THE THIRD WORLD: THE EXAMPLE OF BLACK AFRICA

The Pearson Report stresses the decisive role of agricultural progress at the start of industrialization. One cannot but agree with it on this point. At the start of industrialization, agriculture alone, which employs the majority of the people, provides an important market for industry, just as it must feed the urban population. (Otherwise, it becomes necessary to import food supplies, which obstructs industrialization itself.) It is only at a later stage of industrialization that this double function loses its relative importance, with industry and tertiary activities becoming more and more the essential outlets for industry.[7]

Both during the long period from 1900–1966 and the more recent 1960–67, agricultural progress in the Third World has been extremely inadequate. Such stagnation slows down possible industrialization, *even when it is inward-looking*.[8] Especially since 1960 the growth rates of both light *and* heavy industry have declined in the Third World for this reason. The agricultural productivity index (net calorie production per active male farmer), calculated by Bairoch for the entire Third World (excluding China), on the basis of 100 in 1909–13, fell to 96 for the period 1953–57, and to 95 for 1960–64. Moreover, this productivity was already 30% lower than that of the developed countries on the eve of the industrial revolution.[9] Certainly the situation in India (which produces roughly 30% of cereal in the Third World) showed considerable improvement in 1967–68 after the 1965–66 setback: but this is jumping much too quickly to the conclusion that the miracle of a "Green Revolution" is occurring and the first hurdle has been cleared, as the Pearson Report pretends.[10]

In the Third World there was a deficit of 23 million tons of grain in 1966 (9% of the total production of the developing countries). This is a direct contrast to the 11 million tons of food grains exported from the Third World in 1938. The Pearson Report itself reminds us that while agricultural growth in Latin America, which was 3.5% per annum from 1950 to 1967, exceeded the growth of the population (2.9%), in

Africa the rate did not exceed 2% (less than the growth of population), and in India it just kept pace (2.5%). In the case of Pakistan, although the rate has been 3.2% since 1960, this followed a period of stagnation from 1955 to 1960 (1.4%).

Similar stagnation can be observed in Africa, although there it was the agricultural export trade (and not grain) that experienced a rapid start *in certain areas*. In fact the idea that very poor or zero average rates of agricultural productivity growth, either in the Third World as a whole or in vast sections of it such as Africa, indicate stagnation of the rural world is completely erroneous. These average rates have no *significance* because they include immense areas of stagnation, and occasionally even recession, along with minor areas of rapid growth. It is essential to study the conditions that determined these localized spurts of activity. I have already begun to do this in the case of Black Africa and I believe it possible to show the obvious relationship between the growth of agricultural productivity and the establishment of agrarian capitalism.[11]

There seems to be a close correlation between those areas which did experience rapid spurts of activity and the development of a black rural bourgeoisie. The development of such a bourgeoisie requires that four conditions be met. The first of these conditions seems to be the existence of a traditional society sufficiently hierarchical so that certain kinds of hereditary chiefs possess enough social power to appropriate to themselves important parcels of tribal lands. It is in this way that traditional tribal heads of Ghana, southern Nigeria, the Ivory Coast, and Uganda were able to create, to their profit, a plantation economy.

The second condition is an average population density of the order of ten to thirty inhabitants per square kilometer. Any lesser density makes the private appropriation of lands ineffective and the potential supply of paid labor insufficient. The mechanism of proletarianization is considerably facilitated when there is a convenient source of foreign labor, as is the case with the Voltaics and the Ivory Coast. At a second stage, the younger members and dependents of the families of the original planters can in turn be proletarianized.[12] Densities that are too great, as in Rwanda and on the Bamileke plateau in Cameroon, make it difficult for the chiefs to seize control of sufficient land.

The third condition is the presence of fertile soils, making it possible, with very little mechanization and, hence, with the low rate of productivity in an agriculture that is still largely extensive, to produce, per man-acre, an adequate surplus from the very start of development. It is in this manner that cotton in Uganda or peanuts in the Serer country,[13] and, generally speaking, food produce with low production rates, exclude what coffee and cocoa have made possible elsewhere.

Finally, the fourth condition requires that the political atmosphere not be detrimental to this kind of spontaneous development. The relative ease of private appropriation of land, the freedom of work, and the credit awarded individual farmers have everywhere played an important role in the establishing of this rural bourgeoisie. Very characteristic of this was the abolition of forced labor in the French colonies in 1950. The typically middle-class demand for freedom of work allowed the Ivory Coast planters to profit from a flood of immigrants unparalleled in strength by the number of workers recruited by force and, up until then, assigned solely to the French planters. It also made it possible to organize a great political battle in the country, with the peasant victims of forced labor backing the native planters. On the other hand, in certain areas, such as the lower Congo, the paternalism of the Belgian "pay-sannats" undoubtedly played a negative role in checking the tendency toward the development of a bourgeoisie. Is it not noteworthy that when the political structure of the "paysannats" was swept away after independence such a bourgeoisie was able to clear the way for its own development? In six years, from 1960 to 1966, commercial food production in the lower Congo quadrupled. It should be noted that for the first time, on a large scale, the course of capitalist development had stemmed not from export goods but from food products stimulated by the demand from Kinshasa. It should certainly also be noted that another condition in the lower Congo—the possibility of using foreign labor—was finally met in 1960, thanks to the refugees from Angola. The politics of apartheid and "preserving African traditions," practiced in South Africa and Rhodesia, are obviously obstacles to the progress of a rural middle class.

Does the same hold true for the policies regarding rural mobilization, organization, and cooperative development? These policies, practiced everywhere according to the same naive paternalistic formulas, which undoubtedly arise from the Utopian desire to see the whole country advance equally, at an even, sustained pace, have neither hindered the development of the plantation system wherever it was possible nor brought on any considerable qualitative transformations elsewhere.

In fact, there remain huge areas still outside the movement, because the conditions that make change possible have not been met: this is the Africa that "didn't get off the ground" or "was unable to get off the ground." This is also the rural Africa, "without problems" in the sense that it can adapt to its demographic growth without modifying its structures, simply by extending its traditional subsistence economy. The insertion of this Africa into the colonial world inevitably meant a very limited development of crops for export, often imposed by the authorities for tax purposes. Occasionally, when the terms of exchange between export goods and legally purchasable manufactured goods broke down, or simply whenever the administrative force which imposed them became weakened, these crops were given up in favor of subsistence agriculture. To call such abandonment a regression is superficial, because rationality here was on the side of the peasants and not the administration, which wanted to impose uneconomical crops. The development of a parasitic urban economy and the inflation it entails are often at the bottom of this breakdown in exchange terms, of which the economic setback of cotton production in the Congo Kinshasa provides the most spectacular example.[14]

Exceptional growth rates occasionally occur in the agriculture of some areas: rates of 7% annually are not uncommon. There is no doubt that the transformations undergone by these rural areas in Africa in the course of three decades contrast with the relative immobility of the oriental rural world. We are closer here to the conditions of certain areas of Latin America.

This is why it is a mistake to make universal statements, common to United Nations literature. The analyses of the FAO, adopted by the ECA, underline the fact that, on the average, African food production growth has been very poor (2% as compared to 3.5% for agricultural export goods, which gives 2.4% for agriculture as a whole). But the "exceptions" to which the document draws attention are more interesting: corn in Kenya (3.9%), rice in Egypt (3.8%), livestock in all the savanna countries.[15] Now for all these products, *destined for the domestic market,* better prices have been possible. (This was a necessary, but insufficient condition.)

The Pearson Report stresses the necessity of this condition. For once I share its opinion. For it is quite obvious that cereal production in western Pakistan and rice production in Thailand could not have been undertaken without it (see pp. 302–17 and 330–37 of the Report). However, the analysis is not carried far enough by the Report, as it neglects to mention all the *other conditions*.

From this kind of compelling analysis, completely absent in the Pearson Report, which ignores the real problems, the problems relating to the transformation of the structures of the rural world (including, of course, its social structures which cannot be studied apart from its economic structures), I am led to form conclusions almost always diametrically opposed to those of the Report.

Demographic *pressure* is not always an *obstacle* to the growth of productivity, as is suggested by a very superficial analysis (which consists of dividing the growth of production by that of the population and saying "if the latter had been lower, the growth of progress per capita would have been greater"). On the contrary, demographic pressure is often the engine that sets the intensification and progress of productivity in motion.

Agrarian capitalism based on small family properties (of sufficient size, nevertheless, to be able to support a capitalist form of production, i.e., recourse to wage labor) is potentially more dynamic than that which results from the transformation of the big precapitalist ("feudal") properties into capitalist estates. Now this second form of agrarian capitalist development is the one which occurred most frequently outside Black Africa for historical reasons (the structure of the precapitalist social formations of the Orient and that of the capitalism of the Latin American periphery instituted during the age of mercantilism). In Black Africa, in particular in the Islamic savanna, the precolonial "semi-feudal" formations led, as a result of integration into the world market, to the development of less dynamic forms (such as the Nigerian Sultanates, the brotherhoods: Mourid, Ansar, Ashiqqa, etc). It is this system of land estates which has presented the principal obstacle to agricultural progress—the monopoly held by the great landowners did not compel them to modernize in order to retain their economic privilege. Thus the *political alliances* between the local ruling class and the foreign ruling capital have delayed and are still delaying vital agrarian reforms. It is significant that all the reforms which come under that heading have run up against open hostility from the West. The limited progress realized in this sense (as in Mexico, Egypt, Algeria) has opened the way to the subsequent development of the agrarian capitalism of the rich peasantry (such as the "Kulak"). Developments of this nature, in opening up certain areas of Pakistan, India, and Thailand, have brought about the current limited progress.

Whenever the conditions listed previously are met—and only under these circumstances—economic stimuli (improvement in the relative prices of farm products) will be effective. On this point I agree with the Pearson Report, pronouncing the paternalistic "boy scout" policies advocated and practiced in Black Africa a complete failure. Nonetheless, even on this point, the Pearson Report neglects to analyze the origin of these policies. For the transferring of the *world-wide structures of relative prices* from the center to the periphery—more precisely through that international market which the Pearson Report so adamantly defends— is certainly at the bottom of the failure of the production stimuli. The devastating competition of American "relief aid" is to be noted here. Because of the fact that international prices are imposed upon the periphery, where today the internal relationship between agricultural productivity and industrial productivity is so different from what it is at the center, the farmers are continually left with the short end of the stick. It is this worldwide transferring of price structures which orients producers toward export commodities, thus limiting any possible progress (be it only because the growth of international demand for such products cannot be adequately supported for the entire Third World).

Consequently, the path of progress based on agrarian capitalism is narrowly limited by integration into the international market on which it depends. The nature of the peripheral social systems in fact allows the center to appropriate to itself, through the breakdown of exchange terms, productivity gains made in agriculture on the periphery, while the periphery is concentrating on exports. The Pearson Report remains silent on this subject. The deterioration of these terms for peripheral trade as a whole has been 10% since 1954. For agricultural products, the percentage is higher.[16] Moreover, the economic stimuli have had only limited effects, since they are of interest to a minor fraction of the rural population. In the concrete conditions of the Third World at present, the increasing predominance of the rural poverty-stricken masses (and it is here that the new phenomenon of demographic pressure comes into play) indicates the dire need for rapid progress. This demands the mobilization of the masses. *The direct contradiction between economic stimuli and mass mobilization defines the real conditions of the framework into which rapid agricultural progress must fit.*

THE DYNAMICS AND LIMITATIONS OF OUTWARD-ORIENTED
DEVELOPMENT USING FOREIGN CAPITAL—BARRIERS TO GROWTH:
SOME EXPERIENCES IN AFRICA AND ELSEWHERE

In the area of industrialization, the Pearson Report does little more than draw up a balance sheet of the *overall quantitative achievements* of the Third World during the last twenty years; thus we are told that the processing industry's contributions to the GDP for different countries in Latin America has varied between 15% and 30%, in Asia between 15% and 20%, and that—with few exceptions (Egypt, Congo Kinshasa, Kenya, the Mahgreb)—it has remained consistently below 10% in Africa. We also learn that the less developed countries will henceforth produce 66% of their requirements of manufactured goods, 40% to 50% of intermediate goods, and 20% to 30% of capital goods (Pearson Report, p. 37). The Report lays particular stress on the illusions of the policy of import substitution and those, even greater, associated with the establishment of heavy industries, usually financed by the state. It also stresses faulty options in the matter of choice of techniques (too capital-intensive) which it presumes to be at the root of increased unemployment (p. 59). The Report therefore advocates: giving emphasis to the development of agriculture; promoting the growth of exports (agricultural and industrial, especially minerals); giving the principle of profitability (in a liberal structure open to international competition) greater weight in the choice of investments; basing such choices on a system of reference prices giving greater returns to capital and less to labor (in accordance with the relative "scarcity" of "factors"); putting a tighter rein on the rural exodus.

These recommendations might be described as both incoherent and ineffectual.

"To stand on one's own two feet" is the opposite of sacrificing industry to agriculture or vice versa, for, if inadequate agricultural progress blocks industrialization, *the converse is equally true.* Past experience in world trade, where maximum profit is drawn from *those branches of industry that are the most modern and where the potential growth of productivity is greatest,* has proved that international specialization does not compensate for the profits to be gained from the highest possible degree of industrialization, that is, an inward-looking system.

Opening up industry to international competition would prohibit the development of any inward-looking peripheral industry, or would limit it to the outward-oriented extractive industries (which are not sequential in nature and where "natural" advantages have some meaning). For this reason, the essential recommendation of the Report, based on the axiom of "free, equitable" world trade is contradictory (inequality prevents "free" trade from being "equitable") and has its roots in *ideology* and not *science.* The result is that if certain experiments in inward-looking industrialization have failed for various reasons, notably those related to political structures, the *"stabilization plans"* recommended in various quarters, especially by the IMF, based on a greater degree of external trade, will continue to represent backward rather than forward steps.

The profitability rule encourages the rational entrepreneur (foreign capital) to make the marginal choices he makes, that is, to opt for modern techniques. The problem of the "choice of techniques" is largely *artificial,* one which provides food for discussion in university circles; however, there are really no *efficient* labor-intensive techniques.

It is the outward-oriented nature of "underdeveloped" economies (their links to foreign trade) which is at the basis of the systematic biases in their development that take the form of the *dislocation of such economies and the accentuation of sectoral disparities in productivity.* Such characteristics make it impossible to credit foreign investment with the "transfer of technology" (as claimed on p. 101 of the Pearson Report), which, as is commonly known, is strictly confined to the "modern" sectors. These structural characteristics of "underdevelopment" are even more strongly marked where the level of international integration is higher, that is, where per capita GDP is higher. Thus *outward-oriented development is not development but development of underdevelopment* so that Gabon with its $600 per capita GDP is not less underdeveloped than Rwanda with $70, but more so, in the sense that the structural characteristics of underdevelopment (dislocation and sectoral disparities in productivity) are more marked in Gabon. *This explains why no Third World country has ever "got off the ground" whatever the per capita GDP reached,* and why Gabon is not now at the stage that had been reached by France in 1900, although the per capita GDP may be at the same level. We are not, therefore, justified in equating less developed countries with developed countries at an earlier stage or in claiming, as the Report does, that there is no clearly defined boundary between developed and developing countries.

The record of the development of underdevelopment is, of necessity, one of periods of rapid growth suddenly blocked, of "flash in the pan miracles," of projects which backfire. There is an unavoidable tendency toward a deficit in the external trade figures because, with growing specialization, the narrowing range of goods supplied is offset by the expanding range of goods demanded as GDP increases; exports must increase at a very high rate for even a temporary "miracle" to be possible. If we add that the investment of foreign capital necessarily entails a rechanneling of the profits which must override the flow of incoming capital, it will be understood that the development of the Third World has never been any more than an incoherent series of "flash-in-the-pan miracles."

The African experience largely confirms my analysis. Is rapid outward-oriented growth a feasible concept for the continent as a whole? Seven African countries have shown comparatively rapid growth between 1960 and 1966, thanks to the development of their petroleum or mineral resources (Libya, Algeria, Mauritania, Liberia, Gabon, Togo, and Nigeria), and one other through the development of its agricultural potential, which was still untapped in 1950 (the Ivory Coast). On the whole continent, there has been only one (limited) attempt at inward-looking industrial development: that of Egypt. Most cases of rapid growth have been insignificant. In certain countries of the Sahara (Libya, Mauritania, and, to some extent, Algeria) the extractive industries claim a disproportionate part of the economy's growth (in Libya; 55% of the GDP). Already, however, further expansion of industry is almost entirely blocked by the inadequate growth of the agricultural market and by the inadequate growth of foreign demand, *which does not essentially depend upon the Third World's policy.* The example of the Ivory Coast is illuminating: proportionately, as this country *makes up lost ground in its colonial policy of mise en valeur* to catch up with Senegal and Ghana, which had forged far ahead in this direction, the Ivory Coast is running up against major obstacles (a widening gap in the balance of payments and public finances). This is why there is no justification for claiming, as does the Pearson Report (p. 12), that the rapid growth of certain countries demonstrates that underdevelopment can be overcome, for rapid growth of this kind, due to exceptional circumstances, is necessarily accompanied by stagnation in others.

The dual structural crisis of public finance and balance of payments in less developed countries is the manifestation of these blockages of outward-looking growth. The crisis in public finance is the result of the *necessary* increase in costs arising from the infrastructure and from educational needs brought about by integration into the world market: at the same time this integration limits the expansion of the economy's material basis. This crisis is not, as is too often and too simplistically claimed, the sole expression of political forces which are independent from this integration into the world market (the brain-children of African bureaucrats).

The balance of payments crisis is a further expression of these fundamental contradictions. The falling off of the foreign currency reserves of most of the Third World countries bears witness to that crisis. There is no shortage of data here (see Pearson Report, p. 70, Table 8). The trade deficit of the Third World rose from 5.5% of its imports in 1948–54 to 9.0% in 1960–67; that of non-petroleum-producing countries from 18.5% in 1960 to 24% in 1967.

On the social level, this blockage is manifested by the growing unemployment which the Pearson Report does not even attempt to measure and glosses over, implying that nothing can be done. Yet this factor alone is a witness to the *political failure* of the past two decades. At the same time there is the paradox of the shortage of supervisory staff (for example, in Africa 80% of higher executives are foreign personnel),[17] and unemployment of those holding primary, secondary, or even more advanced certificates in certain countries.

We are told that if the African states united they could go further in the direction of industrialization even within the present framework. This may well be so. But what is forgotten is that the basis of "micro-nationalism" is outward-looking development; for each micro-region of the continent which makes independent attempts at branching out into the world market independently of neighboring areas has *no interest* in promoting integration, which would simply mean that the richer areas would have to subsidize the poorer. Only a voluntarily *inward-looking development* could create the necessary solidarity within the framework of large organized areas, not simple "common markets."

Under these conditions, to tell the developing countries to give priority to stepping up exports is simply to pontificate. The Pearson Report itself points out that for developing countries to achieve a growth rate of 6% over the next decade, their imports must increase at the rate of 7% to 8%, their exports at a higher rate (p. 71). If the reinvestment of profits and loan charges are taken into account, exports will have to be stepped up at an astounding rate: doubtless on the order of 12%. These are, by the way, the figures to be gleaned from the African experience. Between 1960 and 1967, the export growth rates of the eight countries showing the highest expansion ran from 6.3% to 11.6% per annum, and the growth rate entailed by such exceptional performances in the field of exports was between 3.1% and 4.4%. This extraordinary discrepancy between GNP and export growth is easily explained by the fact that such sectors have the character of enclaves: the exporting sectors occupy only 5% to 7% of the work force of the Third World, and this *percentage is bound to decrease* since competition demands the use of modern techniques in these sectors. A sustained 6% per annum growth rate for the African continent would require an annual 12% to 18% increase in exports. This is patently impossible, for even if the supply of primary products could maintain such a rate, demand would not parallel it.

This, moreover, is demonstrated by the concrete analysis provided on certain primary products in the Report (pp. 81–86). It is also demonstrated by its Tables 5, 6, and 7 (Annex II): a strong upward trend in exports requires exceptional conditions with respect to the *development of new resources.*

The Pearson Report suggests, then, that the developed countries should agree to import manufactured goods from peripheral areas, and expand trade in such products among developing countries. There is a rather pious ring to the formulation of such a solution, especially if one reflects upon the attitudes of the developed countries at the New Delhi Conference. At present such exports are minute in volume, and 40% of them are supplied by three less developed countries (Hong Kong, Taiwan, and Argentina), and two which I do not consider less developed (Israel and Rhodesia). Moreover, even should this situation change, it is not at all certain that such a change would be to the advantage of the less developed countries. We are at present undergoing a large-scale scientific and technical revolution; the industries of the *future* (automation, electronics, atomic energy, and space exploration) are based on the relatively massive employment of skilled labor as opposed to the "classical" concept of industry based on the large-scale employment of unskilled labor. A new form of international specialization would arise, reserving the advanced industries for the center, freeing it from the unrewarding tasks of "classical" industry and assigning these to the peripheral areas. This would step up development at the center and accentuate the gap between it and peripheral areas.[18]

There is an alternative which is the true solution. In the Pearson Report it is presented only in its *unacceptable form,* namely, the concept of common markets (p. 95, by an improper extension of the European common market experience), which would tend to accentuate the internal inequalities in the peripheral areas. For this reason, the common markets, which were an inheritance from the colonial era, *have broken up.* The true solution—the planned, voluntary, and simultaneous setting-up of complementary, inward-looking, industrial complexes in *large organized areas*—cannot be financed by foreign capital because the scheme is not profitable within the structure of world prices, and the profits could not be transferred precisely because these would be inward-looking industries not contributing sufficiently toward an improvement in the balance of payments.

This brings us to the heart of the problem: *only outward-looking activities can be developed through the application of foreign capital, and the development potential of such activities is automatically limited;* the manner in which the Pearson Report analyzes this subject is very formal and superficial. Only financial flows which have statistical frames of reference are considered (flows measured by market prices). This does not take into account essential transfers which cannot be represented statistically but nonetheless constitute the *essence of unequal exchange;* this is the case whenever there is *equal productivity* and the wage rate is lower in the peripheral areas than in the central areas.[19] It is significant that even the most superficial aspect of this phenomenon, the deterioration of the terms of exchange, is not given attention in this Report. On the other hand, the Report deals at length with the dynamic of the public debt and demonstrates that servicing this debt will progressively absorb the flow of capital which it produces (pp. 72–76 and Chapter 8). Even if peripheral area exports could increase at the rate of 8% per annum, interest on the debt, under favorable Development Assistance Committee conditions (3%), would, over thirty years, absorb 20% of the income from exports. In 1968, it was already absorbing more than 15% for the larger countries of the Third World (India, Pakistan, Indonesia, Brazil, Argentina, Mexico, Egypt). Now, outward-looking development entails the progressive reduction of the extent to which imports are covered by exports (in Africa between 1960 and 1966 this rate dropped except in the case of six mineral-producing countries). Therefore, to dwell at length on various series of recommendations intended to improve the conditions of "aid" is really no more than wishful thinking, since the *function of such aid* is recognized as being complementary to the investment of foreign capital. Aid maintains the present structures of inequality, the international status quo, and the point has even been reached where maintenance of the present system is no longer possible without aid. It was thanks to this public aid, which increased from an average of $1.7 billion in the period 1950–55 to $7.0 billion in 1968, that private investment also increased from $1.6 billion to $5.8 billion (Report, p. 137). This is the reason for the failure of such aid.

The failure of the system for aid to Africa is obvious (Pearson Report, pp. 260 ff.). Calculated on a per capita basis, this continent received more aid than any other—$6.1 compared with $4.4 in Latin America and $3.2 in Asia (p. 133)—under optimum financial conditions, starting from the lowest GDP levels (so that the aid should have proved relatively more effective); yet it is also the continent where growth has been weakest, and most chaotic (because even more outward-oriented than elsewhere). There is not the shadow of a doubt that this aid was intended to maintain political, state, and economic structures inherited from colonial days—the chief obstacles to development—and that this very fact was the cause of its failure. The Report's claim that

Africa also benefited from belonging to stable monetary zones is indeed laughable when we think, for example, that this integration imposed a systematically deflationist monetary policy on French-speaking Africa and has long enabled Great Britain to support the pound with reserves from its colonies.

If there can be only inward-looking, self-initiated development, development which can be self-financing, is the policy of promoting local private enterprise adequate to achieve this objective? Generalities about "institutional factors" and "attitudes" (Pearson Report, p. 64) are not of much use here. For here again, the obstacle to development of a national private sector is not so much the socialism of the countries of the Third World (a socialism which has never prevented the development of agrarian capitalism wherever the scheme was feasible); it is rather the competition from foreign capital. Taking the particular case of Senegal, I have demonstrated that in the face of an overwhelming flood of foreign capital, local peripheral capital could develop only to the limited extent that *metropolitan policy* permitted it to do so.[20] A bourgeoisie of the periphery that is set up in the wake of foreign capital cannot envisage inward-looking development which implies separation from world markets.

BRIEF CONCLUSION

Africa's experience over the last two decades, largely analogous to that of the other continents of the Third World, demonstrates:

(1) That outward-looking growth is not development, because the latter demands essential structural changes and can only be inward-looking and self-initiated.

(2) That outward-looking growth is of necessity unequal, chaotic, and regularly blocked; in sum, it is too slow to avoid the continuous widening of the gap between the rich and the poor nations, and it is incapable of avoiding repeated misfirings of attempts to get off the ground.

(3) That the structural framework of agrarian capitalism in the contemporary Third World singularly limits the potential of the "Green Revolution."

(4) That the development of the Third World is only possible

within the framework of *socialist* systems organized over large self-reliant regions.

(5) That, contrary to the Pearson Report's point of departure, development *should be regarded as the continuation of the political struggle for independence;* the error is that development has not been sufficiently viewed in this light. The achievements of the past two decades are totally inadequate.

(6) That departing from a set of common prejudices (the bromide of the world market) the Pearson Commissioners prevented themselves from seeing the alternative to the policy they advocated: inward-looking development over large regions.

The Theme of the Debates

Can any one theme be said to have run through the Conference debates? Behind all the details of possible policies, the regional disparities, the varying definitions of realism, the misunderstandings, the shared hopes, one preoccupation insistently recurred—the mystery, the tragedy, the crisis of deepening yet preventable poverty in an inexorably unifying world. It was there, in the beginning, in the Pearson Report's underlining of "the obligation of every government to play its part in cooperation with all others to ensure that *all* people have a reasonable chance to share in the resources of the world, which should be developed for the benefit of all."

It was there at the end in the Columbia Declaration:

"The widening gap between the rich and poor countries of the world has—in the words of the Pearson Report . . . become a central issue of our time. In incomes, living standards, economic and political power, one-third of the world has in recent decades been pulling steadily ahead, leaving the remainder of mankind in relative poverty, in many cases to live without clean water, education, basic medical facilities, or adequate housing. Yet with modern technology and existing productive capacity none of this need continue if mankind would develop the will and organization to use the resources at hand."

It was there in Robert McNamara's outcry against the crime and folly of arms spending:

"The outlook for the 1970's is that the fault line along which shocks to world stability travel will shift from an East-West axis to a North-South axis, and the shocks themselves will be significantly less military and substantially more political, social, and economic in character.

"In view of this, it is tragic and senseless that the world today is spending $175 billion a year on armaments—a sum so huge that it is twenty-five times larger than the total spent in all foreign assistance programs. What is even worse, is that defense spending is increasing by some 6% a year, a growth rate in destructive power that is greater than the growth rate of the world's total production of all goods and services. And the final irony in this litany of irrationalities is that arms spending in the less developed countries is rising at the rate of 7.5% a year, as against the world average of 6%.

"Prudent military preparedness has its place. Prodigal military proliferation is human folly at its worst."

It was there in the address which Paul Hoffman, administrator of the United Nations Development Programme, delivered at the Conference:

"We must, I feel, begin to accept the term 'global' development as being a literal not a figurative description of the goal we seek to attain. For the entire world, and not just some of its parts, is threatened by escalating population growth; by the fouling of rivers, oceans, soils, and air; by a growing alienation of the rich and privileged from the poor and deprived. The whole world, too, is troubled by an excessive and unnatural discord between the generations, and by needless hostility among people who happen to have varying amounts of pigmentation in their skins. I do not see how problems such as these can ever be solved except in a global context. And I am convinced that the whole world stands to profit in a way it never could have profited before from pooling its creative energies and its productive efforts."

It was there, continuously, in the debate between the contending schools of "realism"—the realists who looked to a continuing balance of power in favor of the entrenched, developed, ex-imperial nations and the opposing realists who saw chiefly the gathering storm of revolutionary protest.

At no time did the debate get away from this great question mark of poverty in a planetary context. Within all human communities, certain obligations and interdependencies find recognition and, with recognition, support. The weak, the aged, the young, the sick, are in some way helped. The rich, the fortunate, the strong, accept a duty which reflects their power to act. So, if the planet *were* a human community, a large part of the Pearson Report and of the Columbia debate would have been unnecessary and the time could have been constructively spent on discussing ways of pursuing agreed ends.

But the world is not a community. It has no agreed ends. It still pretends that it can lurch along, divided in wealth, deaf to reason, armed to the teeth, each little sovereignty pursuing its anarchic ends, and still escape the nuclear holocaust. In the face of such irrationality, any complacent belief in survival recalls that ancient judgment of the Duke of Wellington who, when addressed by a stranger as Mr. Smith, remarked "If you can believe that, you can believe anything."

So the ultimate theme was, in reality, human survival. It depends, as it always has, on creative adaptation to new conditions—the radical new conditions of a scientific and a technological planet. It depends upon avoiding the blind alley of ossification in existing forms. It also depends on avoiding the opposite danger of destroying the species from which a hopeful mutation may come. Between the extremes lie the practicable limits of creative change. All constructive debate about survival is an attempt to find what is genuinely the "optimum mix" of preservation and renewal. But here Lester Pearson himself must be allowed the last word.

Address to the Columbia University Conference
on International Economic Development
BY THE RIGHT HONOURABLE LESTER B. PEARSON
February 20, 1970

Those of us who participated in the preparation and production of the Report are conscious of its limitations of scope and substance which, in part at least, we imposed on ourselves by what we considered to be the importance of early publication. We appreciate the examination it is being given by experts in the field, the constructive criticism, as well as approval, which it has received, and the debate and discussion it has provoked. Such discussion, which could help to bring about wise policy decisions by governments, was, after all, a major purpose of the whole exercise; or what is a "grand assize" for?

The Report, in any event, is, in large measure, merely a starting point, from which, hopefully, we can develop a better understanding of the problems; from which we can help to produce better plans and policies and drop those that are no good.

These last months, since the Report's publication, have left me and my fellow commissioners in no doubt about the amount of reinterpretation, redirection, fresh inspiration, and even rejection—at times the best part of inspiration—which the whole aid effort requires.

My chief impression of the various comments made on our report is that opinion is moving toward a considerable degree of polarization over the issues of aid and development. The difficulties and even the dangers from such polarization, however, in this as in so many other matters, seem to be widely appreciated.

On one side of this deepening division (shall I call it another kind of development "gap"?) are those who are inclined to distrust the interventions of government in the economic process and believe that, on the whole, the evidence suggests that official economic assistance has, at best, made little contribution to the recipient nations' growth and, at worst, has seriously distorted it. They cite the difficulty—a very real one, of course—of establishing a direct causal relationship between high aid and rapid growth, and from this they argue the relative unimportance of aid. To prove direct harm, their prize witness tends to be food aid to India which, in their view, has encouraged the Indian government to underinvest in the agricultural sector, thereby hindering sound growth.

As a result of these judgments, they are not unduly worried about any alleged "crisis" in aid or development, or about the downward trend in aid contribution, or about disillusion over results. On the contrary, they argue that an end to cumbersome, badly managed, and usually politically inspired policies of aid would actually speed up the processes of normal growth. Countries which enjoy the stability, economic opportunities, and good administration needed to attract private investment are, for these very reasons, the ones whose development is on the point of becoming a process of healthy, sustained growth. There is no need for special assistance. Profitable openings are present. And if they are not profitable, they won't contribute to genuine development.

It is not as though, the argument continues, private corporations are not willing to venture overseas. On the contrary, one of the phenomena of our day is the fabulous growth in the foreign activities of great American, European, and Japanese corporations, often organized —indeed, increasingly so—on an international basis, with the strength, ability, and wide-ranging vision needed for truly planetary operations, which will result in a fantastic increase in the world's ability to maximize the return on its resources. This is the best hope for a sane, workable, efficiently organized, and soundly profitable development effort, with a maximum of free enterprise and without intergovernmental transactions of doubtful value and wisdom in which any developmental value is buried under an indeterminate and dubious mass of political, emotional, social, ideological, and other extraneous considerations.

It is difficult to picture a viewpoint more completely unacceptable to critics at the other end of the spectrum, who are increasing in numbers and noise. They attack economic assistance for development precisely because it *will* facilitate the extension of private foreign operations and intergovernmental lending of a more traditional kind, as well as the preservation of social systems and economic structures which they feel must be destroyed and replaced before there can be any constructive and supportable international cooperation for development. The present basis for current cooperation, they say, is precisely the network of Atlantic-European domination and imperialism from which it is the prime political aim of the developing nations to escape.

We have been here before, the developing peoples say; or if they don't they should. In any event, this category of critics say it for them. From the seventeenth to the twentieth century, our local economies have been battered by foreign economic interests coming in to "open us up" —to "develop" us—whether we wanted it or not, and without consulting us. Once installed, they gave us modernized export sectors, big ports, and new trade. But the profits went back to the developers, not to us. "Dual economies" grew up: the rich part run for foreigners and a few privileged local followers; the poor part for everyone else. We did not go through the whole process of political liberation—so the argument runs—in order to find ourselves back with the East India Company lightly disguised as the latest thing in a multinational, decentralized, now socially responsible but still efficiency-oriented, billion-dollar conglomerate. Insofar as foreign aid—tied to Atlantic purchases and encouraging Atlantic tastes and techniques, which are becoming increasingly questioned in their own countries—makes the entry of the outside giants more difficult for us to resist—or control—then let us have none of it. It would be even better to seal ourselves off as the Japanese did for centuries. Moreover, our own structures are still too experimental and weak to carry successfully the unholy weight of modern large-scale multinational enterprise. Our values are too vulnerable to confront the whole great, brassy adventure of high mass consumption. We need time. Foreign aid, far from buying it for us, plunges us too quickly into the modern maelstrom of computers, skyscrapers, and miracle drugs.

I hope I have not produced too much of a caricature in this quick sketch of the kind of criticism I find on both wings of the general attack on existing concepts and patterns of aid. I have certainly put in their most extreme form—not, I hasten to add, in a form that appears in the papers for this conference—a series of criticisms which, in many cases, do not yet add up to much more than a certain malaise and dissatisfaction with conventional answers or a reaction against evangelical hopes and rhetorical exaggerations. Yet the trend may well be toward the extreme position on both sides. This could lead to a more or less early end to foreign aid and to all those other policies of special help—in investment, in trade, in technical assistance—which we have brought together under the heading of development strategy. The two extremes, traditionalists and radicals, meet on this point at least: no more special policies or arrangements; no more planned allocation of public money to other peoples' development; in a word, no more aid, in the popular use of the word.

I confess to you that as a liberal of very long standing I am always disturbed when I find conservatives and radicals, traditionalists and innovators, in agreement on the need to reject proposals for reform put forward by people nearer the middle of the political spectrum. I admit to you at once my bias. I am not an "all or nothing" man, and I begin to worry when I find a concurrence of view between those who want to change everything *au fond* and those who do not want change at all apart from a few alterations here and there to make things fit better.

It seems to me that in politics—the issue of foreign aid is plunged into the very center of politics—there are not many occasions on which you *can* change everything. There are perhaps even fewer situations when nothing needs to be changed. I am as certain as I can be that the issue of world development over, say, the next three decades is simply not amenable to the great head-stirring or heart-stirring simplicities of the conservative or radical extremes. This is a belief which I think most of you share—whatever may be your views about specific proposals or solutions or approaches.

Let me give you some of my reasons for this belief. I start with my own estimate of where cooperation for development stands today. We cannot divorce this issue of development from the realities of the world economy in which it has to function and in which it will—or will not—succeed. If to the environment of 1970 we apply, unchanged, policies and attitudes evolved for 1870, or even for 1950, then, I think, the whole effort stands a very good chance of failing. This is the core of my disagreement with those who would abandon officially planned international cooperation for development in favor of greater reliance upon the traditional, international market system. That would require far more confidence in earlier methods and in results than is justified by economic history. It would also gloss over the violent contrasts between our problems today and those of the areas and eras where "normal methods" are supposed to have worked. I believe, on the contrary, that the market system did not work unaided even in the most favorable conditions of the nineteenth-century Atlantic world—that world of Europe and North America on whose axis we once assumed the whole planet revolved. The system will certainly not work, at least not without drastic modification, in the infinitely less favorable situations of our own day.

One hundred and fifty years ago, most economists were dubious about the capacity of the new industrial system of that epoch to survive. What changed mid-century gloom to the long Victorian boom was, above all, the opening up to the Atlantic peoples, those already in America and those to migrate from Europe to North America and other continents, of the world's remaining virtually unoccupied belt of fertile temperate land. This was the biggest bonanza ever to be bestowed upon a single group. It was done with little more cost than that of running the

Indians and the Aborigines and the Bantu off their ancestral lands. It ended, for the time at least, the Malthusian nightmare of people outstripping resources. It was, if you like, manna from Heaven, aid from nature, aid from luck. This vast input of almost "free" resources, which men had the energy and skills to develop, took the Atlantic countries over the borders of modernization and into the new territory of "sustained growth."

Nothing comparable is available to developing nations today—unless we use our abundant capital and technology to provide a comparable form of aid relevant to our times. If we say they must develop without it, then we are really saying "Let them eat cake."

Nor are the effects of this expansion exhausted. It gave the Atlantic people—representing less than 20% of the world's population—a grip on the planet's resources which they have since maintained and even strengthened. As late as 1945, they controlled most of the earth's peoples and engrossed about 80% of the world's resources. They still enjoy that share of world income. Indeed, the disproportion is increasing. Given this relationship of overwhelming, one-sided power, the uncorrected market works—how could it be otherwise?—as inequitably as it does, say, between landlord and Harijan in an Indian village.

Even more alarming is the fact that present inequalities threaten to grow more intractable in the years ahead. The fact that the poorer countries must develop in the wake of the successful giants of modern technology—Europe, America, Russia, and increasingly, Japan—reinforces the differences between nineteenth and late twentieth century development. Public health, introduced ahead of technological modernization and higher living standards, has sent population and the work force shooting upward with the speed of a moon rocket. The relative lack of elbowroom in agriculture has sent despairing migrants away from the farms. But they cannot cross the oceans to new and open land. So they drift to the cities where the scale of industrial employment has not yet developed sufficiently to absorb them.

To me, it all adds up to this. In the world's vast and deepening regional disparity—between North and South—without an exceptional effort, including transfers of a kind to suit the conditions of today and on a scale at least equivalent to the hundreds of millions of acres of available land which supported the growth of developing states in the nineteenth century, we shall face once again a period of deepening crisis and misery, with tragic results for security, ordered progress, and peace in the world.

At this point, I become acutely conscious of critics at the other end of the spectrum. For them, I think, the prospect of disruption and revolution is not frightening. In their analysis of our world situation, it is bound to result. To some, it is even welcome. The unequal relationships of which I have spoken are the consequence, in their view, of the essentially exploitative character of the grip upon the world's resources by a few dominant imperialist powers. In the past, the developing nations, the "hewers of wood and drawers of water," provided raw materials and cheap labor. The profits, the capital gains, and the value added have all flowed back to the original investors. Modernization in developing countries cannot now be achieved by sole reliance on these traditional patterns of commerce and capital. Trade and investment carried on between unequal partners do not produce sustained growth for the weaker party. And since aid, particularly tied aid, is in some measure simply a way of keeping the poorer community in a position of dependence on the aid-giver, this, too, perpetuates an essentially colonial relationship. From this crippling state of subjection, therefore, the only escape is the "clean break"—the kind of break the Japanese imposed on western traders and missionaries in the seventeenth and eighteenth centuries; a stronger version, if you like, of America's revolutionary break with the British trading system in 1776; a break comparable to Russia's turning inward in 1928 and launching the first Five Year Plan.

To this analysis, my reaction must be much the same as it is to those opposite critics who advocate reliance on "normal" economic relationships. I do not believe in its possibility or desirability but find it charged with dangerous implications. The "clean breaks" of the past took place in societies that were relatively simple and uncluttered technologically and economically, with structures that could be knocked down and rebuilt without the devastating disruption and infinitely complicated replacement jobs that would be required in the post-industrial technological society of today. (It's easier to replace an igloo in the Arctic than a twenty-story intercontinental hotel in a new African state.)

These "breaks" also took place against backgrounds of less devastating pressures than those we face today. America and Russia had great
empty continents to develop; Japan was a lively, compact country in which
food and people were still in balance. The developing continents today,
on the contrary, suffer from unbelievably heavy and intensifying pressures of population on food and resources. However effective policies of
family stabilization may be over the next two decades, the next three
billion babies are already, as it were, locked into the reproductive process and over two billion of them will arrive, over the next twenty-five
years, in the areas which can afford them least.

If you are well-educated, well-fed, and reasonably well-employed,
it is easy to speak of a "clean break," it is easy to picture the duties and
splendors and opportunities of total self-reliance; it is easy to warn
against the "Greeks bearing gifts." But we are not the ones who may
suffer from these heroics. We do not witness the death of children and
the misery of parents. We do not carry the despair of the workless or
the hopelessness of the illiterate. If a "total break"—which to a few
must be preceded by, or go along with, a "total break" at home—could
mobilize the scale of effort and resources needed for a "great leap for-
word," a case could be made for supporting the idea. But if, on the
contrary, it would result in more chaos than growth, would deprive developing peoples of essential transfers of capital and skills, then it would
be folly in the name of social change to romanticize policies which could
carry with them the risk of chaos or stagnation or both and of spreading
poverty, hunger, and distress.

This should not and need not mean that present patterns of dependence, where they exist, have to be perpetuated. They should not.
Social progress must be a part of economic growth. So also should new
forms of international cooperation.

External assistance, however, can hasten as well as strengthen these
processes of internal reform which are needed for sound development,
if such assistance is judiciously linked to relevant criteria of performance
which are, objectively—not unilaterally—established. Land reform; revised tax systems; increases in savings and in their local investment;
wider distribution of employment, income, and the benefits of economic
growth; rapid increases in literacy and technical skills—all these are
critical for development and critical, too, for local reform. We surely

despair too soon if we assume that transformation of social structures must, of necessity, be inhibited by rationally devised and carefully coordinated assistance.

The mention of "relevant criteria of performance" brings me to the last point I want to raise. I admit that for one national government to sit down with another national government and suggest the criteria that should be used for external and internal transformation is as difficult as it is unappetizing. It smacks of paternalism and patronage and of two hundred years of colonial guardians "knowing best." It is for this reason, among others, that the recommendations of our report point in the direction of a greater internationalizing of the whole aid process, of making it more genuinely collective and cooperative. What may be intolerable from a single rich government may be more acceptable from a responsible international body on which both donors and recipients are represented and which gives some institutional content to the ideal of partnership, an ideal which, I know, is to some merely unrealistic fantasy.

What we propose in the way of reforms to the whole development effort must indeed look quite utopian if we consider only nations and their governments against the background of today's world. Men are not accustomed to responsibilities—in the absence of war or aggression —that run beyond their frontiers. I know this well. We are not encouraged to make comparisons which include the needs of others. We are all in some measure stuck fast in the inherited tribalism of a past with vast distances and vaster ignorance, with those instinctive fears and suspicions of "lesser breeds" that breed hostility.

But if we try to make the Copernican revolution needed in our day, we must begin whenever and wherever we can. For any beginning, we must see the planet as we now know it really to be: totally dependent on its shared biosphere of soil and air and water; bound together in a way that the carelessness of each can corrupt all; one and indivisible, the only home in infinity of that single species, *Homo sapiens.* It is only within this framework that all concepts of cooperation, partnership, and mutual support find validity. It is within the planetary country named "Earth" that the rich and developed minority can become aware of the degree to which they engross the world's resources and also of the degree to which their control of the major means of consumption and production can inhibit the development of other lands.

It is a concept not easy to appreciate, or even understand, in this time of competition and conflict.

If we go no further than governments, then such a concept certainly will not be sufficiently appreciated to alter the ways of the past, even though those ways lead, inevitably, as I see it, to the explosions of the future. But if the destiny of this century, as it moves to its end, is to balance the effort and the genius that led to the discovery of physical and ecological unity with an equal effort to promote social and moral solidarity, then the reforms such as we propose in our report—altered and improved where desirable—can be seen not so much as inter-governmental arrangements as a modest step toward the building of the human community which now seems so remote but is so necessary for very survival, as a move toward a better planetary balance, more justice, more sharing, more generosity, more real partnership for mankind. No planet can survive half slave, half free; half engulfed in misery, half careening along toward the supposed joys of almost unlimited consumption from unprecedented production with less work; and all in an atmosphere of greater ease and luxury than man has known since the declining days of Rome. Neither our ecology nor our morality could survive such contrasts. And we have perhaps ten years to begin to correct the imbalance and to do so in time.

APPENDIX

SECTION I

Participants Williamsburg Sessions

* BELAI ABBAI, Minister of State; Head of Planning Commission, Ethiopia
* A. R. ABDEL-MEGUID, Chief Advisor, Project Manager, United Nations Development Programme, Special Fund Planning Project, Ceylon
* PETER ADY, Fellow, St. Anne's College, Oxford University
* O. AKINRELL, African Development Bank
* RUBEN D. ALMONACID, Ph.D. Candidate (Economics), University of Chicago
* SAMIR AMIN, Professor of Economics, University of Poitiers, France; University of Dakar, Sénégal
* SARTAJ AZIZ, Senior Economist, Pearson Commission
* WERNER BAER, Professor of Economics, Vanderbilt University
  ELLIOT J. BERG, Associate Director, Center for Research on Economic Development, University of Michigan
* PATRICIA W. BLAIR, Senior Economist, Pearson Commission
* NIELS BODELSON, Head of Project Section, Secretariat for Technical Cooperation, Denmark
* RODRIGO BOTERO, Economic Advisor to the President, Colombia
  DONALD T. BRASH, Senior Economist, Pearson Commission
* JOSEPH BROSSARD, Catholic Relief Services
* LESTER R. BROWN, Senior Fellow, Overseas Development Council
* MICHAEL BRUNO, Chairman, Department of Economics, The Hebrew University, Jerusalem
* HOLLIS B. CHENERY, Professor of Economics, Harvard University
* JEROME F. CHEVALIER, Director of Research at the IRFED, Paris
* BERNARD T. G. CHIDZERO, Director, Commodities Division, United Nations Conference on Trade and Development

* An asterisk indicates those Conference participants who signed the Columbia Declaration. The text of the Declaration is in the Introduction to this volume.

PAUL G. CLARK, Chairman, Center for Development Economics, Williams College

WILLIAM CLARK, Director of Information and Public Affairs, World Bank

ANDREW W. CORDIER, Dean, School of International Affairs and President Emeritus, Columbia University

* GAMANI COREA, Permanent Secretary, Ministry of Planning and Economic Affairs, Ceylon

L. GRAY COWAN, Director, Institute of African Studies, Columbia University

* VALY-CHARLES DIARRASSOUBA, Professor of Economics, University of Abidjan

MOHAMED TIEKOURA DIAWARA, Minister of Planning, Ivory Coast

* CARLOS F. DIAZ-ALEJANDRO, Senior Economist, Pearson Commission

LORETO M. DOMINGUEZ, Teaching staff, Economic Development Institute (World Bank)

* RENÉ DUMONT, Professor, Institut National Agronomique, Paris

HAROLD B. DUNKERLEY, Senior Economist, Pearson Commission

* CHARLES M. ELLIOTT, Assistant Secretary, Committee on Society, Development and Peace, World Council of Churches

MICHAEL FABER, Senior Lecturer in Economics, Overseas Development Group, University of East Anglia

* RONALD FINDLAY, Visiting Professor of Economics, Columbia University

CHARLES R. FRANK, JR., Associate Director, Research Program in Economic Development, Woodrow Wilson School, Princeton University

J. WAYNE FREDERICKS, Head of Program, Middle East and Africa, International Division, Ford Foundation

IRVING S. FRIEDMAN, Economic Advisor to the President, Chairman of the Economic Committee, World Bank

* DHARAM P. GHAI, Senior Economist, Pearson Commission

RICHARD GOODE, Director, Fiscal Affairs Department, International Monetary Fund

* DAVID L. GORDON, Chief, Resident Mission in Pakistan (World Bank)

* JAMES P. GRANT, President, Overseas Development Council

* REGINALD H. GREEN, Economic Advisor to the Tanzanian Treasury

JOHN GRIST, BBC Television

* JOSEPH GRUNWALD, Senior Fellow in Charge of Economic and Social Development Studies, Brookings Institution

RAVI GULHATI, Senior Economist, Pearson Commission

EDWARD K. HAMILTON, Executive Secretary and Staff Director, Pearson Commission

* SVEN HAMRELL, Dag Hammarskjold Foundation

MAHBUB UL HAQ, Visiting Lecturer, Economic Development Institute (World Bank)

ALBERT G. HART, Professor of Economics, Columbia University

* G. K. HELLEINER, Associate Professor of Political Economy, University of Toronto

* ALBERT O. HIRSCHMAN, Professor of Political Economy, Harvard University

* BRANKO HORVAT, Director of the Institute of Economic Studies, Belgrade

* GUY HUNTER, Member of Overseas Development Institute; Visiting Professor, University of Reading

* STEPHEN HYMER, Professor of Economics, Yale University

* ENRIQUE V. IGLESIAS, Coordinator of the Prebisch Commission at the Inter-American Development Bank

* NURUL ISLAM, Director, Pakistan Institute of Development Economics

* CHARLES ISSAWI, Ragnar Nurkse Professor of Economics, Columbia University

* BIMAL JALAN, Senior Economist, Pearson Commission

* RICHARD JOLLY, Fellow in Economics, Institute of Development Studies, University of Sussex

ISAAC KERSTENETZKY, Professor of Economics, Catholic University, Rio de Janeiro

* MICHAEL KIDRON, Yale University Pakistan Project, Pakistan Institute of Development Economics

* PETER KILBURN, Staff, Pearson Commission

TIMOTHY KING, Population Studies Division, World Bank

* APTULLAH KURAN, Vice President, Robert College, Istanbul

* KEMAL KURDAS, President, Middle East Technical University, Istanbul

* JEAN LOUIS LACROIX, Institute for Social Research, Louvanium University

* GASTON G. LEDUC, Professor of Development Economics, University of Paris

* SYLVAIN LOURIÉ, Senior Economist, Pearson Commission

* NICOLAAS LUYKX, Associate Professor, Department of Agricultural Economics, Michigan State University

* GEOFFREY W. MAYNARD, Professor of Economics, University of Reading

* JOSÉ ANTONIO MAYOBRE, H. L. Boulton and Company, Caracas

O. J. MCDIARMID, Chief Economist, East Asia and Pacific Department, World Bank

* MALEK ALI MERICAN, Alternate Executive Director for Malaysia, International Monetary Fund

* JAMES A. MIRRLEES, Professor of (Mathematical) Economics, Fellow of Nuffield College, Oxford

* CECILIO J. MORALES, Technical Manager, Inter-American Development Bank

* JAMES I. NAKAMURA, Associate Professor of Economics, Columbia University

ZAKARIA NASR, Professor of Economics, Ein Shamus University, Cairo: Head of Research Department, Kuwait Fund for Arab Economic Development

PHILIP NDEGWA, Permanent Secretary, Ministry of Agriculture, Kenya

* JOAN NELSON, Visiting Associate Professor of Political Science, Massachusetts Institute of Technology

* DAVID NEWBERY, Lecturer in Development Theory and Mathematical Economics, Churchill College, Cambridge University

MAX NICHOLSON, Chairman, Land Use Consultants, London

BERNARD NOSSITER, *The Washington Post*

* GORAN OHLIN, Senior Economist, Pearson Commission

* SABURO OKITA, Member, Pearson Commission

* E. N. OMABOE, Chairman, E. N. Omaboe Associates, Ltd., Ghana

* H. M. A. ONITIRI, Director, Nigerian Institute of Social and Economic Research

* PITAMBAR PANT, Member, Indian Planning Commission

* GUSTAV F. PAPANEK, Director, Harvard University Development Advisory Service

* JAVIER PAZOS, Senior Economist, Pearson Commission

* ANDRÉ PHILIP, President, OECD Development Centre, Paris

* NICHOLAS G. PLESSZ, Senior Economist, General Agreement on Tariffs and Trade

* WILLIAM R. POLK, Director, Adlai Stevenson Institute of International Affairs

* JONATHAN POWER, Member, Haslemere Declaration Group; writer and broadcaster

ANISUR RAHMAN, Professor of Economics, University of Islamabad

* GUSTAV RANIS, Director, Yale University Economic Growth Center

V. G. RASTYANNIKOV, Oriental Institute, USSR Academy of Sciences

* IDRIAN RESNICK, Assistant Professor of Economics, Albert Schweitzer Research Scholar on Africa, Columbia University

JOHN RIELLY, Senior Fellow, Overseas Development Council

K. N. SAAD, Senior Staff, Arthur D. Little, Inc.

* DANIEL SCHYDLOWSKY, Research Associate, Center for International Affairs, Harvard University

* DUDLEY SEERS, Director, Institute of Development Studies, University of Sussex

* M. R. SHROFF, Alternate Executive Director for India, World Bank; Counselor, Indian Embassy, Washington, D.C.

* THOMAS H. SILCOCK, Senior Economist, Pearson Commission

* RODOLFO SILVA, Executive Vice President, Central American Bank for Economic Integration

HANS SINGER, Fellow, Institute of Development Studies, University of Sussex

SOEDJATMOKO, Ambassador of Indonesia to the United States

PAUL STREETEN, Director of the Institute of Commonwealth Studies, Fellow of Balliol College, Oxford University

MAURICE STRONG, President, Canadian International Development Agency
* R. M. SUNDRUM, Director of Development Programs Study Group, World Bank
* ERIK THORBECKE, Professor of Economics, Iowa State University
DAVID TURNHAM, OECD Development Centre, Paris
* SNOH UNAKUL, Assistant Secretary General, National Economic Development Board of Thailand
* CHARLES VAN DER VAEREN, Chef de Service, European Development Fund, Brussels
* ROGER VEKEMANS, S.J., Founding Director, Center for the Economic and Social Development of Latin America, Santiago
* ABDOULAYE WADE, President, Planning Commission, and Director of General and Analytical Studies for the Economic and Social Council, Sénégal
* BARBARA WARD, Albert Schweitzer Professor of International Economic Development, Columbia University
STANISLAW WELLISZ, Professor of Economics, Columbia University
P. WIGNARAJA, United Nations Asian Institute for Economic Development and Planning, Bangkok
* WAYNE WILCOX, Chairman, Department of Political Science, Columbia University
* PETER WILLIAMS, Ford Foundation educational planning advisor, Ghana
* LAURENCE WHITEHEAD, Fellow of Nuffield College, Oxford University
* W. HOWARD WRIGGINS, Professor of Government, Director Southern Asian Institute, Columbia University

SECTION II

Participants New York Sessions Only

SIMEON O. ADEBO, Executive Director, United Nations Institute for Training and Research
JOHN H. ADLER, Director, Programming and Planning Department, World Bank
SVERKER ASTRÖM, Permanent Representative of Sweden to the United Nations
* DAVID A. ANDERSON, Deputy Representative, Ford Foundation, Nairobi
DAVID BELL, Executive Vice President, Ford Foundation
* JAGDISH BHAGWATI, Visiting Professor of Economics, Massachusetts Institute of Technology
* ROBERT S. BILHEIMER, Executive Director, International Affairs Program and Department of International Affairs, National Council of Churches
* ANDRAS BIRO, Editor, *Ceres,* Food and Agricultural Organisation

HENRY S. BLOCH, Adjunct Professor of Public Law and International Relations, Columbia University

* MARVIN BORDELON, Acting Director, Division of World Justice and Peace and Director of International Affairs, U.S. Catholic Conference of Bishops

SIR EDWARD BOYLE, Member, Pearson Commission

COURTNEY C. BROWN, Professor, Graduate School of Business, Columbia University

ROBERTO DE OLIVEIRA CAMPOS, Member, Pearson Commission

WILLIAM J. CASEY, Member, President's Commission on International Development (Peterson Commission)

L. MAYNARD CATCHINGS, Chairman, Africa Committee, National Committee of Black Churchmen

TERENCE CARDINAL COOKE, Archbishop of New York; Member, Peterson Commission

DANIEL F. CROWLEY, Senior Vice President, McGraw-Hill, Inc.

THOMAS B. CURTIS, Member, Peterson Commission

DANIEL DEGUEN, Director, International Affairs, Ministry of Economics and Finance, France

PHILIPPE DE SEYNES, Undersecretary, Department of Economics and Social Affairs, United Nations

* CHARLES S. DENNISON, Director, Business Council for International Understanding

C. A. DOXIADIS, Doxiadis Associates, Inc.

JOHN DUNCAN, Executive Vice President, W. R. Grace and Company

JOEL FISHER, Bureau of International Organization Affairs, United States Department of State

EDWARD R. FRIED, Executive Director, Peterson Commission

MARTIN GAINSBRUGH, Chief Economist and Senior Vice President, National Industrial Conference Board

RICHARD GARDNER, Henry L. Moses Professor of Law and International Organization, Columbia University

WILLIAM GAUD, Executive Vice President, International Finance Corporation, World Bank Group

ELI GINZBERG, A. Barton Hepburn Professor of Economics, Columbia University

* KENNETH R. HANSEN, Honorary Fellow, Adlai Stevenson Institute of International Affairs

JOHN HANNAH, Administrator, Agency for International Development

JUDITH HART, Minister for Overseas Development, United Kingdom

FELIPE HERRERA, President, Inter-American Development Bank

* PAUL G. HOFFMAN, Administrator, United Nations Development Programme

GEORGE F. JAMES, Dean, Graduate School of Business, Columbia University

HARRY G. JOHNSON, Professor of Economics, University of Chicago and London School of Economics and Political Science

JOHAN KAUFMANN, Permanent Representative of the Netherlands to the Organisation for Economic Cooperation and Development

WARREN J. KEEGAN, Assistant Professor of Business, Graduate School of Business, Columbia University

* DONALD KEESING, Associate Professor of Economics, Stanford University

GRAYSON KIRK, President Emeritus, Columbia University

BO KJELLEN, Office of the Secretary General, Organisation for Economic Cooperation and Development

ANTONIE KNOPPERS, President, Merck, Sharp and Dohme International Division, Merck and Co.

W. ARTHUR LEWIS, Member, Pearson Commission; Professor of Economics and International Affairs, Princeton University

JOHN P. LEWIS, Dean, Woodrow Wilson School of Public and International Affairs, Princeton University

JOHN D. LYONS, President, Chase International Investment Corporation

JACQUES MAISONROUGE, President, IBM World Trade Corporation

EDWIN MARTIN, Chairman, Development Advisory Committee, OECD

EDWARD S. MASON, Member, Peterson Commission; Thomas W. Lamont Professor of Economics, Harvard University

ROBERT S. MCNAMARA, President, World Bank

DONALD MEADS, Chairman, International Basic Economic Corporation

ERNST MICHANEK, Director-General, Swedish International Development Agency

* C. V. NARASIMHAN, Chef de Cabinet, United Nations

GLENN A. OLDS, U.S. Representative on the United Nations Economic and Social Council

RAINER OPPELT, Department Chief, Ministry for Economic Cooperation, Germany

* EGIDIO ORTONA, Ambassador of Italy to the United States

LESTER B. PEARSON, Chairman, Commission on International Development

MANUEL PEREZ-GUERRERO, Secretary-General, United Nations Conference on Trade and Development

JUDD POLK, Economist, U.S. Council, International Chamber of Commerce

SIR DENIS RICKETT, Vice President, World Bank

* STEFAN H. ROBOCK, Professor of Business, Graduate School of Business, Columbia University

* PAUL ROSENSTEIN-RODAN, Professor of Economics, Massachusetts Institute of Technology

W. W. ROSTOW, Professor of Government, University of Texas at Austin

M. R. SCHEYVEN, Minister of Cooperation for Development, Belgium

PIERRE-PAUL SCHWEITZER, Managing Director, International Monetary Fund

TIBOR SCITOVSKY, Professor of Economics, Yale University

* ELLIOTT D. SKINNER, Professor of Anthropology, Columbia University

WOLFGANG STOLPER, Director, Center for Development Studies, University of Michigan

JAN TINBERGEN, Professor, Netherlands School of Economics

TUN THIN, Deputy Director, Asian Department, International Monetary Fund

* ANTHONY THOMAS, Washington Correspondent, *London Times*

* ROBERT TRIFFIN, Frederick William Beinecke Professor of Economics, Yale University

E. VAN LENNEP, Secretary-General, Organisation for Economic Cooperation and Development

TAKESHI WATANABE, President, Asian Development Bank

* NAT WEINBERG, Director, Special Projects Department, United Auto Workers

SIR GEOFFREY WILSON, Permanent Secretary, Ministry of Overseas Development, U.K.

GEORGE WOODS, Director and Consultant, The First Boston Corporation

List of Contributors

Samir Amin is Professor of Economics at the University of Poitiers, France, and the University of Dakar, Senegal. He has served as a Technical Adviser to the Government of Mali.

Lester R. Brown is Senior Fellow at the Overseas Development Council. He was formerly Administrator of the International Agriculture Development Service of the U.S. Department of Agriculture and adviser to the Secretary of Agriculture. His most recent book is *Seeds of Change.*

Hollis B. Chenery is Economic Adviser to the President, World Bank Group. He has been a Professor of Economics at both Harvard and Stanford Universities and Assistant Administrator for Program, United States Agency for International Development.

Mahbub ul Haq is Chief Economic Adviser to the Government of Pakistan Planning Commission and a Visiting Lecturer at the Economic Development Institute of the World Bank. He is the author of *The Strategy of Economic Planning.*

G. K. Helleiner is Associate Professor of Political Economy at the University of Toronto and President of the Committee on African Studies in Canada. He has been Director of the Economic Research Bureau of Tanzania.

Albert O. Hirschman is Professor of Economics at Harvard University and has been a Professor of Economics at Yale and Columbia. His publications include *The Strategy of Economic Development* and *Development Projects Observed.*

Richard Jolly is a Fellow in Economics at the Institute of Development Studies, University of Sussex, England, and an adviser to the Government of Zambia. He is the author of *Planning Education for African Development.*

Harry G. Johnson is Professor of Economics at the University of Chicago and the London School of Economics and Political Science. He has written extensively on problems of trade policy and economic development and is the author of several books in this field including *Economic Policies Towards Less Developed Countries* and *Money, Trade and Economic Growth.*

W. Arthur Lewis is President of the Caribbean Development Bank. Sir Arthur has been a Professor of Political Economy at Manchester University and was James Madison Professor of Political Economy at Princeton. He served as Vice-Chancellor of the University of the West Indies and has been active in a number of UN agencies, including the United Nations Development Programme. His many publications include *Theory of Economic Growth* and *Development Planning.*

James A. Mirrlees is Professor of (Mathematical) Economics at Oxford University and a Fellow of Nuffield College. He was formerly with the Pakistan Institute of Development Studies.

The Honourable Philip Ndegwa is Permanent Secretary, Minister of Finance and Economic Planning, Kenya. Mr. Ndegwa was Permanent Secretary, Minister of Agriculture at the time of the Conference, and prior to that was Permanent Secretary and Chief Planning Officer for the Ministry of Economic Planning.

Joan Nelson is Visiting Associate Professor of Political Science at the Massachusetts Institute of Technology and Research Associate, Harvard Center for International Affairs. She is the author of *Aid, Influence and Foreign Policy.*

David Newbery is Lecturer in Development Theory and Mathematical Economics, Churchill College, Cambridge University. In 1969–70 he was the Cowles Foundation Visitor at Yale University.

Max Nicholson is Chairman, Land Use Consultants, in London. Formerly the Director-General of the Nature Conservancy (U.K.), he is the author of *The Environmental Revolution.*

Akbar Noman is a Research Assistant at the Institute of Commonwealth Studies, Oxford University.

I. G. Patel is Special Secretary, Indian Ministry of Finance. Dr. Patel has served as the Chief Economic Adviser to the Finance Ministry and has taught at the Universities of Baroda and Delhi. He has also been the IMF Alternate Director for India.

The Right Honourable Lester B. Pearson was Chairman of the Commission on International Development. Mr. Pearson began his diplomatic career in 1928 and served as Canadian Ambassador to the United States during World War II. In 1948 he was appointed Secretary of State for External Affairs and became Leader of the Liberal Party and Leader of the Opposition in 1958. In 1963 he was elected Prime Minister of Canada, a position he held until his retirement in 1968. Mr. Pearson has received many awards including the Nobel Prize for Peace and the Freedom of the City of London.

V. G. Rastyannikov is a Fellow of the Oriental Institute of the USSR Academy of Sciences. He is a specialist in the agrarian economies of the developing countries of Asia and has written widely on the subject in Soviet periodicals.

Theodore K. Ruprecht is Professor of Economics at Humboldt State College in Arcata, California. From 1969–70 he was Senior Economist-Demographer with the Population Program of the OECD Development Centre.

Paul Streeten is Director of the Institute of Commonwealth Studies and a Fellow of Balliol College, Oxford. From 1964–66 he was Director-General of the Economic Planning Staff at the British Ministry of Overseas Development. Professor Streeten is the author of *Economic Integration* and the editor (with Michael Lipton) of *The Crisis of Indian Planning*.

Erik Thorbecke is currently Professor of Economics at Iowa State University. He was formerly Associate Assistant Administrator for Program Policy, United States Agency for International Development, and is the author of *The Role of Agriculture in Economic Development*.

Robert Triffin is Pelatiah Perit Professor of Political and Social Sciences and Master of Berkley College, Yale University. A former staff member of the Board of Governors of the Federal Reserve System, the International Monetary Fund, the Economic Cooperation Administration and President Kennedy's Task Force on the Balance of Payments, Professor Triffin has served as a consultant to many United Nations agencies. His publications include *Gold and the Dollar Crisis* and *The Fate of the Pound*.

Carl Wahren is Head of the Population and Family Welfare Division of the Swedish International Development Agency. From 1968–69 he was coordinator of the Population Programme at the OECD Development Centre.

Stanislaw Wellisz is Professor of Economics at Columbia University. He has been a member of the Harvard Development Advisory Service team to Pakistan and is the author of *Economies of the Soviet Bloc* and numerous articles on problems of development and planning.

Laurence Whitehead is a Fellow of Nuffield College, Oxford, and had the same title at St. Antony's College, Oxford.

Peter Williams is currently a Ford Foundation education planning adviser to the Government of Ghana and has previously served in that position in Kenya. He has also been a Research Officer with the Overseas Development Institute in London.

NOTES

1. GROWTH AND STRUCTURAL CHANGE

1. Government of Argentina, Consejo Nacional de Desarrollo (National Development Council), *Results of the Survey on Production and Investment Expectation of Industrial Enterprise,* Buenos Aires, March, 1965, Table 3.

Chenery

1. See Simon Smith Kuznets, *Modern Economic Growth* (New Haven: Yale University Press, 1966).

2. The stability of these development patterns is shown by Hollis B. Chenery and Lance Taylor, "Development Patterns: Among Countries and Over Time," *Review of Economics and Statistics* 50, no. 4 (November, 1968): 391–416; and Hollis Chenery, Hazel Elkington, and Christopher Sims, "A Uniform Analysis of Development Patterns," Economic Development Report no. 148, Harvard University, 1970, multilith.

3. These are the median values for rapidly growing countries shown in Table 2. I assume the growth rate of services to be equal to the average of the other three sectors, since its share is fairly constant and determined by domestic demand.

4. Investment rates of 20% of GNP at this level are sufficient to sustain a growth rate of 6% or more.

5. Although data are fragmentary, almost all studies show a rise in urban unemployment in traditional urban services in less developed countries. (See Erik Thorbecke, "Unemployment and Underemployment in the Developing World" [mimeo. paper presented to Columbia Conference on International Economic Development, February, 1970]. Portions of this paper are quoted in Chapter 2 of this volume.) The annual rate of increase in urban population is typically 5% to 6%. Since the rate of labor absorption with existing technology is only about half the rate of growth of industrial output, growth in excess of 10% (corresponding to a growth of GNP in excess of 6%) would be required under present policies to reverse the trend of rising unemployment.

6. See W. Arthur Lewis, "Economic Development with Unlimited Supplies of Labour," *Manchester School* (May, 1954); and John C. H. Fei and Gustav Ranis, *Development of the Labor Surplus Economy* (Homewood, Ill.: R. D. Irwin, 1964).

7. See R. Solow, "Technical Change and the Aggregate Production Function," *Review of Economics and Statistics* 39, no. 3 (August, 1957); and Edward F. Denison, *Why Growth Rates Differ* (Washington, D.C.: Brookings Institution, 1967).

8. Based on results for: Israel—Michael Bruno, "A Programming Model for Israel," in *The Theory and Design of Economic Development,* ed. I. Adelman and Erik Thorbecke (Baltimore: Johns Hopkins Press, 1966); the Philippines—Jeffrey G. Williamson, "Dimensions of Postwar Philippine Economic Progress," *Quarterly Journal of Economics* 83, no. 1 (February, 1969): 93–109; Japan, Brazil, Mexico, Colombia, and Chile—H. Bruton, "Productivity Growth in Latin America," *American Economic Review* 57, no. 5 (December, 1967): 1099–1116; and Yugoslavia, Branko Horvat, private communication. Such estimates are not yet available for countries below $200 per capita income.

9. See H. Chenery and A. Strout, "Foreign Assistance and Economic Development," *American Economic Review* 56 (September, 1966).

10. See Sherman Robinson, "Aggregate Production Functions and Growth Models in Economic Development: A Cross-Section Study" (Ph.D. diss., Harvard University, 1969).

11. This interpretation is subject to several qualifications. For example, Peru may have a high capital/output ratio because of its extractive industry, which need not be a sign of inefficiency.

12. A similar list is given in the Pearson Report (p. 361) for the longer period 1960–67, but the longer period gives a better test of a successful strategy. I have excluded countries having a population of less than a million people in 1967.

13. Albania, Poland, and Romania also meet the growth rate standard but are omitted for lack of other data. They would fall in my D category. I have shaded the standard in the case of Brazil, which maintained a growth of 5.5% for 1950–65 but fell off in the last several years of the period. The record is incomplete for Malaysia, Iran, and the Ivory Coast, but it is clear that they meet the growth standard.

14. Normal values of exports and other variables are determined from regression equations that allow for country size.

15. Trinidad, Jamaica, Malaysia, and Rhodesia had high inflows of private capital during the 1950's, but they conform to the primary export strategy.

Wellisz

1. Thus, K. N. Raj argues convincingly that the official figures greatly underestimate the growth of the small manufacturing sector. See K. N. Raj, *Indian Economic Growth: Performance and Prospects* (New Delhi: Allied Publishers, 1965), p. 2 and *passim.*

2. Calculated from S. Sivasubramanian, "National Income of India 1900/01–1946/47" (Ph.D. diss., Delhi University, 1965), cited in J. N. Bhagwati and P. Desai, *Planning for Industrialization* (OECD, forthcoming), Chap. 3.

3. Government of India, Planning Commission, *Fourth Five Year Plan: A Draft Outline* (New Delhi, 1966), pp. 14–15. It must be noted that estimates of savings and investment are subject to very wide error.

4. Calculated from figures given in Government of India, *Economic Survey 1967–1968.*

5. The agricultural situation has, *inter alia,* a major influence on India's balance of payments. In 1964/65 agricultural products (including products of industrial agriculture) amounted to 40% of India's imports, and cereals alone accounted for 20% of the imports. Between 1964/65 and 1966/67 cereal imports rose by almost 50%. India's exports of agricultural goods and agricultural-based industries (such as jute manufactures, cotton fabrics, oil cakes) accounted for over 60% of the country's exports in 1964/65 (based on data from the Directorate General of Commercial Intelligence and Statistics). Thus, a major crop failure means a foreign exchange crisis, food aid notwithstanding.

6. Government of India, Programme Evaluation Organization, Planning Commission, *Evaluation Study of the High Yielding Varieties Programme, Rabi, 1967.*

7. For a rapid summary of the new agricultural policy, see J. S. Sarma, "Current Prospects and Trends in Agricutural Development: India," in *Regional Seminar on Agriculture* (Sydney, Australia, April 10–12, 1969: Papers and Proceedings, Asian Development Bank, 1969), pp. 151–59.

8. The current exchange rate for the Indian rupee is $0.1338 cents per rupee.

9. If we take a two-year moving average to eliminate the year-to-year fluctuations, we obtain the following picture of the ratio of government savings to central and state taxes:

1960/61–1961/62	18.4%
1961/62–1962/63	19.0
1962/63–1963/64	18.9
1963/64–1964/65	18.8
1964/65–1965/66	18.2
1965/66–1966/67	14.6
1966/67–1967/68	8.9

10. Land revenue, the major direct tax on the agricultural sector, has declined in importance: in 1955/56, it was 10.2% of total tax receipts, and in 1967/68, 2.9%

11. The Grand Strategy was heavily influenced by P. C. Mahalanobis's theories. See in particular his "The Approach of Operational Research to Planning," *Sankhyā,* Vol. 16, 1955, reprinted in his *The Approach to Operational Research to Planning in India* (Bombay: Asia Publishing House, 1963). Mahalanobis's strategy posits development in a virtually closed economy. Even if it were true that India faced a highly inelastic demand for its exports, the strategy was nonoptimal if one takes into account foreign aid possibilities. For a critique of the approach, see J. N. Bhagwati and Sukhamoy Chakravarty, "Contributions to Indian Economic Analysis: A Survey," *American Economic Review* 59, part 2 (September, 1969): 5–10.

12. Committee on Public Undertakings, 12th Report, reviewed in *Economic and Political Weekly* 3, no. 21 (May 25, 1968): 820.

13. The indirect control approach is preferable from the point of view of economic efficiency: the tax (subsidy) expresses the public valuation of the discrep-

ancy between private and social goals; private resource allocation then proceeds on the basis of the market prices thus modified. (For a statement of optimal tax-subsidy policy given the policy goals, see J. N. Bhagwati and T. N. Srinivasan, "Optimal Intervention to Achieve Non-economic Objectives," *Review of Economic Studies* 36, no. 1 (January, 1969): 27–38. The difficulty of the approach is that it is extremely difficult to calculate in advance the effects of a given tax or subsidy; insofar as the national objectives are quantitative, the direct approach is almost inescapable.

14. Quoted in R. K. Hazari, *Industrial Planning and Licensing Policy,* Interim Report to the Planning Commission, Ministry of Industry, Government of India, 1967, p. 18.

15. *Ibid.*

16. See Bhagwati and Desai, *Planning for Industrialization,* Chap. 16.

17. Government of India, Department of Industrial Development, Ministry of Industrial Development, Internal Trade and Company Affairs, *Report of the Industrial Licensing Policy Inquiry Committee* (Main Report), July, 1969, p. 114. According to the *Ninth Report* of the Estimates Committee the licenses are considered in the order they are received and "provided the location in a particular area is not too uneconomic" preference is given "to the more under-developed areas" (para. 2.46, quoted in Bhagwati and Desai, *Planning for Industrialization,* Chap. 13).

18. *Industrial Licensing Policy Inquiry Committee* (Main Report), p. 74.

19. Prior to September 8, 1969, the ex-factory price of a Premier car was Rs. 13,551; on the free market a 1965 model sold for approximately Rs. 15,250. See the *Economic Times,* September 10, 1969.

20. In the case of coal, government-owned railroads argued their case against private and government-sector mines. In the case of steel, the argument was carried out by "steel consuming ministries" against the (largely government-owned) steel mills.

21. Raj Krishna and S. S. Mehta, "Productivity Trends in Large-Scale Industry," *Economic and Political Weekly* 3, no. 43 (October 26, 1960): 1655–60.

22. The respective planned investment figures are: First Plan, 7%; Second Plan, 14.4%; Third Plan, 23.6%; Fourth Plan, 25%.

23. Most of the gains were achieved by applying the new technology on irrigated large-scale and medium farms; the problem for the future is how to improve yields on smaller and less favorably situated holdings.

24. Between 1961 and 1966 rice output in East Pakistan increased by 30%. See John W. Thomas, "Rural Public Works and East Pakistan's Development" (Ph.D. diss., Harvard University, 1968), pp. 173–75, cited in Gustav F. Papanek, "Comparative Development Strategies: India and Pakistan," Economic Development Report no. 152, Development Advisory Service, Center for International Affairs, Harvard University, 1970.

25. Gustav F. Papanek, *Pakistan's Development* (Cambridge: Harvard University Press, 1967), p. 220.

26. The current exchange rate for the Pakistani rupee is $0.2105 cents per rupee.

27. This was done initially through direct internal controls and export duties. Subsequently, the controls were relaxed and the export duties eliminated, but

export earnings were limited because of the overvaluation of currency which was not compensated, in the case of agricultural products, by export bonuses, so that domestic consumers continued to reap the advantages of low prices.

28. Papanek, *Pakistan's Development,* Table 26, p. 195.

29. In 1954/55, raw jute exports (at prices adjusted for devaluation) amounted to Rs. 857 million and exports of jute manufactures to only Rs. 16 million. By 1964/65, exports of raw jute and jute manufactures amounted to Rs. 926 million and Rs. 320 million respectively.

30. The process of substitution for jute was also caused, in part, by exogeneous factors such as changes in packaging technology; rigid or semi-rigid containers are increasingly favored over sacking.

31. The problem was aggravated by East Pakistan's shortage of entrepreneurs; as a consequence, the major private jute mills established in the East Wing were owned and managed by West Pakistanis.

32. Capital outlays involved in major schemes are not stated in the schedules; moreover, some licenses may not be taken up. According to Papanek (*Pakistan's Development,* p. 136), investment sanctions under the first schedule amounted to Rs. 3,660 million in West Pakistan and only Rs. 1,510 million in East Pakistan. The revised schedule indicates the availability of licenses for new investment amounting to approximately Rs. 800 million for the East Wing and Rs. 359 million for the West Wing.

33. Initially enterprises in the more developed areas were granted tax holidays for periods from 2 to 4 years, and those in less developed areas from 6 to 8 years. Under 1969 reforms, tax holidays will not apply in the highly developed areas of West Pakistan to industries established after June 30, 1970, except for petrochemicals, heavy machinery, and other capital goods industries. In view of the usual "teething troubles" of new enterprises, resulting in low profits in initial years of operation, and in view of low effective corporate income tax rates, the impact of the regional tax differentiation is open to doubt.

34. See Stephen R. Lewis, Jr., and Stephen E. Guisinger, "Measuring Protection in a Developing Country: The Case of Pakistan," *Journal of Political Economy* 76, no. 6 (November/December, 1968): 1188, Table 4. The exact figures are somewhat open to debate, given the complexity of the issues involved in performing the calculations and the data problems.

35. Nurul Islam, "Commodity Exports, Net Exchange Earnings and Investment Criteria," *Pakistan Development Review* 8, no. 4 (Winter, 1968): 593.

Helleiner

1. J. O'Connell, "The Inevitability of Instability," *Journal of Modern African Studies* 5, no. 2 (1967): 181.

2. If, as many believe, it is presumptuous, if not harmful, for foreigners to dispense advice on economic policy to independent African governments, how much worse must it be for them to venture into the delicate arena of social and political change in Africa. I am only too conscious of my proper place in this respect and of the fact that, whether one wants to or not, one cannot easily shuck off one's upbringing, cultural conditioning, and implicit or explicit value judgments.

Yet Africans who prescribe for Africa also have individual biases; moreover, if everyone frets too much about his own, nothing meaningful is ever said.

3. The Pearson Report states that 30 African countries, accounting for 86% of Africa's population, have per capita incomes of less than $160, and 17 of them, accounting for 55% of the population, have per capita incomes of less than $80.

4. See, for instance, H. Myint, "Economic Theory and the Underdeveloped Countries," *Journal of Political Economy* 73, no. 5 (October, 1965): 484–88.

5. This is a very rough figure. Typically, about 15% of the population is under 5 years of age, 30% is between 5 and 14, and 40% to 45% is between 15 and 44. See United Nations, Economic Commission for Africa, *African Economic Indicators* (Addis Ababa, 1968), pp. 27–29; and United Nations, Economic Commission for Africa, *Statistical Bulletin for Africa* 7, no. 2 (March, 1967): 25–36.

6. See Keith Griffin, "Development Myths," *Bulletin,* Institute of Development Studies, University of Sussex 1, no. 4 (May, 1969).

7. A. R. Jolly, "Employment, Wage Levels and Incentives," in United Nations, Economic and Social Council, International Institute for Educational Planning, *Manpower Aspects of Educational Planning* (Paris, 1968), pp. 236–47.

8. "Increases in *real* wages have averaged about 4 percent per year in Africa." (*Ibid.,* p. 238.)

9. The Pearson Report (Annex I) calls attention to the degree of concentration of Ivoirien expenditures in Abijan (p. 265), but it does not make sufficiently clear that this urban bias is a universal phenomenon in Africa.

10. The population of sub-Saharan Africa's largest cities grew during the 1950's at an average annual rate of about 6.8%. (See C. R. Frank, "Urban Unemployment and Economic Growth in Africa," *Oxford Economic Papers* 20, no. 2 [July, 1968]: 253.) The flow has almost certainly accelerated during the 1960's.

11. See J. R. Harris and M. P. Todaro, "Urban Unemployment in East Africa; and Economic Analysis of Policy Alternatives," *East African Economic Review,* n.s. 4, no. 2 (December, 1968): 17–36.

12. Tanzania has experimented with this. One recent survey concludes that this may be one of the best available policies for combating urban unemployment. (*Ibid.*)

13. Calculated from W. A. Hance, *Southern Africa and the United States* (New York: Columbia University Press, 1968), pp. 119–20.

14. Pearson Report, p. 376.

15. There is one passing reference to the defense problem in Annex I (p. 279).

16. Raúl Prebisch used this phrase in his report to the Second Session of the UNCTAD. United Nations, Conference on Trade and Development, *Towards a Global Strategy of Development* (TD/3) New York, 1968, pp. 51–54.

17. United Nations, Economic Commission for Africa, *Report of the Fourth Joint Meeting of the ECA Working Party on Intra-African Trade and the OAU Expert Committee on Trade and Development* (Geneva, August, 18–23, 1969), Annex V, p. 5.

18. Organisation for Economic Cooperation and Development, Development Assistance Committee, *Development Assistance, 1968 Review* (24.637) (OECD, Paris, December, 1968), p. 271.

19. The new Institute of Tropical Agriculture in Nigeria might act as one of the spearheads of the effort in Africa. It has the advantages of being free from

the traditions of earlier institutes created in the pre-independence era and of being able to draw on the recent experience in Mexico, the Philippines, Pakistan, and India.

20. International Monetary Fund, International Bank for Reconstruction and Development, *The Problem of Stabilization of Prices of Primary Products, A Staff Study, Part I* (Washington, 1969), p. 26.

21. National Academy of Sciences, National Research Council, *Agricultural Research Priorities for Economic Development in Africa, The Abidjan Conference, 1968.*

22. Max F. Millikan and David Hapgood, *No Easy Harvest, The Dilemma of Agriculture in Underdeveloped Countries* (Boston: Little, Brown & Co., 1967), p. 27.

23. Ivan Illich, "Outwitting the 'Developed' Countries," *The New York Review of Books*, 13, no. 8 (November 6, 1969): 20.

24. Jon Moris has provided a useful list of objectives which the teaching of agricultural science in the schools should pursue. See Jon Moris, "Farmer Training as a Strategy of Rural Development," in *Education, Employment and Rural Development, The Proceedings of a Conference Held at Kericho, Kenya, in September, 1966,* ed. James R. Sheffield (Nairobi: East African Publishing House [published under the auspices of University College, Nairobi], 1967), pp. 349–50.

25. The case has recently been effectively and succinctly presented by E. R. Watts, "Bureaucracy and Extension," *East Africa Journal* 6, no. 8 (August, 1969): 37–40.

26. Illich, "Outwitting the 'Developed' Countries," p. 20.

27. Archibald Callaway, "Nigeria's Indigenous Education; The Apprentice System," *Odu* 1, no. 1 (July, 1964): 1–18; *idem.,* "From Traditional Crafts to Modern Industries," in *The City of Ibadan,* ed. P. C. Lloyd et al. (London: Cambridge University Press in association with the Institute of African Studies, University of Ibadan, 1967), pp. 153–71.

28. A much-quoted and dramatic estimate is that many African national markets are no larger than that of a European town with a population of about 100,000. See Economic Commission for Africa, "Approaches to African Economic Integration," *Journal of Modern African Studies* 1, no. 3 (September, 1963): 395.

29. W. Arthur Lewis, *The Politics of West Africa* (London: Oxford University Press, 1965); and *Some Aspects of Economic Development; The Aggrey-Fraser-Guggisberg Memorial Lectures, 1968* (Accra: Ghana Publishing Corporation, 1969).

2. THE DEVELOPMENT SECTORS

1. D. Turnham and I. Jagger, "The Employment Problem in Developing Countries" (OECD Development Centre Working Document, December, 1969).

2. Organization of American States, *The Unemployment Problem in Latin America* (October, 1969).

3. Economic Research Academy, "Prices, Taxation and Agriculture" (published by *Finance and Industry,* Karachi, 1969), p. 36.

4. Quoted in *Patriot* (New Delhi), November 29, 1969.

5. *The World Food Problem: A Report of the President's Science Advisory Committee,* Vol. 1 (1967), pp. 86–87.

6. "Prices, Taxation and Agriculture," *The Economic Times* 2 (Bombay, April 2, 1969): 55–56.

7. Calculated on the basis of figures given in "All-India Rural Household Survey," *The Economic Times* 2 (Bombay, April 2, 1969): 52.

8. Republic of Turkey, Prime Ministry, State Institute of Statistics, *Tanim istatistikleri özeti 1967* [the summary of agricultural statistics 1967] (Ankara, 1968), p. 19.

9. U.S. Department of Agriculture, Economic Research Service, "The Agricultural Situation in the Far East and Oceania, Review of 1968 and Outlook for 1969" (ERS-Foreign 262) (Washington: April, 1969), p. 11.

10. S. R. Rose and E. H. Clark, "Some Basic Considerations on Agricultural Mechanization in West Pakistan," *The Pakistan Development Review* 9 (1969): 289, 291–92.

11. U.S., Agency for International Development, "Rice and Wheat in India" (mimeo., New Delhi, March, 1969), p. 118.

12. Inter-American Development Bank, *Eighth Annual Report of the Social Progress Trust Fund of the Inter-American Development Bank* (Washington, D.C., 1968), p. 34.

13. Bruce Herrick, *Urban Migration and Economic Development in Chile* (Cambridge, Mass.: MIT Press, 1966), pp. 53, 103; Bertram Hutchinson, "The Migrant Population of Urban Brazil," *America Latina* 6, no. 2 (1963): 43–44; D. T. Lakdawala, *Work, Wages, and Well-Being in an Indian Metropolis: Economic Surveys of Bombay City* (Bombay: University of Bombay, 1963), p. 159; V. K. R. V. Rao and P. B. Desai, *Greater Delhi: A Study in Urbanization, 1940–1957* (Bombay, New York: Asia Publishing House, 1965), p. 79.

14. William L. Flinn, "Rural-to-Urban Migration: A Colombian Case" (mimeo., Research Publication no. 19, Land Tenure Center, University of Wisconsin, July, 1966), pp. 10, 23; Granville Sewell, "Squatter Settlements in Turkey" (Ph.D. diss., M.I.T., 1966), p. 304; Herrick, *Urban Migration,* p. 49.

15. Gino Germani, "Inquiry into the Social Effects of Urbanization in a Working Class Sector of Greater Buenos Aires," United Nations, Economic and Social Council (E/CN.12/URB/10), December, 1958, Table 10, p. 26; Herrick, *Urban Migration,* p. 91; United Nations, Economic Council for Latin America, "Urbanization in Latin America: Results of a Field Survey of Living Conditions in an Urban Sector" (mimeo. E/CN.12.622), 1963, p. 17; Flinn, "Rural-to-Urban Migration," p. 27; Hutchinson, "Migrant Population of Urban Brazil," Table 12, p. 61.

16. Herrick, *Urban Migration,* p. 92; ECLA, "Urbanization in Latin America," p. 16; Germani, "Inquiry into the Social Effects," Table 37, p. 69; Hutchinson, "Migrant Population of Urban Brazil," pp. 67–68.

17. Robert Slighton, *Urban Unemployment in Colombia: Measurement, Characteristics, and Policy Problems* (Santa Monica: RAND RM-5393 AID, January, 1968), p. 38; Herrick, *Urban Migration,* p. 84; Myron Weiner, "Urbanization and Political Protest," *Civilisations* 17, no. 2 (1967): 6; Rao and Desai, *Greater Delhi,* table 16–1, p. 341, and table 17–3, p. 383; Lakdawala, *Work, Wages, and Well-Being,* p. 481; R. Mukerjee and B. Singh, *Social Profiles of a Metropolis* (Bombay:

Asia Publishing House, 1961), p. 116; G. M. Farooq, *The People of Karachi: Economic Characteristics* (Monographs in the Economics of Development, no. 15, Karachi, Institute of Development Economics, July, 1966), p. 19; N. V. Sovani, *Urbanization and Urban India* (New York: Asia Publishing House, 1966), pp. 154–55.

18. Germani, "Inquiry into the Social Effect," p. 16; Doris Phillips, "Rural-to-Urban Migration in Iraq," *Economic Development and Cultural Change* 7, no. 4 (July, 1959): 417.

19. E. M. Nicholson and A. W. Colling, "Chart of Human Impacts on the Countryside" (presented at the Countryside in 1970 Conference, London, 1963).

20. These have been prepared and were published in the *Annales de l'Institut National de la Recherche Agronomique de Tunisie* during 1967–68.

21. Since the Columbia University Conference on International Economic Development in February, 1970, the World Bank has announced its decision to provide for specialist advice in the ecological validation of projects submitted to the Bank. Following this welcome action in pursuance of the kind of approach here advocated, arrangements have been made for a Working Group of specialists in development and in conservation to meet at the headquarters of the Food and Agriculture Organization in Rome on the lines suggested above.

3. TRADE AND LIQUIDITY

Mirrlees

1. On p. 71 of the Pearson Report crises of the "major industrial powers" are singled out as "perhaps the greatest threat to international development." This appears to refer to world economic growth, which may not be as important for the developing countries as is often thought. In any case, this concern is not developed in the Report.

2. The General Agreement on Tariffs and Trade puts some constraint on the ways in which the degree of protection can be varied but perhaps has the effect of worsening the way in which it is done—by affecting purchases by the public sector (always important), tying aid, not reducing existing tariffs. The balance of payments neurosis can even affect the private sector's behavior.

3. Alisdair I. MacBean appears to have shown that there is no *general* case for supposing export price fluctuations to have affected growth adversely. See *Export Instability and Economic Development* (London: Allen and Unwin, 1966).

4. Ideally, one would be more concerned about fluctuations in the incomes of poor farmers than fluctuations in the profits of large firms or plantations. No easy way of achieving that suggests itself and, in practice, this does not seem to be a serious objection.

5. Preliminary estimates of GNP might tend to be understated, relative to final estimates; but the advantage to the debtor would be small, and penalties for systematic underestimates could be built into the loan contract. If published estimates are reduced, the government's reputation suffers, and aid prospects deteriorate. The difficulty of organizing the "evasion" can hardly be worthwhile for such doubtful net gains.

6. As examples of the kind of formulae that might be used, the two following, rather simple ones may be of interest. In each case, the outstanding debt is calcu-

lated by subtracting the payment made from the previous year's debt and adding an interest charge (say 2%).

(1) Repayment $= aD + b \ (Y - Y_o e^{gt})$, where D is outstanding debt, Y is GNP, Y_o is GNP in the year when the loan is made, and g the expected rate of growth.

(2) Repayment $= \dfrac{g}{\bar{g}} \ \dfrac{D}{T - t}$ where g is the actual rate of GNP, t is the year in which repayment is being made, and T is a year determined as follows. In the initial year, T is the expected term of the debt. It is then adjusted upwards or downwards according to the rule

$$\frac{dT}{dt} = 1 - \frac{g}{\bar{g}} \ .$$

The former scheme is simpler, but does not take very much of the economy's fluctuations onto the donor. It is easily verified that with the second scheme, the actual term of the loan is the period until the GNP of the economy reaches that level it was initially expected to reach at T_o, the expected term of the loan.

In practice, further complications would be desired, and perhaps desirable, to allow for clear cases of mismanagement (when the aid is being wasted). Grace periods are easy to allow for.

7. Not always. For example, they appear to bless research into new uses for primary products (p. 84) more because it would be nice than for its economic value.

8. The definition of developed and developing countries for this purpose is very important. Since a relatively inelastic demand is advantageous to the developing countries, one would like to see most producers included as "developing countries" for the purposes of the taxation. Ideally, the taxing agency should decide whether it would like to include countries not automatically subscribing to it and then negotiate with these outside countries, treating them on the same basis, with the same rules, as other parties to the scheme, for the purpose of the specified commodity.

9. The most thorough treatment is that of J. de V. Graaff, "On Optimum Tariff Structures," *Review of Economic Studies* 17, no. 42 (1949): 47–59.

10. This leads to the—somewhat misleading—necessary condition that the proportion of the tariff in the price of sale should be the reciprocal of the demand elasticity for the commodity, if cross elasticities are negligible.

It would be natural to charge the tax at the port of embarkation of the commodity. Since the f.o.b. price will vary from one port to another, this leads to complications, but they are not essential, and could well be ignored.

11. Harry G. Johnson, *Economic Policies Towards Less Developed Countries* (London: Allen and Unwin, 1967), p. 162. He roughly estimates the gains from only five commodities at $2½ billion per annum.

12. At a time when aid-givers try to impose higher rates on the more competent developing countries, regardless of poverty, a contrary recommendation (that crises should not be the criterion) would have been good.

Streeten and Noman

1. Alternatively, the absolute amount of savings could be traced on the two axes. It is the savings *rate* which is relevant to the growth rate, but it must be remembered that income and savings can go up as a result of an inflow of foreign aid, while the savings rate remains the same or even declines. Whether we trace savings or *a fortiori* the savings rate, aid can contribute to an increase in *consumption*. If the terms of aid are sufficiently soft, this must be reckoned a benefit even if neither the savings *rate* nor even *savings* are increased.

2. We are indebted to Dr. Keith Griffin for discussions and critical comments on this issue.

3. Perhaps the diagram raises more questions than it answers. Implicit in the presentation is the argument that, while there may not be a correlation between aid and growth, growth is positively correlated to investment/income ratios. Yet the evidence shows only very weak correlation. It might, therefore, be that it is the absence of a relation between investment and growth which accounts for the absence of a relation between aid and growth. Further, the data of the critics are taken mostly from intercountry studies. Time series for particular countries might show stronger correlations.

4. It might, of course, be argued that extra aid merely replaces other forms of foreign exchange receipts and, in particular, exports. This would be one way of accounting for the absence of a relation between import capacity and growth. The impact of aid on import capacity would always be negligible, because canceled out by offsetting movements of other credit items.

5. B. S. Minhas, *Fourth Plan: Objectives and Policy Frame* (published on behalf of *Commerce* by Vora & Co., Bombay, September, 1968), p. 14.

6. These are growth rates for commodity exports. The figures for 1950–67 are derived from exponential trend function and those for 1960–66 from compound interest growth rate. See United Nations, Conference for Trade and Development, *Handbook of International Trade and Development Statistics* (TD/STAT/2), Geneva, 1969.

7. See note 6 above.

8. Government of Pakistan, Planning Commission, *Revised Phasing, Sectoral Priorities and Allocations of the Third Five Year Plan* (Karachi, 1967), p. 3.

9. Net value added at world prices in many manufactured exports is very small or negative. See Nural Islam, "Commodity Exports, Net Exchange Earning and Investment Criteria," *Pakistan Development Review* 8, no. 4 (Winter, 1968): 582-605; Joseph J. Stern, "A Note on the Structure of Pakistan's Foreign Trade," *Pakistan Development Review* 9, no. 2 (Summer, 1969): 212-23; and Ronald Soligo and Joseph J. Stern, "Tariff Protection, Import Sustitution and Industrial Efficiency," *Pakistan Development Review* 5, no. 2 (Summer, 1965): 249-70.

10. Whereas India is said to have gone through this "teething period." See Gustav F. Papanek, "Comparative Development Strategies: India and Pakistan," Economic Development Report, no. 152, Development Advisory Service, Center for International Affairs, Harvard University, 1970. We are grateful to the author for making available to us a draft copy of the paper.

11. At current prices and as percentage of GNP, whereas at constant 1959/60

prices and as a percentage of GDP, the savings rate was 9.2% in 1964/65, having risen slightly from 8.6% in 1959/60. (United Nations, Economic Commission for Asia and the Far East, *Feasible Growth and Trade Gap Projections in the ECAFE Region,* Development Programming Technique, no. 7 [E/CN.11/844], Bangkok, 1968, p. 26.)

12. See note 6 above.

13. On the other hand, against the effects of aid on breaking bottlenecks and thus lowering capital/output ratios must be set the greater emphasis on agriculture, on better capacity utilization, and on quick-yielding projects, which, in part, was a response to aid shortage, and which may continue into the seventies, thus lowering capital/output ratio. In this sense, at least, the capital/output ratio is not entirely independent of capital imports. This interdependence is one of the weaknesses of gap analysis.

14. The difference may be due to different definitions of the gross capital/output ratio. Unfortunately neither document attempts precise definitions.

15. These calculations were made before the recent proposed increase in IMF quotas. If all countries increase their quotas to the maximum proposed, the share of India and Pakistan will fall. In that case they will, presumably, receive fewer SDRs in the last two years.

16. See Nicholas Kaldor, *Essays on Economic Policy* (London: G. Duckworth, 1964), Vol. 2, Chap. 19.

17. Another difficulty, which explains the reluctance to move away from import controls which are recognized to be inefficient, is the existence of tied aid. This forms a significant proportion of available foreign exchange in both India and Pakistan. Ways of matching supplies of inconvertible currencies and demand in a system of dual exchange rates are sketched out in United Nations, Economic Commission for Asia and the Far East, "The Implications of Economic Controls and of Liberalization" in *Economic Bulletin for Asia and the Far East* 19, no. 4, supplement, *Economic Survey of Asia and the Far East 1968* (E/CN.11/878), Bangkok, March, 1969, p. 92.

Whitehead

1. Wendell C. Gordon, "Has Foreign Aid Been Overstated?," *Inter-American Economic Affairs* 21, no. 4 (Spring, 1968): 8–9.

2. President Lyndon B. Johnson in a speech to a meeting of Latin American ambassadors in August, 1965. Reported in U.S., Department of State, *The Department of State Bulletin* 53, no. 1368 (September 13, 1965): 426–28.

3. President Lyndon B. Johnson in a speech to the Punta del Este Conference of chiefs of state in April, 1967. Reported in U.S., Department of State, *The Department of State Bulletin* 56, no. 1454 (May 8, 1967): 710.

4. Of course, the Pearson figures were not compiled by the staff of the Commission; they were taken from the OECD's Development Assistance Committee reports. But I cannot call them OECD figures since the Pearson Commission refused to accept the OECD's claim that Portugal is a developed country busy "aiding" less developed countries.

5. Compared with about $9 billion in the period 1946–60. Actually, the $6

billion also includes tourist spending. If Latin America's net earnings on this account were deducted, the cost of remaining services would turn out to be rather more.

6. See note 2 above.

7. United Nations, Economic Commission for Latin America, *External Financing in Latin America* (E/CN.12/649), New York, 1965, p. 82.

8. United Nations, Economic Commission for Latin America, *Economic Survey of Latin America,* Vol. 12, 1967 (E/CN.12/808), Santiago, Chile, 1968, p. 96.

9. Of course, no one should be surprised that a country receiving aid thereby loses some control over its economic policy. This is natural enough, but it does mean that "aid" has political costs which substitute for financial ones. There is evidence that these costs may often be considerably higher than the recipients at first realize: the costs to Bolivia's government were shown in my pamphlet *The United States and Bolivia* (London: Haslemere Publication, 1969).

As for the economic costs of tied aid, the Pearson Report says that the direct costs frequently exceed 20% (p. 172). In some cases the economic costs may be so high that a country simply cannot afford to receive aid. In 1969 the *New York Herald Tribune* stated ". . . the 'additionality' clause . . . seeks to insure that all dollars lent to a country are returned immediately in the form of purchase of American goods. . . . Furthermore the goods purchased must come from a list of US products that are doing badly in international commerce. . . . Last year, for example, as a prerequisite for receiving a $4.5 million budget support loan, the US was urging . . . [Bolivia] . . . to buy American ore carts costing three times as much as a similar Belgian product. . . . The Bolivian government has said . . . it simply does not have the money for the additional purchases from the US." (*New York Herald Tribune,* European edition, February 5, 1969.)

Fortunately, the "additionality" clause was scrapped in 1969, but the question remains whether loans with conditions to them should be called "aid." Finally, aid recipients may be required to attack the donor's enemies. "Relations between the Philippines and the US have become more strained in the past few days following the release of part of the Washington hearings on foreign aid. According to a heavily censored transcript, publication of which was delayed until after the Philippine elections, the US was described as having paid Manila nearly $39 million in return for having sent a small contingent of men to Vietnam."

10. ECLA, *External Financing,* p. 203.

11. *La Brecha Comercial y la Integración Latino-Américana* (Mexico City: Latin American Institute for Economic and Social Planning, 1967), p. 115.

12. ECLA, *External Financing,* p. 214.

13. Albert O. Hirschman, *How to Divest in Latin America and Why,* Princeton Essays in International Finance, no. 76 (Princeton, Princeton University Press, November, 1969), p. 6. The paper is reprinted in this volume, Chapter 4.

14. ECLA, *External Financing,* p. 201.

15. M. Bronfenbrenner, "The Appeal of Confiscation in Economic Development," *Economic Development and Cultural Change* 3, no. 1 (April, 1955): 201.

16. *Ibid.,* pp. 216–17.

17. Keith Griffin, *Underdevelopment in Spanish America* (London: Allen and Unwin, 1969), p. 124.

18. *The Economist para América Latina,* October 15, 1969, estimated that mutual investment funds (such as Investors Overseas Service) alone siphoned off $450 million a year of domestic savings from Latin America (compared to roughly $500 million a year allocated by the United States to the Alliance for Progress). The article says that the Argentine liberalization measures of 1967 (so favorably regarded by foreign opinion) "gave rise to a substantial boom in mutual investment funds," even though these enterprises generally ignore the law requiring at least 75% of the resources they collect to be invested within the country. It adds that the Mexicans were eventually driven to close down the offices of IOS, the largest concern, but even so the outflow has continued. As for Venezuela, companies operating from New York, Switzerland, and the Bahamas drain off about $100 million a year, according to *The Economist.*

The developed countries could help the less developed to reduce this outflow. Through international cooperation these companies could be forced to respect the laws existing in the countries where they raise their funds, even if these laws require 100% local investment.

19. Griffin, *Underdevelopment in Spanish America.*

20. There is no easy way to reduce Latin America's outflow under these headings—national shipping companies might cost the balance of payments more in the purchase of ships than they saved on freight costs, if the ships were constructed in the developed countries. The point is merely that this outflow on invisibles is a very large (and growing) problem. There is a full discussion in the report of the first UNCTAD conference (United Nations Conference on Trade and Development, *Proceedings of the United Nations Conference on Trade and Development* [Geneva, 1964], Vol. 5, *Financing and Invisibles—Institutional Arrangements* [TD/1-64], pp. 123–331). It shows, for example, that in 1961, the nineteen Latin American republics lost $577 million on the balance of payments in freight charges alone, and $87 million in insurance (see pp. 120–21). Recent developments are discussed in *The Economist para America Latina,* 9 February, 1968. The CECLA meeting of Latin American countries agreed at Vina del Mar (point 26) that joint measures to encourage their merchant marine fleets should not be regarded by third parties as discriminatory. Hitherto, when, for example, the Peruvians offered slightly preferential treatment to their own fleet, the United States threatened to cut off aid.

4. PRIVATE INVESTMENT

Hirschman

1. John Knapp, "Capital Exports and Growth," *Economic Journal* 67, no. 267 (September, 1957): 432–44; Felipe Pazos, "The Role of International Movements of Private Capital in Promoting Development," in *Capital Movements and Economic Development,* ed. by John H. Adler with Paul W. Kuznetz (New York: Macmillan, 1967).

2. Pazos, "The Role of International Movements," p. 196.

3. For some interesting remarks along these lines, see Hans O. Schmitt, "Foreign Capital and Social Conflict in Indonesia," *Economic Development and Cultural Change* 10, no. 3 (April, 1962): 284–93.

4. Herbert Marshall, Frank A. Southard, Jr., and Kenneth W. Taylor, *Canadian-American Industry* (New Haven: Yale University Press; Toronto: The Ryerson Press, 1936, for the Carnegie Endowment), pp. 252–62.

5. Joao Frederico Normano, *Brazil: A Study of Economic Types* (Chapel Hill: The University of North Carolina, 1935), p. 157.

6. Raúl Prebisch, "Reflections on International Cooperation for Latin American Development" (mimeo., May 9, 1969), p. 24.

5. THE AID RELATIONSHIP

Jolly

1. Economists will wish to stress a number of important caveats about the meaningfulness of these figures: they refer to averages over groups of countries, and the positions of individual countries within each group may differ widely; they ignore the inequalities of income within countries; they are based on national income data which involve considerable margins of error and which can be compared with income figures in other countries only with further assumptions about prices and exchange rates which can never be entirely satisfactory. It would, however, be a mistake if these technical qualifications were to divert attention from the fact that the world gap in living standards, wealth, and economic power is, given present prospects, likely to widen very considerably. If the gap is a central issue of the 1970's, a gap which by the century's end is three or four times greater than the present one will be much more serious.

2. Consider, for example, the works of John Stuart Mill, Alfred Marshall, A. C. Pigou, and John Maynard Keynes.

3. Many groups have made such calculations in recent months, including the Tinbergen Committee. The present figures are taken from Y. Sabolo, "Sectoral Employment Growth: The Outlook for 1980," *International Labour Review* (International Labour Organization, 1969).

4. See United Nations, Development Program, *A Study of the Capacity of the United Nations Deevlopment System*, 2 vols. (DP/5), 1969. This study was headed by Sir Robert Jackson and has come to be known as the Jackson Report.

5. To be fair, the Pearson Report at a general level makes a number of extremely important points in Chap. 11, including the recommendation of a 1970 conference of heads of the United Nations, multilateral agencies, regional banks, and coordinating bodies to discuss the creation of improved machinery for coordinating aid.

6. With regard to the United Nations agencies, the Jackson proposals may not go far enough toward proposing institutional changes which are significant enough to limit their present independence.

7. At this point, the Jackson Report seems to weaken unnecessarily in its proposal of a strong United Nations Development Program country representative. On p. 20 it refers to the United Nations Development Program as a strong "partner" of other agencies, especially the World Bank and the International Monetary Fund, at the country level. Surely it follows from the Jackson argument that the resident United Nations representative should at the very least become the senior partner, if not the undisputed leader, of all the international groups. Indeed, it

seems that if the service is strengthened as planned, the United Nations representative will necessarily become the convener of all donor consortia, with an increasing proportion of aid channeled through international agencies.

Amin

1. United Nations, Economic Commission for Africa, *The Economic Situation in Africa in Recent Years* (E/CN.14/435), January, 1969.

2. I shall examine these problems systematically in a book entitled *L'accumulation à l'echelle mondiale* (Paris: Coll. Anthropos–IFAN, forthcoming).

3. See also Paul Bairoch, *Diagnostic économique du Tiers Monde 1900–1966* (Paris: SEDES, 1963); and *Révolution industrielle et sous-développement* (Paris: Gauthiez-Villars, 1967).

4. ECA, *The Economic Situation in Africa*.

5. Ester Boserup, *The Conditions of Agricultural Growth* (London: Allen and Unwin, 1965).

6. Nazhat Chalaq, "The Structure of African Economy" (mimeo., United Nations, Economic Commission for Africa, n.d.).

7. This thesis was brilliantly demonstrated by Bairoch in *Révolution industrielle et sous-développement*. Adam Smith had already understood the problem, which the later Ricardian analysis was to overlook.

8. The word used in M. Amin's French original is *auto-centré*. There is no exact translation in English; "inward-looking" is closer to the author's thought than "self-centered" or "autonomous" and has been used throughout this translation.

9. Bairoch, *Révolution industrielle et sous-développement*, p. 12.

10. Gunnar Myrdal is considerably less "optimistic" than the Pearson Report. See Gunnar Myrdal, *Asian Drama* (New York: Twentieth Century Fund, 1968).

11. Samir Amin, "Le développement du capitalisme en Afrique noire, l'Homme et la Societé 1968," in *En partant du capital* (Paris: Anthropos, 1968).

12. See my study, *Le développement du Capitalisme en Côte d'Ivoire* (Paris: Editions de Minuit, 1967).

13. District of Sénégal which, contrary to the Wolof country, has retained less hierarchial systems of social organization.

14. The IMF, in helping to institute a convertible zaire, contributed greatly to making this delicate recession equilibrium possible. See B. Ryelandt, "Congolese Inflation, 1960, 1968" (thesis, Lovanium University, Kinshasa, 1969).

15. ECA, *The Economic Situation in Africa*, pp. 67 ff.

16. See, for example, our figures relating to the UDEAC countries for the period 1960–68 in Samir Amin and C. Coquery, *Du Congo Francais à l'UDEAC—1880–1968* (Paris: Anthropos—IFAN, 1969).

17. See ECA, *The Economic Situation in Africa*.

18. See R. Richta, *La Civilisation au carrefour* (Paris: Anthropos, 1968).

19. See A. Emmanuel, *L'échange inégal* (Paris: Maspèro, 1968).

20. Samir Amin, *Le monde des affaires Sénégalaises* (Paris: Editions de Minuit, 1969). See also my submission "La politique coloniale francaise à l'égard de la Bourgeoisie commerçante Sénégalaise (1820–1960)" (paper delivered to the International African Institute talks at Freetown, 1969).